Aquation 4/24/06

WEST POINT

CHARACTER, LEADERSHIP, EDUCATION

a book developed from the readings and writings of
THOMAS JEFFERSON

by, NORMAN THOMAS REMICK

RPR • New Jersey
2003

For comments or information contact:

Norman Thomas Remick
P.O. Box 200
Barnegat, N.J. 08005
Fax: 609-698-5117

*For Victoria Narodzonek Remick ORR and
Ralph ORR – Mom and Dad – who showed
us how to raise kids.*

*Something helped Mom give up all the good things in life so her kids might have
what she didn't have. To be there and do that with Mom, something helped Dad –
as T/Sgt. Ralph ORR – survive the following brutal action in W.W.II:*

<pre>
                    HEADQUARTERS XXIV CORPS
                          APO 235

                                            8 March 1945
     GENERAL ORDERS)
                    :
     NUMBER   44)

                          EXTRACT
                           ***

          SECTION II - AWARD OF THE SILVER STAR

        Technical Sergeant RALPH H. ORR, (33177551), Infantry, United
States Army. For gallantry in action at Leyte, Phillippine Islands
on 8 December 1944. When his platoon leader fell seriously wounded
Sergeant ORR crawled under heavy enemy fire to administer first aid
He then unhesitatingly assumed command, reorganized the platoon
and aggressively led it forward in the assault, seizing the objec-
tive and annihilating many of the enemy, eleven of which were
killed by Sergeant ORR personally. Sergeant ORR's display of
courage and leadership reflects great credit upon himself and the
military service.

              BY COMMAND OF MAJOR GENERAL HODGE:

                                        CRUMP GARVIN
                          Brigadier General, General Staff Corps
                                       Chief of Staff

     OFFICIAL:

             s/ W.H. Biggerstaff
             t/ W.H. BIGGERSTAFF
     Colonel, Adjutant General's Department
                Adjutant General   A TRUE EXTRACT COPY

                                            Theodore D. Bielfeld
                                            THEODORE D. BIELFELD
                                            Captain, 306th Infantry
                                            Personnel Officer
</pre>

This book is dedicated to Mom and Dad.

Second only to the support of my loving wife, **DIANE ELIZABETH GOSSETT REMICK**, I wish to extend my grateful thanks for helping me produce this book to:

Richard P. Ruocco
A Friend

CONTENTS

INTRODUCTION: A MUST READ
(The Story Behind The Book)

This book is, virtually, by Thomas Jefferson. It was developed from books in his personal library that he read, and letters and documents he wrote.

In this book, "West Point" is a metaphor for "America". The book could have been named "America: Character Leadership ... Thomas Jefferson", for, telling you the real story behind the founding of West Point (my first aim in writing this book) takes you on a fantastic journey through history that brings into clear focus the true meaning of America, and what it means to be an American during this time of terrorism and soul-searching.

Your journey also reveals the treasure of great moral stories from history that shaped a young America, Thomas Jefferson, and West Point, and teaches us character and leadership by moral imitation (my second aim for this book).

The story behind the book began when my son received the Offer of Admission from West Point. I challenged him with the question, "why West Point?". To answer that question, we found it necessary to first answer the question, "why does America still have a West Point?". The usual answers were neither convincing nor compelling. Then, "why was West Point founded in the first place?". I read everything available, and found not a single reason squared with the facts. Okay, simply find out what the founder said. "Who <u>was</u> the founder?". We know that President Jefferson signed an 1802 Bill, a tiny piece of which established a corps of engineers, but, he was never credited with being the founder, the prime mover behind West Point. So, who was? I could find no answer. This was becoming a mystery. I was becoming a detective trying to solve that mystery.

Now bitten by the history bug, I kept researching. One day, deep in the archives of the Library of Congress, I uncovered information that proved Thomas Jefferson was, secretly, the prime mover to found West Point. Now I just had to answer the question, "<u>why</u> did Thomas Jefferson found West Point?". I poured over the official documents and thousands of his writings in the archives to dig up just one single sentence saying why he founded it. There was none. So, detective-like, I proceeded to develop a profile on what shaped his mind and influenced his thinking. I got inside his head and heart by reading his own words, and the same books (on history, philosophy, character, and leadership) that he read. I got to know Thomas Jefferson. As you read this book, you too will be reading what he read and learning what he learned. You'll get to know him, too. You'll be getting the same education (in history, philosophy, character, and leadership) that he got, except made easier and more interesting, of course. And you are there when I give the world formal notice (my third aim for this book) of my history-making discovery that it was Thomas Jefferson who founded West Point, and, more important, <u>why</u> Thomas Jefferson founded West Point.

To make this book fun, easy, understandable, and educational for, not just scholars, but people of all ages and educations (my fourth aim for this book), I decided to write it as a creative nonfiction story, presenting true history and philosophy within the framework of a fantasy. The story begins, fantasy-like, in heaven when a guardian angel, Thomas, is sent down to America to visit a Congressman, Harry, in his sleep. Thomas takes Harry -- and you, too -- on that fantastic journey through history that winds its way from ancient to post-Revolutionary times to witness, "firsthand", history being made. To draw you into this unusual reader participatory role of "being there", I chose a dramatic dialogue between Harry and Thomas as my narrative vehicle, and, I intentionally wrote in a colloquial vernacular way that guides you to read the text like it sounds when we talk to each other in everyday life, complete with innovative punctuation, contractions, underlining, slang spelling, exclamation points, and other devices (grammatical "flaws" included), much like the script of a play or movie. I painstakingly converted the difficult philosophy in Jefferson's books into ordinary language, and blended-in hundreds of poems, anecdotes, and "miniatures" (scenarios from history with pen-and-ink cartoon sketches), to make it light and refreshing. And, take note. Though I present the history and philosophy within the framework of a fantasy, it is true and accurate history and philosophy for which I read 170 complete books, over 10,000 Jefferson letters, and hundreds of other sources during 10 years (over 10,000 hours) of work I did, philanthropically, for America and West Point.

Now, let me say a few words about the mechanics of the book. To keep the dialogue between Harry and Thomas flowing, I simply use an asterisk to tell you when one or the other is beginning to speak. For example:

* Have you seen enough, Harry?
* Yes, Thomas, I have.
* Good, then we can go on.

I put the text of the "miniatures" in quotations to indicate conversation, not to imply the text is a direct quotation from history. Each miniature has an endnote so you can know whether its setting is actual documented history, or, imputed from history. For example:

"Come away from here with me, dear Rebecca."
"Sir, like fine china, reputation is easily fractured."
"You have nothing to fear from an honorable British Officer."[22]

And, I use circle quotations, °o °O, to show someone is thinking, not speaking.

My venues for research were the Library of Congress, National Archives, West Point Archives and Library, and Rutgers University Library. I use "West Point" to mean The United States Military Academy, unless otherwise noted.

West Point is like a piece in a jigsaw puzzle. You don't know its significance until you see how it fits into the whole puzzle. There is only one book that puts together the whole jigsaw puzzle of history and shows how West Point fits into it in order to reveal the true significance of West Point to America. This is it. And, there had never been a book to inform current issues like, "why attend West Point?", and, "why have a West Point at a cost per officer (allegedly) four times that of ROTC?". Now there is. This book revolutionizes thinking on West Point by linking West Point, America, Thomas Jefferson, character, leadership, and education into a single chain.

1.
PROLOGUE

In the Prologue you find out who Thomas and Harry are, and how this story came about. Remember, these °o °O mean thinking, not speaking.

CHAPTER 1: OUTSIDE OF SPACE AND TIME (HEAVEN)

* ∞Thommmmmas. ...... Are ...... you ...... there? ...... Come ...... in, ... Thomas. Ah! There you are! ∞

* ∞Yes. I am here. And I am surprised to meet you again out here ... where shall I say ... outside of space and time? ∞

* ∞On Earth you called it Heaven, Thomas. You may still call it that if you wish. We know what you mean. And yes, I know you are surprised to meet me again. We had to make contact with you quite urgently. It seems we have a problem. One of our eternal bedrocks — Virtue — has come under threat. That is a sign of trouble for our eternal order of things. ∞

* ∞What can I possibly do? Only ... you know **WHO** ... can do something about that. ∞

* ∞You can help us, Thomas. This threat happens to be at one of our outposts that you come from. Earth. The threat is to your United States Military Academy at West Point, New York. ∞

* ∞Oh? ∞

* ∞Yes. An unusually great number of "requests" about it are coming in. ∞

* ∞About West Point? Is that so? ∞

* ∞Yes. Almost 15,000 so far this Earth year. ∞

* ∞Requests? I take it you mean prayers? ∞

* ∞That is correct. But they are not the usual kind of requests — prayers. This year, many are prayers requesting that we give special guidance to the Congressmen of your American government in their decisions regarding West Point. ∞

* ∞Prayers for politicians? That is unusual! ∞

* ∞Perhaps it is. However, you would not consider it so unusual if you heard the stories behind those prayers. I cannot tell you every story, of course. There are thousands of them. And they are all different But let me give you one example. I shall tell you the story of one young man we just recently heard from. We shall call him, Kyle. His story began when he received an unexpected letter from the West Point football coach. His S.A.T. scores, high school grades, and athletic ability made him a top prospect. West Point was interested in him.

Kyle was, likewise, interested in West Point. He had lived in England with his family for five years because of his Dad's business. During holidays and Dad's business trips, they would visit with "extended family" from America who happened to be in West Germany with the U.S. Army. "Uncle Carl" and other Officers stationed with him in Heidelberg would often talk about their days at West Point. That is how Kyle first heard about West Point.

When his family moved back home to America, they occasionally visited his Uncle Conrad who lived near West Point. They would drive through the West Point grounds or catch Army football games. Also, his Grandmother mentioned that his Uncle Tom was once offered an appointment to attend West Point. So, when Kyle got that first letter from the football coach, he was familiar with the place. He opened a file, the first step in the long procedure of applying to West

Point. Several months later he received an appointment and nomination. He also had acceptances from other top colleges. His Dad was thrilled with the one from M.I.T. Kyle was thrilled with the one from West Point. That surprised his Mom and Dad. West Point is a serious, difficult, life changing commitment for an eighteen year old — especially when he does not know what West Point is <u>really</u> all about. They decided it was time for another serious discussion with him about college.

Now. Instead of my telling you about that discussion, it would be better if I were to take you straight back to that time so you can see it for yourself. Seeing is a thousand times better than hearing, you know. ᵒᴼ
* ᴼᵒ Can you do that? ᵒᴼ
* ᴼᵒ Why of course I can. Surely you must know by now that **WE** can do anything! Watch!

See? Here we are! That is Kyle, doing his homework. Now let us witness that discussion for ourselves. ᵒᴼ

"Kyle! Did you finish your homework?"
"Just about Dad. Why?"
"Your Mom and I want to sit down and have a little talk with you."
"Uh oh! About what?"
"About college …. especially West Point."
"Oh!"
"You wanna be an Officer, Kyle? How come? We're not really a military family."
"I know, Dad. But what I like is the idea of not just going to an ordinary college with all the drugs and other stuff. I like the idea of being with a bunch of people that think like me. And I like the idea of doing something more than you can do at other colleges. Have you guys read the West Point brochure yet?"
"Pretty much. But tell Mom and I what you mean by something more."
"Well. I like the leadership. The clean lifestyle. The challenge. I like the idea that I would face the exact same challenges that Lee and Grant and MacArthur and Eisenhower and a lot of other great Americans faced when they were my age. And just think, I would be doing that on the exact same ground they did it on. That's really something! Right?"
"That's for sure. But they were at West Point to be career Officers. They were interested in the military for a career. You're not … are you?"
"Maybe. By the way, remember when I talked to the Army recruiter on career day at school and applied for ROTC? I just got a scholarship! That was quick, wasn't it!"
"Well, I'd say ROTC would be your better bet. You can go to M.I.T. or Penn or Princeton or Dartmouth, still become an Army

3

Officer, but also have your civilian job."

"I know. Right now I'm keeping all my options open."

"Don't forget, Kyle, West Point is meant for people who think they might want to be in the military full time."

"I know, Mom. Don't worry. I won't do anything until I find out what West Point is really all about."

"That's good, Kyle. But, that's a lot of work!

"Maybe you could help me, Dad? Right now, between baseball and calc. and bio. and all my other subjects, I don't have much spare time."

"I know. And funny you should ask. I just happened to be reading something about West Point. So I kind of have a head start, already."

"Ohh yehh! Just happened? I should have known ... Dad.

So. What is the story about West Point?"

"I've only just begun. But as usual, it already looks like good news and bad news."

"Uh ohhh! Give me the good news, first."

"The good news is: it's a great education; it has a major in biological sciences; and it awards more than a college degree and commission as an Army Officer. It's supposed to be the premier institution in the world for teaching leadership!"

"What's the bad news?"

"The bad news is that it's a hard four years. And the worst thing, it seems there's always someone in Congress with the bright idea of shutting it down to save money."

"Oh no! Shut it down?" Really? Why is that?"

"I'm not sure, Kyle. But I'll find out! So leave it with me for now. I think we've talked enough about it for tonight. You have a baseball game tomorrow, right? Aren't you on the mound for this one?"

"Yeh. It's at home again, too. You and Mom coming?"

"Yep! How's the arm feel?"

"Good. Good. ... I guess I better go to bed."

"Me too. And, I don't know about you, but being that you're interested in West Point, Mom and I are going to pray those Congressmen don't cut the legs out from under it!"

"Yeh! Me too ... and that we can find out what the story is with West Point so I can make the right decision. Right, Dad? Right Mom? Right?"

"Right, Kyle!"

Oo So there you have it, Thomas. There are thousands of such stories. But it seems that some influential people don't care. They have gotten one of the Congressmen to "tamper" with West Point. And the worst part of it is .... this Congressman does not have a clue as to what West Point is really all about. **WE**

4

want you to tell him the true story of West Point. **WE** want you to contact that good soul while he is still asleep so he does not remember you when he awakens. Tell him everything about West Point so he can form his own judgment. And ... oh yes ... be sure you speak to him in the particular style of the English they are now using in America. It will make him feel more comfortable with you. I believe they say you are speaking in the vernacular when you do that. Do you understand what I am intimating? ^{oO}

* ^{Oo} Of course. I fully appreciate your intimation. Or perhaps I should start practicing right now by saying ... I hear you ... I'm on my way ... what's this guy's name, this Congressman, I'll have to be contacting? ^{oO}

* ^{Oo} That is very good, Thomas! Ohhh, we can make the Congressman respond to any name we choose. So we shall call him ... ohhh ... how about ... Harry? ^{oO}

* ^{Oo} I've got ya! But I'd still prefer to simply fill him in on West Point. Why can't I simply put all the information about it straight into Harry's head? ^{oO}

* ^{Oo} Ah, ah, ahhh! You know better than that, Thomas! That is against the RULES! We are not allowed to work that way! We must not do that! Why that would be ...... crossing the threshold! ^{oO}

CHAPTER 2: ON EARTH IN AMERICA

* H a r r .... ry.
* Oh God! Oh my God! Get away! Who are you? What do you want here? Oh my God!
* I'm not God, Harry. I'm Thomas. But don't be afraid. I won't hurt you. Ah! You're looking over at your body. Don't worry about your body. It's still sleeping. And, it'll be alright. We'll just let it sleep there for a while.
* Let it sleep there? What do you mean? What do you want ... uh ... Joseph, did you say? Where did you come from? And do I know you? You look familiar!
* The name's not Joseph, Harry. Thomas is the name. And you know me now. I just want to talk with you. So don't be afraid. I'll help you.
* Help me? Talk with me? Talk with me about what?
* It seems that you have gotten something into trouble here on Earth that is near and dear to us.
* To us? What do you mean ... us? Is there someone else here? Is someone else around here somewhere with you?
* No, there's no one else here. But you can't fool me, Harry. I know that you know what I'm talking about!
* You do? Can you read my mind?
* You know that I'm talking about West Point.
* Oh! West Point! Yes! The West Point agenda! Well, that's nothing personal you know. But I have to keep some pushy folks happy. They're the ones who got me where I am today in Congress. Politics is my game. I can't always do what's right. Without their ... umm, help ... my election campaign is dead on arrival. Then my career in Congress is over. You know how it is, don't you.
* No, I don't know how it is, Harry. It wasn't supposed to work that way in America. And, West Point is something more important than politics. Do you actually know anything about West Point?
* I must confess I don't have the time to find out about it. My aides are working on it. I only know we're supposed to put an unfavorable "spin" on it. But you probably know all about West Point ... don't you! You're probably an Army man. Right?
* No, I'm not an Army man. No, I'm not a West Point graduate. No, I have nothing to gain or lose by it. But, yes, I do know about West Point. Yes, I do know the facts about it. And that's why I'm here — to give you the facts about it. I just want you to know the true facts. Have you ever been to West Point?
* No. I'm afraid not.
* Well that's what we shall do first then. I'll take you there. We'll do a tour so you can get a feel for the place. Then after that, I'll tell you what West Point is really all about.
* How can I do that? I'm over there sleeping! Oops! See that! Now you have me saying that, too!
* It isn't a problem, Harry. That's only your body over there sleeping. You're going with me. I'm taking you fifty miles north of New York City to West Point, New York.

And here we are!

* What happened? Where are we?

* Like I said, we're at West Point. We're at the spot where West Point, the <u>place</u>, began. And, as you remember, Mom and Dad of that young man, Kyle, told him they were praying for Congress to not cut the legs out from under West Point. If you listen carefully, I'll now let you hear what else they're praying for:

A PARENT'S PRAYER

Build me a son, O Lord, who will be strong enough to know when he is weak, and brave enough to face himself when he is afraid; one who will be proud and unbending in honest defeat, and humble and gentle in victory.

Build me a son whose wishes will not take the place of deeds; a son who will know Thee --- and that to know himself is the foundation stone of knowledge.

Lead him, I pray, not in the path of ease and comfort, but under the stress and spur of difficulties and challenge. Here let him learn to stand up in the storm; let him learn compassion for those who fail.

Build me a son whose heart will be clear, whose goal will be high, a son who will master himself before he seeks to master others, one who will reach into the future, yet never forget the past.

And after all these things are his, add, I pray, enough of a sense of humor, so that he may always be serious, yet never take himself too seriously. Give him humility, so that he may always remember the simplicity of true greatness, the open mind of true wisdom, and the meekness of true strength.

Then I, his parent, will dare to whisper, through all eternity, "I have not lived in vain".[1]

* That was powerful.

* Believe it or not, Harry, there are thousands of requests, prayers, like that one, coming in to us each earthnight from parents for their sons, and, for their daughters.

2.

WEST POINT: THE PLACE

In this part you see West Point as it looks to a visitor today. You can use it as a tour guide when you visit West Point. Note that the points of interest along the tour are generally arranged in chronological order of history.

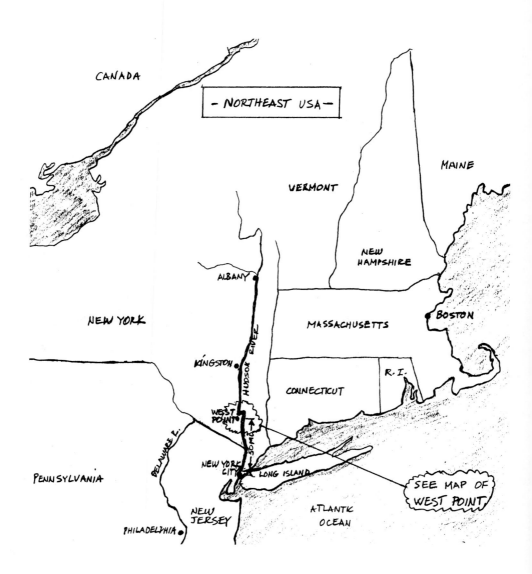

- NORTHEAST USA -

CANADA

MAINE

VERMONT

NEW HAMPSHIRE

ALBANY

NEW YORK

BOSTON

MASSACHUSETTS

KINGSTON

HUDSON RIVER

R.I.

CONNECTICUT

WEST POINT

DELAWARE R.

50 MILES

NEW YORK CITY

LONG ISLAND

SEE MAP OF WEST POINT

PENNSYLVANIA

NEW JERSEY

ATLANTIC OCEAN

PHILADELPHIA

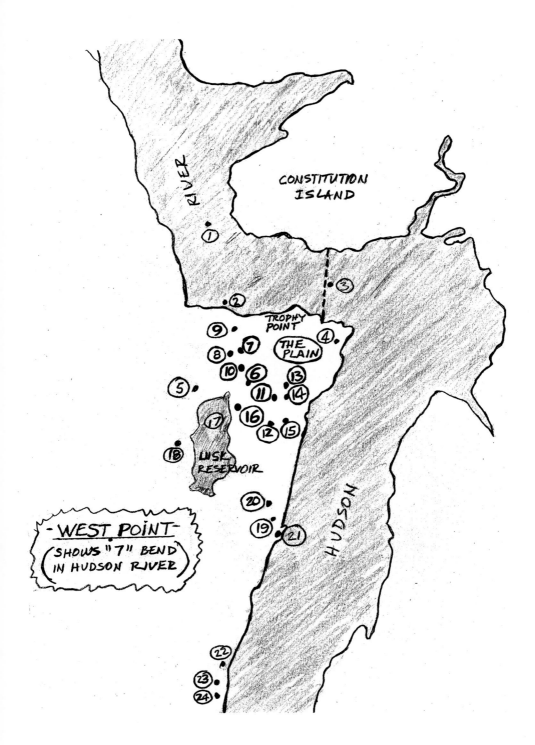

CONSTITUTION ISLAND

RIVER

TROPHY POINT

THE PLAIN

LUSK RESERVOIR

HUDSON

-WEST POINT-
(SHOWS "7" BEND
IN HUDSON RIVER)

11

THE TOUR

We will begin our tour with what <u>geologically</u> created West Point. The River! Showing no respect, the River had throughout the geological ages ruthlessly cut its way southward through the mountains and carved out the river canyon we see in the view before us (1).

(1) Geological "River Canyon"–view from river bank

But the River had also met up with a formidable obstacle — a mass of solid granite rock! Showing great respect, it had gone eastward around the mass of granite rock before continuing on its way south toward the ocean (2).

(2) River turning eastward around "Granite Rock"

The sharp bend due to its detour around the granite rock made the River's path look like a "7". Therefore the west bank of the "7" in the River, being the mass of granite rock, jutted out to form a point — the west point of the bend in the River.

* It's a stunning view of the Hudson River!
* The view from this west point of the bend in the River is called the "million dollar view". It was from this west point on the river that the great chain was stretched to the opposite bank during the Revolutionary War to halt British warships (3).

(3) Where the chain was at the "7" in the river

Up the steep bank from the River are the remnants of Fort Clinton (originally called Fort Arnold), built by the Polish patriot Thaddeus Kosciuszko to guard the chain and the River (4).

(4) Statue of Kosciuszko at Fort Clinton (originally called Fort Arnold) above chain

13

If we go behind Fort Clinton, away from the River, across The Plain, and look up the next steep embankment, we can see Fort Putnam (5), built to protect the back door of Fort Clinton below.

(5) View from Fort Putnam guarding Fort Clinton below–shows the "7"

In the mountains behind Fort Putnam are a series of small forts, called redouts, that protect the back door of Fort Putnam. This entire complex of fortifications on the mass of granite rock at the west point in the river was simply called — West Point! Commander-in-Chief George Washington also called it "the key to the Continent". He considered it the Gibralter of America. So did the British. And during his visit to West Point in 1841, Charles Dickens would say that a military academy "could not stand on more appropriate ground, and any ground more beautiful can hardly be".

Back down on The Plain we see the statue of Washington that shows him expediting the work in 1779 to get his Gibraltar of America finished before the expected British attack (6).

(6) Statue of Washington expediting the fortifications in 1779

In the end, West Point deterred an attack, but couldn't deter a disgruntled Benedict Arnold from almost turning the whole place over to the British. Arnold barely escaped from being hung by rowing down river from near what is today's West Point Boat Docks, which we shall see later.

Not far from Washington's statue we can visit with the statue of someone called Sylvanus Thayer. He's also called "The Father of the Military Academy"! His methods nurtured the Academy to international prominence during his thirteen year watch as its Superintendant. His work is the reason Charles Dickens said "at West Point the course of education is severe but well devised and manly", and Andrew Jackson simply said "West Point is the best school in the world"(7).

Thayer's statue is next to the house he was the first to occupy, the oldest building at West Point and now the Superintendant's living quarters (8)

(7) & (8) Statue of Sylvanus Thayer looking at oldest bldg. at West Point that he was the first to occupy in 1820 (now superintendant's house)

While we're at this end of the "post", let's depart from chronological order for the moment. To the rear of Thayer's statue, the neat little house you see in front of the huge Eisenhower Hall cadet center is the one used in the famous film about West Point called "The Long Gray Line" (9).

(9) Marty Mahr's house in "The Long Gray Line" movie

15

Now, we go back to Thayer's statue and look in the same direction he's looking. We see the parade ground that takes up a big chunk of "The Plain" of West Point. If we go to the far left side of the Plain and walk along that side just uphill from the River, called Trophy Point, we'll see relics such as the Great Chain, the cannons from 1812 and the Mexican War and the Civil War, and the tall monument to the Civil War called Battle Monument — the largest column of polished granite in the Western Hemisphere (THE PLAIN).

(The Plain) Battle Monument

Now let's go from Trophy Point away from the River to the parade ground of The Plain and stop in front of the bleachers. Looking to our left (not walking there) we see the baseball stadium that houses Doubleday Field, named for the West Point grad Abner Doubleday who is renouned for having invented baseball. Most people don't know he's also the one who fired the first shot from Fort Sumter to start the Civil War that would put many West Point grads such as Robert E. Lee, Ulysses S. Grant, William Tecumseh Sherman, and Thomas "Stonewall" Jackson into the history books!

Turning our sights back to the far right end of The Plain (not walking there) we see West Point grad Douglas MacArthur's statue in front of the barracks named for him. It's the one to the left of Thayer's statue and the Superintendant's house. Shortly before MacArthur's class graduated, President Theodore Roosevelt had said, "no other institution in the land has contributed so many names as West Point to the honor roll of the Nation's greatest citizens". And he should know. He and his Rough Riders were with some of them in the Spanish-American War (10).

(10) MacArthur statue and barracks to the left of the superintendant's house.

16

If we now go across the parade ground away from the bleachers, we come to the statue of West Point grad Dwight David Eisenhower who went on to be the President of the United States after leading the victory in Europe in World War II (11).

(11) Eisenhower Statue with academic buildings in background

West Point is connected with several Presidents, starting with George Washington after the Revolution, Thomas Jefferson who founded the Military Academy, Jefferson Davis (The Confederacy) during the Civil War, Ulysses S. Grant after the Civil War, Dwight D. Eisenhower, and several foreign students who went on to be President of their countries. And speaking of Grant, down the road behind Eisenhower's statue is historic Grant Hall. Also down there are Lee, Sherman, Pershing, and Bradley Barracks, named for those famous graduates (12).

(12) Looking toward Lee, Grant, Sherman, Bradley, and Pershing Barracks

17

Nearby is the statue of General George S. Patton — the one opposite the library. He hardly used books from the library to sharpen his grades. However, he did sharpen his military knowledge by becoming a fanatical reader of military related books. And that later proved to be crucial. For Patton became America's answer to the ingenious German General, Field Marshall Erwin Rommel, during World War II! An Academy grad who started at the Virginia Military Institute (VMI), Patton had come to revere West Point so much that he called it "a holy place" (13).

(13) Patton Statue, opposite USMA Library, the "Plain" in the background

I would like you to note, if you havn't already guessed, the Library is the most extensive military library in America, if not the world. I would also like you to note the clock tower on the right. That's the one on which MacArthur as a cadet hid the reveille cannon one night. It took him just that one night to smuggle the cannon up there. It took military personnel one week to get it back down (14)!

(14) USMA Library, most extensive military library. Clock Tower where MacArthur hid the reveille canon as a cadet, on right

Although four of the five men ever to hold the rank of five star general — "Hap" Arnold, Omar Bradley, Eisenhower, and MacArthur — are "grads" (George Marshall was a V.M.I. grad), West Pointers have gained prominence in other fields as well. Leslie Groves ran the Manhattan Project that built the atomic bomb to end World War II, saving hundreds of thousands of American soldiers' lives. George Washington Goethals built the Panama Canal after everyone else had failed. Buzz Aldrin and Mike Collins were two of the three astronauts on the first moon landing. West Point has the fourth highest number of Rhodes Scholars of the thousands of colleges in the United States, only following behind Harvard, Yale, and Princeton. Even non-Rhodes Scholars, in fact non-grad West Pointers, such as James Abbot McNeill Whistler and Edgar Allen Poe are amongst America's greatest artists and writers, respectively. And besides the unique Battle Monument, West Point also has the highest all-stone office building in the world. It's located a few buildings down on the left side of the road from Eisenhower statue (15)!

(15) Highest all-stone office building in the world

And from down here we can see the Cadet Chapel with its gothic steeple if we position ourselves between the buildings and look uphill. The Cadet Chapel is noted for having the largest church organ in the world (16)!

(16) Cadet Chapel, which has the largest church organ in the world, seen between academic buildings from the Thayer Hall

You can't see them from here, but also uphill past the Cadet Chapel are Lusk Reservoir Area, as well as, the famous Michie Stadium where Army football powerhouses and many All-Americans such as Heisman Trophy winners Doc Blanchard, Glenn Davis, and Pete Dawkins played. Many tourists take the trouble to get back to their cars, take a break, then drive uphill (using Mills Road) to get a closeup look at the Cadet Chapel (16), Lusk Reservoir (17), Michie Stadium (18), and Fort Putnam (5).

(17) Top of Cadet Chapel below as viewed across Lusk Reservoir

(18) Michie Stadium next to Lusk Reservoir

Then they head all the way down to the River to the West Point railway station (19) and the steep uphill road from the station (20) by which excited young men for many decades arrived and departed.

(19) West Point Train Station–thousands arrived here, thousands left for war

(20) Road up to central area from train station. Used in filming "The Long Gray Line".

Down here is also the West Point Boat Dock area, I previously mentioned, from which Benedict Arnold made his escape downriver to the British side (21).

(21) West Point boat docks–Benedict Arnold escaped from near here

And finally, if we go uphill with the River to our left, we will come to three impressive military gothic-like structures. The first is the Thayer Hotel, still located on post and owned by West Point (22).

(22) The Thayer Hotel right on post at West Point

The second is the main gate, Thayer Gate, which continues to be guarded by Regular Army military police stationed at West Point (23).

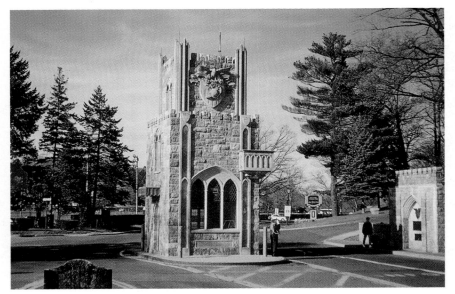

(23) Thayer Gate at south entrance to West Point

The third is the West Point Museum, located just beyond Thayer Gate on the lefthand side behind the Visitor Center (24).

(24)

3.

VIRTUE, LEADERS, AND LEADERSHIP

Before getting into the story behind West
Point, you need to first know what the
important but misused terms known as virtue,
leader, and leadership really mean.

CHAPTER 1: A FEELING OF PRIDE

That should give you a better feel for West Point, the Place, Harry.
* That was fun! It makes you feel proud. I never realized that's what West Point is all about.
* That's not what West Point is all about! I'm about to tell you what it's all about.
* It's a military college steeped in proud tradition. What else can you say?
* You've only seen West Point, the Place. I need to tell you about West Point, the Idea. The unseen West Point. The one few know about. The one you can't see by merely touring these famous statues and buildings and forts and million dollar view. The one that will give you an even greater feeling of pride than when we toured West Point, the Place. It's the real story behind West Point!
* I don't get you.
* What it boils down to is ... West Point is really about "putting old souls into young bodies"!
* Surely you jest. Old souls? Into young bodies? Me thinks you're getting into some pretty heavy stuff here, Thomas. And me thinks you're about to drop me in way over my head.
* Hmm. I see. °oI had better make it easier then.°O ..... I know what I'll do. I won't just tell you the unseen real story behind West Point. I'll show you! Someone once said that seeing is a thousand times better than hearing!
* Show me? How can you show me history? You made a believer out of me by showing me — while my body was sleeping — West Point as it stands today. But how can you show me history? How can you show me the past?
* We can do anything, Harry. You'll see. I shall take you through a ... well ... it's a timegame.
* Timegame? What's that? This is Harry you're talking to, you know! I wouldn't know a timegame from a toothbrush!
* Yes. Of Course. You couldn't understand. But you don't have to understand. You just have to think of it as a journey. I'll be taking you on a journey through time ... a super-special journey ... a journey through history. And we'll be seeing the "other side" of history, too, which can be fun — sometimes even funny! But, before we embark on that journey, Harry, I have to clue you in on something.
* Oh? On what?
* On leadership — especially West Point leadership.
* Leadership? Why? Everyone knows what leadership is.
* That's what you think! People toss that word around very loosely, you know.
* Oh! Okay! Tell me about leadership, then! But make it easy, will you!
* I promise I'll take it slowly ... one step at a time.

CHAPTER 2: NON-LEADERS, HEADMEN, BAD LEADERS

You need to know about leadership, Harry, — especially West Point leadership. I promised I'd make it easy. I said we'll take it slowly, one step at a time. So my first step is to tell you what appears to be obvious, but isn't. That is, the United States Military Academy at West Point is not your ordinary college. I don't mean it's different because of the spiffy uniforms and the magnificent military-Gothic, gray-granite buildings. I don't mean what would be obvious to even "Mr. Magoo" — that it's a military college. I mean the "Johns" and "Janes" of America are not at West Point just to earn their "sheepskins" — their diplomas. They are not there just to earn their "butter-bars" — to be commissioned as 2nd Lieutenants. And they are not there to be made into Rambos and Wonderwomen. Sure, Cadets get a top education and the West Point bachelor of science degree. They have the premier military science "curriculum". And they get a pile of practical training. They do, indeed, grunt and grind their way toward getting a lock on military and physical skills. So yes, Cadets are at West Point for all those things. But not <u>only</u> those things. The chief, foremost, paramount, unique reason they are at West Point is to learn leadership — to become good-leaders for our Nation. That's the name of the game. LEADERSHIP!

* Ah, I see. Then what <u>is</u> leadership?
* Leader and leadership are very slippery terms. They are among the most mis-used words in the English language. The way most folks and the American media use them makes them, well, almost meaningless. They throw around those words like halloween candy.

There are people with <u>zero</u> leadership ability, but are well known, and are therefore referred to as "leaders". Look at the sportsworld. We see ballplayers who lead the league in homeruns, for instance. That by no means makes them what the real world should call leaders. They're just at the top of the heap as home run hitters. Then we see professional basketball high scorers and top rebounders ... pulling down big money for doing something as insignificant to mankind as pulling down rebounds. They're certainly at the top of the league in scoring and rebounding ... and money ... but not certainly leaders. They may not have a clue about what it takes to be a <u>real</u> leader. Unfortunately, all of these peo-ple are often referred to as leaders! Here's a good example. .... We're now at a "pro" basketball arena.

* Wow! Here we are! Like the speed of light!
* Better, Harry! But you couldn't understand! Anyway, look at that rowdy bunch of fans carrying signs. The signs say, "We Want Mr.Basketball". And listen to what they're chanting as they march outside the arena!

> "Elect Mr. Basketball to Congress! We want Mr. Basketball for
> Congress! Elect Mr. Basketball"[1]

See what I mean? They think he's a leader just because he's a star basketball play-er. It's "idolship" ... not leadership!

Athletes are not in charge of a single person. Yet, their popularity gets mistaken for leadership. And the same can be said about people in the movies, television, and other media. They're necessarily well known. But they're not necessarily leaders. They're what **WE** would call — "non-leaders"!

Then, unlike non-leaders who are popular but not responsible for anyone, we'll next look at people who <u>are</u> responsible for other people, but are still not really leaders. Whether they're bosses over a few or many people, they are in fact the bosses. So they're mistakenly called leaders when they're often nothing but dead-beats. For example, we see politicians who get where they are because they're actually merely followers. You've seen that, right Harry? Many politicians get their "marching orders" from rich fat cats, don't they. They're just pawns in a power political chess game. Then we see the management types, running large corporations, who get their jobs because of their golf records, not because of their track records as leaders. It's worse than using "pull". It's "bootlicking". We'll visit a golf course so you can see what I mean. For instance, look at that "bootlicker" over there sucking up to the boss, probably the company president. As usual, he has the boss' ear. Now the boss is whispering something to him. Is it big, secret, important stuff? Let's listen and find out:

> "How did you do last year? Do you have the final 'numbers'?
> I'm corporate president. You can tell me."
> "Yes. I certainly do. Did quite well, in fact! Got my game
> down to a 5 handicap!"
> "Marvellous! You should win the big golf tournament then! °°I
> knew I hired the right person.°° That deserves a stock option!"
> "Thank you sir."[2]

Then we see the big boss who got where he is because he's already a rich fat-cat. His money may have fallen into his lap through dumb luck, or a megabucks inheritance, or even through crime! And, there are even bosses who are, unfortunately, losers as leaders even though they're skillful, or well educated, or hard workers. The bottom line is, there are a lot of bosses out there in charge of people who shouldn't be!

Now we'll go back a few years. We'll visit with Ohio State researcher, W.H.Crowley. Guess what he says about all those make believe "leaders" — those bosses in charge of people who shouldn't be. He says they're not real leaders. They're merely "headmen". That's an interesting term. Crowley says they're guys who are bosses merely because of: wealth; or connections; or a license; or a commission; or maybe even special knowledge in some subject. The unlucky folks who have "headmen" as bosses have to follow them anyway. They are, in fact, the bosses. Leadership has nothing to do with it. "Headmen" are no better than "non-leaders"!

Crowley gave a lecture about leaders to a group of peers in his profession, many years ago. If we go back in time and listen to this particular lecture, we hear him say that <u>one</u> of the important things a real leader as opposed to a headman has is the knack of <u>persuading</u> people to follow.[3] Crowley is brilliant in his field. But, there are always critics who misinterpret even the words of experts. Listen to what those three critics over there are quietly saying about his speech:

> "Crowley's got it all wrong you know! It takes more than
> <u>persuasion</u> to make a leader!"
>> "Well, he doesn't have it <u>all</u> wrong. He's just pointing out one
>> thing of major significance."
> "He made it sound like it's the <u>only</u> thing to me!"
>> "We all know better than that, don't we."[4]

They should know better than that. Good leadership is more than just persuasion. Look at Hitler, Mussolini, and Saddam Hussein to name a few. They had charisma. They stirred the masses into frenzies of "followership". They had the knack of persuasion. People followed them — even if for the wrong reasons. And they all came pretty close to getting their evil work done. The most successful "bad-guys" are always great at persuading people to follow. They're among that rare species in the world that are called "born leaders". But they're not good-leaders. We can all do without those kind of born-leaders. They're nothing but "bad-leaders". Who needs them!

* Yes. I see what you mean, Thomas. Now I understand why you say leaders and leadership are slippery terms. Your examples of "non-leaders", and "head-men", and "bad-leaders" are enlightening. So let me ask you about the young Cadets at West Point. You said they go there for one purpose. That's to become good-leaders for our Nation. How do they do that? What do they have to do? What qualities do they actually need to learn? In fact, what in heavens name are the qualities that anyone needs, deep down inside, to be what you call a good-leader ... in any field?

CHAPTER 3: VIRTUE

* We don't need to visit all the experts on leadership to tell us the qualities good-leaders need. I'll summarize what they all agree on. They say, first, good-leaders need that rare commodity called VIRTUE — morals, ethics, and character! That's things like honor, trust, courage, loyalty, compassion, integrity, and many others. Second, intelligence is needed. So it's Virtue — morals, ethics, and character. And it's intelligence.[5] Got that, Harry?

* Yes and no. I think I know what's meant by morals, ethics, and character. But the <u>difference</u> between them isn't all that clear to me. How do they relate to each other? In fact, what actually is Virtue?

* Good question. Before we go on, I'll clear it up. "Virtue" is an eternal, universal, never-ending <u>ideal</u> having to do with right and wrong, good and evil. Morals, ethics, and character are like three branches of Virtue.

"Morals" — shown by the "moral virtues" — deals more with your relationship to what you call God. Moral virtues are never-changing things like truth and honor and duty. Lying, cheating, stealing, lusting, and so on are their opposites.

"Ethics" — shown by the "ethical virtues" — deals more with your relationships to what you call society. Ethical virtues are things like justice and freedom and fairness and liberty.

"Character" — shown by the "character virtues" — deals more with you, the individual. Character virtues are things like courage and loyalty and discipline and sincerity and perseverence and responsibility.

* So morals, ethics, and character make up the overall ideal called Virtue?

* Yes. And "the virtues", as distinguished from the overall thing called "Virtue", are sometimes called "traits" — moral traits, ethical traits, and character traits!

* Ah! I see! All of the virtues you mentioned are also called traits.

* Right. But I have to warn you that the lines between morals, ethics, and character are not bright, sharp lines. They're blurred in many cases. There's overlapping. Take adultery, for example. Adultery is bad morals (lieing and cheating) <u>and</u> bad character (disloyalty). In the Army it's also bad ethics — it's illegal! But no matter. Morals, ethics, and character are still all a part of Virtue.

* I see. I think I understand now.

* Good! Then we'll get back to looking at good-leaders.[6]

CHAPTER 4: GOOD-LEADERS

So, Harry, good-leaders need that special thing called Virtue — morals, ethics, and character. Plus they need to have intelligence and the right kind of education. That's what the experts on leadership say![7] We can go back and sort through all the research on leaders and leadership. But, we won't. Instead, I'll give you a summary of all the conclusions.

* That works for me!

* And I hasten to assure you that their conclusions were sifted from mountains of data. But it all boils down to this. You should use the mix of different virtues that are most important to the particular field and situation you're working in. With different jobs, some virtues required of you as leader will be more important than others. Again, it all depends on the job, the situation, and the kind of people who are the "followers".[8] I'll take you around to show you examples of what I mean.

First look at this union leader. He can fire-up a bunch of grumbling employees real well. He's just now telling them to down tools, stop work, and use their "power in numbers". He's telling them not to worry about this month's pay. He says it's the dream of the future that counts. And he's gotten them into a full blown strike. The wife of a worker is watching. She's holding their small child, and there are two others at her side. Let's hear what she has to say about it:

> "Now look what he's gone and done! I <u>told</u> Daddy not to join that Union! Future dreams don't put bread on our table, do they kids!"[9]

Traits, like persuasion, used by that union leader are not the same as those needed by the next leader we'll look at. He's a scientist ... about to light the fuse of his brainy research team by challenging them to solve a problem. That'll push them toward exploding open a longtime mystery of science! Achievement and dedication and perseverence are the types of leadership virtues that are important here.

Now we'll visit with yet another kind of leader — the Army Officer. You can see he's working with a somewhat different mix of qualities and traits. But mostly, people under him have to trust him. And he has to hang onto that trust even from tired and scared and sick young soldiers ... perhaps in the heat of battle or the height of chaos. Listen to what he's telling them during a recent struggle:

> "Come on men! You'll be alright. Just follow me. This is what
> you trained for. You'll do just fine! You know you can trust
> me!"[10]

If this Officer's men are to believe him and follow him, they have to <u>trust</u> him. If they don't, he fails! The mission fails! The Army fails!

Speaking of trust. It reminds me of a landmark study made by theorist R.M. Stodgill. He sifted through <u>everything ever written</u> about leadership!

* Everything? Really? That's incredible!

* It is. And he spared others the pain of having to do all that research. He gave up the bottom line. His study concluded that Virtue, especially trust and integrity, is what's crucial in a good-leader![11]

So, we can see that morals, ethics, and character are important to everyone, not just the military. Why? Because everyone has a boss, a leader. Leaders in every walk of life — business, industry, academics, civil service, and even politics — need lofty morals, ethics, and character. Leaders having bad morals, ethics, or character can kill jobs, dreams, careers, families — and even men, women, and children. Yes, in some cases they can cost people life and limb!

CHAPTER 5: GOOD-LEADERS FOR THE MILITARY

Now I'll tell you the part leadership plays in the last thing I just mentioned — life and death! You may not believe there are some leaders who hold life and death in their hands. But there are. Take Court judges. They may have to some-day decide on the death penalty. Take doctors. Their work could mean life or death to patients. And then there are America's military leaders — Officers. Their decisions could mean life or death to people they know and see every day under their leadership![12]

Most judges and doctors will never have to make a life and death decision dur-ing their careers. Most career military Officers will! At sometime during their careers, Officers will be in a life-and-death situation. History and statistics prove that to be true. They must be prepared for it![13]

It's true. Officer-leaders have to know the art of war. But they also have to know the "art" of life-and-death decision making. That's why moral, ethical, and character training is important at West Point. That's why they learn about con-cern for others at West Point. That's why putting up with stress is crucial at West Point. In short, that's why the name of the game at West Point is producing good-leaders!

Making a decent living is important to everyone. Making a profit is important to a corporation. Hitting the budget goal is important to an executive. Complet-ing a job is important to a manager. Getting good shipments out is important to an industrialist. All of these things put great pressures on leaders in the civilian world. But the pressure on a leader in the military world is actually greater!

* How do you figure that?
* Well, for example, are there board meetings or budget goals or production goals that call upon civilian leaders to put their own lives on the line like military Officer-leaders have to?
* Of course not.
* How many civilian leaders are here to defend the security of our nation like Officer-leaders are? In fact, how many are expected to put the greater good of society and the nation above themselves?[14]
* A few civilian political leaders, perhaps. But that's it.
* Right. And do civilian leaders besides those in political office have to swear an oath their first day on the job to keep our nation free? How many swear to commit their "life, fortune, and sacred honor" to the job?[15]
* None that I know of.
* How many civilian leaders can go to jail if they don't do what their boss tells them to do, whether the boss is a good-leader or not?
* None.
* Do top civilian leaders have the kind of technological power under their con-trol to take over America, if they wanted to? And how many would you trust not to do so if they did have that power?
* Hmm.

* And again, how many civilian leaders hold young peoples' lives in their hands like Officer-leaders do?

* I see what you mean.

* Good! Because all of these things are the reasons why Officer-leaders must be good-leaders. That's why West Point is important to America. In that respect, it's more important than terrific places like the Harvard Business School and Yale Law School and other great Schools![16]

CHAPTER 6: THE OFFICER'S COMMISSION: A LICENSE TO LEAD

Cadets who make it through West Point are appointed by the President of the United States as Officers to act on his behalf in military matters. They receive a legal Commission for that purpose. Most people don't realize it, Harry, but it's actually a "license"!

* You mean like the licenses-to-practice that civil agencies give to doctors, lawyers, architects, engineers, and so forth?

* Correct. Like those licenses, it says Officers have the required skills in their field. And therefore they have the legal right to go out and flog their skills on other people. But, unlike civil licenses, the military Officer's license isn't just a legal license. It's also a moral license! This license truly grants the authority to decide who will live and who will die in certain circumstances!

* That's pretty heavy baggage to carry!

* Americans put the lives of their sons and daughters in the hands of Officer-leaders commissioned by the President! Those leaders should be intelligent and should be trained in morals, ethics, and character. The Commission — their license — should be taken very seriously. And it should be given only to good-leaders!

CHAPTER 7: MAKING GOOD LEADERS

So who would not want to see America's military leaders trained in morals, ethics, and character? Only America's enemies. Right? The Saddam Hussein's of your modern world would just love for America to have Officer-leaders with poor morals, ethics, and character.

* But in making <u>good</u> leaders that have good morals, ethics, and character, how do we know <u>what</u> is good morals and <u>what</u> is good ethics and <u>what</u> is good character, Thomas? Who's to say what is moral or ethical behavior? Who am I or anyone else to tell others what's right or wrong, what's good or evil, what's moral or immoral, what's ethical or unethical? Why should anyone believe anyone else? Who set the standards? And why should I believe them? In fact, why should I even care about morals and ethics? And therefore, should I care about a place like West Point in the first place? Unless I should meet God[17], who can I believe?

* Unless you meet God, as you say here on Earth, wouldn't you think you can believe the greatest thinkers and prophets that God has put on this Earth for that purpose?

* Hm. ...... I guess there's no one better to believe!

* Good! For that's who I'm about to show you — the greatest thinkers and prophets of all time! And whether they're religious or non-religious — no matter <u>how</u> they come at the questions — we're talking about **philosophers**! The questions you just asked are age old questions. The greatest thinkers and prophets in history have agonized and struggled over them. They're basic questions about life. They're about who you are. They're about what life is all about. They're the heavy questions of ... dare I say it ... philosophy! But don't worry, Harry. I promise I'll lighten the heaviness of philosophy. You'll see. Like the other side of history, philosophy can also be fun — sometimes even funny. It can even be poetic, like this piece of philosophy on being a leader:

YOU'LL BE A LEADER, IF

from: Rudyard Kipling

If you can keep your head when all about you
    Are losing theirs — and blaming it on you;
If you can trust yourself when all men doubt you,
    But make allowance for their doubting, too;
If you can dream — but not make dreams your master;
    And you can think — but not make thoughts your aim;
If you can meet with triumph and disaster
    And treat those two imposters just the same;
If you can talk with crowds but not lose Virtue,
    Or walk with kings — and keep the common touch;
If you can stand when nothings left inside you;

And all men count with you, but none too much;
If you can fill the unforgiving minute
   With sixty seconds worth of distance run —
Then yours is the Earth — and everything that's in it,
   What's more — a Leader of man you'll be, my son!

The virtue is: Character. It's a whole branch of Virtue that's
needed by leaders.

* I see what you mean.
* So now you're ready, Harry. I've given you some background on leaders and leadership. We're ready to begin our adventure — our journey in time — that tells us how the United States Military Academy at West Point came about. You're about to see why young leaders from West Point have a little deeper insight into American values — deeper than most people have. You're about to see the real story behind West Point!

4.

THE STORY BEHIND WEST POINT: THE IDEA

The roots of West Point go all the way back to ancient times, and even before! You are taken back to ancient times to see how those roots grow through the Middle East, Greek civilization, the Roman Empire, Europe, 1700's America, and finally, to West Point.

CHAPTER 1: PUTTING OLD SOULS INTO YOUNG BODIES

The story of West Point begins a long time ago during ancient times in the Near East. So that's where we're off to now, Harry.

*   Why all the way back to ancient times? Can't we just see how Americans thought back in 1802 when West Point was founded?

*   I <u>will</u> show you how Americans, especially Thomas Jefferson, thought in those days. But for you to understand how Americans thought in those days, I'll first have to show you how people in Europe thought in those days.

*   Why?

*   Because their philosophy books are the ones Americans learned from. And for you to understand why people in Europe thought the way they thought in those days, I'll have to show you how <u>their</u> philosophy books developed. That'll take us back to the Middle ages, and then even further back to the Roman Empire. But Roman philosophy was little more than the old Greek philosophy warmed over and written in Latin. So we'll continue back to ancient Greece, and even before that. Like I said, modern West Point is about the mysteries of morals, ethics, and character — about "putting old souls into young bodies". People throughout history have been on a quest to understand those mysteries. And that quest began in ancient times!

*   I see. You're saying West Point is a product of history.

*   That's right. <u>All</u> institutions are products of history and the history of philosophy. Everything throughout history is inter-connected. Think of West Point as a single piece in a giant jigsaw puzzle of history and philosophy. A single piece in any jigsaw puzzle only has meaning when you see it as part of the whole jigsaw. Therefore we must first put together the whole jigsaw of history and philosophy before we can see the meaning of the single piece we're interested in — in this case, West Point. But, again, don't let that scare you, Harry. I'll make it easy. You'll see. As I said, we're going on a fun journey. And our journey begins in the ancient Near East ... sometime after The Beginning!

CHAPTER 2: THE BEGINNING

In The Beginning ... God[1] created the sun, moon, stars, wind, water, earth ... and therefore ... atoms, sub-atoms, particles, and everything else out there that people know about, and don't know about. Then God wondrously used atoms, sub-atoms, particles, and whatever ... and created man and woman![2] Then man and woman created "god" — the "god" you imagine here on Earth!
* Come again?
* How close the "god" that you imagine comes to God will be argued ... probably forever! But back here in the ancient Near East where the West Point story really begins, man and woman create their "god" to explain what's been happening around them in life. And you can't blame them. First the world seems friendly and providing. Then it gets hostile and terrifying. It's either feast or famine. Just when things are going well ... bang! There's thunder and lightning. There's earth quakes. Then comes floods. Crops are ruined. Herds die. Fish are killed. There's nothing to eat. And sometimes it's scorching hot. The soil dries up. There's fire. There's disease. There's nothing to drink. People die of thirst. These hardships make people steal each other's food and water. They fight over little patches of land. They should really sit down together and learn to deal with nature and with each other. But they're too busy trying to get their "god" to do it for them! And they continue to fight!

Various peoples have their own versions of "god", but some peoples push the notion of one supreme "high god". It's what they call the "Sky God" ... somewhere up there in the heavens above. Belief in this Sky God even spreads all the way south into the heart of Africa. And by the way, Harry, the Sky God is still mentioned in the religions of many African tribes in your century.[3]

The Sky God bumps along together with other versions of one "god" for a long time. By 3000 BC, however, people are getting more and more into nature worship and its many so called "lower gods". They believe that nature worship with its many lower gods helps them. For instance, listen to what those two wretched looking farmers over there are telling each other as they turn over their soil with sticks:

> "Yeh mate — that's what I said! I drew this
> little picture of a dark cloud on this stone.
> Everyday I made a wish to it for rain. And guess
> what? It rained yesterday! You saw for yourself!
> There's something to this worship stuff, I tell
> you!"[4]

Well, coincidence is usually the architect of superstition! And it's no different back here. They're convinced that these lower gods give a boost to daily life — help with farming, fishing, herding, and so on. So the idea of one "god", such as the Sky God, becomes unfashionable!

Pretty soon people are into inventing a lower god for almost every purpose. And what's important to us, Harry, they make a crude attempt at "putting old souls into young bodies" for the first time ever. They invent a lower god for moral guidance! But they're still not into "Reason" — not into reasoning things out.
* All this worshipping, and I haven't even heard the word "religion" yet?
* The word isn't needed, Harry. That's because life and worship are one and the same thing! <u>Everything</u> in life is religion to these people. Take one of their typical festivals, for instance. The latest craze at festivals is art. All the paintings and carvings are about their lower gods. And listen to their music. It's hymns of worship. The same with dance. The choreography honors their lower gods. And dramatic acting is also about one god or another.[5]

That's only art. They also have a system of laws. It's not much. It's basically what the guys in the new industry called "priesting" say is the will of the gods — what we would call superstition. But this new industry of so called priests doesn't have much of a moral and ethical branch yet. They haven't gotten into convincing people what they <u>should</u> do — how they <u>should</u> behave. They're still bogged down with convincing people about what they <u>shouldn't</u> do.[6] For example, the "priest" we see over there is right now telling that man and woman what they shouldn't do — that they <u>shouldn't</u> do the "goddess of fertility ritual" in public:

> "Hey! You lot over there! Yes you! You can wash
> your dirty laundry in public! But kindly cease
> your celebrating to the 'goddess of fertility'
> in public! That's for the privacy of your own
> digs!"[7]

* He doesn't sound like what I would call a priest.
* No. And he's not. But those so called priests who try to interpret the gods' wishes are amongst the world's first leaders! They're starting to scratch the surface of questions about morals and ethics. That's why we're back here in ancient times — to see attention to morals and ethics in its infancy. And these so called priests also show us a basic leadership character trait in its infancy. Leaders become leaders by trying to help other people!

CHAPTER 3: HAMMURABI AND AKHENATEN

Along comes Hammurabi and Akhenaten. They both stand out like sore thumbs among all the so called leaders for thousands of years in what's called "the fertile crescent" in the Near East.[8] We'll first go to Babylon around 1792 BC to see why Hammurabi stands out.

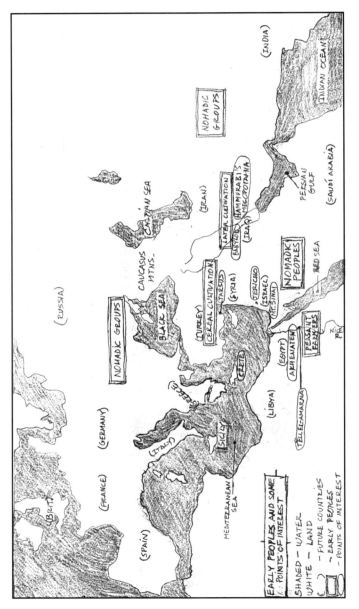

* I know why he stands out! Who wouldn't ... with that name!
* True! But besides the name, Hammurabi also stands out as a ruler.
* Why?
* Because he's a serious thinker. He's a <u>good</u>-leader. Perhaps he's the world's first good-leader!

For centuries before Hammurabi, folks thrash about, stealing each other's food and grabbing each other's land. People wander far and wide to find new lands and get a fresh start in life. Remember? Raw survival is the name of the game. This leads to a few creative individuals gaining power through nothing less than a protection racket that works something like this:

> "I'll help you and you and you protect the little caches of food you
> have squirreled away. And I'll supply you wretched ones there
> with the needs of life."
> "Oh yeh! And what do I have to do for the pleasure of your
> protection?"
> "You just have to be loyal, and fight for me!"[9]

This protection racket is the way kings and rulers are made! Centuries pass. Kings and rulers rise. Kings and rulers fall. Then along comes Hammurabi.

Hammurabi isn't your run of the mill ruler. He <u>refines</u> the protection racket! How? With a new legal code. Why? It helps him protect the good guys. It helps him punish the bad-guys. Believe it or not, Harry, that's original! And it's not based on the priesting industry's superstition of what the gods want. He works out, through experience and innate moral sense, 282 rules and laws to control society! And he has these laws chiseled in stone — a stone pillar called the "stele"! It's the first time in history that folks are told how they should behave and what they <u>should</u> do — not just what they <u>shouldn't</u> do.[10]

So for the first time here in 1792 BC, we see a written rule of law taking over. Most people like it. But there are some guys who always complain. In this case the complainers are mostly the liars, cheats, thieves and other law breakers being herded off to jail because of Hammurabi's "stele". For example, let's listen to what that guy who's passing by is grumbling about:

"Whose big idea is this set of laws, anyway? What happened
to the old law of the jungle? What's wrong with might
makes right? °°If this keeps up I may have to get a job!°°
I'm innocent I tell you! This is a frame-up!"[11]

* That doesn't surprise me, Thomas. What else would you expect a liar, cheat, or thief to say to get out of being tossed into the slammer. Some things never change.
* The stele is not just about lawbreaking, however. In fact, it's not just laws. It's also about morals, ethics, and character! The stele has a remarkable appreciation for justice and honesty and fair play in both commerce and personal life built into it. And remember, this is still only 1792 BC! Some people even think Hammurabi's moral and ethical principles may have been used by Moses ... centuries later![12]

Now we'll skip to 1375 BC and Egypt. Akhenaten inherits the Egyptian throne when his father dies. He later becomes the father-in-law of the famous Tutenkamen. I'm sure you've heard of Tutenkamen, right Harry?
* Yes. That's the mummy that was a big hit with archaeologists around the 1920's I believe? And I thought "Hammurabi" was a funny name? What genius came up with "Akhenaten"? Even "Harry" is better than that!
* You're right. And speaking of genius. Akhenaten is one — the only one in thousands of years of Egyptian dynasties.[13] He's also a religious pioneer. He decrees that his kingdom must worship only the One God instead of the pagan lower gods. That takes guts. For that means he's wiping out the powerful industry of priests. That doesn't help him keep many old friends. But he does win new friends with the jobs he creates building a new capital city and religious center in

Egypt called Tell el-Amarna.

* So, out with the old ... in with the new?
* That's right. Still, Akhenaten tries to keep everything low profile. He tries to hold down the public's shock ... and the powerful priesting industry's outrage. And speaking of keeping things low profile, let's visit his old palace to see if his servants are managing to tiptoe away with the old statues and images of the lower gods:

> "Shhh! (whispering) This is top secret stuff! No one knows we're getting rid of these images and statues."

* Look there, Thomas! There's some other servants just around the corner, out of sight from the ones we just heard.
* Right. They're also tiptoeing out with statues — but in the opposite direction! What they're saying is a bad sign of things to come:

> "Shhh! (whispering) We're not supposed to know about the servants around the corner tiptoeing out with the lower gods. They want One God? It'll never work! Akhenaten is crazy! We'll have to worship our lower gods on the quiet — on the blackmarket!"[14]

Most people <u>do</u> try to comply with Akhenaten's wishes to worship the One God as creator and ruler of Heaven and Earth. But, old habits die hard. Blackmarket worship of lower gods continues.[15] At the same time, Akhenaten continues along his track. He personally writes and teaches his principles of God. His theology compares real well with any religion in your era, Harry. And what's interesting to us, it has a section on morals and ethics! For instance, he asks: How do you be an honest person? How should a preacher teach? How do you be a good father and good husband? How do women be good wives and mothers? What should men of arts and men of sciences put their efforts into? He answers all of these, and many other, questions in his <u>Eternal Life and Light</u>.

Akhenaten is also practical. He'll write his own scriptures! No one else who pioneers so broad a religion will ever do that! For instance, the Old Testament will be written long after Moses is gone. The New Testament will be written years after Jesus is crucified on a cross. But Judaism and Christianity will both survive. Akhenaten's religion won't. He dies just ten years after writing <u>Eternal Life and Light</u>! His ideas about One God die with him![16]

His followers are not clever enough to carry on with his work. The toppled priesting industry smells blood. Priests see the chance to get their old jobs back. They pounce on it. They buzz like a swarm of horseflies around Akhenaten's followers with stories like this:

> "Did you know people all around are dying of thirst because we have no god of rain? There's blood all over the streets from people fighting over water!" °°Does this clown believe me?°°

They twist arms and make threats:

> "You had better bring back the old gods, for your own sake. Do you know how it feels to be left out in the desert on foot?" °°This guy should be cut loose in the desert, regardless!°°

And they make deals:

> "How would you like our inside support? You'd like to have your job for life, wouldn't you? You want more power, don't you?" °°If <u>you</u> don't, <u>I</u> do!°°[17]

The pressures are too great! Akhenaten's followers cave! They re-establish pagan worship of the lower gods!

Akhenaten's theology doesn't completely die with him. People for all time can see his original text on the walls in Tell el-Amarna, Egypt. And even Moses will someday catch Akhenaten's spirit of <u>Eternal Life</u> and gleam of <u>Eternal light</u>. That's because Moses will luck out. He'll be raised by the pharaoh's daughter. So he'll get a chance to study in Egypt and learn about Akhenaten. Years later, he'll borrow principles from Akhenaten's <u>Eternal Life and Light</u> for his famous <u>Laws</u>![18]

* Let me ask you this, Thomas. We're now in 1350's BC Egypt. You said that Moses studies Akhenaten's principles of God. Is Moses alive — right now as we speak?

* Not yet. He's here later. But only decades, not centuries later. In fact, we're pushing forward to that time right now — the time of Moses. We wouldn't skip <u>him</u>! Not when so many people through the ages think he influenced more human beings than any other man who ever lived!

CHAPTER 4: MOSES

The Laws of Moses and his Golden Rules are bold and strict and vengeful.[19] Moses is a hard taskmaster. He's a tough old cookie. And it's not surprising, Harry. He learned discipline and leadership in the Egyptian army's school for military training. This is the same school Egyptians will later claim the Spartan's famed military program is copied from.[20] And, as he was raised the son of pharoah's daughter, he became a top officer in the Egyptian army.

Now, years later, things have changed. It's 1245 BC. Gritty old Moses decides to convert from military leader to religious leader. He leads fellow Hebrews out of Egypt to help them escape the pharoah's heavy handed treatment. The event is called The Exodus. But it doesn't take long for well intentioned Moses to see he may have bitten off more than he can chew. His so called "army" of the Exodus is no harmonious community of Hebrews. It's no army, period! It's a motley bunch of complainers!

* Is that <u>really</u> Moses I see over there?
* That's him, Harry. He starts before dawn every day, trying to mold his motley bunch into a real army. But that's not easy. These folks are very independent. Listen to Moses trying to train those scruffy guys with him over there:

> "All right. Now that I <u>finally</u> got you to line up, you're going to learn how to march. Ready? Left foot first now. ..... No! Not right foot! I said <u>left</u> foot!"
>> "Why? Why not right foot first? What's wrong with right foot first?"
> "Don't ask why! Just do it!" ᵒᵒGod help me with this bunch. No wonder pyramids take so long to build!ᵒᵒ [21]

50

Moses is in for a long uphill struggle! These folks come from a lot of different tribes and groupings. They not only dislike the Egyptians, they don't even like eachother! They fight like cats and dogs. Finally, Moses' Egyptian education and military leadership pays off. He lays down the Laws and gets everyone pulling in the same direction. He enforces order out here in the wilderness — even from guys with attitudes like this:

> "If it isn't one thing it's another. First it's Pharoah keeping us
> under his thumb. Now it's even Moses!"
> > "First you guys complain about lining up. Then about starting
> > with the left foot first. Now this. How come? ᴼᵒSome guys
> > are never satisfied.ᵒᴼ
> ᴼᵒSome guys don't have the guts to complain.ᵒᴼ [22]

There may be complaints. But Moses' Laws — moral and ethical codes — maintain order for forty years! They later become the Pentateuch — the first five books of the Bible!

The moral codes that Moses cobbles together will echo through the centuries. They will become the roots of Islam and of Christianity. They will inspire future philosophers. England's King George III will someday blame those philosophers for giving American colonists the idea of starting a revolution against him. But that's three thousand years from now. What happens now is one of the most important stories of all time. It takes place during the forty years that Moses and the Hebrews are in the wilderness. Moses is tough and gritty. He prides himself on having the broad shoulders of leadership. He lets everyone come to him for help. But this time he needs the help. Who can he go to? He climbs to the top of Mt. Sinai to get help from the only one that can help him. God! Moses is up there forty days before we finally see him making his way back down. He has two stone tablets in his arms.

* They would be the Ten Commandments, right?
* That's right. They're the ten covenants given to him by God. As you know, they're the basic laws of moral conduct for all human beings. They're meant to guide the world for all time.[23] But, as usual, there's always one in the crowd to complain:

> "Is that Moses? I didn't recognize him with the long beard!"
> > "Are you kidding? He's had a beard before! And what can
> > you expect. He's been up there forty days! What's that he's
> > carrying?"
> "Uh oh! Another batch of laws? And now we're really in for it.
> We'll never get around this batch. See what he's done this time?
> Chiseled them in stone! Let's see what they are:

THE TEN COMMANDMENTS[24]

1. Thou shalt have no other gods before me and make no graven image.
2. Thou shalt not take the name of the Lord thy God in vain.
3. Remember the sabbath day, to keep it holy.
4. Honour thy father and thy mother.
5. Thou shalt not kill.
6. Thou shalt not commit adultery.
7. Thou shalt not steal.
8. Thou shalt not bear false witness against thy neighbor.
9. Thou shalt not covet thy neighbor's wife.
10. Thou shalt not covet thy neighbor's house.

The virtue is: Self-discipline. Living by moral standards requires discipline.

They're too hard!" ⁰⁰We can't get away with anything anymore!⁰⁰
   "There a piece of cake!"
"Your kidding? I'm registering a complaint!"[25]

Like I said, Harry, there are always complainers in the crowd! But for the rest of the Hebrews, and the future Western world, the Ten Commandments are the foundation of <u>faith-based</u> morals!

Years later Moses climbs to the top of 4000 ft. high Mt. Nebo. From there he can see his "promised Land" across the Jordan River. It's actually the walled city of Jericho. He finally gazes upon the land of milk and honey he sought for so many decades. He's there with his General and likely successor, Joshua. Suddenly, a cloud comes rolling by. It ... rs everything — including Moses. 't find him anywhere. He has van-

y will see the herculean job he did. successful army and lawful com- military victories, beginning with ccessors — Saul, King David, and ses had gazed upon from atop Mt. Israel![26] nake Israel famous. The moral and ll. The following story about King at I mean:

TWO MOTHERS

e Old Testament–Kings.

claimed a certain child f the women, whose aby next to her's as her vith the living and dead ir stories. Then he

ng child in two, and nic, one of the y lord, do not kill my ut let the child en willing to take mon then wisely nan who would not er."

leader, King of being their leader. truth.

problems wisely and

Stories like this will eventually be gathered up into one big religious "history book". The world will come to know the book as "The Old Testament" of The Bible.

We've now seen some great leaders from ancient times. They planted the seeds of morals and ethics. Morals and ethics are now on the cultural map, thanks to Hammurabi, Akhenaten, Moses, and other leaders. And by the 900's BC, the cultural map is getting bigger. It's spreading from the Near East to far away places. One of those far away places is Greece. So that's where we'll be off to next. **Ancient Greece**!

CHAPTER 5: ANCIENT GREECE

When you had ancient history in school, Harry, I'm sure you must have touched on Greece.

* Oh yes. It was one of my favorites. The land of Homer. I like his stories: the Illiad and the Odyssey; the Greeks defeating Troy to rescue beautiful Helen who had been kidnapped by Trojan warrior, Paris; the story of Achilles, hero in the Battle of Troy. Yes, I do remember some of that history.

* Good. Then I don't have to fill you in on a lot of background information. We'll dive right in.

* Oh! You're not going to do some background? I don't mean to mislead you. I don't know that much about Greek history.

* I see. Well, we're really only interested in how morals, ethics, character, and leadership evolved. However, if it will help you, I'll set the scene for you.

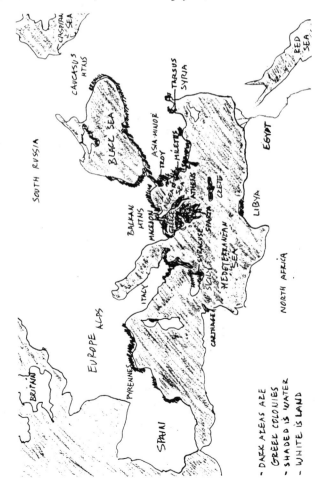

The first European civilization was Crete. That's the island south of present day Greece. The Mediterranean Sea was a natural barrier to invading armies. So Crete was safe. It prospered. By 1700 BC it was riding high. That's about the time Hammurabi was pushing his ethical code of laws over in Babylon.

Crete's country cousins in what is now Greece were becoming prosperous too. They were the "Helladic" culture, made up of people who migrated down from what is now eastern Europe. These peoples settled down all through Macedon, mainland Greece, and the Peloponesian islands south of mainland Greece. Later, they were collectively called ... "Hellenic".

By the mid-1300's BC many settlements were popping up around Greece. They were places like Mycenae, Athens, Sparta, Thebes, and others. "Country cousins" Crete and Mycenae were competing to set up colonies all around the Aegean Sea. That's the sea between Greece and Asia Minor to the east (modern-day Turkey).

The Mycenaeans weren't very loving "country cousins". To them, kinship stopped with race and language. They got fed-up with competing for colonies. So they snuffed out their competitor! They overran Crete and burned it to the ground![27]

We won't actually go back again to the 1300's BC, Harry. But imagine the irony of it all. Here comes this unkempt, bearded Mycenaen warrior. He bangs on the door to his Creteian cousin's house, holding a deadly spear in his hand, and shouts:

"Attention! I'm looking for my long lost country cousin from up
   North! She's supposed to live here! She here?"
   "You're from up North? Now I recognize you behind that
      snarl, cousin! I'm your long lost cousin!"
"Good. I can put this down, then. How about catching up on the
   family gossip over a flask of wine. For, come mornin', we have
   to torch the whole town!"
   "But we're only women and children here now. Why do you
      have to torch the whole town?"

"Orders, dear cousin. You know how it is!"
   "No. I don't know how it is. There's no need for it. What
   can we do?" ᵒᵒYou scruffy vermin.ᵒᵒ
"Hmm. ... Alright! I'll not lift a finger against your house dear
   cousin!"
   "Thank you". ᵒᵒPerhaps you're not a vermin, after all!ᵒᵒ [28]

By the middle 1300's BC the largest mainland settlement, Mycenae, became
the center of the entire Aegean Sea region. That would be shortly after the time
that Akhenaten, across in Egypt, purged away pagan gods and wrote his Eternal
Life and Light. And remember I told you Moses' general, Joshua, booted out the
people of Canaan in about 1200 BC so the Hebrews could start Israel? Well, at
about the same time, Dorian Greeks from up around Macedonia in the north of
Greece booted out the people of Mycenae Greece! Most of the Mycenae people
fled in all directions. They scattered to the four winds around the Mediterranean
Sea. But there were some that toughed it out and stayed home. They were the
ones around what is now Athens and Sparta. When all the dust of battle settled,
Greece had a new look. There were hundreds of independent little countries.
They were self-ruling states, each only the size of a little city. They were called
"city-states"!

The people who fled all around the Mediterranean pioneered new colonies or
joined existing ones. So Greek civilization had been forced to expand. And during the next 500 years it expanded to Spain in the west and to the Black Sea in the
east.

* I didn't know the Greek Empire had been so large.

* It wasn't an Empire. There was no central control over all the places. The
biggest city-states would go around setting up colonies all over the place. Their
colonies were linked only to them. So there was no empire.

The Greek city-states were loosely connected through race, religion, and language. They "confederated" loosely for military defense and security. Greek culture was present throughout the vast Mediterranean area. And all the colonies
were located on a coastline. So there was a free flow of ideas and information by
sea between the colonies and city-states. The Mediterranean had become a Greek
lake, so to speak! [29]

That sets the scene for you in Greece, Harry. We're in the 900's BC again —
the age of Homer. Homer tells us about legend and history and mythology and
multi-gods. The Greeks use stories from mythology to teach morals, ethics, and
character. Here's one about Zeus and Hermes, who the Romans called Jupiter and
Mercury:

BAUCIS AND PHILEMON

from: Thomas Bulfinch's, Age of Fable

Once upon a time the gods, Jupiter and Mercury, took
human form and visited the land of Phyrgia in what is

57

modern time Turkey. It was late at night. They were tired. And they sought a place to sleep. They knocked on many, many doors, but no one bothered to answer. Finally, an older man and woman peeked their heads out of their small cottage. Baucis the woman and Philemon the man kindly invited Jupiter and Mercury to come inside.

As poor working class people, they could not offer much. But, they scurried around to lay out whatever food and drink they could find. Baucis and Philemon began to be astonished at the wine in their pitcher. It never went down! It stayed full! Only then did they recognize their guests. Terrified, they begged the forgiveness of Jupiter and Mercury for their meager hospitality. Jupiter and Mercury told them not to be afraid. Because of their kindness, they would be spared when the rest of the greedy villagers were destroyed. As Baucis and Philemon watched, the rest of the village was sunk under a torrent of water. But, their meager little house was turned into a magnificent mansion!

Jupiter and Mercury asked what wishes the kind old couple wanted granted. It took them but a few minutes of thought. Baucis and Philemon asked that the end of their lives come at one and the same moment, so that they be taken together.

Years later, their wish was granted. Their hour had come. They kissed each other and said, "Farewell dear spouse". In a moment they were both gone. And in their place stood an oak tree and a linden tree — side by side.

The virtue is: Compassion. You don't have to be rich to be kind and compassionate.

It's stories like this that will cause Belief in myths and multi-gods to live on. Myths and multi-gods will have lives of their own!

* I can understand why, Thomas. It's a nice story! But it's a strange way to teach morals, ethics, and character. Isn't it?

* It's the only way in Greece. For the next couple of centuries mythology flourishes. By the 600's BC, mythology is one and the same as art, drama, and literature. For example, listen to those two Athenian guys who are sitting over there. They're dressed in their best attire, sitting around with chin in hand, trying to decide what to do on their night off:

"What should we do tonight, Uly?"
"I don't know, Archi. What do you want to do?"

"I don't know. But I asked you first, didn't I!"
    "How about we take in a play. I hear the Battle of Titans is on
    at the amphitheater. You know, 'Zeus' verses 'The
    Generation of Heaven and Earth'? How's that sound?"
"Sounds alright."
    "Maybe we should do that, then?"
"Yehhh, okkkay."[30]

This scenario is probably repeated thousands of times in Athens and other places.
The old idea about myths and multi-gods still enters everyday Greek life.

As we enter the 500's BC, Harry, we'll see that some new ideas enter everyday
Greek life, too. Each city-state is a proud, individualistic, self-ruling community
of only tens of thousands of people, or less. Everyone knows what's going on.
They want a voice in making decisions in their own backyard. So a new and revolutionary idea surfaces. It's a new kind of government. They call it ......
"democracy"!

Democracy starts in Athens. It's limited in many ways. Only citizens have it.
And not many people are citizens. Slaves, servants, women, young-men, and
bonded-men all are not citizens. They can't vote. But the word — democracy —
is a winning sound bite. Leaders of the hundred or so city-states recognize the
value of a winning sound bite. When Athens makes democracy fashionable, leaders of other city-states follow. They want to show they're up on this latest fashion. It's a good ploy to help them stay in power. So democracy begins to blos-
som. And it blossoms all around the Mediterranean world!

So does culture. Greek city-states are in the right place at the right time. Either
they or their Asia Minor colonies are on Mediterranean seacoasts. They're on trade
routes between the eastern and western worlds. Thus, they can soak up knowledge
and discovery all the way from the Orient to Egypt, Persia, and the rest of the
Middle East. They can pinch ideas and pick brains from all over the world![31]

This is when Sparta pinches ideas for leadership training from Egypt, as I mentioned when we visited Moses. Remember? The Spartans build on Egypt's basic

ideas and develop their own renowned military regimen.[32] It's important to us because West Point will pick up on many Spartan military ideas! Here's how famous historian, Plutarch, will write about the Spartans and their pioneering good-leader, Lycurgus:[33]

DEVELOPING MILITARY LEADERS IN SPARTA

from: Plutarch's Lives

Plutarch's Lives is biographies of fifty notable people of ancient Greece. In this biography he described how the Spartan, Lycurgus, who was King for a short time, visited many nations on both sides of the Mediterranean. It is during these visits that the Egyptians claim Lycurgus admired their military training so much that he transferred it to Sparta.

In Sparta every young man was enrolled in a military school for training in a stern and disciplined lifestyle, and learned the virtue of courage and heroism. The most outstanding of these young men would, after several years of such training, become the leaders of the Spartan city-state.

It was some of these young men who were the 300 Royal Bodyguards of King Leonidas who held off the invading Persian army of thousands of men at the famous Pass of Thermopylae in 480 BC. They all perished in doing so ... but saved Greece! Here follows a description of the training that Spartan leaders received.

Returning from abroad, Lycurgus at once undertook to change the existing order of things and revolutionize the civil government of Sparta. All sons of those who earned Spartan citizenship would be arranged at military schools into companies. The boy who excelled in judgement and was thought by elders to be the most courageous in fighting and most naturally disposed of boldness and aggressiveness in sports that mimicked battles was made captain of his company. Academically, they were made to learn all the proper subjects in the correct amount needed to achieve the purpose. The rest of their training was calculated to obey commands of superiors, endure hardships, become physically fit, and conquer in battle. Their hair was close-clipped, although later in battles it was long and managed. They had to make their own pallet-beds and provide for their own warmth from surrounding woodlands and plant life. Their diet was kept spare to promote physique, and, they often gathered their own food. Those who had been two years out of the class of boys, young men of twenty years old or more, were so-called "Eirens". Eirens were tutors, mentors, governors, and big brothers to all the younger boys. They commanded their subordinates in practice battles, made subordinates serve them at meals, and commissioned them to such chores as fetching wood and gathering diet from nature. The training of Spartans lasted into the years of full maturity. They had been mentally trained to have neither the wish nor ability to live for themselves. They made themselves integral parts of the entire community, clustering about their leaders and belonging entirely to their country. When people asked why Sparta was so safe and secure compared to other city-states, they were told it was because their leaders are trained and know how to command. Men do not willingly consent to obey those who have not earned the right to lead. It takes good-leaders to hold the trust of good followers!

People of other city-states did not send requests to Sparta for ships or money. They requested Spartan commanders! When they got them, they treated them with honor and reverence. These men, and the city of Sparta from which they came, were regarded as teachers of well ordered private and settled civil life.

Lycurgus produced not only writings and treatises, as others did. He left behind an example of an entire city-state beyond imitation, dedicated to love of wisdom and virtue. Future philosophers will say that the honor and fame given to Lycurgus are considerably less than he deserves!

The virtue is: Dedication. It requires dedication to do the things that make a good-leader.

* It's surprising. Lycurgus is not exactly recognized as a "cause celebre" by modern historians.
* Imitation is the most flattering recognition of leadership, Harry. And Lycurgus' Spartans will have a lot of imitators. As I said, West Point will be one of them!
* I guess that's good enough. Afterall, he did get the basic idea from Egypt.
* True. But we all get our ideas from somewhere. For example, there was a short, crude experiment with democracy in the Middle East over 1000 years ago! So maybe Greece borrowed the idea of democracy, too. Who knows? But one thing we do know. Greece doesn't borrow the Middle East's tradition of using pagan priests to censor free speech!
* They have no censors here in Greece?
* No. Democracy brings freedoms! So you're free to talk about things without

using myth, religion, or superstition. For example, let's listen to that group of young folks sitting over there having a "rap session":

> "I'm about to be off to the polls to vote. Who are all of you vot-
> ing for?"
> > "I can't vote. I'm in the 'young-man' category."
> > "Me neither. Women can't vote!"
> > "I can't either. I'm not from Athens".
> > "Nor I. I'm a servant, not a citizen".
> > "And you know I can't. Slaves don't vote".
> "You're a slave? How did that happen. You're Greek!"
> > "Back when Athenians overran our village they made every-
> > one slaves!"
> "Well then! I know a way around this. I'll represent you at the
> polls. How's that! So here are the voting choices. By a show of
> hands, all in favor of #1? #2? Right! Then #1 it is. I'm off to
> vote for #1! Wait here! I'll be right back!"[35]

Freedom of speech is a hallmark of Greek democracy. You may not be free to vote, but you're free to "rap". And what better language than Greek for "rapping"? It's great for <u>details</u>. Just read some of Homer's literature, Sophocles' dramas, or Xenophon's histories. You'll see. Homer uses four pages in his <u>Illiad</u> just to describe the scenes and events shown on Achilles' shield![36]

Greek is also great for describing <u>change</u>. Just read some of Simonides' poetry about "change and life's opposites". You'll see. War and peace. Honor and shame. Courage and cowardice. Life and death. Simonides made a career out of <u>lamenting</u> over "change and life's opposites". His theme will turn up in the Old Testament:[37]

LIFE'S OPPOSITES

from: The Old Testament: Book of Ecclesiastes

For everything in life there is a season, and a time for
every purpose under heaven:
> A time to gather, and a time to cast away stones;
> A time to gain, and a time to lose;
> A time to love, and a time to hate;
> A time of war, and a time of peace;
> A time to kill, and a time to heal;
> A time to weep, and a time to laugh;
> A time of our youth, and a time to grow old;
> A time to be born, and a time to die;

The virtue is: Self-confidence. It's needed to deal with
change and life's opposites.

Someday in the 1800's AD the great German scholar, G.W.F. Hegel, will <u>also</u> make a career out of, not lamenting, but <u>celebrating</u> "change and life's opposites". He'll use "change and life's opposites" —- his "dialectic" —- to explain all of history and all of the world's knowledge. So his "dialectic", that boils down to "think change, cause change", will also explain the big cultural change back here in 500's BC Greece. The change is from teaching about morals, ethics, character, and the world by using mythological **Belief**, to teaching about those things by using ... **Reason!**[38]

* So, to Simonides' <u>Life's Opposites</u> we can probably add:

"A time for **BELIEF** and a time for **REASON!**"

* Very true, Harry. But let me point out that the Greek world is doing all the changing right now! Persians, Egyptians, and Judeans are still into using blind Belief — myths, multi-gods, and religion — not Reason.[39] Greek scholars are the only ones trying to dump the old myths and multi-gods. They're trying to kill the old messenger — Belief, without killing the old message — morals, ethics, character, and the world. And they don't just call the <u>new</u> messenger, Reason. They also give it a new name. They call it ..... **PHILOSOPHY!** It means "love of wisdom". And they call the people who do it ..... **PHILOSOPHERS!**

CHAPTER 6: EARLY PHILOSOPHY

During most of the 500's BC, pioneering philosophers are busy helping people to understand life and the world by trying to get them to <u>reason</u> things out instead of just <u>believe</u> all the old mythological tales. But old tales, like old habits, die hard. Mythological <u>Belief</u> has been passed from father to son for centuries now. It gets in the way of <u>Reason</u>. Belief and Reason keep getting tangled up. Pioneering philosophers have their hands full keeping them untangled!

* You say "pioneering" philosophers. Who is the pioneer — the <u>first</u> philosopher?

* Funny you should ask! For that very question is being hotly debated right now in late 500's BC Athens. We'll pick up a discussion about it between two philosophy "freaks":

"I don't fancy any of these we've discussed so far as possible first philosopher, do you?"

"No, not really. I have to agree with you on that."

"Should we consider someone not from Athens in that case?"

"Well, we know Athenians are best. But ... why not!"

"Right then! How about Thales from across the Aegean Sea in the colony of Miletus?"

"Thales. I've heard of him. What did he do again?"

"Didn't you hear about the stir he caused in 585 BC? He predicted the Sun God would stop shining — disappear before their very eyes. They said he was nuts! But sure enough, it happened! The Sun disappeared right before their eyes! Thales gave it a name. Solar eclipse — I think he said. What's more, he told everyone not to worry ... the Sun would return. And it did!"

"That shows he's a great astronomer. But it doesn't mean he's a philosopher."

"Well that's not the end. They badgered him to explain <u>why</u> it happened. He dared to tell them that there's <u>no</u> Sun God! But he knew he'd be in trouble if he just left them hanging out to dry like that. So he needed explanations. That got him thinking about everything, not just the sky. How did the world come about? Where do we come from? To make a long explanation short, he concluded the origin of everything to be ... water!"

"Water? If you don't mind my saying, that sounds all wet! And it doesn't make him a philosopher!"

"It's not as all wet as it sounds. Forget actual <u>water</u>. His inquiry into the origin of things amounts to a <u>real</u> explanation!"

"True. But backers of religion and superstition do that too. And they're <u>not</u> philosophers."

"No they're not. But Thales explains things <u>without</u> using gods or myth or religion or superstition."

"So what? So he parts ways with religious and mythological type people."

"Oh. And I was about to add this important point. His explanations are based on the new way of looking at things — observation and reason. He uses, <u>REASON NOT BELIEF</u>!"

"Ah. You're right. <u>That</u> is different. And it is indeed philosophy! Not astronomy!"

"Do you think our search is ended? Need we go further? I for one pick Thales as the first philosopher!"

"Yes. You're right. You've convinced me. I agree on Thales! Now we have to sell it to the <u>rest</u> of the world!"

"It's not a problem! Thales sells himself!"[41]

Thales of Miletus (624-546 BC) <u>does</u> sell himself in his writings. He <u>is</u> considered the world's first philosopher![42] And he touches on many things I've shown you so far — from city-states and democracy, to free speech and Change, to Reason and Belief.

* What about morals, ethics, and character?

* Thales, and others who follow hot on his heels, kind of say you have to first understand the world around you before you can understand morals, ethics, and character. Like Thales, they keep plodding along untangling Reason from Belief and science from magic. Like him, they're brainy enough to talk about the world without first talking about myths and multi-gods. And like him ... they're all in Miletus!

* Hmm. Why all <u>there</u>?

* Fish hatch where the eggs are laid, don't they. Thales, the leader, makes his nest in Miletus and gains people's respect and trust. So a bunch of his followers — a so-called "school of Miletus" — ends up doing their thing right there, too. Then one day a marauding Persian army comes along. You can imagine that the old boys must get scared out of their sandals:

"The Persians are coming! Run for your lives!"
   "Oh gods! What do we do now! Wait. Don't answer! I
   know! Thales said water is the source of life. So follow me
   boys! Run for your lives! Head for the water!"
"Right! Let the people 'fall in' to defend Miletus. We philosophers and politicians had better 'fall out'! Let's head for the
   water and take the next boat out!"[43]

They flee to the island of Samos, off the coast of Miletus. The Persians wipe out
the city. That wipes out the so called school of Miletus!
   Samos is the native land of Pythagoras (572-500 BC).   He inherits the
Miletians' philosophy. But like them, he also inherits their bad luck. For Samos
has one of the last dictators left in the Greek world. The place hasn't been bitten
by the democracy bug yet. The dictator has a cozy little gig going for himself. So
when Pythagoras talks to the people about democracy, the dictator talks to
Pythagoras about getting out of town ... real quick ... or else! He does like the
Miletians did. He hops the first boat off the island to save his skin![44]
   Pythagoras wanders to all the Mediterranean hot spots! He finally stops at a
Greek colony in Italy. His "school" of followers there becomes the center of
mathematics and deductive reasoning. He invents the Pythagorean Theorem of
geometry. He also invents religious philosophy .... he believes he has mathemat-
ical proof of the "migration of the soul" into other living creatures when you die.
In other words he's saying, people who kill and eat animals may be killing and
eating deceased friends and relatives!   No wonder they're vegetarians at
Pythagoras' school! Some people believe there's something to his Migration of
the Soul philosophy. Most people say its nuts![45]

THE PYTHAGOREANS ARE FINE. EXCEPT THEY DON'T EAT MEAT BECAUSE THEY THINK YOU'RE EATING A PERSON, REINCARNATED! THAT'S KINKY!

Pythagoras's vegetarian lifestyle turns a lot of people off. But his mathematics and deductive reasoning will turn someone named Plato and a lot of other philosophers on in the future. And his school will last another 400 years![46] So, nuts or not, Pythagoras has a place in the history of philosophy. He deserves it. He's brilliant with numbers. But he's not brilliant with morals, ethics, and character. And no wonder. It's a sticky problem. In spite of democracy, city states still give most people few ... or no rights. Therefore, philosophers avoid morals, ethics, and character. They'd sooner try to sell a pet fox to a chicken farmer! The subjects of life and the world get all their attention, for now!

Heraclitus, for example, is still hung up on that old Greek passion for Change in the world. He comes up with some clever stuff on how everything is being slowly created and destroyed. His favorite example is, "You can't step in the same river twice". Get it? It's not hard. He means the river is already different the second time.[47]

Then comes Parmenides. He does Heraclitus one better. He says, "You can't step in the same river once". Now that is hard ... I guess because Parmenides is very smart. Zeno, Anaxagoras, and others are also very smart. And they're all smart enough to avoid the problem of morals, ethics, and character![48]

Then there's Empedocles (500-440 BC) over in Sicily. This old boy doesn't avoid anything and isn't afraid of anything. So with him, the good news is ... we finally have our best hope to tackle morals, ethics, and character. The bad news is ... he thinks he's a god ... and his critics aim to make him prove it! The way he decides to prove it says that he must know the story about the "Fiery Furnace of Babylon".

* The what?

* And that says you must not know the story about the "Fiery Furnace of Babylon"! It happened in 586 BC, the year before Thales predicted the solar eclipse. King Nebuchadnezzar of Babylon conquered Jerusalem that year:

THE FIERY FURNACE OF BABYLON

from: The Old Testament Book of Daniel

King Nebuchadnezzar took the captured Jewish hero, Daniel, and his close supporters to Babylon. A ceremony was held to dedicate a gold coated 100 foot high statue as an image of worship. Everyone present kneeled to worship the idol, except the Jews. Nebuchadnezzar became furious that someone would dare to disobey his order. He again ordered the Jews to kneel and worship the golden idol. They were told they would be put into the fiery furnace if they refused to obey. Again, they refused. With that, the King told the soldiers to seize three young supporters of Daniel and put them into the furnace. The soldiers dragged the three Jews to the mouth of the furnace and threw them into the fire. The flames were so strong that they even shot out and burned to death the soldiers who had held the three young Jews. In sight of all, the three Jews emerged out of the furnace! Everyone could see they were not burned, or scorched, or even singed! They were alive as before. The king was filled with astonishment over what he saw. He ordered that no one in all his kingdom shall, hence forth, prevent the Jews from worshipping their Most High God.

God had intervened to reward the Jews. For being loyal to their faith and to their leader, Daniel, God spared their lives!

The virtue is: Loyalty. This is loyalty, and loyalty rewarded.

So when critics make Empedocles prove he's a god, he just sneers at them ... strange old boy that he is ... and says he'll show them all. He then proceeds to jump straight into his own fiery furnace — the volcanic fires of Mount Etna!

Our best hope gets roasted alive! He's not a god![49]

Life goes on. Philosophers go on avoiding the problem of morals, ethics, and character that they're inheriting from mythological Belief. It's a problem they <u>must</u> eventually deal with. It's like they're inheriting a pet lion cub. Perhaps they don't want it. But they get it. If they don't deal with it, soon it will become a raging three hundred pound lion that gets <u>them</u>!

As our "pet lion cub" gets bigger and bigger, Democritus (460-370 BC) hits the philosophy scene talking about things that are smaller and smaller! He sees everything on earth as vast numbers of tiny indivisible particles called "atoms", from the Greek word "atmos". Using his theory of atoms, Democritus looks at both the world outside and the world inside of people, including the soul. And looking at the soul is a step in the right direction as far as we're concerned. That means he's getting the scent of our morals, ethics, and character problem. However, he never gets into it or becomes famous for it. He <u>will</u>, however, become famous for being the first man to get the scent of an "atomic theory"![50] Meanwhile, our pet lion keeps getting bigger!

* So if I'm an Athenian, who can I turn to for advice on moral, ethical, mental, or any personal problems I have?

* Believe it or not, you can still go to an "Oracle" for some mythological mumbo jumbo, or seek out what we'll call your local philosopher. But I can't imagine what good either would do you at this point in time. However, let's see what happens with this ordinary guy named Bonkerius who's talking to a bunch of so called philosophers:

> "My name is Bonkerius. I just came from the Oracle. He was
> useless! I'm told you're the ones who give advice?"
> "Yes. We're the ones. What's the problem?"
> "Well, I lost my job. Then my wife ran out on me. Now I have no
> food for the kids ... so they were taken away. I'll have to shoplift
> some food to get them back. My landlord wants to evict me. I'll
> have to steal some money. Now even my dog has run out on me."
> "Is that it? Is that all that's bothering you Bonkey?"
> "The name is Bonkerius! And yes, that's it." ∘∘Isn't that enough?∘∘
> "Well. I have the answer to your problems. Want to hear it?"
> "Of course". ∘∘Why do you think I'm here?∘∘
> "Come closer then. It's confidential. I want to w h i s p e r
> i t. T h e a n s w e r i s, s h h h .... w a t e r."
> "W a t e r?"
> "Y e s, W a t e r."
> "S o w h a t d o I d o w i t h w a t e r?"

> "I disagree with him and his water theory! You can't have the
> same water twice"!
> "I also disagree. You can't even have the same water once"!
> "Why not?"
> "Because it's not actually water! It's spaces and atoms!

69

There's actually no such thing as water! Just spaces and atoms!"

ᵒᵒWhat the heck does this all have to do with my problem, you bloody eggheads?ᵒᵒ

"How do you all know for sure?   Maybe it's air, maybe fire, maybe even seeds!"
   "Seeds? I think it all comes down to numbers! Without numbers, it's impossible to determine!"

ᵒᵒRight then. That's it! I got nothing outta this! These guys have my head spinning. I'm outta here! If I wasn't nuts when I came in ... I am now! Now what I need is directions to the looney bin.ᵒᵒ "Thank you for your ...umm ... help. ᵒᵒWhat a joke!ᵒᵒ Can I leave?"
   "Of course you can. You can go ... Bonkers!"[51]

So people are now looking to philosophers for advice on morals, ethics, and character. But as your generation would say, Harry ..... they ain't it! Not yet, anyway. But they will be. For moral and ethical philosophy are just around the corner![52]

CHAPTER 7: THE ATHENIAN PERIOD

By the 400's BC, our "pet lion cub" — symbolizing the subject of morals, ethics, and character — has become a raging, full grown problem. Philosophers will no longer be able to avoid it. The pressure is too great. Here's how it breaks out into the open and finally begins to get their attention.

A lot of so called philosophers in Athens have been knocking themselves out trying to figure out the world. One day, someone bothers to "hear" the messages ordinary people — like Bonkerius — have been screaming out to them. Forget the world! Go with people! That's where the action is! People are the future! Many of the so called philosophers step back and see there is a big demand for dealing with people and their problems. So they turn their sights in that direction. They call themselves "Sophists" ... from "sophos", meaning wise. Some of them are "wise". Others are just "wise-guys"!

The "wise" ones help people to read, write, debate, make speeches, register complaints, and so forth. They're dedicated teachers. The "wise-guys" are frank, cynical, and sarcastic. They say power and success are all that matters. Might makes right. Justice is the play thing of the powerful. Facts and truth are not important. Eloquent arguments that win are only important. They help people to win court decisions any way that works. They cleverly lie and use twisted justice. But they win. That's good for business. And that's all that matters to them!

* They sound like lawyers! I've seen some like that in my day. You know. Greedy. I guess some things never change.

* And greed is like sea-water, Harry. The more you drink, the thirstier you get! So the Sophists get more and more "thirsty"! They grab more and more money by passing the hat around for "donations" as they're doing their pitch out here in the streets of Athens ... and pass it twice if they can get away with it.

* I don't blame them. You can't live on philosophy alone.

* True. The problem is, a lot of these guys are nothing more than money grabbing con artists. For example, listen to the "wise-guy" Sophist giving his speech in this city square:

> "My point is, I just proved an absurd thing to all of you. And you
> believed me. If I can do that, I can prove anything on your
> behalf in court, can't I? And guess what? It's because I drank
> from this bottle I'm now holding up. It's a bottle of genuine,
> pure philosophical snake oil. That's brain juice. If you want to
> gain a little more brains, I have this little bottle for 2 drachmas.
> If you want a lot of brains, I have this bigger bottle for 5 drach-
> mas. Or, you can hire me. I'll just be your brains and your
> mouthpiece for you". °°If these halfwits believe that, they'll
> believe anything. I was really off my game today, too!°⁰ 53

* All Greek speechmakers aren't "wise-guy" Sophists. Some really <u>are</u> "wise".[54] The following passage taken from the Athenian historian, Thucydides, is a good example:

THE FUNERAL ORATION BY PERICLES (431 BC)[55]

from: Thucydides

The leader of Athenian democracy in the mid 400's BC is the great statesman, Pericles. He gives what the historian, Thucydides, makes into a famous funeral oration over Athenians being killed in the battles against Sparta. In this oration Pericles describes the greatness of Athens. He says a city-state like Athens can only be good if it has people and leaders who are good in respect to character and virtue. This speech raises the morale of Athenians.

"We enjoy a form of government which is not the rival of our neighbors but rather the example. We are also different from most because of our benevolence. To sum up: I declare that each of us, in my opinion, can exercise the most varied activities with greater

ease and grace than those in our neighboring cities.
That this is no passing boast, but actual truth, is
shown by the power we have acquired because of
these outstanding traits of ours. I remind you that it
was due to courage, duty, and honor that we won our
greatness.

It was for this city of ours, then, that these dead
warriors of ours so nobly gave their lives in battle.
Every man who survives these warriors should gladly
toil, on behalf of them and their city."

The virtue is: Duty. We have a duty to maintain principles our forefathers died for.

Meanwhile, wise-guy Sophists have turned philosophy into a money harvesting
business. Now they don't even bother passing the hat. They charge admission.
And they make big money. They also make big enemies. One of them is Socrates
(470-399 BC).

Socrates has just one thing in common with the "wise guy" Sophists. He lectures out here in the streets of Athens. Other than that, they're as different as
chalk and cheese. He's not into money. Just the opposite. He looks real shabby,
sports a scruffy beard, and often goes around barefooted. In fact, that's a trademark he owns and flaunts — humble appearance. But this gadfly of Athens is a
brilliant old boy, and not just in philosophy. While teaching the benefits of marriage, this fourty year old military hero actually persuaded a nineteen year old girl
to marry ... him! That's another trademark he owns — ace teacher and persuad-
er. The Sophists are no match for him. Someday historians will say that no one
who ever walked the face of the Earth was a match for him!

Socrates has a nifty little method of teaching going for himself. It's questions
and answers. His questions are so clear and simple, you have to answer "yes".
He has you answering "yes" to a string of questions. Before you can decide
whether to agree with him or not, you already have! What's more important, by
then he's taught you what he had set out to teach you!

That's the "Socratic Method". It requires a lot of time. It also requires a lot of
"thick skin", as you'll realize when you hear these two students talking about how
tough Socrates is:

"Greetings. My name is Plato. I'm new around here. Have you
ever engaged in a dialogue with Socrates?"
"Yes. Why? Are you scheduled to talk with him?
"Yes I am. In a few moments from now".
"Well, let me give you a bit of advice. Don't try to show him
how much you know. In fact, don't try to show you know anything at all. If you do, he'll cut you to ribbons. His comments
can be vicious and cynical. You know, like some of those

73

Sophists are. I've even seen him reduce people to tears."
"Even though he's supposed to be a good, kind, virtuous human
   being?"
   "Yes. He hates know-it-alls. Here he comes now. Good
   luck!"

"Are you Socrates — the philosopher?"
   "Hm. My hearing must be failing! You did address me as
   'Sir', did you not? You did say 'Socrates, Sir'. Correct?
   And what might they call you?"
"I'm Plato .... Sir"!
   "Well, Plato, I see here in my notes that you are a leader.
   Then you can tell me all about leadership. Is that correct?"
"Me? No, Sir! I couldn't do that, Sir! Sure. I played athletics.
And, I certainly got the highest grades. Thus far, no one can beat
me up. And I do, indeed, have a lot of money. But, I know I'm
not a leader just because of those things. That's what I wanted to
ask you about, Sir. What it takes to be a leader. And by the way,
can I take notes on what you tell me?"
   "Absolutely not! I shall start by telling you how things stand.
   Never, never put anything into writing! It is because of those
   nasty Sophists! They will drag you into court over what you
   may write. They twist everything around. They turn you
   into dogmeat ... and collect big fees for doing it. They are
   strictly in it for the money, not for what is right or wrong. So
   you must be smart about it. Do not put any of your own philosophy into writing while you are alive. Let someone else
   do it after you are gone. If you want to write about philosophy, write that of someone else. Then you are in the clear."
"Yes Sir. But ... whose? Whose can I write about?"
   "Well, for example, perhaps someday you can write about the
   things I say. And along the way, you can stick in a few
   things of your own. But at this point, who is to know
   whether you shall prove yourself worthy? It is too early to
   know. Do you catch my drift?"
"I catch your drift, Sir!"[56]

Socrates breaks you down. Then he builds you back up by feeding you —
"knowledge"! But it has to be true knowledge. A diet of phoney information
won't do. He says getting true knowledge is the only way you can know what's
really right and wrong, moral and immoral, ethical and unethical. So Socrates
backs straight into becoming our first bonafide moral philosopher. We finally
have someone who takes on that raging full grown lion — takes on explaining
morals, ethics, and character. And more than explain them, he aims to teach them
to people!
   Socrates puts a new method of education into play. It's the "academy" method.

He says, if you want good-leaders, you have to train them the right way. The right way means you not only feed them job knowledge, you build their moral, ethical, and character muscle. That way, they'll be able to earn Trust and get their followers to willingly follow. That's real important for leadership!

* Thats also real hard!

* It is hard! That's why Socrates says the right way can't be just weekend lectures. People aren't going to change overnight. You have to get them to work at it. They have to live their leadership training. They have to make it a way of life. These are things that make the academy method different. They're the hallmarks of Socrates' educational philosophy. And someday they'll be the hallmarks of West Point's educational philosophy!

* I didn't know the "gadfly of Athens" is into leadership philosophy, too. That makes him the first philosopher to do that also ... besides being the first moral philosopher!

* Yes. In both cases, it's because he's the first philosopher with enough guts to take on the problem of morals, ethics, and character. And it brings him big trouble. It breeds enemies. It offends snobs, Sophists, and politicians. They band against him. They warn him he'd better join their team. But Socrates tells them ... straight to their faces ... he wouldn't lower himself to the standards of their team. So here's the irony of it all. He's far superior to them as a moral and ethical human being. Yet they get him anyway ... can you believe this ... on a claim that he's immoral!

Plato knows the whole story of how they get Socrates. In fact, he'll put all of Socrates' stories into writing. You see, in the end Plato will prove himself worthy to write the biography of his teacher and friend Socrates. Here's a small piece of it — Plato's account of the death of Socrates:

THE DEATH OF SOCRATES

from: Plato

Socrates' own morals and ethics and character were
complete. He tried to convert others. Because of his
quest for promoting individual morality and truth, Socrates
offended many of the most influential and powerful figures of Athens. He was indicted on fabricated charges of
teaching "irreligious" and false doctrines. They intended
to humiliate him by forcing him to beg for mercy and his
life. Far from begging for his life, he lectured them about
their ignorance in a manner that humbled them. When
asked what punishment he deserved, Socrates told them
they should erect a statue in his honor in the main square
and give him free meals for life! The jury was so enraged,
they condemned him to death. But some feared the popular opinion in favor of Socrates, and, others were ashamed
to put to death their most intellectually eminent citizen.
So they were willing to allow Socrates' friends to arrange
his escape, and thus, he would voluntarily exile himself
from Athens to avoid the death penalty. He refused to
compromise his honor and integrity. Nothing less than a
reversal by his accusers would do. As prescribed, he
drank the hemlock to bring about his own death. Thus, he
became a martyr.

The virtue is: Honor. Many have even died before com-
promising their honor.

Socrates becomes a martyr. It makes him world famous.[57] His martyrdom is only
surpassed by the martyrdom of Jesus, 400 years later!

Jesus and Socrates were curiously similar. Both were humble in appearance.
Both were teachers. They were interested in morals, and left it to others to explain
the world. They both lectured in the streets. Their favorite audiences were the
poor and the downtrodden and the ordinary masses of people. Both had the
opportunity to save themselves. Both refused if it wasn't on their own terms.
Both were put to death because they refused. Neither left his own written doctrine. Someone else wrote it. For Jesus it was Paul of Tarsus. Socrates had Plato.
There was one gigantic difference between them, however. Socrates was a mere
mortal human being. Jesus was the Son of God. Therefore, Jesus' agenda caught
fire. It later became Christianity. It was morals by Divine Command. Socrates'
agenda — morals, ethics, and character for their own sake — well, it continues to
struggle even in your time, Harry.

* More than ever, probably.
* Yes. And that's why I'm here on Earth with you!

After his teacher Socrates dies, Plato (427-347 BC) decides to see what's going on in the rest of the world. He crosses the Mediterranean to study in the Middle East — particularly in Egypt. Then he decides to check out the Pythagoreans across in Sicily. He realizes the grass isn't greener on the other side of the Mediterranean. True, he learns a lot. But he finds himself teaching others more than others teach him ... thanks to what he learned from the master, Socrates. It's a wake-up call. He realizes how lucky he was to have Socrates as his teacher. He returns to Athens, armed with new confidence. He's heard his calling ... pick up where Socrates left off. Teach!

Old Socrates had put the academy method of teaching into play. Plato keeps it in play and adds a move of his own. He turns the academy method into a college! It's the world's first college. He calls it ... The Academy! And he puts it in Athens — right smack in the middle of Sophist territory! It's an instant success. It's the Sophist's best competitor. It'll become the Sophist's worst nightmare if they don't do something real quick ... like copy it!

"I thought when old man Socrates drank the poison hemlock we'd
   have the field all to ourselves. Now this upstart, Plato, comes along
   and throws a spanner into the works. Who is this guy, anyway?"
      "Plato? He was a student of Socrates. He's not been around
      for a while ... off studying abroad they tell me".
"If this Academy of his catches on ... we're out of business!"
      "Not to worry! It's just another hairbrained idea. You know, a
      flash-in-the-pan. It won't last. When it goes under, we'll get
      all that business he recruited ... thankyou very much!"
"Yes. You're right. We've seen it before. They come and they go
   ... don't they".[58]

77

* It sounds like the Sophists are already sloughing The Academy off. How long does it last?

* More than 900 years! But more important, its <u>spirit</u> still lives on. Your Academy — West Point — will lift students of your era to a "higher level" by feeding them knowledge and building their moral, ethical, and character muscle, just like Plato's Academy does in this era.

* So I take it that "higher level" means what you described to me a while back as Virtue ... with a capital "V".

* That's right. I'm glad to see you get it, Harry. Let's see if the "wise-guy" Sophists get it enough yet to make them copy The Academy. We'll listen in on what a couple of their paying customers are saying while they're waiting for a lecture:

> "How come you're not across the way studying at the Academy?"
>> "It's too hard! And it takes too long! Astronomy and mathematics? Who needs them? Who needs star-gazing and number-crunching!"
> "What about those other parts I've heard about though? You know — truth, honor, trust, integrity and so on?"
>> "No problem. We learn them right here from the Sophists. I come here every week. And, I hear about truth and honor ... uhh ... quite a lot".
> "That's <u>not</u> the truth! I come every single week, and they <u>never</u> talk about any of those things. And you're <u>not</u> here every week!"
>> "Oh! Uh, I do come ... well ... a lot, anyway".[59]

The Sophists aren't copying the Academy. It's pretty obvious they aim to ignore morals, ethics, and character. Plato, on the other hand, is going the other way. He aims to show us that morals, ethics, and character are immortal — constant and unchanging — for all eternity. He collectively calls them ... "The Good".

* "The Good"? That sounds the same as Virtue.
* For our purposes, we can say it is the same. The Good is where "good" in "good-leaders" comes from. Plato tells us a ton of stuff about Good leaders in his Education and his Republic, like this example from the Republic:[60]

GOOD-LEADERS AND PHILOSOPHER-KINGS

from: Plato's Republic

Plato said that a just ruler (Good-leader) needed "philo-sophical knowledge" about The Good. He said it in numerous dialogues. The following is in his Republic:
"Until philosophers are the kings, or, the kings and princes of the world have the power and spirit of philosophy — so that political leadership and wis-dom meet in one person — their cities will never have rest from their evils, nor will the human race, I believe."

The virtue is: Knowledge. Knowledge breeds wisdom, wisdom breeds Good-leaders.

So what it boils down to ... Plato's aim for The Academy is, roughly:

"to educate and train students over a long period of time so they will obtain Virtue — The Good — that is fundamental to good leadership for their city-state and their military; and to encourage some to carry on training and educating others at the Academy."

* I think I saw something similar to that during our tour of West Point.
* Probably. Except for West Point's Spartan military way of living, it is roughly the same as The Academy. Like Plato's Academy, West Point believes they can mine the depths of your subconscious soul, through special training, and raise to your conscious mind the morals, ethics, and character — Virtue, The Good — that you're born with. Like Plato's Academy, the idea at West Point is not just to study and know about morals, ethics, and character, but to have them. Like Plato's Academy, West Point says you need, not just months, but years to have them.
In the Republic, Plato touches on the amount of years it takes. He divides city-states into three classes of people: "Guardians" — we call them rulers or politi-cal leaders ; "Soldiers" — we call them military leaders; "Masses" — we call them ordinary folks.
The "Masses" are laborers and artisans who do all the "heavy lifting" and sweating that creates wealth. They also do most of the fighting and dying in wars started by bad leaders!

* That's always been the case, Thomas. Unless someone can come up with a better idea, that will never change.

* Plato thinks he <u>does</u> have a better idea. In <u>his</u> city-states there are no bad leaders! The leaders — Guardians and Soldiers — are trained and educated the right way! The "Guardians" — the ruling class of leaders — study to be philosophers. And they're trained until they have virtues — The Good. The "Soldiers" — the military leaders — study the arts of war. They're also trained until they have virtues. The study and training for both takes many years. Based on what Plato's experience has shown him, it takes at least fifteen years for "Guardians". It probably takes several years less for "Soldiers", as military leaders don't need all the liberal and cultural subjects that political leaders do.

* That's an incredible amount of time.

* I know! But the product is worth it. The "Guardians" will run a city-state. They had best be world class. The "Soldiers" will risk people's lives. They had best be world class, too! Unfortunately, until West Point comes along, the academy method will be all but forgotten. It will mean nothing to many centuries of rulers and political "leaders"! They'll happily ignore all the good stuff Plato is telling us. They'll only be interested in grabbing power and keeping it! They couldn't care less about mining the depths of anyone's soul for Virtue! They'll be too busy mining wealth and power from the sweat off the backs of the "Masses"!

* Oh well. So much for Plato, and his ideas on good-leaders.

* Only for now, Harry. Besides, Plato writes on a whole bunch of other subjects, such as, life, politics, theology, mathematics, the arts, analytical methods and so on. And they're not textbooks, but a massive forty-two volumes that are lively dialogues and are often written in the style of thrillers. He introduces his <u>Dialogues</u> allegorically — symbolically — with his <u>Myth of the Cave</u>. It's his way of trying to make philosophy a little easier to understand.

* See! Even Plato knows people can lose their marbles over this stuff if he doesn't simplify it!

* In the <u>Myth of the Cave</u> prisoners are chained inside a cave facing a wall in front of them.

They can't turn around. They can only see shadows on the wall in front of them of real things behind them. So that's their idea of what people and things are —

those shadows on the wall! One prisoner is unchained and let out to see the real world behind him. When he returns to clue the other prisoners in about his new found knowledge it only angers them. It blows all of their ideas and illusions. They prefer the pleasant deception of the shadows on the wall!

* What is Plato saying there? Is it a clever criticism of Socrates' accusers because they didn't <u>want</u> to see the truth?

* You decide, Harry. He goes on after <u>Myth of the Cave</u> and creates an entire system of philosophy. However, he never gets to create a "philosopher-king". He comes close. He's invited to tutor young Dionysuis II in Syracuse, Sicily. But the political climate there turns ugly. His invitation is scrubbed. Bad luck robs him of his only chance!

* That's sad. He must have held back a few tears of regret over that!

* Perhaps. But tears of regret are legacies of things <u>not</u> done. Plato has a huge legacy of things he <u>has</u> done! His philosophy is like a jeweled timepiece. It ticks on forever. Even in your era the well-known philosopher, Alfred North Whitehead, will say that all philosophy is merely a series of footnotes to Plato![61]

So Plato dies without the top prize — being tutor to a philosopher-king. But he wins a consolation prize. His star pupil <u>will</u> become tutor to a philosopher-king. That star pupil is named Aristotle (384-322 BC). The future king that Aristotle will tutor is King Philip of Macedonia's son who will someday become known as ... Alexander The Great!

* Who gets Plato's number one slot at the Academy?

* It isn't his star pupil Aristotle! And that turns on all the gossipy students here at the Academy. They're milling around amongst themselves speculating about Aristotle. If we listen to them, maybe we'll pick up the inside story:

    "Have you heard about Aristotle? He's leaving the Academy!"
      "No. Really? That's just incredible! After being here for
        twenty years?"
    "I hear he expected the number one job. They wouldn't give it to
      him."

81

"That's politics for you. It's that Sophist-like clique — those lawyer types. When is the last time you've seen them give the best man the job?"

"Well, I hear Aristotle was passed up because he's not a home grown Athenian. Sure, he's a Greek, but he's from Stagyra in Thrace. That makes him a foreigner to some of these local Athenian rednecks. And this place is loaded with Athenians. They wield most of the political clout around here. There's probably a lot of prejudice involved."

"Yes, you're right. I think not being from Athens weighed heavily against him. But, no matter what the reason is, I hate to see him go."

* Prejudice? That's surprising! Don't you think so, Thomas?
* Perhaps there is prejudice. But I suspect jealousy is also involved somehow. Aristotle was always one of Plato's favorites. Here's some more scuttlebut from a couple of other students:

"Did you know they dug up Aristotle's old records? They discovered he wasn't the perfect student he's knocked up to be. He once got a "C" for his grade in mathematics."

"Well, he never claimed to be a Pythagoras — you know — a mathematical genius! But he is certainly a heavy hitter when it comes to philosophical thought. He would have no trouble filling the sandals of Plato and Socrates with a brilliance at least equal to theirs."

"Yes, and now that Plato is gone, Aristotle is the number one crowd pleaser — the number one draw. He's the star who can keep the Academy full."

Here come a few more students to join the conversation. Let's see if they have anything else to offer.

"We agree with you. Aristotle can fill Plato's sandals. And we hear he'll also follow in Plato's footsteps."

"Yeh. We hear Aristotle is going abroad to study for a few years now that Plato is dead. He's going to Assos in Asia Minor. Maybe also Egypt."

"That's what Plato did after Socrates died. He went abroad. And we hear he wants to come back to Athens and set up his own school — do his own thing — just like Plato did!"

"I predict he sets up a school right across the street from the Academy to compete with his old Athenian colleagues."

"Well, if anyone can do it ... Aristotle can! He'll syphon off a lot of students from the Academy."

"Would you switch to his school?"

"Maybe. But, he doesn't have a school yet. So its all pure speculation."[62]

Those last two students called it right, Harry. Aristotle <u>does</u> leave the Academy.
He studies in Asia Minor. Just when he's about to return to Athens to set up a
school, he gets hit with a bolt from the blue! King Philip of Macedonia asks him
to tutor his only son, Alexander! Aristotle accepts the job. His school in Athens
will have to wait. It will turn out to be a seven year wait. Aristotle knuckles down
to making young Alexander into the philosopher part of a philosopher-king.

Alexander becomes King Alexander of Macedonia six years later when his
father is mysteriously bumped-off. Aristotle continues knuckling down to philosophy. Alexander doesn't. We can imagine what they say to each other, and
ᵒᵒthinkᵒᵒ, after this unforeseen turn of events.

"You've made solid gold progress during these six years,
Alexander. But remember the master, Plato, said it takes fifteen
years! I notice your fire for philosophy is dying out. ᵒᵒYou've
been playing as much the jock as the genius for the past three
years now.ᵒᵒ You've been spending almost as much time at your
father's Spartan military school as you have with my tutoring."
"Don't worry Aristotle. I'm fine. I will soon be off to conquer the rest of Greece ... and then the rest of the Greek
world! ᵒᵒSix years of this is enough, anyway!ᵒᵒ Besides,
Plato didn't figure on <u>you</u> being the tutor when he said it
takes fifteen years!"
ᵒᵒYou're a clever boy, Alexander.ᵒᵒ [63]

Aristotle stays on in Macedonia for another year to guide his young friend.
Alexander successfully makes the transformation from philosopher-boy to
Philosopher-king. He next completes his father's plan to control all of Greece by
crushing the last major resistance at Thebes. At age twenty-one, Alexander is
now the ruler over Greece, including Macedonia!

One of the first things he does as ruler is assure the loyalty of his officers by strengthening his father's military school.

ALEXANDER THE GREAT'S MILITARY ACADEMY

from: The Army of Alexander The Great

Alexander the Great's father, King Philip, started with a Spartan concept of military school for training leaders in his Macedonian army. This was furthered after Philip's death by Alexander who became ruler of the Greek confederacy of city-states called the League of Corinth. Alexander combined philosophical education he received from Aristotle with existing Spartan techniques. He established a "court" military academy for officer training that was called the Royal Pages.

Sons of Greek nobility, especially those from Alexander's Macedonia, would be enrolled in the Royal Pages, a court based military academy. The young men received their education and were trained for leadership. At the same time they served as a guarantee of their parent's loyalty. The noble youths were given a general education, undoubtedly based on Aristotle's philosophy. There was emphasis on the manly pursuit of hunting, and on "sphaira" — a violent ball game similar to football. The most important role of the institution, however, was to imbue the noble youth with obedience to their ruler. Consequently, they were called upon to perform duties not very different from those of slaves. They served at the dinner tables, stood guard, poured the baths, prepared food, and, under the watchful eye of trainers, they performed many other menial duty-motivated functions. They would next receive more professional training as officers in the elite Royal Bodyguard or the Companion Cavalry regiments. In these they were called upon to fight as an active unit so as to gain practical experience in soldiering. They were then distributed throughout the army.

It is highly probable that the entire corps of Alexander's Generals had gone through the academy and seen service in the Royal Bodyguard or Companion Cavalry. The functions of an officer training corps and of a staff and general officer corps were combined. Thus, Alexander developed his leaders in the mold he desired, and assured his own security and their loyalty. He used a military academy concept to do so.[64]

The virtue is: Loyalty. If it isn't natural, it can be taught.

Aristotle now returns to Athens. His reputation soars. He's the tutor and friend of the first-ever philosopher-king of Greece! Finally, redneck politicians of Athens can no longer deny him. Who dares deny the tutor of King Alexander? He opens his own school — The Lyceum. Seven years with Alexander should itself assure the Lyceum's reputation. But let's hear what students in the squares of Athens are saying about the new school, anyway:

"There's a new School here in Athens called the Lyceum. My father's pushing me to go there."
   "Mine is too. The tutor of Alexander, Aristotle, is the one who started it. I remember him, vaguely, when I was young. And a lot of people always talk about him being great when he was at the Academy twelve years ago."
"Right. My father said all of Aristotle's former students will send their sons to the Lyceum."
   "But, the Academy must surely still be the best School. The Academy says that a lot of the philosophy they teach was made by those they taught!"
"Yes, I've heard that. But, have you heard Aristotle's answer? He says the Academy is right! Much of the philosophy they teach was made by those they taught — namely <u>him</u>! Then Aristotle goes on to say, therefore at his Lyceum, much of the philosophy is <u>taught</u> by those who <u>made</u> it — again, namely him!"[65]

85

* Well, where do they go, Thomas? The Academy or the Lyceum?
* It doesn't matter. Both Schools rub along together for a long time. They both have plenty of students. The Academy continues to use the academy method. Aristotle gears the Lyceum more to research. And they pick up this little quirk there:

THE PERIPATETICS

Aristotle had a habit of walking around when lecturing or when thinking. He was role-model to student and teacher alike. They wanted to be like him. So they all began to walk while talking or thinking. Wandering while talking or thinking became the touchstone of the Lyceum. Those at the Lyceum became known as the Peripatetics ... from the Greek word meaning "walking about."

They say that imitation is the ultimate flattery. Well, being imitated is also the hallmark of a leader and role-model. Aristotle demonstrated how teachers become role-models. And he showed they should be role-models!

The virtue is: Trust. If others trust you, they will imitate and follow you.

* One of the students said Aristotle teaches only his own philosophy at the Lyceum. He must also use some of Plato's ideas, too. After all, he was with Plato for twenty years!
* Of course he does. Some of Plato's philosophy is taught in the Lyceum school. But Plato always kind of wore two worlds on his sleeve. One world was some perfect, lofty world — he called it The Good. Remember? The other world was our real world — he called it a poor imitation of The Good. On the other hand, Aristotle would tell you there's just one world that concerns him. And you're in it!

Don't get me wrong. Aristotle does believe there's something greater than the world — what he calls the "Prime Mover". But he also asks, do you know what it is? There's no way you can know. It's beyond your brain's capability to know. So why should you bother to mess around with it? Concentrate on the world you're in!
* I don't get what he means by "Prime Mover".
* It's just a name. Like your name is the word for you, it's just a word for the idea of some higher cause of everything. In the world of 300 BC, some folks use the word "God" to represent that higher cause. Others use "the gods". Plato chose "Ultimate Good". Aristotle prefers "Prime Mover". The words don't matter. Folks are just trying to find a word for some ideal, perfect, other-worldly "something". Your era, Harry, will settle on using the word "God"!

* I see. And does Aristotle have the guts to take on the problem of morals, ethics, and character?
* He becomes famous for it! It's in his <u>Nichomachean Ethics</u>. He starts by talking about the virtues. You remember, they are things like truth, honor, kindness, compassion, discipline, loyalty, perseverence, responsibility, and so forth. If you have the virtues, then you have what Aristotle calls "goodness". For example, anyone can be a father, a teacher, a leader. But the idea is to be a <u>good-father</u>, a <u>good-teacher</u>, a <u>good-leader</u>. These "good" versions are a lot harder to be — but a lot better. And if you go on to become a "good" version of everything you do in life — make virtues and "goodness" a way of life — then you'll have what Aristotle calls "Happiness"!
* So by "Happiness", Aristotle doesn't mean fun and joy.
* Heavens no. "Happiness" is a kind of inner peace. It means you have a virtuous heart and soul. It's as close to Virtue — with a big "V" — as you can get in order to prepare for what comes next after this life ... whatever that is!
* So "Happiness" means you're pretty close to having Virtue — with a big "V". And, as you told me once before, Virtue is made up of three <u>branches</u> of virtues ... moral virtues, ethical virtues, and character virtues. Am I right?
* You're right, Harry. Though Aristotle does take it out one more step. He says there are two <u>classes</u> of Virtue, also. That means two <u>classes</u> of moral virtues, ethical virtues, and character virtues. Basically, you have the <u>Intellectual</u> class and what we'll call the <u>Mortal</u> class.

You get your <u>Intellectual</u> virtues through <u>inheritance</u> and through <u>education</u>. You're born with them, and you can read about them to understand what they are.

You get your <u>Mortal</u> virtues by <u>imitating</u> role models who have them, and by <u>practicing</u> them until you turn them into habits! You have to practice doing things that are like the virtues you want to make into habits. For instance, you become honorable by living according to an honor code. You become just by following a code of justice. You become loyal by practicing loyalty. You get to be efficient by paying attention to details. You couldn't trot out onto the court and win a Wimbledon tennis match without years of practice, could you? And so it is with the virtues you're not born with. Aristotle tells us it's easy to do a virtuous thing, once, but not easy to acquire a settled habit of doing it always. He says it takes study and practice measured in years, not months, to make the virtues into habits:

ARISTOTLE ON HABITS OF MORALS, ETHICS, AND CHARACTER

from: The Nichomachean Ethics

Without demonstration and practice, says Aristotle, no one
has any prospect of reaching a state of Virtue.
"Most people think they can take refuge in theory
alone and think they will become virtuous [good].
But they will not be made good in soul by a course in

philosophy alone. It makes not a <u>small</u> difference,
then, whether we form habits of one kind or another
kind. It makes a very great difference or rather, it
makes <u>all</u> the difference"!

The virtue is: Dedication: It takes committed dedication
to form virtues into habits.

*   I'm left with the impression that there's no difference between Plato and
Aristotle when it comes to morals, ethics, and character — Virtue. I know that
Plato claimed to know the "other world" ... and Aristotle doesn't. I know that
Plato talked about both the other world and this world ... and Aristotle only talks
about this world. However, it looks like they both think Virtue is the key to all
worlds. Right?
*   You're right! But to prove or disprove things in <u>this</u> world, Aristotle doesn't
use the Socratic method of questions and answers like Plato did. He invents a system of Logic. I'll tell you how it works:

(true premiss)   - The figure has three straight sides
(true premiss)   - Only triangles have three straight sides

_____

(true conclusion) - The figure is a triangle

If the first two statements — premisses — are true, and if they're logically connected to eachother — valid, then the conclusion that follows is absolutely guaranteed to be true! This three statement "syllogism" in Aristotle's logic is called
deductive reasoning. Stash it away in your memory bank, Harry. We'll use it later
in our journey through history!
    We'll also use Aristotle's work on morals, ethics, and character later in our jour-
ney. His <u>Nichomachean Ethics</u> is a "must know" for anyone interested in virtue
and leadership. And his monumental work in logic, science, politics, metaphysics,
and linguistics will be a "must know" for all future philosophy scholars. A thousand years from now, a chunk of his philosophy will be alloyed with Christianity
and Islam! Religious philosophers will all but canonize him as a saint.[66]
    Aristotle will leave a gigantic footprint on the world. And thanks to his pupil,
Alexander, the footprint will be deeper and broader than you first imagine. That's
because Alexander, the king, doesn't just hit the brakes when he becomes ruler of
Greece and Macedonia. He drives on toward Greece's arch-rivals, the Persians!

King Darius <u>III</u> of Persia has ruthlessly overrun the Greek city-states along the
coast of Asia Minor. And he's eyeing the disunited, warring city-states on the
mainland of Greece. But our twenty-one year old Alexander is now ruler of
Greece. He's not some young royal upstart. He's a Philosopher-King. And he

has other ideas. He's savvy enough to know he can't just sit around and wait for an enemy attack. Sometimes the best defense is a bold and clever offense. This is one of those times!

Alexander crosses the Hellespont! That's the narrows in the Aegean Sea — later to be called the Dardanelles. He kicks the Persians' butts out of the Greek city-states on the coast of Asia-Minor. And he doesn't want to do it all over again sometime in the future. The city-states are still surrounded by Persian lands. So he doesn't stop at the city-states. He pushes deeper into Asia-Minor to Phyrgia — later to be Central Turkey!

Besides philosophy, Aristotle taught Alexander history, literature, and the sciences. So Alexander has heard about something called the "Gordian Knot." It's a legend with a life of its own:

THE GORDIAN KNOT

from: Greek mythology

The Oracle in Phyrgia said the Ruler would be the first person who could reach the public square in a wagon. A Phyrgian peasant, Gordius, got there first and became King. He dedicated his wagon to the god, Zeus, and tied the wagon to a yoke. He used an indestructible rope of bark to tie an intricately entwined knot, as instructed by the gods. No one could undo the knot. Whoever could undo the knot would become ruler of all Asia, according to the legend. During the centuries that went by, many tried to untie the Gordian Knot. All failed to do so!

The virtue is: Justice. The opportunity for anyone to "make it" is one form of justice.

* If Alexander is smart, he won't risk trying to untie the Gordian Knot!
* Alexander is smart. But he's also bold. Maybe a little too bold this time, Harry ... for here he is! That's he and his generals arriving at the public square in Phyrgia. Does he think he can take on a legend? We'll see. He and his generals are now walking into the grove of the Temple where the wagon is tied to the yoke with the Gordian Knot. An excited crowd is gathering. Alexander is heading straight to the Knot to look it over. He's backing off! That's not good! He can't lose face now! The huge crowd is watching every move he makes! You can feel the tension mounting!
* Uh oh. I think he's dropped himself in it! He probably didn't expect this big an audience.
* You're right. The people of Phyrgia will never support him now, unless he deals with the Gordian Knot. You can't fight superstition, you know. And he's

nobody's fool. He must feel that in his bones. Because look what he's doing now. He's walking back up to the Knot for a closer look. And he's only taking a few steps back this time. And this time he's also drawing his sword.

* I wonder why! Didn't you tell me the legend says the Knot has to be unravelled?

* It also says the Knot is made of stuff from the gods that is impossible to cut. Alexander obviously doesn't buy that ... he's raising his sword! I can't believe it! I think he's fixing to take a big wind-up so he can lay a mighty blow onto the Knot! What a risk he's taking! Here ... he ... goes! ... UH! ... Incredible! Look at that! He slashed right through it! It only took him one shot! He cut it in half! The two halves have fallen apart! They've unravelled themselves! He's done it! Alexander has cut the Gordian Knot![67]

This is a whopping psychological boost to the plan Alexander is cooking up for Asia Minor. For, true to the legend, many of these folks now consider him their king. Now they'll follow him anywhere ... or at least they won't oppose him!

* This place is buzzing with excitement, Thomas! The people love Alexander! We haven't seen anything like this since Aristotle packed it in at the Academy! Can we do our usual thing and listen in on what the common people are saying?

* I was about to suggest that, Harry. Let's put an ear to the conversation right next to us here:

"Good gods! If I didn't see it with my own eyes, I wouldn't have believed it! He's done-in the Gordian Knot! This Alexander is, um, ... Great!"

"He must be a descendant from one of the ancient gods. Only someone who's descended from a god could do that!"

"Maybe. And, I hear he also had that philosopher Aristotle as a teacher."

"Aristotle? Who's that?"

90

"You never heard of Aristotle!? Are you that backward?"

"I'm not too backward to know Alexander's star is rising. In fact, it's going to shoot straight up! I'm not too backward to know that! And when it does, I'll be hanging on to his coat-tails! I'm getting over to sign up with his army! I want a piece of the action! I'll be able to retire on my share of the spoils of his victories! How about you ...... Mr. Philosopher! You coming?"[68]

This conversation gets repeated many times around Asia-Minor. Alexander's reputation spreads like wild-fire. Superstitious throngs of men trample over eachother getting to the place where they can sign up to join his army. Opposition melts away. The way is clear for him to go after Darius and his Persian armies.

Alexander chases Darius into and out of hiding all around the Middle East. He has to get him. Otherwise, Darius can stay in hiding until Alexander is gone, then re-surface and take over everything again. One by one, Alexander smashes the Persian armies. Darius goes into hiding again. But, this time is the last time. His own Generals bump him off!

* Do you think it was Aristotle who suggested that the Gordian Knot could be cut ... must be cut ... in order to take Asia-Minor?

* Well, I'll give you the facts, Harry. You can decide for yourself. First, Aristotle lived in Asia Minor for five years ... he had firsthand knowledge of how important the Gordian Knot is. Second, Aristotle was Alexander's tutor ... anything Alexander knew about the Gordian Knot came straight from him. Third, Aristotle was Alexander's advisor ... he was in Macedonia when Alexander was cooking up his military blitz into Asia Minor. And last, Aristotle was a sage forty-nine year old philosopher ... he had the wisdom to predict the consequences of unravelling the Gordian Knot. His nineteen year old pupil didn't.

* This has Aristotle's fingerprints all over it! I think the Gordian Knot was in Alexander's military game plan right from the start. It's a brilliant stroke of psychological warfare!

* It's also a brilliant story of leadership! Alexander now has a healthy dose of myth, legend, and superstition going for him because of it. Many more men join his army. Most local populations in his path just roll over and play dead. But his enemies don't. He still has to beat them in the field. And he does. He smashes every single army he comes up against ... from Egypt all the way to India!

Alexander is one of the great military leaders of all time. He's also one of the great social and political leaders! He doesn't just trample over everything in his path, leaving carnage behind. He builds new cities. Leaders from his army — all trained at his Royal Pages military academy — stay behind to govern and to plant Greek culture. They marry into influential local families. In fact, he encourages all his men to marry eastern women so he can cement a new civilization of locals and Macedonian Greeks. Alexander joins together 9000 soldiers and eastern women in one stroke at the historical "marriage of East and West"!

* Incredible!

* If you pull a man up from his neighborhood by the roots, he'll transplant that

neighborhood wherever he settles again. And that's the whole idea. Alexander ends up transplanting twenty-five new "neighborhoods" — cities — along the path of his victories. One of them at the mouth of the Nile River in Egypt, Alexandria, blossoms into one of the greatest of all cities. It makes dazzling breakthroughs in science, medicine, astronomy, geography, and mathematics. The Alexandria Library gathers up books and manuscripts by the tens of thousands. Alexandria becomes the known world's unrivaled center of research and study!

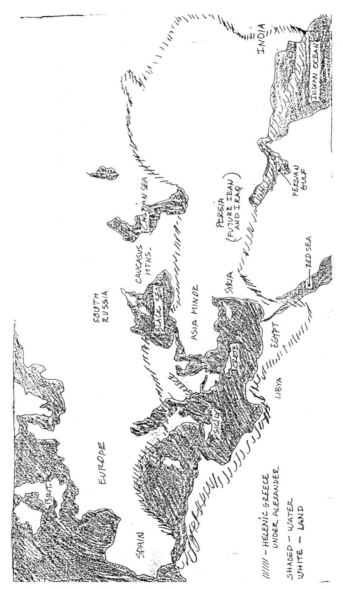

People from the new cities begin to spread Greek culture all around Asia and the Mediterranean. Without stepping a foot outside of his Lyceum, Aristotle now influences more people than he ever hoped he could! The entire known world is becoming "Hellenized" through Greek enlightenment. Aristotles' Lyceum is churning out the culture while Alexander's Royal Pages academy is churning out the leaders for this "Hellenization"!

Alexander has always been driven by youthful ideals — missionary zeal to spread Greek culture and need to prove himself to a forceful mother, his greatest fan. He's done both. But he never gets to enjoy the hero's homecoming welcome from the mother and hometown that proudly await him. He never gets home again! At age thirty-three, just ten years after he began his mission, he dies from fever!

As you might guess, that ends Greek missionary zeal. But Alexander took it far in ten short years. And his success wasn't just luck or ruthless determination. Alexander was a special kind of leader — a good-leader. He was a "whole person" — a guy who had natural intelligence, Spartan character virtues, and Aristotle's education! When all is said and done, Aristotle's greatest accomplishment will be having made Alexander, the boy, into a great leader! For Alexander was philosopher-king of the entire Hellenized Western world. He was worthy of being called Alexander the Great![69]

Now that Alexander the Great is dead, the Athenian fathers are going back to shedding Macedonian domination. You can see Aristotle's fame quickly turning to blame! The Athenian fathers "blame" Aristotle for Alexander's meteoric rise to power. They also trump-up charges of impiety against him, saying he fails to worship their multi-gods. Aristotle tells them they're right, both times! Of course he helped to "produce" Alexander the Great. And of course he's not a worshiper of the pagan gods. That's what philosophy — the stuff he's teaching their own sons — is all about! So they've got him. They decide he has to drink the poison hemlock, like Socrates did. Not one to be force-fed on poison hemlock, he beats a hasty escape. He "saves Athens from sinning a second time against philosophy"![70]

About a year later on the island of Chalcis ... Aristotle dies! With him dies the flourish of Greek culture. It's been called an "axial age" of civilization — an "ancient enlightenment". And Greece was its center. It was the "axis of civilization"!

* What happens to Aristotle's Lyceum? Do they close it down?

* It continues, just like you and I saw the Academy go on after Plato's death. But they don't do much of anything that's new at either the Lyceum or the Academy. They make no new advances ... only changes. And the Academy, not the Lyceum, suffers the most painful of all changes — a Sophist comeback. But these are more sarcastic and cynical than the old Sophists were. They infiltrate the Academy and take non-conformism to the extreme. For example, one guy is so ridiculous ... he lives in a barrel. Of course, a barrel is too small to have a toilet. So what does he do? He relieves himself just outside the barrel — to the public's full view and outrage![71]

* Poor Plato! His Academy now sounds more like a house of horrors, than a house of philosophy, doesn't it Thomas. Where's a young person to go for his education now?

* I think we'll get the best answer to that question down at the market square in Athens where all the young folks hang out:

> "Have you decided where you're going to study?"
>   "No, not yet. I haven't started looking. Have you?"
> "Yes, I've considered a few Schools."
>   "Well, how are they?"
> "So far, not good! Take the Pythagorean School. They don't eat!
>   Then there's the Lyceum. I like Aristotle. Who doesn't? But
>   they don't sit down! They just keep walking around all over the
>   place."
>   "How about the Academy?"
> "I hear they're becoming a little weird over there. One philoso-
>   pher supposedly lives in a barrel! Can you believe that?"
>   "How about Zeno's new School — The Stoics?"
> "Yes ... I've heard about them. Zeno lectures the students from up
>   on a porch — the stoa. So they're called "Stoics". It's rumored
>   they believe in suicide though! That turns me off"!
>   "I agree. That would turn me off too. I want to enjoy life —
>   not die!"
> "Me too. Then you'll be interested in the one I'm going to see
>   next. It's the Epicurean School. They push inner peace in this
>   life. No fear. No pain. No suffering. Only pleasure. I hear
>   Epicurus acts as the role model by lying on his hammock, wal-
>   lowing in the pleasures of food and drink while lecturing. But, I
>   don't know how true that is!"
>   "That's for me! Give me some good old-fashioned gluttony,
>   debauchery, and physical titillation anytime!"

"I wouldn't go <u>that</u> far. However, the Epicureans do sound interesting".[72]

The Epicurean School <u>doesn't</u> go that far. Not at all. In fact, Epicurus (341-270 BC) teaches: 1.) Prudence; 2.) Temperence; 3.) Fortitude; and, 4.) Justice. They're the "cardinal virtues". He'll tell you that some good man sees everything you do in life. Therefore you should live like you know the good man is watching you.

* Then what's this pleasure mentality?

* Harry, the Epicurean meaning of "pleasure" is wildly mistaken. It's <u>not</u> orgies of food, drink, and luxury. Epicurus clearly says pleasure simply means not having pain and not doing wrong. If you study Epicurus' writings, you'll see he's a lot tougher than the mistaken term, "Epicurean", calls to mind. He pushes the cardinal virtues real hard. That means he expects you to be disciplined. They're the reasons Epicurus doesn't catch on with most people. In a future age he <u>will</u> catch on with someone who does bother to study what he really says. That someone will be Thomas Jefferson! But for now, Plato and Aristotle are tough acts to follow for any philosopher![73]

A guy in Greece named Zeno (334-262 BC) pioneers the new philosophy called "Stoicism" that finally catches on big. Zeno likes to study people's morals, ethics, and character. Like Plato and Aristotle, the Stoics say you have to live a life filled with the virtues to prepare for what comes next. But the Stoics put spe-

cial emphasis on courage, honor, prudence and temperance as the hot virtues that lead to ideal Virtue, with a capital "V". And he says that students at his School have to live a simple, self-denying life to acquire those virtues. Greek Stoicism will travel West to Rome.[74]

CHAPTER 8: ROMAN PERIOD AND CHRISTIANITY

Meanwhile, Harry, dark clouds are gathering to the West of Greece! They're around Sicily and southern Italy in the great "Greek lake" — the Mediterranean part of the Helenic Greek civilization. Rome and Carthage have been at eachother's throats for decades. Rome finally emerges the victor in what becomes known as the Punic Wars. So while the Greeks thought, the Romans fought ... and built a powerful war machine.

Now, like Alexander, the Romans keep going. Their war machine drives onward to take on other armies. And first up is Greece. Our once great Greek civilization is about to be chewed up and swallowed by an emerging Roman Empire. But, unlike Alexander, the Roman conquerors don't have a cultural mission. They can't add anything to Greece's culture and philosophy. In fact, you'll see that Greece actually adds to Rome's culture and philosophy. The conquered teaches the conqueror, you might say. From the cultural and philosophical standpoints, Greece takes its captors captive!

* I don't get it. Why do the Romans pick on Greece first?
* Because Alexander's Helenistic civilization fractured into three parts when he died. One was on this side of the Aegean Sea — Greece and Macedonia — where we are now. Another was across the Aegean Sea from us in Asia Minor. And the third was across the Mediterranean Sea from us in the Middle East. The two across the Seas are ruled by Alexander's former generals. They still have bonafide armies. But here in Greece the army is rather a myth! It's weak. As I said, the Greeks thought while the Romans fought. So the Romans chose to dispose of the thinkers before taking on the fighters.

When the Romans eat up the Greek army, Stoicism is the going philosophy in Greece. The Romans eat that up too! They love it! So they import it to Rome. Stoicism becomes the rage among authors and writers, not only in Rome, but all around the expanding Roman Empire. Rome is building a mighty Empire. But its philosophy is all Greek!

* It seems like everything in Greece is migrating to Rome!
* And that includes us, Harry. The next stop on our journey is Rome!

There's a thriving bunch of homegrown writers and philosophers here in Rome. But most of the things they do are actually reruns or remakes of Greek history, mythology, and philosophy. The remakes are well done. But they are copies! For example, if you read what Cicero (106-43 BC) says about moral and political philosophy, you'll see he is eloquent. But he says almost exactly what the Stoics in Athens have been saying ... and what our friend Aristotle said 200 years earlier. And take Virgil (70-19 BC). He writes an epic about Ulysses. But Ulysses is, really Odysseus of Homer's Iliad and Odyssey. You can see example after example of copycat Greek culture in Rome!

You can imagine what philosophers at the exclusive Maecenas literary circle in Rome must be saying while sitting around, sipping too much wine:

"What's new mate?"

"New? What does new mean?"

"I hear you have a new work coming out".

"If you mean not a copy of a copy — but only a simple copy … then yes … I do have one coming out."

"What do you mean by that?"

"Come now. You know. We all do it. Change the names. Write in Latin. Use different construction. But all made with the same old Greek toolkit!"

"So what? What's the difference?! As long as they sell!"

"The difference is, you're not practicing the Stoic virtue called honesty. Ever hear of it?"[75]

Most Stoics really do practice the virtues. And the virtues are even woven into history. If you read <u>History of Rome</u> by Livy (59-17 BC), you'll see what I mean. He uses history to teach moral and ethical lessons. So he's not just a historian. He's a philosopher!

HISTORY OF ROME

from: Livy (Titus Livius)

Early in his <u>History of Rome</u>, Titus Livius tells the story of Horatius At The Bridge in much the same way as Greek historian Herodotus told of the Spartan's stand against overwhelming numbers at the Thermopylae Pass. Livy's lesson in it was the virtue of courage. The story goes like this:

Horatius, first with two other officers known for their gallant exploits, and finally by himself, held off the invading Etruscan army. He did so at the entrance to the only bridge across the Tiber River that leads south to Rome. He held off long enough for his fellow soldiers to destroy the bridge, escape to safety, and thus save Rome! Horatius then almost miraculously swam the river to safety, in spite of wearing full armor and having lost an eye in the fighting!

Livy's History tells how the small "city" of Rome went on to break away from the dominant Etruscan civilization (around 500 BC) and form a republic. He tells how they began to subordinate all of the neighboring cities of Italy, and eventually, even put their own Roman rule into the powerful Etruscan state in central Italy. Over the next few hundred years their military power steadily grew. They finally defeated Carthage in the three Punic Wars that went on from 264 BC to 146 BC. So the boundaries and rule of Rome grew too. But Livy unfolds his lesson of how an ominous situation was developing between the military legions and the civilian Republic. The Romans, unlike Alexander The Great in Greece, had no military school to shape the minds and morals of military officers into loyalty to republican ideals. In fact, officers had become quite the opposite of loyal by around 100 BC! Why? Because expansion of Roman rule to territories outside of Italy was giving opportunities for governors and generals in the new provinces to make immense fortunes for themselves from the spoils of war. Although there was some looting and theft, much was actually legal. A new tradition grew. Generals bought their leadership loyalty by distributing some of the spoils of victory to their troops. An outstanding general, Marius, actually got those under his command to swear an oath of allegiance to him personally!

The Empire had originally been built by the Republic with early Roman ideals and morality. Now military power was the ultimate reason for its existence. And Marius was gaining substantial power over the Senate. When he died, Sulla, a general who had been wildly successful in Asia, returned to Rome and began to launch a dictatorship over the Senate. The power of his army made this possible. Then, Sulla's protege, Pompey, conquered huge Asian Territories. He returned to Rome to gain prominance over the Senate.

Years passed. Disorder in Roman streets and official corruption grew. By the time Julius Caesar, the nephew of Marius, had conquered the territories north of Italy in Europe and Britain, political factions were fighting against eachother in Rome. Caesar decided to use his now formidable military power and civil support to do something about it. In 49 BC he took his army across the forbidden boundary between the Northern and Roman provinces, the river Rubicon. The resulting civil war with Pompey and supportors lasted four years. After his victory, Caesar brought order to the streets and curbed corruption. But, just fifteen months later he was dead. Caesar was murdered in the Senate on March 15, 44BC ... the Ides of March!

Julius Caesar had, wisely, adopted his great-nephew to be heir to his political connections and military support in case of his death. This was the one to be called Caesar Augustus. And, a wise legacy it was that Julius left to his beloved Rome. Augustus continued Julius Caesar's reforms of disorder and corruption. The virtues of "ancient" Rome almost seemed to come alive again under Augustus. He revived most of the old republican traditions and the concern for ethics and morals. The examples and lessons taught by Livy on morals, ethics, and character in his histories were implemented by Augustus to promote his reforms. The lessons were especially valuable when coming from someone like Livy. For he was from Northern Africa and thereby outside of Rome's self-serving literary and military circles. Augustus even made an apparent attempt at something like the military school of Alexander the Great when he formed his Praetorian Guard. But it didn't go far enough. For, professing trust, honor, and loyalty are not the same as acquiring them permanently from a long period of training. The Praetorian Guard turned into nothing but a palace guard. It did not have the strong foundation of Aristotle's philosophy. It failed to stay uncorrupted when all else was becoming corrupted. It was eliminated by a later Roman Emperor.

Livy had pointed out that Rome's troubles did not start when Caesar crossed the Rubicon. Rome was already seriously damaged a long time before that! Although the Romans had seen great material wealth, they could not see their government was becoming morally and ethically bankrupt! Augustus tried to turn things around! But the Romans of his day had ceased to resemble the Romans of the early Republic in all but name.[76]

The virtue is: Integrity. A nation lacking integrity is a
nation who's days are limited!

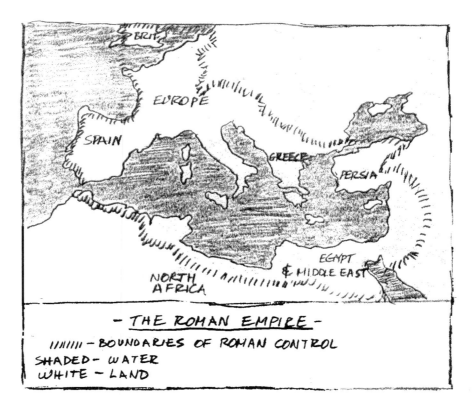

- THE ROMAN EMPIRE -

//////// - BOUNDARIES OF ROMAN CONTROL
SHADED - WATER
WHITE - LAND

* That's a good way to teach history. Instead of giving a lot of dates and details, Livy tells a story and throws a little philosophy into it.

* Actually, Livy is more philosopher than historian. He's out to have folks learn Virtue, not just history. He's merely using history as a learning tool. Like us. We're using history as a learning tool for seeing, firsthand, the importance to West Point of "putting old souls into young bodies".

We're about to see how Julius Caesar also learns, firsthand, the importance of "putting old souls into young bodies". He could do with a few virtuous old souls around him on the Ides of March in 44 BC. That's the day he gets assassinated while entering the Senate in Rome! Shakespeare will give us his take on what Caesar says at the moment his murderers plunge their knives into his back. Can you imagine what Caesar himself must also be °°thinking°° at that moment?

> "Uh!" °°Stabbed! From behind!°° "Cassius. My trusted General. You disloyal snake!" °°I should have paid attention to my tutor in Rhodes. He told me you can only teach virtues like loyalty at an academy.°° "Uh! You too Brutus?" °°Even you? You should have had training in trust and loyalty — instead of law. I should have known not to trust anyone.°° "Uh"! ... °°Uhhh ... now it's too late.°° [77]

The Romans have been lifting a lot of Greek culture and calling it their own. But they never lifted ideas like Plato's philosopher-king or Alexander's military academy, unfortunately for Julius Caesar. And it's unfortunate for us, too. For now we'll never know whether or not Caesar was going to be a benevolent dictator — a philosopher-king — and restore the old Roman Republic once he restored the old Roman virtues!

* Perhaps the course of history would have been different.

* Perhaps, Harry. Perhaps. But Roman philosopher Seneca (4 BC-65 AD) <u>does</u> later stumble into the philosopher-king business. He's hired to tutor Emperor Claudius' young adopted son, Nero. And let me tell you, this kid is a little scoundrel! If you met him, you'd probably say Claudius would be better off hiring a warden instead of a tutor! And guess what? In the end, he comes close to doing just that! He brings in the commander of the Praetorian Guard, Burrus, to help Seneca discipline the kid!

Nero becomes emperor at seventeen years old when Claudius dies in 54 AD. Believe it or not, the first five years of the young scoundrel's reign are actually idyllic. That's because he's not involved! Seneca and Burrus are the ones running the show. They're defacto co-emperors. Rome actually has a "philosopher-king" and a military leader-of-virtue in charge for a few years! Then Burrus dies. Seneca can't handle Nero. And he can't get through to him as a tutor. The undisciplined Nero has no "Will" to learn about the virtues, much less have the Will to work on making them habits. The young scoundrel drops straight to the bottom of the heap as a human being!

Speaking of "Will", that's one of the few original twists the Romans add to Stoic philosophy. Another is "Fate". They believe that life gives everyone a predetermined destiny — a Fate. Will and Fate are the things that make Roman Stoicism different than Greek Stoicism. Roman Stoicism finally takes on its own flavor. That's because Plato, Aristotle, and Zeno all but ignored Will and Fate. They considered them to be things that are natural and unchangeable.

Seneca thinks that besides having natural Will, you can also be <u>convinced</u> to have the Will to do something. But he'll never prove it by Nero! For Nero will be an epic example of the old saying, you can lead a horse (someone) to water but you can't convince him to drink. He'll lead Nero to the pure waters of Virtue. But he'll never convince him to drink! He'll learn a lesson about Will from Nero. So will we!

If we make our way down this stately hallway of Nero's palace, Harry, we can hear Seneca lecturing inside one of the chambers about Stoic Will and Fate:

"We must have the Will to face destiny with courage and dignity.
It's beyond our control. We should accept and be happy with our
lot in life."
    "Yes, sire. I understand."
"Remember. Everything happens for the good. We should not try
to get what we want — we should want what we get."
    "And I also understand, sire."
"There's a reason for what we get — a divinely determined reason! So don't worry! Start living! Get on with your life! Is that
clear to you?"
    "Yes, sire."

Let's just peek inside the room, shall we Thomas? Which one is Seneca?
* I'm afraid to say that's him lying back on the couch, cooling his feet in the basin of cold water while being fanned with that huge feather!
* Why he's surrounded by platters of roasted poultry and fresh fruit! He's feeding his face while three servants wait on him hand and foot! Listen to what he's saying!

"We must be resigned to our Fate — want what we've got."
    "I'm resigned to my Fate, sire." ᵒᵒYeah! Just what I always
    wanted — to cool someone's stinking feet for the rest of my
    life!ᵒᵒ

"And what about you?"
    "I'm resigned to my Fate too, sire." ᵒᵒI always wanted to fan
    you with this big, dumb feather, didn't I!ᵒᵒ

"And you?"
    "And I'm also resigned to my Fate, sire — and want what I've
    got." ᵒᵒWhat a liar I am. The last thing I want is to wait on
    you hand and foot! I wish I was born man instead of
    woman!ᵒᵒ

"So we are all resigned to our Fate then — are we?"
    "Yes sire. We are." (everyone together)

"Yes, and I too." (sighing, and ripping a big hunk out of a huge chicken leg with his teeth.)[78]

* Seneca's words are always steadfast Stoic. But his lifestyle is sometimes blatant baccanalianism — pigging out on food and wine. And guess what, Harry. That's how most politicians and uppercrust Romans are here in the first century AD. It's the fashion. Sadistic Nero knows it bothers Seneca's conscience, however. So he mercilessly badgers and berates him. He pretends to pick on Seneca's lavish lifestyle. But he's really insanely jealous that Seneca is pulling down big money from investments. Nero goes from being pampered punk to maniacal madman! It gets very ugly! Seneca is fed up! Enough is enough! He resigns!

Now he's free of Nero. He's free of the madman's endless whims and badgering ... he thinks. But we're about to find out he's not free of the <u>final</u> whim! Nero whips up a lie that says Seneca is plotting against him. He issues Seneca an ultimatum with two options. Option one: Seneca must return to Nero's "stable". Option two: If he refuses option one, he'll be forced to poison himself to death!

* Some options! He's boxed-in!

* Seneca says, "the dirtiest death is preferrable to the daintiest slavery." And he <u>does</u> have a guilty conscience over not practicing all the Stoic virtues because of his lavish lifestyle.

* But a person can <u>believe</u> in the virtues without yet having perfected them all himself. Right?

* It's true that you don't have to be a saint to go to church — unless, of course, <u>you're</u> the preacher. And that's the rub in Seneca's case. He <u>is</u> the preacher, so to speak. He's the role model. So should Seneca become a martyr to prove his beliefs like philosophers in the past did? Remember Empedocles? He jumped into the volcanic fires of Mount Etna to prove he was a god.

* Yeh. And it only proved he wasn't!

* And dear old Socrates drank the poison hemlock to defend truth.

* He could have escaped, and defended truth on many other days!

* Right. But the Stoics have a peculiar belief about suicide. They believe suicide is desirable in certain situations. Seneca concludes that this is one of those situations. He says, "to die well is to escape the danger of living badly". He chooses Nero's option two. He poisons himself! And no self-respecting Stoic

would let other philosophers outdo him at suicide. So he not only takes the poison. He slits open the veins in his wrists, knees, and ankles! Then he steps into a hot bath to hasten loss of blood, and death!

* That's groddy! It sends a chill up my spine! And it's dumb!

* What Empedocles did was dumb, Harry. What Socrates did was tragic. But what Seneca did? Well, there are two opinions. One opinion says he was a philosopher, dying for his beliefs. The other says he knew that Nero would kill him, anyway. So he had the last laugh. He deprived Nero. He killed himself!

The lesson I told you we'd learn about the Will from this whole sordid affair with Nero is — not everyone can be made into a good-leader. You need the Will to be one. Nero is our firsthand living proof of that. And he won't be living proof very much longer. For he's about to be overthrown by his own Praetorian Guard. Before they can execute him, he commits suicide! Like Seneca, he has the last laugh! I guess he did learn something from Seneca, afterall!

* I'm hung up on something! Stoicism says accept Fate? Want only what you have? Does that leave any room for ambition, Thomas?

* It's true, the Stoics say you should bully your own Will, learn the virtues, accept nature and destiny, be happy with your lot, and recognize your own limits. Yes. That's all good Stoic wisdom. But within your own limits you can still have ambition to be the best that's possible for you! You should still be the best that you can be! For instance, if you're cut out to be a farmer ... be a good one. If you're cut out to be a soldier ... work hard to be a first-class soldier. Nothing comes easy. You have to work at it. And it takes time. Lots of time. The Stoic philosopher, Epictetus (60-125 AD), is known to harp-on about how much time, work, and Will it takes to acquire good morals, ethics, and character![79]

EPICTETUS

from: The Encheiridion (Handbook)

The Phyrgian-Greek Epictetus was born a slave! He later earned his freedom. This affected his philosophy. He was one of the Greeks who carried Stoicism to Rome. Because he worked hard to earn his freedom, he preached that it takes determination to capture traits of character that represent virtues and principles. And, recognizing how much time it takes to capture virtues and principles, he said:

"You must know that it is no easy thing for a principle to become a man's own, unless each day he maintain it and hear it maintained, as well as, work it out in life."

And he said:

"To obtain virtues the work of every man would have
to be like the service of a soldier — long and
arduous."

The virtue is: Determination. Good results require time,
effort, and determination.

Here's an interesting tidbit about Epictetus, Harry. He's interested in how virtues
are used in everyday life. Take Truth, for example. He never concerns himself
too much with explaining Truth. He simply says that he "holds Truth to be self-
evident." You and I will see Thomas Jefferson say that 1700 years from now!

While Nero and Seneca were playing out their tragedy in Rome, an epic story
was in progress across the Mediterranean. It went along kind of unrecorded at the
time. But, its after-shocks will be earthshaking! It was the rise of Christianity!

JESUS: "SUPERSTAR"

based on: The New Testament

The original ingredients of Christianity were all in
place. They started with ancient myths, Hammurabi's
laws, Akenhaten's One God, and Moses. Then came the
Old Testament, the Prophets, the Birth of Jesus, and the
teachings of Jesus during his life on earth. While philosophy across in Greece searched for answers, religion had
the answer to everything. That answer could usually be
summed up into one word. God!

Jesus, the man, can certainly be considered the greatest
leader of all time! He was the ultimate good-leader. He
was the only true "Superstar"!

Jesus, the Son of God, performed many divinely guided
miracles. And he miraculously rose from death after being
crucified on a cross! The miracles should have guaranteed
that his religious teachings would not die out, as other
sects and variations on Judaism died out in the past. But
the religious teachings of Jesus nearly did die out ... until
St. Paul got into the picture!

The virtue is: Faith. It's the missing piece to life's puzzle.

* Are you telling me that Christianity faded after the death of Jesus? I thought
that's when it began to flourish and spread.
* When Jesus died there still was no such thing as Christianity, Harry. Jesus was

105

trying to change Judaism — not start a separate new religion. Jesus and his followers were all Jews trying to work within the framework of Judaism. For decades after his death the followers of Jesus were busy putting together everything in writing. It all finished up as the New Testament. Now let me tell you about St.Paul and Christianity.

PAUL OF TARSUS (ST. PAUL)

based on: The New Testament and Romans 5: 1-5

As a Jewish Pharisee and himself a persecutor of the followers of Jesus, Paul got to know the new Jewish sect which was not yet known as Christianity. He soon became a follower himself. His insistance that Jesus was the Son of God threatened the structure of existing Judaism. There was simply no place in Judaism for such an idea! Jesus' followers were forced out of the Temple!

Paul found Jesus' emphasis on moral and ethical sincerity, rather than strict Jewish ritual, to be compatible with many aspects of Greek philosophy, especially Plato's. He combined them, and began to teach the new and winning doctrine. It was called Christianity! Paul had saved Jesus' teachings from dying out, or from becoming unrecognizably dissolved into Judaism!

In about the year 47 AD, Paul began a long series of missionary treks to teach Christianity far and wide. He paid particular attention to a seemingly unlimited number of religiously non-committed people around the Mediterranean. His new Christianity even began to compete with the philosophies of Stoicism and Neo-Platonism for the hearts and minds of Romans! A colossal structure of religious-philosophy was being built! Christianity and philosophy would intimately be related for the next 1,200 years!

As a leader who did not have benefit of divine guidance as Jesus did, Paul of Tarsus has to be considered one of the greatest good-leaders of all time! He had no armies. He was not a king or a ruler. But he had a cause. It was a cause greater than himself. He was well versed in what he taught and he had intellectual wisdom. He helped people. He filled their needs. And he succeeded in doing these things because he embodied Virtue. Thus he commanded the trust of others. He got people to follow him willingly. Millions would follow willingly!

In his famous letter, Romans 5:1-5, St. Paul described how those who train to survive hardship will develope sta-

mina and mental endurance! Stamina and mental
endurance make for proven character and tested virtues!
And all of these in turn make leaders who have hope —
hope that holds up during time of crisis! He said:
> "We can even <u>boast</u> of our hardships (afflictions)".
> We know that hardship makes for mental
> endurance, mental endurance for tested virtues,
> and tested virtues for leadership under stress (to
> give hope)!"

The virtue is: Determination. St Paul's determination
created Christianity!

* Incredible! I didn't know St Paul was the one who founded Christianity ... long
after Jesus died! And his letter to the Romans endorses <u>hardship</u> as the way to
develope virtues and leadership![80]
* That's right, Harry. You'll see later in our journey how West Point picks up on
the idea of hardship. But at the moment, back here in Rome, the Christians are
bearing <u>grave</u> hardship! They're getting badgered and blamed for everything in
sight! Nero even blamed the fire of Rome on them. He set the precedent. Now
even Emperors who come after Nero blame them for everything. The Christians
are scapegoats for fire, flood, and famine. They're lightning rods. They nicely
attract public attention away from the <u>real</u> problems. Democracy is crumbling.
The Senate is losing its grip on power. Barbarian hordes are circling the Empire.
Yet the Christians get all the attention!
* I can understand how philosophers might see Christians as competitors. But
what does Rome have against them?
* Rome sees them as the enemy! Christians refuse to sacrifice to pagan gods.
They refuse to swear an oath to the divinity of the Emperors. So, as punishment,
Rome makes them part of the "contests" at the Coliseum. The wrong part! The
sacrificial lambs! These "Christian martyrs" are either eaten by lions or beaten by
gladiators! You'll see for yourself. We'll now go to one of these so-called contests. You can judge for yourself whether they're as callous as everyone says they
are. ......
* So this is the Coliseum! It's better than pictures I've seen of it! Check out the
gladiator down below us. What a great looking shield, sword, and suit of body
armor he has! But who's that other guy?
* He's the Christian.
* Poor devil! His gear is pretty grubby looking! I guess it's better than nothing,
though.
* It's better than nothing. But, not much better. You probably don't realize it,
but these gladiators are trained professional killers. They can kill you in a hundred fancy ways.
* That gladiator over on the other side of the arena isn't very fancy. He's about
to kill the Christian real bluntly — chop off his head! See him? What's he doing

with his thumb?

* He's asking the spectators if he should kill the poor devil. Thumbs down means do it. Thumbs up means let him live. Listen to the remarks from spectators up here in the galleries:

> "Oh heavens! ... Oh no!"
>> "What's the matter, mate? Can't bear to watch? Turn your head then."
> "No, it's not that. I just remembered! I left my sandwiches outside in the chariot!" ∘∘You think it's the first time I'm gonna see a head roll?∘∘

> "Thumbs up! Thumbs up! Hold the blood for now! I'm still eating!"
>> "Yeh! Me too!"

> "No! Thumbs down! Finish him! The wife's waiting at home with supper. I have to split!"
>> "Yeh! ∘∘And I have to go to the toilet.∘∘ Come on, finish it!"

> "This Christian is useless! I didn't pay to see a one minute fight! Throw him to the lions and bring on another. He's too easy!"
>> "They already did that with a bunch of them before you got here."
> "Then cut him up into pieces for us! Go on, throw us a souvenir! A hand or finger will do for me!"

That's an off-duty gladiator in the audience over there. Let's hear what he has to say:

"Am I glad I played the matinee! This evening crowd's tough!
And I thought it was bad this afternoon!"
    "You're a gladiator? What happened this afternoon?"
"Yes, I am. This afternoon they gave my wretched Christian ... if
you can believe this ... an old bronze breast plate. A real relic.
From the Etruscans or something. Poor wretch. I ran my hard
iron sword straight through it!"

"That's it! I've seen enough! This isn't sport! I'm getting out of
here! I'm history! From now on it's the wrestling matches for
me!"
    (whispering) "He's a bloody whimp!"

"Wait up. I'll go with you. I've decided. I <u>will</u> get my sandwich-
es out of the chariot! I'm staying for the next show. This is
exciting!"[81]

It's ironic that inside the Coliseum they're killing Christians because of their
beliefs. At the same time outside the Coliseum, they're using the Christian's
beliefs in their philosophy!
* I don't get you.
* Remember I told you that St.Paul mixed Plato's philosophy with Jesus's teachings to create Christianity? Now, mixing Christianity into current Roman philosophy has become all the rage. You might call it ... the Christianization of philosophy!
* Christianization of philosophy? Isn't that just the opposite of why the Greeks
invented philosophy in the first place? Wasn't finding <u>Reasons</u> for things, not just
<u>Belief</u>, the whole point?
* For sure. But there's a different aura here in Rome than there was back in 400's
BC Greece. Back then, the flower of Greek culture was just starting to bloom.
Greece was buoyant and optimistic. But here in second century Rome there's a
feeling of hopelessness. The Roman Empire hasn't expanded for fifty years.
Neither has philosophy. Roman legions at the Empire's furthest outposts can
barely hold on to the lands they occupy. And then there's the growing moral and
ethical decay. You saw one type of it inside the Coliseum. Outside the Coliseum,
you can see other types of it all over the place!
    Even good emperor Marcus Aurelius (120-180 AD) can't rein-in the immoral-
ity going on all over the place. He's the closest thing to a philosopher-king since
Caesar Augustus. He bullies himself into being fair, kind, honest, trustworthy,
hard-working and so on. He even adds "social obligation" to his menu of virtues
in his <u>Meditations</u>. He's amazing. Here he is, a mighty Emperor. Yet, he has simple virtues. He sets a good moral example as the leader and role-model of his people. He's known as the last good Stoic philosopher. He'll also be known as the
"last good Emperor". He devotes his entire life trying to use Stoic philosophy to
rein-in the decay and immorality going on all over the place. But it doesn't work.
Something else is needed. And that brings us back to the Christianization of phi-

losophy. In the future, the only morals, ethics, and character taught will use some form of Christianity ... the very same Christianity that has been persecuted in The Coliseum for so many years!

Plotinus (200-270 AD) is our main man when it comes to the Christianization of philosophy. He's a follower of Plato. But he doesn't talk about Plato's "Ultimate Good" as the reason you should work on your morals, ethics, and character. He talks about Christianity's God!

* Hm. How can he be a follower of Plato and not talk about the "Ultimate Good"?

* Because he says Christianity's God is what Plato meant by the "Ultimate Good"! And to boot, Christianity's God is a lot easier to picture in your mind. So he proceeds to blend the best bits of Plato, Aristotle, and Stoicism with Christianity. The result is Neo-Platonism — the Christianization of philosophy. Just like Christianity is really philosophy with emphasis on Jesus, Neo-Platonism is really Christianity without emphasis on Jesus. Either way, Christian thinkers are the ones trying to guide folks back again to good morals, ethics, and character.[82]

By 313 AD, Rome's own barbarianism — feeding Christians to lions or gladiators in The Coliseum — has ended. Christian martyrs have not died in vain. Their sacrifice finally pays off. Emperor Constantine is so impressed with them that he converts to Christianity himself that year! That makes Christianity the official religion of the Roman Empire! It will someday stop pagan religions from taking hold in Europe. Unfortunately, it will not stop pagan decadence and immorality from taking hold in Rome today. Christian thinkers may guide, but Roman morals still slide!

* When Christianity became the religion of the Roman Empire, why couldn't Constantine halt the slide?

* He tried. But Rome was already into the endgame of decline. It's been in a downward moral and ethical slide for over three centuries now. Halting the slide was too big a job for even an emperor once it went too far. Julius Caesar tried. You saw what happened to him. Caesar Augustus tried. And so did Marcus Aurelius. No one was able to stop the inexorable decline of the Roman civilization once morals and ethics went downhill. Neither economic wealth nor military power made any difference. And that's why you're on this journey through the history of philosophy — to see firsthand why morals, ethics, and character are vital!

Pax Romana is a Roman tradition. It's Rome's slogan for "a secure and peaceful Empire". But by the mid 300's AD the tradition is dying. Huge armies of barbarians are on the move. Goths, Huns, and Vandals penetrate border defenses. The Roman legions are spread too thin to stop them. And Pax Romana isn't the only Roman tradition that's dying. So is the once proud and efficent Roman civil service. It had once held the vast Roman Empire together. Now it can't even hold itself together! It's collapsing under its own weight! Layers of bureaucracy that rub along in different directions are finally siezing up. The civil service simply has too many bureaucrats living off of it and not enough taxes to pay for it. So Rome is like a car full of people that gets stuck in the mud. Some folks have to get out and push to get it moving. If everyone sits inside waiting for the next guy to push, nothing happens. It doesn't move. Like the car, Rome has too many people going along for the ride and not enough people pushing!

By the end of the 300's AD, people are flocking into Rome from the countryside by the thousands. Some are freeloaders. Others are seeking jobs. Still others are seeking protection from the barbarians. The city of Rome bloats to over one million people. One million! That's huge for this time in history! Freeloaders, civil servants, and well-connected fat cats ... all sitting in the car, not pushing ... are draining away Rome's wealth. So the government gets lawyers to cook up ways to squeeze more taxes out of people. Rich folks get other lawyers to cook up gimmicks to avoid or cheat on those taxes. Ordinary folks get the shaft! Even back here, only the dead ... and the rich ... get out of their taxes! So ordinary folks have to pay up. But they're stuck for the money. They can't pay. Therefore Rome is also stuck for the money!

There's not enough tax money to rebuild the Roman military. That leads to second-rate recruits. It leads to lower caliber officers. It leads to low morale. The result is a cut-rate Roman army that can't defend its own borders. Rome actually resorts to bribing whole barbarian armies onto its side to fight other barbarian armies on the borders.
* You're kidding!
* I'm not. I'll show you. We'll go there. ......

We're now at the northern frontier where the Goths have been threatening. Those two guys you see there, believe it or not, are two Goth Generals talking to eachother before moving their barbarian armies into position to fight — against eachother! Listen to the confusion ... and the surprise!

"Max! What the devil are you doing here with your army?"
  "I'm here to fight the Goths."
"How can that be? You are the Goths!"
  "No I'm not. Not today! I'm the Romans today! You're the
  Goths!"
"Uh Oh! I was told I'm to be the Romans. I'm here to fight the
  Goths. And you're the only other army here. So I'm here to
  fight you!"
  "I don't think so. Hold it! How much is Rome paying you?"
"One thousand ounces of gold. How about you, Max?"
  "Five thousand."
"Really? Then you must be the Romans. You're the one getting
  paid more!"
  "Agreed. We'll be the Romans. We'll be the ones with the 2-
  horned hats!"
"Okay. And we're the Goths. We'll be the ones with the pointed
  hats!"
  "Right. Any other rules of war you want to talk about?"
"Yeh. Win or lose, you have to send the story to Rome, Max.
  You're the Romans here. Right?"

111

"Right. Then let's get on with the fighting!"[83]

You can read well documented history about how sick and confused Rome's security, finances, and morality are. Sure, the Romans have done great things in construction, engineering, and so on. They're not short on material progress. What they're short on is morals, ethics, and character. Rome never will regain the republican virtues its founders had!

In 410 AD the barbarian Goths are finally at the gates of Rome! You'll now see how the Goths bust them down and begin to sack this city in which republican virtues like courage and honor began.

* Rome looks like its in chaos! I don't detect much courage and honor around here. Am I wrong?

* Let's see. We'll listen to what the shopkeepers and people gathering around the street in front of us are talking about. Maybe they're organizing a Home Guard to fight against the Goth onslaught.

> "I hear the Goth is seven feet tall! With piercing eyes! And big
> iron teeth!"
> "Your kidding!"
> "No, he's not kidding. And the teeth are in double rows!"
> "Oh my god!"

> "We'll soon see for ourselves. The hour has finally come.
> They've busted down the gates of the city. They're ravaging
> through the streets right now."
> "God help us! What are we to do?"
> "Fight them to the death. What else!"
> "You've got that right, mate … the death part. I guarantee you
> that! They've slaughtered our legioneers. Imagine what
> they'll do to us! What can we do? Oh God!"

"Leave it with me. I've prepared for this for many months now."
   "What do <u>you</u> have, the sword and shield of Achilles or something? (looking at the others) Maybe he has some kind of magic sword. Or maybe his Christian God will save us? Hah! What is <u>He</u> going to do?"

"You'll see. Just keep your mouth shut and leave it with me. It all comes down to business!"
   "Uh Oh. Here come the barbarians now!"

"Accueil a Rome ... et mon magasin! Comment allez-vous? Que desirez-vous?" (Welcome to Rome ... and my shop! How are you? What do you wish to have?)
   "Tout!" (Everything!)
"Tres bien, Monsieur." (Very good, sir)[84]

Well, they're not organizing a Home Guard. They're rolling over!
   In the future, experts will debate endlessly over the fall of the Roman Empire. At this time, however, the world is simply stunned. People are asking how Rome could let this happen. They're looking for explanations. And they get them from one of the most powerful minds of this time. The sacking of Rome inspires St.Augustine (354-430 AD) to write his masterpiece, The <u>City of God</u>.
   Augustine sets up <u>The City of God</u> as a tale of two cities — not real cities but symbolic cities. One is Evil, one is Good. Struggle between them represents struggle within people, or even within empires. Augustine says the City of God — the Good city — will always win. But he likens Rome to the Evil city because it had become wicked. In Rome, politicians ripped off ordinary folks to make themselves rich. The well-born only became military leaders to grab power and gobble up wealth from the spoils of war. Playing around during marriage was accepted because everyone did it. Lying, cheating, and carnal lusting were

viewed with a wink and a nod. Parents had to have their children escorted home from school by a special service to protect them from homosexuals along the roads. People used any means necessary to get, and keep, power … even if it meant staging the "accidental deaths" or "suicides" of competitors. Cicero, Seneca, and many others learned that the hard way! Some people married, or even murdered, for ambition. Like Nero. He poisoned his half-brother and rival, Brittanicus. And can you believe he had his own mother put to death for bugging him to get rid of his mistress, Poppaea, because he already had a wife, Octavia! The irony is, he went on to marry Poppaea anyway … after first killing wife Octavia! Nero, like other Roman rulers, had thousands of Christians mauled in the arena for the sport of it. He also rubbed out eighteen prominent Romans who he accused of plotting against him. His own nephew, the poet Lucan, was one of them. He went on to kick to death his wife, Poppaea, in order to marry Messalina … but only after bumping off her husband, of course!

Not every ruler was as vile as Nero. But lust, greed, and even murder were common from the top to the bottom of Roman society. That's why Augustine says all aspects of life were morally and ethically already in the toilet long before the Goths burst through the gates of Rome. He says the sacking of Rome was God's way of telling the world it was an Evil city.

Then there's the other one of Augustine's two symbolic cities. This one is heavenly, honorable and full of virtue. He says it's a city you should do everything you can to get into. With help from the Church you can leave the Evil city with all its vices and get into the Good city — the City of God — with all its virtues.

Rome is only a small part of the story Augustine tells us in the City of God. As a bishop, he talks about the Creation, the rules of Moses, the teachings of Jesus, and so on. As a philosopher, he also talks about the ideas of Thales, Socrates, Plato, Aristotle, Cicero, and Plotinus. The City of God is a fascinating story of leadership. Augustine's life is, itself, also a fascinating story of leadership. I'll give you the short version of it.

THE STORY OF ST. AUGUSTINE – (354-430 AD)

from: Augustine of Hippo: A Biography

Augustine was the greatest of the four theologians who are called the Fathers of the Church. The others were Ambrose, Jerome, and Gregory. Perhaps he was the greatest Church Father because he was the only one that was truely also a philosopher.

He was born in the North African area of the Roman Empire that is now Tunisia. It was Cicero's writing's about the Greek philosophers that first caught Augustine's attention while studying, not in Rome, but in the North African coastal city of Carthage. He completed his education in Latin at Carthage.

The next few years of his life were a celebration of manhood! He endlessly chased around society after women, and became well known to the city's brothels. He was involved in wild affairs of the heart. But he gradually got into thinking about the soul, and afterward, about the evil lurking within himself. Along the way he also did a little teaching for a living!

Augustine next moved to Rome and Milan where he was hired to teach rhetoric. He began to live his religion. That gradually led to a celebic, spartan lifestyle. Willing years of this self-conditioning went by. Then one day he made a momentous decision. He joined the Christian Church — not to just worship — to study! He was already thirty-three years old by that time!

From there he saw it all the way through to be ordained as a priest. His combination of philosophy and practical life-experience propelled him up the ladder of the Church. He was sent back to his childhood origin in Carthage — as a Bishop!

Augustine had internalized wisdom and virtue only after being well into the mature years of his life. He showed it can be done — you're never too old! He and St. Paul are the most important leaders of Christianization in the West. His doctrines, and life-story, provide lessons that are just as important for modern times as they were 1500 years ago!

The virtue is: Hope. Where there's the will there's hope.

* That's interesting. But Augustine isn't in Rome. He's out in the boonies some-where. I can't see him being part of the mainstream of Christian thought.
* Augustine is not just part of the mainstream of Christian thought. He is the mainstream of Christian thought! And he has come along just in time! For every-thing in Europe is falling apart after the Roman Empire falls apart. Roman law and order has not just declined, it has melted down and disappeared. Society is in chaos. So to take the place of laws to keep order, people turn to religion to keep order. They turn to the basic morals and ethics that, after all, are what the former laws were based on in the first place. That means they turn to the Church!

The Papacy — the Pope and those who help him run the Church — are able to respond to the chaos, thanks to Augustine. His philosophy, in which neo-Platonism is absorbed into Christianity, wins the hearts and minds of people to the Church. It helps the Papacy restore and maintain order in society. Others in the Church follow Augustine's leadership. For example, Ambrose uses the barbar-ians' fear of God to have them make the Church spiritually supreme over every-one — including the Emperor. Gregory works out a ritual of worship — the

Mass. Jerome translates the Bible into plain Latin that most can understand — the Latin Vulgate. The Church puts on what is probably the greatest show of an institution's leadership of all time:

THE GREATEST SHOW ON EARTH: CHURCH LEADERSHIP

from: Edward Gibbon

The Decline and Fall of the Roman Empire by Edward Gibbon could also have had the subtitle, "The Rise of Christianity." The rise of Christianity did not cause the decline of Rome. But, the decline of Rome enabled the rise of Christianity. At first the Church did not recognize the opportunity that rose out of disaster. They identified more with what was collapsing — civilization and the Empire itself.

It quickly became evident that the Church was the sole institution that survived in most places — right down to the municipal level of government. They were the only authorities left when imperial armies went away and imperial administration just dried up. Bishops had intellectual and administrative experience. They were educated men among the new barbarian, uneducated ruling class in many places. The new semi-pagan population looked to them with awe, and thought they had near magical power. Thus, the Church took the leadership role in local communities.

The Church took the lead in making order out of chaos by creating two new institutions. The first was a system of Christian monastery communities. These communities attracted many from among the well-born who sought refuge from the changing world around them. They could live, work, and pray in security, guaranteed by the respect the barbarians had for the Church!

The second new Church institution was the Papacy — a cadre of administrators that executed the policies of the Pope and the Church. Located in Rome, the office of the Papacy — The See — drew prestige from Rome's legendary guardianship of St. Peter the Apostle's bones. It could claim to be directly descended from the first Apostle. So, this was the setting of the Church's leadership and its emergence as a great historical force.

In the 400's AD, Pope Leo got the emperor to declare papal decisions to have the force of law. Leo also asserted that the Pope spoke in the name of St. Peter. The emperor

116

gave the Pope a title that emperors once kept for themselves. The Pope would be "pontifex maximus" — supreme religious authority.

Gregory later became the first Pope to fully recognize barbarian Europe. He started the first great missionary campaign to convert all of Europe. Gregory was sowing the seeds of the future — a Christianized Europe.

Gibbon said the five causes of the rise of Christianity were: the inflexible zeal Christians inherited from Judaism; the idea of life after death; the miracles and superstitions within the Church; the pure morals and ethics of Christians; and, the leadership of the church which created The Vatican, a state within a state in the residual Roman Empire. This last cause was, politically, the most important. For while everything was falling apart around it, the Church was able to provide a steady hand of order and control.

The virtue is: Initiative. Nothing ventured, nothing gained. Take the initiative.

* What you're telling me is the Roman Empire gets bagged by barbarians who haven't the first clue about how to run a civilized nation. So the Church steps in to help restore order.
* That's right. The laws of the Church kind of become the laws of the land! Christianity will dominate life and philosophy for the next 1000 years — until the Renaissance in the 1400's AD! During those 1000 years, plain philosophy will be very diluted. Reason will be watered down with Belief ... like it was before Thales in 500 BC Greece. But it won't be lost! The ideas of Socrates, Plato, Aristotle, and others will still be there. They'll just be so well alloyed with religion that it will take innovative refining processes to recover them.
* How about Augustine? Will the Papacy try to make him water down his philosophy too?
* No. Augustine dies! He succumbs to old age in his cathedral at the very moment the barbaric Vandals cross over from Spain into North Africa and burn everything in sight! His death ends the last plain philosophy permitted by the Church. He had made his philosophy palatable to the Papacy. It passed through their filter. No one else who can do that will come along for a long, long time. You can say philosophy and Augustine are laid to rest at the same time! The long dark night of philosophy and Western culture that's called the Dark Ages is about to begin![85]

CHAPTER 9: DARK AGES AND CHRISTIANITY

During the next 400 years, very little philosophy, watered down or not, seeps through the Papacy's filter! And we have but a mere handful of brave souls, well out of the Papacy's sight, to thank for what little <u>does</u> seep through. These brave souls, called "Encyclopedists", secretly study and write philosophy in far off corners of the old dead Empire. They're hidden away in isolated monasteries in Spain, Britain, and islands in the Irish Sea where few people care to venture.

The Encyclopedists had secretly squirreled away all the Greek and Roman works they could lay their hands on. For example, Bede The Venerable (673-735 AD) in England knows enough Greek and Roman classics to inspire him to write a total of fourty biographies, commentaries, and histories of the English peoples! We have him to thank for most known information about England before 800 AD. His works prove there <u>is</u> an "Ancient Culture" based on Greek and Roman political philosophy back here in Saxon England during the Dark Ages. That will be important to Thomas Jefferson, and therefore to us, a thousand years from now in America. You'll see why when we get there.

So you can still find a bit of philosophy on the isolated fringes of Europe. But throughout the mainstream of Europe, the Papacy wheels and deals to implant religion. In the process the Papacy shapes-up society. It turns chaos to order. To do so, it bangs heads with all those who are trying to carve out pieces of the former Roman Empire for themselves. The Christian Church takes on all challengers, be they Italian princes, Greek emperors, barbarian Vandals, or warring Franks and Lombards. It becomes rich and powerful. It also becomes rigid and intolerant!

* Rigid and intolerant are a lot better than the persecution they themselves as Christians formerly had to suffer!

* Indeed. But when the shoe is on the other foot, sometimes the formerly persecuted become the new persecutors. And that's what a tiny faction of militant Christians become — persecutors. Look at the story of Hypatia across in Alexandria, for example. She was a learned philosopher, scientist, and political figure. But, because her morality was lustfully pagan, a tiny faction of militant Christians persecuted her ... to death!

* Wasn't there an outcry from the public? From women?

* From women? Back in these times? Most young women in Rome who know about Hypatia probably react like these two:

> "Hello there! Fancy meeting you at a market with all these house-
> wives. Are you still pursuing your career ambition?"
> "Yes ... the ultimate ambition. Staying alive! You've heard
> about our female role model, no doubt."
> "Who?"
> "You know. Our favorite pagan, scientist, philosopher, and
> female political figure over in Alexandria. The woman we
> said we wanted to be like someday. Hypatia!"

"You think I said that?! I never said that! Homemaking is <u>my</u> bag!"

"Well then you <u>have</u> apparently heard. It's awful how she was dragged from her chariot by some intolerant Christian zealots. They stripped her naked and cut her up alive with sharpened seashells! She didn't die, so they burned her at the stake like a witch! You of all people must have been shocked."

"Me shocked? Why would I be shocked? Don't get that around, whatever you do! I'm not interested in this Hypatia you speak of. It's a homemaker's life for me. And you'll do the same if you know what's good for you!"

"So then, it's like the Stoics said. Accept your lot in life. It's your fate. Want what you have. Is that the way it is with you? Well then. What can I say, except, if you're going to be a homemaker ... be a good one!"

"I hear someone's giving lessons in cooking and knitting. Are you Interested?"

"I should be. That someone is me! It's my new kick. Don't laugh. As you said, it's better than ending up like Hypatia did!"[86]

See what I mean, Harry? No outcry. Only fear!
* Interesting. But how does that connect with our journey toward the founding of West Point?
* You're seeing the start of a strain of zealous Christianity that will continue in

one form or another right up to England in the 1600's. That's when an army of zealous "Puritan" Christians led by Oliver Cromwell in an English Civil War will whip the King's army, abolish the monarchy, and set up a Protectorate. Cromwell's victory will in many ways lead to the American Revolution which, in turn, will bring about West Point.

* I see.

* Right now we see another zealous Christian, the warlord Charlemagne, come out of what is now France to whip the warring Lombards, take over Rome, and conquer Germany. As a convinced fan of St. Augustine, he spreads Christianity by fire and sword! He even gets the Pope himself to crown him Emperor. His coronation on Christmas day in 800 AD marks the beginning of what becomes known as the Holy Roman Empire!

Almost overnight, Charlemagne has gone from warlord to emperor. Now he wants to go from barbarian to statesman. To do that, he dreams up a grandiose scheme in three parts. Part one: restore an imperial line of new "Caesars". That's easy. He makes himself the first "Caesar" in the line! Part two: build St. Augustine's City of God here on earth. He comes close. There's a long period of peace and cooperation between Ruler and Church. Part three: start a statesman-like imperial court ... with him as a statesmanlike philosopher-king. He has big problems there. But he goes for it. He hires a philosopher from England named Alcuin. Pupil and teacher alike have their work cut out for them. Here's how these two very different guys hit it off:

"Before this I didn't even know the word 'emperor'. Now I are one. And now I learn how to read and write word from you, Alcuin."

"Very good, Mighty Charlemagne." ᵒᵒAnd that's about it. You might learn to write one word — the word, emperor. I'd consider it a success if you do just that!ᵒᵒ

120

"How long take it before I write like you?"

"It depends on how hard you work, Mighty Emperor."

ᴼᴼBecause your brainpower sure won't do it!ᴼᴼ

"I work just as hard at learning as do at conquering."

"If you do that, then you will learn very fast, Mighty One."

ᴼᴼLearn how thick you are!ᴼᴼ

"And like good warrior, I work to the death to become philosopher-ruler."

ᴼᴼUh Ohh! Looks like I'm stuck here for life!ᴼᴼ [87]

Just when Charlemagne is starting to get the hang of reading and writing in 814 AD ... he dies! Alcuin's job as philosopher to the Emperor dies with him. But it was never really the job for a philosopher. It was more the job for an elementary school teacher — grades K thru 2! And that gives you an idea of what's ahead. The new breed of neo-Caesars after Charlemagne will bring no scholarly baggage with them. The only scholarly souls in the former Empire will still be buried away all around within the monastery system. The Church's leadership of society will continue to go unchallenged!

Charlemagne actually started something of a renaissance for a while. But when he died you could have written the history of the next 200 years right then and there. The former chaos returns! Fighting between Church and "neo-Caesar" emperors starts up again. That brings back plague, poverty, and ignorance to go along with the feudal system's enslavement. The Holy Roman Empire becomes nothing more than a stylish name. It's neither Holy, nor Roman, nor an Empire. The Papacy throws the wildest parties in town. They blemish the record of a sacred and dedicated institution. So much for the "Holy" part of "Holy Roman Empire"! The Roman Empire used to be peoples of the world controlled by Romans. Now it's peoples of the world controlled by assorted other peoples of the world. So much for the "Roman" part of "Holy Roman Empire"! Kings, princes, and rulers are running around all over the place doing their own thing, not Rome's thing. So much for the "Empire" part of "Holy Roman Empire"!

* So you're telling me the long dark night of culture and philosophy called the Dark Ages continues on?

* That's right ... except for a crack of light that shines through from the pure philosophy of John the Scot — John Scotus Eriugena (800-877 AD). Other than that, the culture of Europe is still all religion. When John the Scot says that pure philosophy is just as important as religion, the Church labels him a heretic. And as you know, heretics would usually get persecuted by some zealous faction of Christians. But somehow — perhaps by luck of the Irish — John the Scot escapes that fate!

* Irish?

* That's right, Harry. Irish! Only during the Dark Ages could they be so nutty to call an Irishman — John the <u>Scot</u>! But even <u>his</u> luck runs out. After he dies they condemn him posthumously! His books end up on the scrap heap! And, want to hear something else uniquely nutty? Only in a "Dark Age" would they call an increase — a cut!

* I don't get you.

* The Dark Ages are a period of intellectual stagnation in culture and philosophy. But in the late 1100's, interest in philosophy returns. A school of thought called "Scholasticism" emerges. It represents new found interest in what St. Paul and St.Augustine had done centuries before — alloy Jesus's teachings with Greek philosophy. Scholasticism extends Church leadership to culture and philosophy. So it's an increase in the Church's influence beyond religion and social control ... not a cut. Nevertheless, the Church doesn't like it.

* Why?

* Because the Church has always kept Christianity's Greek philosophy connection a dark secret. Scholasticism lets that secret out of the bag. And if that isn't bad enough, the ones who are responsible for Scholasticism being able to let the secret out of the bag are the so-called "infidel" Arabs!

* The Arabs? Why the Arabs?

* You have to remember that even the little bit of philosophy in far off corners of the old Empire is written mostly in Greek. But Latin is the language of what's still called the Holy Roman Empire. On the other hand, the Arabs have been big fans of Aristotle and the Greeks for centuries now. They're part of Alexander the Great's former empire. Greek culture is inbred in them because of it. The Syrians had first translated Greek philosophy into Arabic. Then, during the Roman Empire, they also translated it into Latin. It kept spreading throughout the Arabic world long after the Greeks and Romans were gone. The Arabs turned Aristotle into the authority on almost everything in life. Many folks considered him a prophet! So now centuries later, the Arabs are able to use the works of Plato and Aristotle, already translated into Latin, in trade and cultural exchanges with Europe.

For the next 200 years religious scholars in Europe will gradually change the mix of Plato, Aristotle, and Jesus that makes up Christianity. Religious doctrine will be gradually reformed. The Church will also reform. The Papacy will stamp out "simony" and "concubinage". Simony is selling jobs and positions of power. That's now banned! From now on if the brother-in-law wants a job, he'll have to get it on his own! Concubinage is keeping mistresses. That's also banned! You'll see no more wild parties at the Pope's Lateran Palace! The priest at the door to the Lateran Palace would inevitably find himself in the following embarassing situation as a crowd lines up for confession:

> "Confessions are changed today my children. They can now be
> heard here in the Lateran Palace. Does everyone know the way?"

Everyone shakes their head and says no ... except, to the embarassment of the priest, several tart-looking, pretty, young ladies who piously reply in unison without hesitation:

> "Y - e - s   F - a - t - h - e - r."[88]

Having cleaned their own house, Church reformers now think it's their calling to clean other peoples' houses. They set out to reform and convert the "infidel" Arabs to Christianity. That panics the Turks who, at this time in history, rule the roost in Syria and Palestine. To keep out the reformers the Turks close Jerusalem. That panics the Christians. They say that Jerusalem — the Christians' Holy City — must be kept open. European Christians send armies to the Middle East to open it back up. It's the beginning of what will be called "The Crusades"!

It's ironic. European warriors are, through fire and sword, helping the Church spread Christianity in the Arab countries. At the same time, Arab philosophers are, through Scholasticism, helping the Church spread Christianity in European countries. So when the Crusaders invade, here's roughly what the man on the street in Jerusalem is saying:

"Say, what's going on here? Who are you, anyway?"
    "I'm with the Crusaders' Army".
"Crusaders' Army? What's that?"
    "We're here to bring Christianity to you."
"Why?"
    "Because we're bringing civilization to you backward
    infidels."
"Backward infidels, are we! Who do you think is helping your
Church scholars? Who do you think is translating Aristotle into
Latin for them ... so they can write their new books on
Christianity? It's none other than us — us infidel Arabs, as you
call us! You ... Crusadermen, or Crusaders, or whatever you call
yourselves ... are like students trying to teach the teacher!
Before you swing those big swords of yours you should get your
facts straight!"
    "The only fact I know is: Christians are right! Pagans are
    wrong!"[89]

123

The Crusaders never do get their facts straight. They massacre Jerusalem! At the very time in history when so called infidels' translations of Plato and Aristotle alter Christian theology in Europe, Christian crusaders "alter and purify Jerusalem by washing it in the blood of infidels". It's one of the darkest hours in history!

* When you think of the Crusades you think of England's King Richard the Lionheart. He's famous for being a good human being. Yet, he's a Crusader. How do you square that with the massacre of Jerusalem?

* The massacre of Jerusalem takes place at the end of the <u>first</u> Crusade. But did you know there will be <u>seven</u> Crusades over 200 years? King Richard doesn't get into the fray until the <u>third</u> Crusade! There are no such massacres under him. For King Richard is a moral and ethical leader — a <u>GOOD</u>-leader. And that's one of the lessons we learn from the Crusades. If we have GOOD-leaders in charge, we won't have such things as the massacre of Jerusalem. But we're not here to pass judgement on mankind, Harry. We all know mankind is capable of horrible imperfections. We're here so you can learn lessons from looking at bad examples, as well as, good examples of leadership. Our quest is to brighten the eyes of the future, not blacken the eye of the past!

* I understand.

* The brightest of eyes in the 1100's AD are at Italy's University of Bologna — the world's oldest University, and at the University of Paris. European scholars are finally into reading Plato, Aristotle, and other classical philosophers. The sons of English Barons and laymen are drawn to the University of Paris. Many Englishmen even stay on to teach there. Then one day a political quarrel erupts between the French and English rulers. That ruins everything. All Englishmen get expelled from the University!

English intellectuals are now scholars without a University. But they hear that, back home, the towns of Oxford and Cambridge are trying to become centers of learning. So they turn crisis into the mother of innovation. Armed with their books and knowledge, they bring the latest culture and philosophy to Oxford and Cambridge. They build their own universities. And when they do, others come! Englishmen can now get into the mainstream of higher education ... right here in England!

It's now 1215 AD. England is having internal problems. The good King Richard the Lionheart is off on the Crusades. His sly mouse of a brother, acting-King John, is bulging through his limits of authority. All in England are fed up with him. That includes England's Barons. They don't trust him. They fear what move he may make next. So they make the next move! They meet in secret at the Abbey in Bury St.Edmunds, the old Roman town in East Anglia. All the Barons swear an oath before God to join in fighting King John. And here's where education at Oxford and Cambridge come in. Some of the Barons, their sons, and their scholarly collegues attended Oxford and Cambridge. They know about ancient philosophy, Saxon Law, and England's so called "Ancient Constitution". So they do something unheard of. They draw up a charter of laws, rights, and liberties that they call the "Magna Carta", meaning Great Charter! Not just the title but the entire thing is written in Latin.

* I know about the Magna Carta.

* Good! For the Magna Carta is one of the greatest documents of all time! And as you might expect, it doesn't go over in a big way with King John. Historical events surrounding the Magna Carta are well established. But, imagine what an eye-witness's account would sound like:

> "What's this you have, knave?"
>   "M-m-message for you, King John".
> "From my self-rightious, goody-two-shoes brother, no doubt."
>   "No, Your Highness. It's from the Barons. They told me to
>   wait for your signature and return the original."
> "Hmmm. Rather long in the tooth, isn't it. How can I sign this? I
> can't even read it!"
>   "It's in Latin, Sire."
> "Ah! Trying to slip one by me are they? Leave it to those clever
> Barons and their intellectual cronies! Take it back! I shan't sign
> this!"

A few months later, during the heat of battle with the Barons:

> "Where the devil have we retreated to now?"
>   "We're at Runnymede — on the Thames River right in
>   London, King John. I knew we had big problems when the
>   Barons withdrew their allegiance. The chain of loyalty that
>   ties together our feudal system has completely come undone!
>   The Barons have gotten seemingly everyone to march on
>   London against us! And they've captured the City! You're
>   now actually their prisoner, Sire! That is, unless you sign
>   their Magna Carta."
> "Alright! I'll do it, I'll do it! I'll sign the bloody thing! Just fetch
> me that useless Latin teacher I threw out a while back. I'd like to
> know what the devil it is I'm signing at least! And get me a

bloody lawyer!" °°What a turn of events! This has bloody well thwarted me for good! There go all my schemes for power!°° 90

King John signs the Magna Carta on June 15, 1215! It's the grandfather of all documents having to do with the rights of life, liberty, and property, including the Declaration of Independence and Constitution of the United States of America. So you can see, America's greatest documents are soaked in moral and political philosophy! They have their roots in the philosophy of the ancients — from Greece, to Rome, to Saxon Law, to the "Ancient Constitution", to the Magna Carta!

Classical education's influence on the Magna Carta doesn't immediately sink in to King and Crown. Finally in 1264 AD, Royal servant and English Bishop, Walter de Merton, undoubtedly looking back to the Magna Carta, sees the light. He establishes a special program at Oxford on behalf of the Crown. It's purpose is to develope leaders to serve the Crown. But not just any old educated people to be in charge. These leaders are conditioned to be loyal and obedient to the Crown in handling Royal affairs. Then, Kings College is established at Cambridge. This is an entire college dedicated to the same purpose!

* It's not a new idea. It reminds me of when Alexander the Great set up the Royal Pages academy, except Oxford and Cambridge are not military.

* Exactly. Alexander the Great saw the advantages in an academy to teach his military officer-leaders virtues such as loyalty and obedience. That's why he established his Royal Pages academy program. Unfortunately Caesar and the Roman Empire had no such academies. After that, the Church became the great teacher. It became the custodian of European law and culture. And it became the keeper of moral and ethical standards. So the Church will also latch on to Bishop de Merton's idea. It will setup hundreds of schools and colleges in the coming centuries. Those schools will commit students to both knowledge and religion based morals. So after Oxford and Cambridge lead the way in education to produce loyal and obedient leaders, so do other Schools around Europe — especially the Church's schools!

Meanwhile, Scholasticism in Europe is cut and patched and revised in bits and pieces. But no one can wrap it up into one neat package. No one can turn it into a tidy philosophical system — like the systems of Plato, Aristotle, and Augustine! Then along comes Thomas Aquinas:

ST. THOMAS AQUINAS (1227 - 1274 AD)

Modern psychologists say a life is colored by emotional shocks of childhood. The life of Thomas Aquinas is a good demonstration of that. For, Thomas the child, witnessed startling and emotional incidents. And he became one of the most unusual and remarkable good-leaders that ever trod this earth! He was like a precious diamond! The ingredients given him at birth were made into a diamond-in-the-rough by the heat and pressure from emotional events of childhood. Then the diamond-in-the-rough was wisely shaped to give it the many facets of morals and character. It was then polished to the gem-quality of a good-leader — in his case a good-leader in teaching theology and philosophy.

He was born to the Castle Roccasecca in Italy, family stronghold of the Counts of Aquino. As a three year old boy, lightning struck the castle and killed his little sister, right by his side! He was miraculously unharmed, physically! But it was a shock, emotionally! A little boy was bound to absorb the sense of a Great Power beyond human control! It's no wonder he had an unquestioning faith in God his entire life! The family conversation for months thereafter surely fixed in his mind that he was spared by God for some special destiny. And his mother, Theodora, thought she knew what that destiny was. Her son would be Abbot of their ancestral monastery across the valley from them — Monte Cassino!

At five years, Thomas' parents took him across to Monte Cassino to be taught and trained by the monks. So there he was, among dull, cloistered, reverent men who invoked God's blessing before every aspect of daily life. They say Thomas the boy kept pestering monks with the same question: What is God? He never got an answer that satisfied his inquiring mind. Many years later Thomas the man would come nearer to an answer than any man has ever come!

For seven years the same discipline as the Benedictine order of monks was required of Thomas. When he was twelve years old, Monte Cassino was captured by King Frederick's soldiers in his war against Pope Gregory. Thomas witnessed the terrible fighting during which some of the monks were killed. Again he escaped without physical injury! But the death of his pious friends and teachers had to be another emotional shock for a twelve year old!

Not many years went by before his parents sent him to the University of Naples. At sixteen years old he shocked his parents by joining the Dominican order. Dominicans were preaching-type friars who vowed poverty and begged for their livelihood. He had to renounce all his worldly prospects and don the white woolen garment of poverty. All of his mother Theodora's hopes for her son to be Count of Aquino and the Abbot of Monte Cassino were taken away by what she considered a rash decision. She pulled him out of Naples and put him under lock and key until he could be convinced by his father, brothers, and sisters ... and even a young brothel girl ... that he made a mistake! This went on for more than a year, but he never changed his mind. Theodora appealed right up to Pope Innocent who offered young Thomas a deal. He could remain a Dominican friar and also be Abbot of Monte Cassino. He flatly refused the offer!

Thomas travelled to Cologne and Paris to study under renowned theologion and philosopher, Albertus Magnus. This would shape the remainder of his life! The diamond was being polished! First, at twenty-five he was ordained as a priest. Then he worked on a doctorate degree. After he received his Doctor of Divinity degree he went to work as a Professor of Philosophy at Paris University. His lecture hall soon was packed with students demanding him as lecturer! The Pope got wind of this and called Thomas to be his lecturer in the Papal University, a travelling school that went wherever the Pope went. He became a treasured scholar, and most prolific writer of theological philosophy. But toward the end, he had visions and revelations of "heaven". He said words are "mere straws in the mind". He completely stopped writing!

When he died at forty-seven, quarrels erupted over possession of his body. The body was divided! Most of it is now in Rome, parts are in Salerno and Naples, and his right arm is in Paris! Almost fifty years after his death he was cannonized as St. Thomas Aquinas, and he was pronounced the fifth Doctor of the Church, with Jerome, Ambrose, Gregory, and Augustine![91]

The virtue is: Sacrifice. Sometimes immediate pleasure must be sacrificed for long term good.

* How do you come to know so much about St. Thomas Aquinas, Thomas? It's a fascinating story.

* And if you read a complete biography of St. Thomas's life, you'll see that it's even more fascinating. So that's something else for you to read after our journey, Harry. However, we'll look at his philosophy right now. For he's the one who finally gathers all the bits and pieces of Scholasticism together. He wraps them up into one neat system that joins together Christian theology and Greek philosophy. It becomes encyclopedic — a massive fourty volumes of his written philosophy. And it's big on what we're interested in — morals, ethics, and character!

Thomas Aquinas is an original thinker, make no mistake. But almost everything he writes is grounded in Aristotle. And he chooses to prove things like Aristotle did. He only tries to prove something is true after (post) seeing and experiencing it [called "a posteriori"]. That puts him on thin ice with Church doctrine that says faith and belief in something eliminates the need to actually see and experience that something. Church theologians question why he chooses not to rely on prior faith. He's accused of being like the Arab philosopher Averroes. And Church theologians do not like Averroes! Anything that hints of him and his ideas is taboo with them!

* Why is that?

* Because Averroes blows off religion! He says all religion is merely nice stories that make philosophy easier to understand. Therefore he doesn't use God in his ideas. He uses Aristotle ... and considers him a prophet.

So, Church theologians are shocked when Aquinas uses Aristotle in his theology. But Aquinas pulls off a brilliant move. He shows them that Aristotle's moral philosophy actually supports the Church's moral beliefs. He proves they are really one and the same thing. And opposite to Averroes, Aquinas says that philosophy is merely a nice tool to back up divine stories of God and religion. He says Reason and Belief arrive at the same conclusions, even though they arrive there in different ways. Aristotle and Christendom are actually in harmony. Reason and Belief are united! For all life and knowledge springs from just one eternal thing — God! And there's no need to only believe it. He'll prove it!

Once again using seeing and experience as his starting point [a posteriori], he not only proves the existence of God ... he finishes with five such proofs! It's his renowned <u>Five Ways to God</u>! It becomes the first part of his <u>Summa Theologica</u> (Summary of Theology).

The second part of <u>Summa Theologica</u> deals with morals, ethics, and character. It again begins with firsthand seeing and experience [a posteriori]. It arrives at conclusions about morals, ethics, and character very close to those of Aristotle!

* Really!

* For one thing he says anything you do ... do with a goal in mind — like Aristotle's "telos"! Remember? First choose the goal, the desired good. Then learn and perform virtues that lead to reaching that goal. Take the military, for example. The goal is to win battles with the minimum number of dead and wounded. How do you do that? In addition to other things, you must have good-leaders! The military must train their officers in virtues that make good-leaders!

Aquinas goes on to analyze Virtue — morals, ethics, and character. He proves they come from one eternal thing. And Aquinas has just finished proving in the first part of <u>Summa Theologica</u> that the one eternal thing is what we call God. Thus Aquinas proves that Virtue — morals, ethics, and character — comes from God and theology!

* I can see why he's called the diamond of his era in religion, education, and philosophy.

* But even a diamond isn't perfect, Harry. It has small flaws. Thomas Aquinas' flaws are more like little eccentricities. We'll hear about his flaws by listening to the gossip of his students:

> "Well here it is, the second time Father Aquinas is late for his lecture. I wonder what's happening to him?"
>
> "I don't think he's sick. He certainly doesn't look it. Not with that ... let's say ... ample girth he carries around in front of him. I hear he even has a half-moon shaped niche cut out of his dining table that his stomach fits into!"
>
> "Really? That's what I call bellying-up to the table! And he should be <u>thin</u>. He works himself to death! Did you know he keeps four scribes going at the same time, writing down his thoughts on four different subjects at once?"
>
> "Incredible. No wonder he's getting a bit eccentric. Like his last lecture about angels. Do we need to concern ourselves with how many angels can stand on the point of a needle?"
>
> "You think that's eccentric? I hear he has begun to lock himself inside a cell and beat himself with an iron chain as penance! Now <u>that's</u> drastic penance!"
>
> "Yeh. He's probably beating himself for giving that wacky lecture about angels on the point of a needle!"
>
> "And have you noticed how old he looks lately? He's aged twenty years in the past several months. He looks a lot older than forty-six. You would think he's seen a ghost!"
>
> "From what I hear he says he <u>has</u> seen a ghost! He's been terribly shaken by visions and revelations of Heaven lately."
>
> "Revelations? Really? Maybe this is <u>big</u>! Maybe he's being visited from Heaven — like Moses and the burning bush or something! Maybe we're witnessing theological history being made here! Perhaps it's the Second Coming?"
>
> "Whatever it is, they tell me he has stopped writing the third part of his masterpiece, <u>Summa Theologica</u>. And the third part is about Jesus Christ. He's leaving it unfinished — open-ended!"
>
> "Hmm. That <u>is</u> curious."[92]

We'll never know what Aquinas sees in his visions, Harry. In 1274 AD ... he dies! His visions die with him. Now he belongs to the ages.

Aquinas' work is the culmination of an entire age in the history of philosophy. It summarizes all the theological and philosophical thinking up to his time. He "married" Reason to Belief! The "wedding" brought everyone together: Aristotle and classic philosophers, Augustine and Church Fathers, Averroes and Islamic scholars, Maimonides and Spanish-Jew sages, Scholasticism and the Schoolmen. They were all there. They all had their role to play in joining Reason and Belief. And the marriage was strictly a Church wedding. The union of Reason and Belief got the Church's blessing. That puts Aquinas at the pinnacle of the last thousand years of theology and philosophy. His writings will be the backbone of religious education for seven centuries to come!

* In my century, people in education have undone Aquinas' work. They've split up Reason and Belief. They've pitted biology against religion. Evolutionists and creationists are at eachothers throats!

* So you should be forever hopeful that another Thomas Aquinas will come along to perform another philosophical "marriage" — this time between biology and religion. But you and I are not concerned with that. We're concerned with the "marriage" of people to Virtue that creates good-leaders. It doesn't matter whether its through using scientific philosophy or religious philosophy!

Throughout the Dark Ages, kings and princes have been pitted against the Church for power. Kings and princes have used the feudal system's slavehold over the "masses" to compete for power with the Church's religious hold over the "masses". And Kings and princes have used the feudal system's honor, loyalty, and self-interest to compete with the Church for power over "aristocrats"! But, by the 1400's AD, the feudal system is breaking up. So Kings and princes grab power through war or wealth or politics ... or however they can get it! To them it doesn't matter how, as long as they can grab power and hold on to it. It's therefore not surprising that someone comes along who exposes the raw and seedy facts about power. He's Nicolo Bernardo Machiavelli (1469 - 1527)!

CHAPTER 10: RENAISSANCE

By the mid-1400's AD, the long dark night of civilization that we call the Dark Ages has ended. People are beginning to do things like start businesses, come up with scientific inventions, sail on voyages to discover new lands, revive classical art and literature, and think progressively about philosophy. It's like awakening after a long night's sleep. This renaissance — this great awakening — that began in northern Italy is spreading throughout Europe. We'll pick up what becomes known as "The Renaissance" with Niccolo Machiavelli (1469-1527 AD).

It's 1500 AD. Superstitious quacks who predicted doom and gloom and the end of the world at the turn of the century are wrong, as usual. In fact, the Renaissance is in full bloom. So is Niccolo Machiavelli. He has landed his biggest job yet on his meteoric rise in government. It's a political appointment to work for the "Council of Ten" — the ten men who kicked out the long ruling Medici family in Florence and set up the first Florentine Republic. He's their Secretary, their Diplomatic Missionary, and their Defense Minister.

Machiavelli has been working hard at his profession during the day and playing hard in Florentine society during the night. Along the way, he has witnessed corruption, political intrigue, and complicated shifts of power. But thus far in his life he has not written a scratch about it. He has written absolutely nothing on political philosophy. He will not begin to write until he's past forty years old.
* That's interesting. What makes him begin at that age?
* I'll show you. We'll jump ahead to the darkest day in his life ... the day his world collapses ... the day his whole life completely changes. It's totally unexpected, as we'll hear from the folks who work for Machiavelli at the government palace:

> "There's a lot of excitement around here today. After fourteen
> years the Medicis are back!"
>> "Did you see what happened? Two of the Medici toughs
>> grabbed Machiavelli right away. They said to him, 'the
>> Council of Ten is out ... the Medici's are in!' He said, 'oh?'
>> They said, 'now the Medicis will also need someone with
>> your qualifications.' He said, 'ah hah ... sounds inviting!'
>> They said, 'but you ain't it!' He said, 'uh oh-ohh!' And he
>> was correct in saying uh oh! They carted him off to jail!"
> "Well, take down all the pictures. Put up the old Medici family
> portraits again. Hang up their family crest. And lay out the wel-
> come mats. It's time to put on another welcome celebration. The
> Medicis are back!"[93]

Machiavelli gets tossed into prison! The authorities torture him for information. It looks like they're going to leave him there to rot for the rest of his life. Then one day they make him a surprising offer. They'll release him, but only on the condition that he go into forced exile in the country. It's an offer he can't refuse. He leaves Florence. That's when he first puts pen to paper and begins to write. And, as you'll soon see, he does it vengefully and cynically!

* I can see why he'd be cynical. Who wouldn't be?

* In The Prince, Machiavelli intentionally looks at the dark side of political life. But you have to be careful when reading it. It's easy to misunderstand him when he talks about political power. He doesn't tell you how he thinks it ought to be, but how it actually is. He tells you what he has seen firsthand in the trenches of power politics. He tells you, complete with corruption and seediness, how people have gotten power in the past. And he tells you the best way to get it in the future … if … you're prepared to stop at nothing, and … if … you're prepared to abandon all morals and ethics. He gives you a practical guideline … if … power at any cost is what you want.

* "If" can be a big word.

* Indeed it can. It brings to mind the story of Philip of Macedon's bid to capture Sparta in 300's BC Greece:

PHILIP AT THE GATES OF LACONIA

from: Greek history[94]

King Philip of Macedon had brought all the city-states of Greece under his control, except Sparta. The Spartans lived in southern Greece in an area called Laconia. So they were sometimes called Lacons. They were people of a few carefully chosen words. That tendency came ever

133

more to be known as being "laconic".

When Philip was at the gates of Laconia he sent the following message to the Spartans, demanding their surrender:

> "You must submit! Otherwise, I will invade your
> City-State! If I succeed, I will burn and pillage
> everything! If I burn and pillage everything,
> Laconia will be levelled to the ground!"

A few days went by. Then Philip received the reply. He was startled! The Spartan's answer to his message was the following one word reply:

> "IF"!

> The virtue is: Self-discipline. It takes self-discipline to
> withstand pressure.

Machiavelli goes on in The Prince to expose corrupt politicians for what they are. He examines the phoney claims they use to grab power, such as, divine right, hereditary necessity, the Church's blessing, and so on. The facts he leaks out — not his own opinions — show all these claims on power are self-serving rubbish. The real reasons politicians grab power is to profit from it. And he exposes how they hold on to power through the seediest of means — through lies, deception, and corruption. They cultivate a double standard by living immorally, but talking morally. They secretly act unethically, but loudly hold opponents to high ethical standards. They say things to be loved in public, but do things to be feared in private. And they are convincing fakes and frauds and phonies, even if they ruin people's lives being that way. It may all sound cynical, but it's more realistic than anyone wants to admit. It's an exhaustive investigative report on what really goes on in the world of politics. Because of it, we can probably consider Machiavelli the world's first investigative reporter![95]

Then comes his Discourses. It's like a sequel to the last chapter of The Prince. In that last chapter Machiavelli had changed from cynicism to passionate concern for better morals and ethics. The Discourses is a commentary on the monumental History of Rome that Livy wrote over the fourty year period from 25 BC to 15 AD. Remember?

In his Discourses, Machiavelli is on a mission — like the one Livy was on. For as cynical as Machiavelli is in The Prince, he is moral and ethical in his Discourses. And, like Livy, his mission is to teach lessons and expose evil. Corruption caused by political power is his main target. The Roman Empire had crumbled because of it. On the other hand, stoic virtues had transformed early Rome into a republic. Machiavelli envisioned the same for the city-state of Florence. A great Roman Empire had grown out of a small, virtuous city-state called Rome. Why not a great Florentine Empire out of a virtuous Florence?[96]

Machiavelli then writes The Art of War. It describes how to raise a mighty army for a Florentine Empire. He writes Mandrake, a well-meaning satire about things that are wrong in society. He pinches another idea from Livy when he writes The History of Florence. It's another vehicle to teach morals, ethics, and character. But in all his writings, he avoids bashing the Medici family.

* I don't blame him! They might lock him in jail again and throw away the key this time!

* Let's listen to what the government palace bureaucrats and politicians in Florence are saying about it:

"You're new around here, aren't you?"
> "Yes, I just started work. Castracani is the name. I've worked
> under four different rulers in the same principality in the last
> few months! I had to get into something secure!"

"Unbelievable. Principalities change hands every five minutes
these days! But you may not be so secure around here either!"
> "No? Why?"

"Because of Machiavelli. Have you read his work, The Prince?
He's obviously currying favor with the Medici family to get his
old job back."
> "And if they reinstate him, we'll all get the sack? Is that what
> you're telling me?"

"Yes. Because in the process of currying favor with the Medicis,
he is bashing us! He makes all our perks, and plots, and strate-
gies sound sinister! He's sure to turn public opinion and the
Medici family against us. And if he does, the Medici's will make
believe that they're surprised and outraged. Then we'll all end up
in the slammer! Ask our friend the Priest over here."
> "Is that right what he says, Father?"

"I'm only a Priest. I don't know about those things. I don't like
one thing about Machiavelli, however. He has no intention of
bringing God into his thinking. He's not like the Scholastic
philosophers!"
> "And what do you say my good friend deep in thought over
> there?"

"I say Machiavelli's book, Art of War is also dangerous. He wants
conscription? That means they draft our sons into the army.
Maybe the Medicis like it because it shows how they can raise a
powerful army. But that also means they can become dictators,
like in Roman times. He trashes the volunteer army, and a lot of
other things."
> "I agree. He wrote a biography about my namesake,
> Castruccio Castracani. It trashed my family name! It's my
> solemn duty to get even with him for that!"

"His Discourses and History of Florence say we politicians all must be replaced with more virtuous people. And who knows, maybe those writings even inspired the recent sack of Rome by the Hapsburgs! Maybe Florence is next!"

"Then we must do something about Machiavelli. He not only trashed my good family name, he's trashing us!"

"Right! This can't go on! We have to stand together! We have to put our heads together and come up with a plan to ... let's say ... 'silence' or 'discredit' him!"

(All) "Agreed!"[97]

* It sounds like they hate Machiavelli!
* They do! His enemies want to get rid of him! They believe he's currying favor with the Medicis to get his old job so he can get rid of them and their corruption. Perhaps that's true. Who knows? The one thing we do know, however, his renewed esteem with the Medici family will give him safe cover to continue his explosive revelations. It will keep his enemies from the door so he can continue to trash them as corrupt politicians ... unless they can get him and stop him. And that's just what they do. The "get Machiavelli" movement goes to work. They spread fear and hatred of him. Their dirty tricks finally work. They trump up false charges against him. He's in big trouble again!

Machiavelli is headed for the slammer again! But this time he's older. This time the pressure on him is more than he can handle. So fate steps in to "save" him. Before they can lock him up and throw away the key ... he "conveniently" dies!

Machiavelli was a pioneer. He was like an investigative journalist — exposing "spin", corruption, and immorality. He opened up political philosophy to discussion. He exposed how politics is at odds with ethics. He reinstated a standard of virtues by bringing Livy's, History of Rome, into the 1500's. He talked about leadership. He showed how leaders of morals, ethics, and character can get followers to voluntarily follow. He also showed the same can be done, unfortunately, by bad leaders who are often no more than wolves dressed in sheep's clothing! That's why his story is valuable to you and me, Harry.

Machiavelli left us raw descriptions of politics. He did it in plain language. He "wrote the book" on political philosophy. Thus, he wrote himself into history. No one else ever did it in such bold terms! And do you want to hear something else incredible? Way back here in the 1500's AD he said a republic with a democratic constitution is the best solution to political corruption. Though not a disciple of Machiavelli, someday even Thomas Jefferson will agree with him ... 250 years from now!

What Machiavelli said and the way he said it was <u>reality</u>. He was part of the cultural awakening we call the Renaissance! It was at the core of what will become a cultural revolution in all walks of life. And it all started in the commercial city-states of Northern Italy in the 1400's AD before spreading northward into France and the rest of Europe.[98]

In France, Michel Montaigne (1533-1592) could be called a disciple of Machiavelli because of his skepticism. However, he's not just skeptical about politics. He's skeptical about <u>everything</u> — especially education. He studies everything ever written about the philosophy of education. That's why he's so interesting to us ... and why someday he'll be so interesting to, again, Thomas Jefferson. He concludes that a "whole person" philosophy of education is best. His whole person philosophy combines moral, physical, and intellectual education. West Point will borrow Montaigne's whole person philosophy. But unlike Montaigne, they'll put it to practical everyday use. For, although Montaigne is a brilliant intellectual, he unfortunately never had the ability to put much of anything to practical use.

Unlike Montaigne, Francis Bacon (1561-1626) across in England tries to put <u>everything</u> to practical use. In his <u>Advancement of Learning</u> he explains <u>how</u> to learn. He says learning comes, not only from seeing and experiencing something (Aristotle's a posteriori), but <u>also</u> from philosophically assuming something (Plato's a priori). During Bacon's time, <u>scientific</u> philosophy is dawning. And Bacon is the one who ushers in the dawn. For he is no less than the pioneer of what's called practical scientific philosophy ... later known to us as "science"!

As Machiavelli's pioneering expose' on politics had shocked everyone, Bacon's pioneering work leads other "scientists" to expose's on science that shock everyone. For example, scientists dispel the old legend that metals can be turned into gold. In doing so, they transform alchemy into real scientific chemistry. Next, medical philosophers finally silence claims that there's a magic pill to cure all illnesses. They do so by hatching the science of human anatomy. It will lead to England's William Harvey squelching belief that bleeding is like poking holes into little bags of blood inside the body. Harvey will work out the body's circulation of blood. In Poland, Copernicus also works on the circulation of bodies. But his bodies are the heavenly bodies in the sky. He bursts a lot of star-gazers' and Church cosmologists' bubbles by showing the Earth is <u>not</u> the center of the Universe. In the process he turns astrology into a science. It's called — astronomy!

Back down here on Earth again, change is even more exciting! Geographers fire-up the curiosity of seafaring nations. What's across the oceans? Probably land and riches say philosophers. New land and new riches mean new power for Europe's Kings and Queens. So the race is on. Great voyages will leave from Europe in the 1500's and 1600's, after Columbus broke the ice in 1492!

Meanwhile science marches on. Universities will be awash with discussions between students like these at Paris University:

"Do you understand Galileo's new 'Theory of Motion'? It's got us stumped! What's it all about anyway? Come on. Tell us. Do you know?"
   "You two are pains in the neck! I'm studying! But I'll tell you, if it will get you both out of my hair! It means this: I push your big 150 kg body off the edge of the leaning Tower of Pisa. At the same time I push the little 120 kg body of your buddy here off the edge. "Thump"! There's only one thump when both of you hit the ground. You both hit at the same time — theoretically! It's like you're twins! Get it?"
"Really? And what about Kepler. He disproved Aristotle and Ptolemy on astronomy?
   "Yes. They said paths of planets were circles. Kepler proved that planet's paths are elipses — eggshaped. The skeptics now call him a scientific 'egg-head'! Get it?"
"Dare we ask you about William Gilbert?"
   "He showed why Columbus didn't fall off the edge of the earth. The earth is like a big round magnet. It holds everything on. And now you two clear off, will you! I'm trying to write a paper about the social affects of Gutenberg's printing press!"[99]

In 1500's and 1600's Europe, fascination with science captures everyone's imagination. Great technological advances are made in mining, pumping, hydraulics, gunnery, metallurgy, and a lot of other good things. And it will continue. A century from now, Boyle will work out the physics of gases. And Leeuwenhoek will put his powerful little microscope to good use. He'll confirm his suspicion that "tiny bugs" cause diseases. He'll call those tiny bugs "bacteria"! But the invention that changes Europe more than any other was already made back in the 1400's. It's what that student said he was writing a paper on — Gutenberg's printing press!

Before the printing press in the 1400's, they had to write everything by hand. Books came from scribes, encyclopediasts, and monks in the monasteries. So you wouldn't see many topics. And you wouldn't see many copies of each topic. The ones available went to a few privileged people. Can you believe that even priests didn't have copies of the Bible in many cases? That's why we've been seeing public notices — bulletin boards — in the market squares of towns throughout our journey ... ever since the days of ancient Greece. By the 1500's AD, however, Europe has millions of books! They're printing books on poetry, history, science, religion, and philosophy almost daily. But its the ones on religion and philosophy that will have a monumental influence on ordinary folks' lives. And guess which book is the bestseller?

* The Bible?
* Right! The Gutenberg Bible is the first book that Johann Gutenberg, reputed inventor of the printing press, ever printed. And it turns out to be deadly to the Church's "Inquisition".
* What's the Inquisition, again?
* It's a Council of Church scholars. They examine people's words and deeds. If the words or deeds are immoral or out of sync with Church doctrine, the offenders are blackballed, or ex-communicated ... or even thrown into jail if the offense is serious enough![100]
* I see. But how do they know what is serious enough?
* That, Harry, is the big problem!

CHAPTER 11: REFORMATION AND COUNTER-REFORMATION

What offenses are serious enough to be punished by the Inquisition? It's a big problem for the Church in the 1500's AD. And believe it or not, <u>The Gutenberg Bible</u> turns out to be part of the problem! More people can now read the Bible. That's good news for the Church. But people can now challenge how priests interpret it. That's bad news for the Church. It's disastrous for the Inquisition!

The Inquisition Brothers were already thought to be too strict as it was. But most people had to accept them. Now people are better informed. Now The Inquisition brothers are seen as, not only too strict, but also unfair. Consequently, the Church has a lot of unhappy campers who "protest" very loudly. You'll come to know them as "Protestants"!

Protestants try to reform the Church. But the Church won't reform. The Papacy isn't about to loosen its hold on power. They won't change anything. So guys like Martin Luther and John Calvin take matters into their own hands. They start their own church! These Protestant Christian churches become spearheads of a movement to make entire city-states Protestant. Small wars for control of city-states break out all around Central Europe. Catholic Christian princes stand squarely behind the Church. They take up the fight against Protestants. But Christianity relentlessly re-forms itself, anyway. Protestant Christian churches pop up all over Europe. The time in history during which this happens will be called "The Reformation"!

The Church wins its share of military victories for control of city-states. But Protestant Christians win all the philosophical victories for control of peoples' hearts and minds! That's because they're into public relations. The Church isn't. The Papacy does none! And the Church already has a major public image problem because of the brothers of the Inquisition. So it keeps getting beaten up on the public relations front!

Finally, the Papacy wises up. They realize, if you want to win, you have to take the initiative to help yourself, as Goethe will so eloquently say in the following passages:

TAKE THE INITIATIVE

from: Johann Wolfgang von Goethe

We must not hope to be mowers,
   And gather the ripe gold ears,
Unless we have first been sowers
   And watered the furrows with tears.

It is not just as we take it,
   This mystical world of ours,
Life's field will yield as we make it

A harvest of thorns or of flowers.

The virtue is: Initiative. It's the first step toward success.

The Papacy finally begins to change the Church. First, they revisit Church doctrine and restore discipline. Next, they make plans to nip new Protestant movements in the bud, and snuff out as many Calvin and Lutheran churches as they can.

* How can they do that?
* They counter attack! They take the initiative to finally begin their own public relations effort by launching the Society of Jesus — the Jesuits — whose founder is a Spaniard named Ignatius of Loyola. This public relations mission by the Jesuits in the 1540's to win the hearts and minds of people is known as the "Counter-Reformation"! It's a crucial mission to stop the Protestants and win back God's "flock" for the Church! And our Ignatius is nobody's fool. He knows you don't win back God's flock by criticizing, condemning, and complaining like the brothers of the Inquisition have been doing. That's how they screwed things up in the first place. He believes you win peoples hearts and minds by <u>helping</u> them! That's how you become a leader. He believes helping people and having Virtue gets people to willingly follow you. Take note, Harry. West Point will someday adopt those ideas as leader development tools!
* How does someone like Ignatius, all the way over in Spain, become involved in the Counter-Reformation?
* It's an interesting story ... and important to our journey toward West Point. For it's about leadership and discipline and the virtues. It's about someone who educates and trains a "core" of men to become a "corps" of leaders having morals, ethics, and character. It's about developing leaders whose mission is to win the hearts and minds of people. It's the first time anyone formally takes on the task of "putting old souls into young bodies"!

IGNATIUS AND THE SOCIETY OF JESUS

based on: <u>Ignatius the Theologian</u>[101]

As a young man, Ignatius (1491-1556) was a Page in training for military leadership at the court of Ferdinand the King of Castile in Spain. He then became a military officer and was seriously wounded at the siege of Pamploma. While recovering, he read a book on the lives of Saints. That changed his life. From that time on, he devoted himself to education and a spiritual life.

At 37 years old, he entered the University of Paris. While there, he started a pious fraternity of students. It later developed into the Society of Jesus which was confirmed as a new Order by the Pope in 1540. Its mission was to produce leaders — special priests — for the Church's fight against Protestant expansion. These leaders were the point men of the Counter Reformation! They were sworn to go as missionaries to any place the Pope directed them, much like soldiers!

The Order rapidly expanded. Its members became the leaders in European education. By 1640 these leaders were running more than 500 schools and colleges! They founded over twenty Universities! Missions were established in Europe and then all around the world. And they provided military training where necessary!

The academy that trained candidates for the Society of Jesus was organized along military lines. But preparation of a candidate copied Plato's fifteen years training for his top leaders — his Guardians. First came two years of austere, regimented life as a novice — a plebe — to ingrain the basic faith. Then the candidate took his oath of faith, loyalty, and obedience. Next came two years of studying the Classics. Then three years of studying philosophy, mathematics, and sciences. Finally he engaged in three years of studying theology, followed by five years out in the "field" as role-model and teacher of new candidates for the priesthood. He was then ordained a Jesuit priest and took his final solemn oaths of the Order — vows to the Pope — in which he renounced holding any office outside of the Jesuit Order.

Ignatius organized the entire Society of Jesus like a military heirarchy. His <u>Constitutions of the Order</u> which lays the whole thing out has never been modified! He also wrote the <u>Spiritual Exercises</u> which lays out his philosophy on the meaning of life and development of the right way of life. Ignatius was the first Superior General of the Order.

The Society of Jesus produced dedicated missionaries, energetic fighters of Protestantism, and the best schools in Europe. But it was the target of prejudice, not only from outside, but also from within the Church!

The virtue is: Committment. Becoming a good-leader takes years of committment.

* Why is everyone in the Church prejudice against Ignatius?
* The reasons probably boil down to jealousy because he's singlehandedly stopping the Protestants. But it doesn't matter. In 1556 Ignatius dies. He never gets a chance to bring all Protestants back into the Catholic Christian fold.

Nevertheless, he's finally recognized for having saved Catholicism when in 1622 he's posthumously canonized as Saint Ignatius of Loyola by Pope Gregory. We'll visit his canonization ceremony to hear for ourselves what priests and politicians think about him. Maybe we'll find out if there's still prejudice against his Jesuits:

"We politicians and you priests should be beholden to Ignatius. Jesuit priests are not just preachers. They're doers. They're leaders. They're teachers. They represent the core values of the Organization — the Church. And, they did in fact halt the spread of Protestantism!"

"They also think they're better than the rest of us priests, you know. Why should they foist their standards of ethics and discipline on the rest of us? I see no difference between them and us. Do you? We're just as good!"

"Well, Jesuit priests do come with papers that say they certainly have a lot more preparation than you do, don't they. And they have proven they can bear up under stress and a hard life, as measured in years. You have not had to show you can do that."

"Ah! But look at what it costs to train your elite Jesuit leaders. We local priests are sending hefty tributes of money to Rome each year to support the Papacy. Why should the Jesuits get some of it?"

"That's very true. But how do you think we politicians must feel? The Society of Jesus is devoted only to the Pope. They have no respect for us. Jesuits teach a political philosophy in their colleges that drags us politicians through the mud. All because we pocket a little tax money for ourselves from time to time. And so what if we do? We make sure the tax money keeps rolling in, don't we. Still, unlike you Priests, we haven't called for abolishing the Society of Jesus. Why do you Priests do so?"

"I can't speak for the Church hierarchy, but we Priests can do without the Jesuits!"

"How would you go about abolishing them?"

"Cut their influence. Don't promote them. Abolish their academy. Their discipline is a real pain. We Priests like some fun too, you know. Protestants found a way to have some fun. They started their own churches. Now their training is easier; they can do anything they want to; and, they're still considered men of the cloth. They've got it made! And besides, did you know Jesuits are teaching that new thing called 'science' in their colleges? Did you know that's dangerous?"[102]

You can see that other priests are still prejudice against the Jesuits. They seem jealous because the Pope puts Jesuits on a higher level. But why shouldn't he? The Jesuits came through for him! And they did it in a new and unique way. They taught and they fought. Both "the word" and the sword were their weapons to conquer people's hearts and minds. They used "the word", printed books, to educate folks their way — the Catholic Christian way. They were wildly successful! It's one of history's great examples of leadership. And it's an example of the power of **EDUCATION** that will be followed by other leaders on other days, such as Thomas Jefferson!

Nevertheless, here in 1600's Europe, prejudice toward the Society of Jesus sticks. That thwarts their effort to completely wipe out Protestantism. The Reformation sticks ... especially the German Reformation. The old Holy Roman Empire is now smaller and less influential. The Church's influence on people and nations has been diluted. It's been a bloody dilution. And Christianity has changed forever![103]

Although the Church's influence is diluted, it still produces strong scholars and scientists ... thanks to the Society of Jesus. And the Church, complete with its Council of Inquisition, still holds on to power in many places. One of those places is France. And one of the most outstanding scholars the Church ever produces is a Frenchman. He'll later be known as the founder of modern philosophy. His name is Descartes!

When you look at Rene' Descartes (1596-1650) he's plainly unimpressive. In fact, he's plain. Period. But what a brain! He attends the Jesuit college, LaFleche. The Church runs on faith. And Rene' has faith. But faith is like a leap in the dark compared to the certainty of science. So he's the typical Catholic Christian of his era who's torn between science and the Church. Except, his era doesn't know he also happens to be a whiz at science, especially physics and mathematics. Did God give him that gift so he can bring science and faith into harmony, as Aquinas had brought Aristotle and Christendom into harmony? We'll see.

When Descartes graduates from college he wastes no time before showing his era his gift for mathematics. He carves out a niche for himself among intellectual giants of all time by developing Analytical Geometry! That's the combination of geometry and algebra that mathematicians, ever since Pythagoras, dreamed of finding!

Next, he goes to work on a manuscript on physics. After many months of writing, he finally finishes. He sends the manuscript off to his publisher for printing. But there's a last minute hitch. Just as his manuscript is about to go to print, a courier delivers this ominous news to him:

> "Monsieur Descartes. Your friend Galileo has been arrested by the Inquisition!"
>> "Arrested? Heaven help him. Why?"
> "For teaching his views about science."
>> "Then Heaven help me too! His views are close to those in my manuscript that's right now — as we speak — being published! What did they get him on?"
> "Well, all Galileo did was peer through his new telescope and discover planet Jupiter has three moons orbiting around it. So big deal. Who cares? Why should the Inquisition Brothers get bent out of shape over three moons?"

"Because Church doctrine says the Garden of Eden is like the Earth's bellybutton. Earth is the center of the Cosmos, and everything orbits around the Earth in concentric rings. So if three moons orbit around Jupiter, the Earth is <u>not</u> the center of the Cosmos! That kicks the legs out from under the Church's whole geo-centric doctrine!"

"Well I guess that's more than the Inquisition Brothers could take. Galileo has just been carted off to jail!"

"What a jolt! I'm a good Catholic. But I can see that the Church will be swept away by science if it fails to change its theories and become realistic. Far be it from me, however, to follow Galileo into the slammer to convince them of it!"

"If they carted away Galileo for his mere observation, heaven only knows what they'll do to you for your theories on physics. You're in big trouble, Monsieur! What in the world are you going to do now?"

"I'm going to run down to my publishers, as fast as my skinny little legs can carry me, and stop them from printing my manuscript. I don't fancy a career writing from the bowels of a crowded jail cell!"[104]

* Did he make it in time to stop his manuscript from being published?

* He sure did. And he wasn't about to waste all that work, either. He decided to slip his ideas on physics into his manuscript on philosophy. That manuscript turned into his famous book, <u>Meditations On First Philosophy</u>.

He had actually begun <u>Meditations On First Philosophy</u> while in the Army, isolated in a tiny cabin somewhere in Bavaria. One day, while huddling up next to a pot belly stove to keep warm, he got to thinking about math and physics and that other passion of his ... philosophy. For some unknown reason his mind sort of ran wild and his philosophical thoughts became sharp and clear. For the first time, he clearly realized he had begun his prior thinking on philosophy with questionable assumptions about life and knowledge in order to make his ideas pan out. The more he thought about it, the less he trusted those assumptions. He decided he would have to start all over again from scratch with a new approach. But how? He thought and thought ... and thought some more. Finally, he came up with a more honest, trust-worthy approach than had ever been done before. With his new approach — his "method of doubt" — when an idea would pop into his head, he would have to first test it by doubting it's truth. Then he would only trust the idea, and possibly use it in his philosophy, if he could prove it was true afterall. No more assumptions. Just proof. Then trust. Trust would come to mean everything to what would become Descartes' new modern philosophy. And as you'll see later, Harry, West Point will follow the Descartes model of trust. Trust will come to mean everything to what will become West Point's new leadership philosophy. In fact, a unique West Point honor system will be created in order to develope trust in leaders!

Using his "method of doubt", Descartes was finally able to boil his entire philoso-phy down to one solid, bare bones starting statement that he could prove and trust — not assume. It was the irrefutable statement, "I think, therefore I am"! You can call it his simple first bedrock of philosophy. On that bedrock he then went on to build a solid structure of philosophy that deals with everything ... life, the world, right and wrong, and so on. And he didn't ignore God! He took the short leap from his "I think therefore I am" to God's "I am Who I am" — the answer God gave Moses from the burning bush — and proved the existence of God. Now his philosophy was based on Reason, yet included God! Therefore, he dedicated his book to the faculty of Theology at the University of Paris in hopes of buttering-up the Council of Inquisition.

* So Descartes not only slipped his physics into his philosophy. He also sweetened it up with a proof of God?

* That's right. Read <u>Meditations On First Philosophy</u>, Harry. You'll see it's brilliant stuff. Descartes does bring science and faith into harmony! He shows there's a reli-able relationship between God, physics, mathematics, and morals and ethics. It's as reliable as one of his geometric proofs. It's so good, at the Council of Inquisition trial over <u>Meditations,</u> Descartes convinces <u>almost</u> everyone they can have both Galileo and God — both Science and the Supreme Being!

* Uh oh. You say almost everyone? What happened?

* We'll find out from the Council of Inquisition when they come out of chambers with their decision. Meanwhile, you and I can listen to what these other defendents waiting for trial are saying about it:

"What did they get you on?"
   "My parish priest told me I had to give more to his church. He
   kept on me. I finally told him to kiss off! So he reported me.
   How about you?"
"I told my college clergy that Jesus and the Apostles had no property.
   So the present day clergy should have none either. I'm accused of
   heresy!"
   "What do you think will happen to the good Monsieur
   Descartes? Were you here during his trial? What was said?"
"Well, the Brothers of the Inquisition looked him straight in the eyes
   when leaving the room to deliberate."
   "That's good!"

146

"But their faces didn't look very happy."

"That's bad!"

"During the trial they hailed his work as fresh, eloquent, and carefully written."

"That's good!"

"But they said his sugarcoated eloquence didn't fool them. They know he tried to slip his ideas on physics into it."

"That's bad!"

"Then they said they know he's a devout Catholic. So they won't mete out the same decision as they did to Galileo."

"That's good!"

"Look! They're coming back in now. They're about to give their decision. Here it is. Listen! .... Oh, no! Do you believe that! They said, good Catholic or not, Descartes' isn't a good theological ally of the Church. So they're putting him on the 'Index'!"

"What does that mean?"

"That means all of his work is now blacklisted! It means he can write his guts out, but he can't publish a word of it!"[105]

* So he hasn't convinced, or fooled, the brothers of the Inquisition.

* Unfortunately not. They do recognize his brilliance. But he hasn't slipped a thing past them. The effort he made to do so, however, rates him right up there with Plato and Aristotle on the all time list of top philosophers. And his "method of doubt" is a turning point in philosophy, if not civilization. It gets people to think and question and open up the world to new ideas and knowledge. So Descartes' "method of doubt" in which people first doubt, then become enlightened, really boils down to "doubt and enlightenment"! It will be used for many decades to come as a benchmark that future philosophy buffs can start from.

One of those philosophy buffs is Queen Christina of Sweden. She invites Rene' Descartes to Stockholm to teach her. As you know, it gets real cold in Stockholm. And ever since his hitch in the army in Bavaria, he has hated the cold. But, as you also know, the age old dream of every philosopher is to create a philosopher-king — in this case — philosopher-queen. So off goes our man Rene' to Sweden to take up the philosopher's "dream job" of a lifetime.

OH WELL. I'M ALL WASHED UP AROUND HERE, THANKS TO THE INQUISITION. SO I'M NOW OFF TO SWEDEN TO MAKE CHRISTINA A PHILOSOPHER—QUEEN!

It doesn't turn out to be such a great "dream job"! Queen Christina insists on starting her lessons at five o'clock in the morning. Our man Rene' isn't used to frigid 5 AM Scandinavian air. And he also doesn't like that ungodly hour because he's still forever hopeful of becoming handsome, by some miracle, if he gets his beauty rest. Well, he still doesn't get his miracle. He only gets his death of cold. The frigid morning air does to him what years of the Inquisition's pressure couldn't even do. It wears him down. After less than a year of being worn down, Rene' Descartes unexpectedly ... dies![106]

It's 1650. The Thirty Years War between Catholic Christians and Protestant Christians has just ended in Europe. In England, Oliver Cromwell has won the English Civil War. He has captured King Charles I, chopped off his head, and made himself Lord Protector of England. Across the Atlantic, Europe's colonies in America are rapidly growing. And back in Europe, "doubt and enlightenment" is rapidly growing as the preferred approach to invention and discovery amongst thinking men. It's leading them to make new progress in morals, ethics, science, politics, and economics. Descartes has started a growing wave of "doubt and enlightenment". And catching that wave is Amsterdam-born Baruch Spinoza (1634-1677) in Holland!

Spinoza was born of Jewish Portugese parents who had fled Spain's Inquisition. His major work is Ethics. Like Epictetus back in 100's AD Rome, Spinoza has a Stoic view of morals, ethics, and character. He says you have to practice them day after day in order to internalize them. Then, and only then, can you really be a good leader — a leader of Virtue. His motto that sums it all up is, "all excellent things are as difficult as they are rare". Epictetus and Aristotle had said the same thing. And Ralph Waldo Emerson will later say it better than anyone:

GREAT MEN

by: Ralph Waldo Emerson

Not gold, but only man can make
   A people great and strong;
Men who, for truth and honor's sake,
   Stand fast and suffer long.

Brave men who work while others sleep,
   Who dare, while others fly —
They build a nation's pillars deep
   And lift them to the sky.

The virtue is: Conscientiousness. Hard work day after
            day makes a person and a nation successful.

148

Another favorite saying of Spinoza is, "virtue is its own reward". And he proves he really believes it. For he's one of those rare philosophers out of all history who lives his philosophy. He actually practices what he preaches! For instance, he shuns offers of University professorships and lives the humble life of a lens-grinder. It's enough to support him while he does more important things, such as, lay out his ideas on morals, ethics, and character.

Like Descartes, Spinoza doesn't make assumptions. He proves his ideas. And like Descartes, he uses mathematics plus "doubt and enlightenment" to do so. His Geometry of Philosophy shows that philosophical ideas have the same step by step logic as a geometrical proof. Can you believe he even manages to show, mathematically, how to live a moral and ethical life? Isn't that incredible? He actually shows that virtues like truth and honor are as precise and unchangeable as mathematics. That's why you will see mathematics and deductive reasoning weigh in heavily in leadership education at West Point someday!

In his Ethics, Spinoza shows he's a God-fearing man — like Descartes did. He says God is part of everything, and everything is a part of God. God is nature. God is the cosmos. That's Spinoza's way of having both God and Galileo. But some people think those ideas go too far. They shock the religious types of Amsterdam. His synagogue ex-communicates him. Christians trash his reputation. He's lucky he's in Reformation Holland. There's no Council of Inquisition to pack him off to jail. He can go on writing to his heart's content. And he does!

Next he writes his Treatise on Theology and Politics. This book is a trial balloon on freedom of speech — the freedom to speak or write your ideas. This time, not religious types, but ruling class types are shocked. They also think he goes too far. The book doesn't fly. In fact, it's a rock. It kind of comes back down to clock him on the head. The ruling class trashes it ... and trashes him. Now it's unanimous. Everyone is trashing him. He's an outcast. Ordinary folks would probably love him. But most of them can't read or write. So they can't help him. No one can. Powerful people now pressure him to leave Amsterdam.
* Why should he give in and do that?
* Because he's viciously attacked in numerous publications and news articles. And someone physically attacks him. It's not just a beating. It's an attempted assassination! So they win! Baruch Spinoza packs himself up and gets out of town ... while the gettin' is good! This good soul who makes a modest living out of grinding lenses has actually made enemies just because he's a humble and virtuous philosopher. He learns not only are "all excellent things as difficult as they are rare." He learns that finding an excellent human being among society's ruling class is also as difficult as it is rare. And that will be the story of this rare and noble philosopher's life. But he will rest in peace. History will reward him. His philosophy of morals, ethics, and character will be a model for philosophers in England and Europe. His ideas on freedom — of the spoken and written word — will eventually reach America and be at the core of Thomas Jefferson's ideas on a Bill of Rights.[107]

Speaking of England, Thomas Hobbes (1588 - 1679) is over there across the Channel also adding to the ever growing wave of Descartes' "doubt and enlightenment". He's the first one to look at political philosophy that way. And you can see why it's easy for him to doubt everything. He was a firsthand witness when the "undestructible" royal pillars of society were destroyed. He saw a king, Charles I, beheaded. He was there when Oliver Cromwell and his "people's army" took over England. So now he says that politics and government come down to little more than raw power!

* Machiavelli already said that back in the 1500's.
* Machiavelli exposed how raw power works. Hobbes analyzes it. He assigns blame. And he blames human nature. He says man is like a wolf. Man is pitted against man out of greed. Everyone is fighting against everyone else. We have to find a solution or mankind will eventually destroy itself. Hobbes' solution is what he calls a "Mediator" whose job it is to prevent chaos, preserve peace, and protect the people. The Mediator can be anyone … King … Emperor … Parliament … even a Lord Protector, like Cromwell. Oliver Cromwell loves it. It gives him a philosophical blessing he can add to his Puritan religious blessing. Hobbes has unintentionally endorsed Cromwell, even though he was never a friend of Cromwell's English Revolution. Still, knowing cynical old Hobbes, here's what his conversations with Oliver Cromwell would be like:

> "You're a right hero now, so you are, Lord Protector Cromwell.
> You pulled off the biggest win over the Crown ever. You risked
> everything you have, including your life, to do it. Why?"
> "I did it to restore the liberties of Englishmen!"
> ᵒᵒYeh! As long as those liberties fit into your plans.ᵒᵒ "What
> about Puritanism? Didn't that have something to do with it?"
> "Yes. That was also a factor. Puritans should be free to wor-
> ship as they please!"
> ᵒᵒAnd you want to eliminate the Pope as your competitor!ᵒᵒ
> "Wasn't a bit of class struggle also part of your English
> Revolution?"
> "Indeed! I support the plight of poor people!"
> ᵒᵒYeh! You'll take any warm body into your army as long as
> they're willing to die for you!ᵒᵒ
> "And don't forget the class struggle of us 'Country' producers
> of wealth against the bloodsuckers of the King's 'Court'!"
> ᵒᵒYeh. You 'Country' people want all the money!ᵒᵒ "You reckon
> you did no less than save England? Is that an accurate summary
> of the way you feel?"
> "Of course! It was my moral duty to do so! I was following
> God's law! I love God! I love England!"
> ᵒᵒAnd you love power, too!ᵒᵒ [108]

You can argue ... forever ... whether Cromwell leads England as a Mediator or as a dictator. It won't matter. Fifteen years from now, in 1658, Lord Protector Cromwell dies. And with him dies ... forever ... his movement against kings and monarchies. There's no one to replace him. So a King and a Parliament get back into power. And both hate the concept of a Mediator!

* Why? Hobbes said either a King or a Parliament would make a good Mediator.
* What rubs King and Parliament the wrong way is the "Social Contract" that goes along with having a Mediator.
* What's that?
* The Social Contract is an agreement between the Mediator and all the people of the country. It prevents the Mediator from abusing power. The Mediator is there to keep people from eachother's throats — not milk them! The Social Contract calls all the people of the country (taken together collectively) the "artificial man". It says this "artificial man", not God, gives the Mediator — in this case, King or Parliament — authority to run things. That's what rubs the King and Crown the wrong way. They always pretended the King got his authority to run everything from God. No way would they agree it comes from lowly ordinary people! It also rubs Parliament the wrong way. They consider a Mediator's sweeping authority to be tyranny. So now Hobbes rubs everyone the wrong way! His Social Contract gets buried! We won't see it again for forty years — until a guy named John Locke will dig it up!

In his work called <u>Leviathan</u> (monster government), Thomas Hobbes had cynically said that "life is short, poor, nasty, and lonely". However, the old codger's life ended up being just the opposite — long, prosperous, pleasant, and social. He managed to avoid "the brutish life of human nature" that he had always insisted was unavoidable. But in spite of his good fortune, he was still cynical about human nature when he went to his grave at ninety-one years old. He was convinced you can't enlighten most human beings. A society, or any organization, must be led by "Mediators" that are trusted leaders who earn their trust from the "artificial man" — from all the people, taken collectively.[109]

CHAPTER 12: ENLIGHTENMENT

As we approach the 1700's in Europe, the wave of people using Descartes' method of "doubt and enlightenment" in which you first doubt, then prove, then trust, then become enlightened is growing into a tidal wave! This tidal wave of "doubt and enlightenment" will bring people great opportunities. Philosophers will have the opportunity to learn new things about science, politics, economics, morals and ethics, and so on. Ordinary folks will have the opportunity to pull themselves out of poverty and join a rising "middle class" that's neither poor nor privileged. The great William Shakespeare had told someone: "There is a rising tide in the affairs of men which leads to fortune ... you must not miss the opportunity to catch it". In other words, "old man opportunity" doesn't knock twice, as "he" tells us himself in this personification:

THEY CALL ME: OPPORTUNITY

from: John James Ingalls

Master of human destinies am I!
Cities and fields I penetrate passing by,
And I knock unbidden but once at every gate!
Rise before I turn away, for you who hesitate,
Will seek me in vain and uselessly implore.
But I will answer not, and return no more!

The virtue is: Prudence. Be prudent enough to recognize
that opportunity may only knock once.

The rising "middle class" of people will join a rising class of philosophers who dare to agitate for reform of monarchies, and thus, challenge the "ancient regime" — the old social and political order. The foremost agitator is a philosopher who subscribes to Descartes' ideas about trust and "doubt and enlightenment", but gives trust a special twist. He only trusts something after (post) seeing or experiencing it [a posteriori]. He's an Englishman called John Locke. His special twist to trust is called "Empiricism"!

John Locke (1632-1704) has philosophical ideas that will someday set off sparks in the hearts of Americans that will catch fire and turn into an American Revolution. Those same ideas will also catch on with a small band of French philosophers who will help to inflame a French Revolution. But that's all a bit down the road from now, Harry. Right now, John Locke is still young. He never dreams he'll someday be a philosopher. He only dreams he'll someday get into college. You see, he's not your typical rich, 1700's, Oxford-bound, blue-blood. But he is smart. So he gets into Oxford anyway. He studies chemistry. Then he goes on to become a Doctor of Medicine. As a doctor, he eventually lands a position as private physician to the Earl of Shaftsbury. The Earl is your typical rich, 1700's, blue-blood!

* Sounds like a nice job! Good pay, good hours, and plenty of time to do other things.

* Right! And John Locke does do other things. He reads a ton! One day he picks up Descartes' Meditations on First Philosophy. It turns the good doctor's attention from the body to the mind. And it's a timely turn. For his boss, the Earl of Shaftsbury, is in big trouble. He's at the center of hot political controversy. The good Doctor Locke gets drawn into defending him. And he does a good job. But the Earl's views against the King and Crown are so radical, he gets accused of treason! One step ahead of the hangman, the Earl steals away to Holland! Locke wisely follows!

It's the 1680's. John Locke is already the wrong side of fifty years old. He's becoming more philosophical. He gets to thinking about what he's seen in his lifetime. He remembers how the revolutionary spirit against the Monarchy in mid-1600's England was traced straight back to The Magna Carta and Ancient Saxon Law. He remembers how a revolutionary army that was hurled against the Monarchy had fallen straight into Parliament's lap in the form of a massive Puritan uprising. Like Thomas Hobbes, he had witnessed all the events of the English Revolution: Cromwell and Parliament defeating Charles I; Charles I getting beheaded; Cromwell becoming Lord Protectorate of an English Republic; Puritanism becoming the religion of England for a time; and, Parliament's "Restoration" of a Monarch, King James I, after Cromwell died.

Now in the 1680's, there's a secret plot to oust James I. The plan is to pressure him to step down in favor of both his daughter in Holland, Princess Mary of Orange, and William of Orange. Then a constitutional monarchy would be formed by contract with William and Mary. It's to be a peaceful "Glorious Revolution" in which no heads roll! That's the plan. But in England, nothing is happening. King James I is still there.

Here in Holland, however, John Locke is working on it! He's putting his philosophical views on paper. Those views will become his Essay Concerning Human Understanding, and, his Two Treatises of Government. They're his best weapons against James I. They're easy to understand. Europe's "middle class" loves them. Europe's philosophers love them. Europe's royalty hates them. And the latter is no surprise. For Locke bluntly says the power of Kings and royalty should be curbed. He pushes stunning new powers for parliaments. He pushes religious freedom. In short, he's on a crusade against the monarchies. But, until King James I gets the push, he has to do his crusading from Holland.

Finally, the secret plot to oust James I is ready to come off. Locke has a hand in it. And it works to perfection. It is a "Glorious Revolution"! King James keeps his head and peaceably departs. Mary of Orange and William of Orange return to England. They sign on to having a constitutional monarchy and become King William and Queen Mary.

Locke returns to England where, at fifty-eight years old, his Essay and his Treatises finally get widely published. They set off a firestorm of public debate. We'll listen to the pundits in and around the Parliament buildings in London to get some idea of what actually is being said:

"They say the <u>Two Treatises of Government</u> by Locke inspired those who ousted that tyrant James I."

"Locke?"

"Yes. John Locke. The one who escorted the Princess of Orange — now Queen Mary — into London during the Glorious Revolution." ᵒᵒWhere have you been, mate ... on some deserted island?ᵒᵒ

"Oh yes, I'm with you now. He's one of those blokes who helped get rid of James I and set up this secondhand monarchy we've now got. But why the devil do you say the revolution was glorious?"

"Why? Don't you think it was? I reckon the Revolution was unusually glorious! No one's head got chopped off!"

ᵒᵒIf they chopped your head off it would be no big loss!ᵒᵒ

"Personally, I reckon it makes little difference one way or the other."

"Why doesn't that surprise me? Cheerio then!"...ᵒᵒNo use bothering to talk to you ... blockhead!ᵒᵒ ¹¹⁰

* Interesting. But what's their reasoning behind again choosing a monarchy after half a century of revolution against monarchies?

* When you're raised in a cage, even a cage feels like home. In other words, it's often what you're used to that sways your practical reasoning. However, their philosophical reasoning for a monarchy goes all the way back to Plato. His <u>Politics</u> had "Guardians-Soldiers-Masses" fulfilling his model for government of "One-Few-Many". Remember? Well, now Locke thinks you can have "King-Parliament-Citizens" fulfilling Plato's model. But he adds some new twists that even Plato didn't have. One of them is "checks and balances" to divide power between King, Parliament, and Citizens. He calls the King's power "executive" power. The Parliament's power is "legislative". The Citizens' power is a "citizen force". He says that citizens must have the means to remove the executive or legislative by <u>force</u> — by a "citizen force" — if either should become tyrannical!

* Like Oliver Cromwell's citizens removed King Charles I by a citizen force?
* That's right. And "the means" doesn't mean chucking snowballs at them, or bashing them on the head with pots and pans. It means weapons! Arms! Without them, even Cromwell wouldn't have stood a chance against the King's armies!
* Is that the root of America's Second Amendment right to have guns?
* Perhaps. Like Locke, the Second Amendment also promotes having a "civilian militia". A militia is defined as citizens, collectively enrolled and drilled in military-type organizations other than a formal government standing army — and other than a reserve militia (such as the National Guard).[111]
* It actually sounds more like a private club or organization.
* That's exactly what it is. But take care! Locke also says, "a citizen's force is to oppose only unjust or unlawful authority [or force]". It's his "Theory of Justifiable Revolution"!
* But when is authority unjust and unlawful so that a "citizen force" should be used? And who decides?
* That's the problem, Harry. It usually boils down to force itself that decides the question! Like the English Revolution!
* It sounds like we've gone around in a circle. We've come back to power again — like Machiavelli said. He keeps popping up, doesn't he!
* Machiavelli also pops up when Locke talks about understanding humans and "natural law"! Machiavelli said natural law is based on pure power. Locke says natural law is a moral thing! He says natural law bestows us all with "natural rights" such as "life, liberty, property, and rebellion". He says they're "unalienable" rights that derive their authority through God's natural law!
* Hmm! Our "founding fathers" use those same words!
* His words and ideas will not only be used by America's founding fathers in 1776, they'll be Adam Smith's root moral principles for his <u>Wealth of Nations</u>! That's the classic work on capitalism and free enterprise that will be published eighty plus years from now in … believe it or not … also 1776! You know the <u>Wealth of Nations</u> is America's economic "bible", right Harry?
* Yes. So how do Locke's natural rights do in 1690's England?
* We'll listen to some discussions in the halls of Parliament and find out:

> "I hear a fair lot of people are against Locke's ideas!"
>   "Who could be against <u>these</u> ideas: <u>One</u>, the right to life so
>   long as you don't threaten the life of others; <u>Two</u>, the right to
>   liberty if it doesn't infringe the liberties of others; And <u>three</u>,
>   the right to accumulate property — provided it doesn't spoil
>   in accumulation, and enough is left for others, and accumula-
>   tion does no harm to others. It would be like being against
>   motherhood, plum pudding, and Rule Britannia! Everyone
>   wants life, liberty, and property … don't they!"
> "Well, two out of three 'in't bad, I reckon!"
>   "Oh? Which one don't you like?"
> "I bloody well will not give up my life's accumulations just
>   because some rabble come skulking around claiming they haven't

enough for their meager needs! Locke's rules don't suit me!"
   "Ah, but you'll be glad to hear Mr. Locke said you can hoard
     as much gold and silver as you please!"
"Did he just? Now there's a rule that suits me! It's somewhat like
   that old Golden Rule, so it is. You know the one. The chap who
   has all the gold makes all the rules. So, if we finish up rather
   cool toward Locke's rule's, then bugger it all! We'll just change
   them! We'll start from scratch with new ones!"
   "I guessed you'd fancy that last one about gold and silver!"
"Sure!" Why not throw the rabble a few little tidbits of rights!
Keep them barefoot and happy! I reckon it's like insurance
against another Cromwell!"
   "You know there's a tidal wave of change approaching don't
     you? We must not be swept away by it. If we breast the tide
     to our advantage, it will raise all our boats!"
"Just so! And the more little dingeys bobbing about our big
   boats, the safer we are!"[112]

* Oops! Those guys don't sound real inspired by Locke, do they?
* No. And they know, if you want to gather honey, you don't upset the beehive.
So you notice that they never talked about Locke's idea of rebellion against unjust
laws and rulers — his Theory of Justifiable Revolution. But you'll see a lot of
folks in America talk about that idea in the future. America's Spirit of 1776 could
just as easily be called the "Spirit of Locke!" The year 1776 will give birth to the
spirit of political reform with the Declaration of Independence in America, and to
the spirit of economic reform with the Wealth of Nations in England.
   Right now in the 1690's, however, America is still a group of colonies busily
churning out wealth. And Britain is busily churning out laws to collect and swal-
low-up that wealth. That's what will rub some men in the colonies the wrong
way, someday. But at this point in time those men — America's "founding
fathers" — have not even been born yet![113]
Just born across the Channel in France is the great French political theorist

156

Baron Montesquieu (1689 -1755). He'll one day be first among the collection of French philosophers and scientists called "Philosophes" — French Enlightenment thinkers.

Montesquieu immerses himself for fourteen years into absorbing political philosophy. He emerges a follower of John Locke. Like Locke, he'll be fifty-eight years old before he publishes his famous <u>Spirit of the Laws</u> in 1748. It'll reach clear across the Atlantic Ocean to educated American colonists. Much of John Locke's ideas will be in it. Remember how ancient Rome was a conduit for transmitting Greek culture to Europe? Well, Baron Montesquieu will become a conduit for transmitting John Locke's philosophy to America.

* Are the Locke-Montesquieu ideas the ones Thomas Jefferson used in the Declaration of Independence?

* It depends on who you talk to. Rationalists would "reason" that Jefferson was born with the ideas [a priori]. Empiricists would "observe" that they were put into his mind only after (post) reading, seeing, or experiencing them [a posteriori]. The truth is, it's probably a little of both. Either way, the ideas are America's most important moral and ethical anchors:

THE DECLARATION OF INDEPENDENCE

by: Thomas Jefferson

When in the course of human events, it becomes necessary for one people to dissolve the political bands which have connected them with another, [then] We hold these truths to be self-evident: That all men are created equal, that they are endowed by their Creator with certain unalienable Rights, that among these are Life, Liberty, and the pursuit of Happiness. — That to secure these rights, Governments are instituted among Men deriving their just powers from the consent of the governed, — That whenever any Form of Government becomes destructive of these ends, it is the Right of the People to alter or to obolish it, and to institute new Government —.

The virtue is: Courage. It took courage to stand up for
what's right against England.

Besides Locke's ideas, Montesquieu spins new ones into his <u>Spirit of the Laws</u>. For example, his legal branch of government, the judicial, is to be independent. Modern America still embraces and protects that idea. And he says, though the cement of a monarchy is loyalty, a republic needs more than loyalty. It needs all the moral, ethical, and character virtues to cement it together and keep it together. All the moral, ethical, and character virtues, as you know, are collectively called Virtue!

Montesquieu rejects the approach to trust called Rationalism. Rationalists say you can know and trust something to be true by (prior) "inborn reason" [a priori]. Like Locke, he says that only after (post) "seeing and experiencing" something can you know and trust it to be true [a posteriori]. That approach to trust is Empiricism. He agrees with Locke that the mind at birth is like a "clean slate". He says that information, even Virtue, is put on the slate through our senses of seeing, hearing, and so forth — after (post) "seeing and experience". So like Locke he thinks that Virtue — the cement of a republic — can only be learned, not inherited!

* That only partly agrees with Plato and Aristotle. They said you both learn and inherit Virtue. Right?

* Yes. The bottom line for us, however, is that Montesquieu, like Locke and Plato and Aristotle, concludes that you need to have good-leaders if your republic is to survive! And you can only get good-leaders through training! You'll see later ... Thomas Jefferson will agree with them![114]

Contemporary to moral and political specialist, Montesquieu, is all around star philosopher, Francois Voltaire (1694-1778). He's brilliant. He's also a worrier. Luckily, he's an ambitious worrier. For he sees The Enlightenment's social and political philosophies are beginning to corrode France's morals. That's his biggest worry. So he sets out to single-handedly reform and enlighten France in his own way. He writes tons of plays, poems, novels, histories, and philosophical works to do so. They amount to a massive seventy volumes! Most of them contain his new moral philosophy.

The idea for his new moral philosophy had been inspired by his friend over in England, scientific philosopher Isaac Newton. Voltaire calls it "natural philosophy"! Many people say that Voltaire is trying to change, or compete with, Christianity's religious philosophy. Voltaire doesn't agree. He explains his natural philosophy this way:

NATURAL MORAL PHILOSOPHY

taken from: Voltaire

God created everything. That includes our natural
world and free will. Then our natural world — Nature —
took over from there. It produced human beings. So
organized religion and natural philosophy should cooperate hand to glove. Natural moral philosophers should lead
people to the virtues. Clergymen should lead people to
religious morals. That should produce humans having
Virtue, not humans pitted against other humans!

The virtue is: Patience. Cooperation requires patience on
all sides.

Unfortunately, France's so called leaders in the late 1700's will prefer a bloody revolution that pits humans against other humans. They won't be interested in Virtue and Voltaire's natural moral philosophy![115]

Instead of forging his own moral philosophy, Voltaire could have simply tapped into Joseph Butler's. Though contemporary to Voltaire, England's Butler (1692-1752) had already written an extensive treatise on moral and natural philosophy called Fifteen Sermons! In Fifteen Sermons he says that morals and ethics are about Conscience! What sorts out good and evil, right and wrong? The answer is Conscience! What's even more effective than laws concocted by man? Again, the answer is Conscience! And what helps moral philosophers, such as Voltaire, guide people's free will toward Virtue? Yet again, Butler's answer is Conscience! He says your Conscience is what gives you the will to make the virtues into habits through disciplined lifestyle. It doesn't matter who's philosophical story you listen to. Plato's. Aristotle's. The Stoics'. Spinoza's. Voltaire's. To Butler, all their stories boil down to Conscience![116]

* Then why doesn't Voltaire use Butler's Fifteen Sermons for the moral reforms he's pushing?

* Because Joseph Butler is none other than — Bishop Butler of Durham in England! That means he's a man of organized religion. And Voltaire is challenging organized religion. Voltaire dismisses organized religion as Church rules and ceremonies made by man, not made by God. But he still needs the Church. In fact, at the very time he's criticizing the Church, he's also sucking up to the Church to make room in the pew — find a place in Church doctrine — for his natural religion. Voltaire needs the Church's blessing. He has a moral dilemma!

Jean Jacques Rousseau (1712-1778) knows all about moral dilemmas! He is one! For example, he says that "man is born free, and everywhere he is in chains". He's accusing the "ancient regime" of being hypocritical. But Rousseau, himself, is hardly another Spinoza. Unlike Spinoza, he doesn't live up to his own philosophy. He doesn't practice what he preaches. He often does just the opposite! So even though he's brilliant, energetic, and original ... he's a big hypocrite! That's one of his moral dilemmas. Listen in on some back-fence gossip about him in his Paris neighborhood. You'll see what I mean:

> "There goes Monsieur Rousseau and that ex-servant girl from the hotel he lived at in Paris. After all those classy dames I hear he lived with, I don't know what he sees in this creature."
>
> "He must see something!"
>
> "Yes. And we can guess what that is. This is the fifth Rousseau baby they're carrying off to the Foundling Home. It's a shame!"
>
> "He's just too busy to raise children. He's doing more important things — like writing about how to raise children!"
>
> "No! Really? Is that what his book Emile is about? I read his first book, Discourses."
>
> "Ah yes. Discourses. He lamented about how arts and sciences — the decadence of culture all around him — corrupts the virtues and morals that humans are naturally born with."
>
> "And it looks like he's out to prove that point ... all by himself!"

"In his next book, <u>Discourse in Inequality</u> he cited such 'noble savages' as the Huron Indians as examples of natural morals unspoiled by society. But everyone thought he was just advising people to act like savages or animals back in nature!'"

"And it's no wonder they thought that! He already does a lot of that himself!"

"That's because he stresses feelings and emotions rather than science and reasoning. He talks in terms of a new 'romantic sensibility'."

"He obviously has a lot of <u>that</u> — romantic sensibility, I mean!"

"Well, you must admit, he's never dull!" [117]

* It sounds like Rousseau has a big moral dilemma, Thomas! His life contradicts his words, assuming what we just heard is true.

* It's true alright. But Rousseau is good at living with moral dilemmas and contradictions in his personal life. They have no effect on his work. So his writings still inspire people. In the future, they'll inspire patriots like Samuel Adams over in America. And they'll fire up revolutionists like Robespierre here in France. In fact, he'll be on Thomas Jefferson's personal list of the best philosophers of modern times ... along with Bacon, Locke, and Newton. Rousseau has his contradictions, idiosyncracies, and moral dilemmas. But he <u>is</u> brilliant!

* We heard the book by Rousseau called <u>Emile</u> mentioned in connection with raising and training youngsters. It sounds like it could be important to us.

* It's important enough to read cover to cover! <u>Emile</u> is about education. It talks about the natural process through which children mature from infant to adulthood. In it, Rousseau says everyone has inborn, natural virtues. So he's close to Aristotle on that. And Rousseau says it's important not to disturb those inborn virtues through the early maturing years. In that way they remain intact as people mature. He believes that "nature wants children to be children before becoming men"! Let children mature gradually. Then they'll become diamonds in the

rough. Furthur training and education in the virtues will polish them. And for us, Harry, that means they're ready to be made into good-leaders. Rousseau is telling us how he would go about "putting old souls into young bodies"!

* Rousseau sounds like Butler. He relies on Conscience.

* That's right, Harry. He says we know right and wrong through our hearts, our feelings, and our emotions from birth. And he's also like Aristotle. He says virtues are both inborn and learned. He brilliantly and originally tells us (not shows us!) how to connect moral philosophy to real life, like no one has ever done before.

Rousseau also tells us how to connect political philosophy to real life. In his work, The Social Contract he begins by giving us a blow by blow description of his political philosophy. Then he goes on to explain how society should be like a family. What we'll call, the "ruler", is like the dad of a family. The people yield to the "ruler" just like the kids yield to dad, because dad looks after their safety and best interests. And that's what keeps order in society — like it does in the family.

In a family, kids and dad come together by accident of nature. They don't choose eachother. It doesn't have to be that way for people and "ruler" in society, however. Their union can be, and should be, designed. Rousseau says it must be designed. And how do you do that? What's the best way to design a society? Rousseau has the answer. It's a new design of government. He calls it self-government ... true self-government!

* True self-government? As in a republic?

* Not quite. He says a republic isn't true self-government. It's a good start. But with a republic, you can elect your representatives every four years and end up with nothing but a series of four-year dictators! So a republic is only half of what he means by true self-government!

* I see. What's the other half?

* Democracy! Direct participatory democracy! Rousseau ditches the idea of elected representation — what he calls "elected aristocracy"! Everyone, not just representatives, participate in his self-government!

* Hmm. How's he think that can ever work?

* Here's how it would work. You vote on an issue directly. That's what Rousseau calls your individual will. The net of all individual's wills, added and subtracted, finishes up as the net will of society. It's the collective will of all people in "association" with eachother. So the "ruler" of society is the "association" of all people voting according to their individual wills. You, as part of this "association", make the laws. And you are also subject to the laws. You yield to the "ruler" — the "association" — just like kids yield to dad in the family. "Ruler" and "subject" are simply the same people in different roles. It's true self-government. It's truly of the people and by the people and for the people!

* It's a 100% poll! If you ask me, it's romantic fancy.

* Perhaps. But now here's where Rousseau really becomes a Romantic! He isn't satisfied merely with the simple "will of all the people" — the net of their self-interested wishes. He says you should vote for what's best for society — not just for what's best for you! He calls this the "virtuous will of all the people" — the

General Will! And he says the General Will is always right!

* That is romantic! Why would I put aside my own self-interest?
* That's a challenge alright! You retain your self-interest on your private day-to-day affairs, but not when you vote on public issues. Therefore, you must be virtuous, educated, and well informed on the issues. That's the ideal. But even Rousseau, the Romantic, is troubled that people won't know what's best for society. And we know he's already troubled that moral decay is corrupting the natural virtues of growing kids. So everyone will have to be educated as he describes in Emile! Then society will be a virtuous, well informed "association" of the people. But that takes time. The great ship of society alters course only very slowly. He needs a temporary solution to this problem. And he finds one. His solution is leaders of Virtue — leaders having morals, ethics, and character. He calls these leaders "Legislators".
* Are we back to elected representatives again?
* No, not at all. Here's what Legislators are:

ROUSSEAU'S LEGISLATORS

Rousseau's Legislators are good-leaders who guide and advise people about what's best for society as a whole, and therefore, what's ultimately best for each. This leads to the "virtuous will of all the people" — the General Will — that most people seek, even though most only half understand. Legislators are good-leaders who lead society in the right direction.

Individuals who were educated in youth according to his treatise on education, Emile, would be selected. These individuals would still have natural virtues — like what he called the unspoiled "noble savages". Then their moral and political awareness would be further enhanced through additional education. In the end they would possess the highest of moral, ethical, and intellectual qualities. They would be good-leaders with character and competence who could be trusted to guide and advise all of the people in society. But they would be outside of the legislative structure. They would have no decision making authority! That would still be in the hands of the people, through direct participatory democracy!

The virtue is: Cooperation. It's required to make anything work.

* So education is the key to self-government.
* Right! You can't make good crops if you don't learn about farming ... can you,

Harry? Likewise, you can't make good votes by merely learning about the arts and sciences. You must learn to be a moral, ethical, well-informed voter. And don't forget ... everyone is a voter! So everyone must be educated, and learn to be a moral, ethical, well-informed voter. That means role models — leaders, parents, and teachers — must be that way.

Rousseau's political ideas are a major turning-point in the Enlightenment. In fact, The Social Contract will be the "bible" for many leaders of the French Revolution, such as, Robespierre! For that reason Rousseau is blamed by some for the bloody parts of the French Revolution. But his ideas are more complex than that. They beg for more than the instant gratification that revolution brings. He's out to turn the ship of society ... not sink it![118]

In France the upper classes are convinced by Rousseau to get back to basics — get back to nature. In Scotland, the dean of the Scottish Enlightenment has become convinced to get back to basics also. Basic philosophy! His name is David Hume (1711-1776). He's: author of the History of England; tutor to the Marquis of Arrandale; secretary to the Earl of Hertford at the Paris Embassy; greatest writer in Britain according to Boswell; intellectual darling of Paris; and, host to political exile Jean Jacques Rousseau in Britain!

Hume starts out trying to prove all of philosophy is a genuine science. He uses Descartes' method of "doubt and enlightenment". But he runs into trouble! Somewhere along the way he ends up trashing (prior) "inborn reason" [a priori] — Rationalism — as a way to trust something is true. He also muddles up (post) "seeing and experience" [a posteriori] — Empiricism — as a way to trust something is true. It's very complex, Harry. So, let me just say he finishes by getting philosophy tied up into a knot!

Even grateful guest, Rousseau, can't agree with David Hume on very much. Rousseau is optimistic about the future: Hume has become pessimistic about everything. Rousseau believes his moral and political ideas will lead to a wondrous turning point in the Enlightenment: Hume believes they'll lead to disaster. Rousseau thinks philosophers are making great contributions to mankind: Hume thinks philosophers are useless. And, Rousseau's political ideas could lead to the end of monarchies in the future: Hume's ideas could lead to the end of philosophy, right here and now! For, destroying (prior) "inborn reason" [a priori] and (post) "seeing and experience" [a posteriori] means that very few things can actually be proven and trusted to be true by using philosophy. He's gotten the previously well-defined strands of thought in philosophy tangled up. He's tied all of philosophy into a kind of "Gordian Knot". He himself can't even unravel it. He concludes that no one can. He says the brilliant and original mind it would take, doesn't exist. He's thoroughly discouraged, and says philosophy should be abandoned![119] But Hume is wrong! That brilliant, original mind does exist! It's in the person of a quiet, contented, fifty-year old professor at the university in Konigsberg, East Prussia. His name is Emmanuel Kant (1724-1804).

Kant is strictly small-town, even though he's smart. He grew up in Konigsberg. He went to lower school and higher school in Konigsberg. He went to University there. He spent his whole life teaching there. And he'll probably die there. Nothing exciting happens in his life. No marriage. Little romance. No serious illness. He lives alone. He doesn't even keep a pet.

* It sounds like he's what my era calls socially challenged.

* Not really. He is personable. He has his stable of friends. But he's dull. Plain dull. He's as dull as his contemporary, Jean Jacques Rousseau, is exciting. He's as methodical and reliable as Rousseau is flamboyant and unpredictable. He's as true to his moral philosophy as Rousseau is hypocritical. In that respect, Rousseau can't touch him. But Rousseau manages to touch him in another way. He provides one of the few dramatic flusters in Kant's life!

* Don't tell me. He visits Kant and takes him beerhall hopping.

* No. It's nothing that racy and exciting.

* Then what's this dramatic fluster?

* Let's see for ourselves. We'll let that neighbor and that coachman talking about it over there tell us:

> "Is there an epidemic of illness going around? There's been no one at this coach stop for the past three days!"
>> "The only epidemic is the neighborhood's dependence on Herr Professor Kant."
> "I don't get you! ∘∘Speak plain German, man!∘∘ Who's this Kant?"
>> "Well, Professor Kant has incredibly regular habits. His reputation for punctuality is legendary. The neighborhood actually sets it's clocks by his daily walk."
> "So what's happened! He run off with the neighbor's wife or something?"
>> "Heavens no. Nothing like that. He's an honorable man. To him excitement is getting a boil cut off his butt. Having a tooth fixed also put some excitement in his life a few years back."
> "He hasn't breathed his last then, has he?" ∘∘Might as well have done!∘∘
>> "That's what we all thought, at first. So I went to check on him. There he was at home engrossed in a book called Emile ... by that Frenchman, Rousseau."
> "Well you can just tell your Herr Professor he's caused a lot of trouble around here!"
>> "I know. The neighborhood's been in a tither — late for everything."
> "Not just your neighborhood. I kept the coach standing here overtime to wait for people. That made me late all along the line! It disrupted the whole Principality ... because of someone's daily walk!"
>> ∘∘Because of Rousseau's Emile!∘∘ [120]

Kant was so fascinated with what Rousseau's book, Emile, had to say, he stayed inside for three days! That disrupted half the town that sets its clocks by his daily walk!

* That's the dramatic fluster in his life? As a philosopher, it can't be the first book on philosophy he's been fascinated with.
* No it isn't. He reads everything that's written by scientific philosopher, Isaac Newton. And he's a disciple of Gottfried Leibnitz, the dominant intellect of Prussia back in the early 1700's. Like Voltaire, Leibnitz had written on a variety of subjects. He had invented differential calculus at the same time Newton did in England. They shared the credit for that stroke of genius. And he had stuck by his Rationalism when, because of Empiricism, Rationalism was no longer the trendy approach to proving and trusting whether something is true. So Kant has his Newton and Leibnitz. Just add Locke, and he's professionally content. His philosophy is well squared-away those days he stays home to read Emile ... and makes the whole town late.

But Rousseau isn't the only one who touches Kant's life. One day, a copy of David Hume's Enquiry lands on his desk. Kant is shocked out of his socks when he reads it! He had not been aware of Hume's powerfully destructive arguments. They undermine everything Kant has spent his entire life getting so squared away on. He says Hume's arguments must be torn down. If not, trust in philosophy can never return. Kant comes face-to-face with Hume's "Gordian Knot" that esentially says all philosophy is a load of rubbish! The argument begins!
* Kant should ignore him! Why should he get spooked into arguing with Hume?
* Well, a person usually has two reasons for doing something: a noble good-sounding reason; and a real reason. In this case Kant is no different, Harry. His noble reason is to save philosophy. His real reason is to save his life's work, his reputation, and probably his job. So this quiet, courteous, bookworm takes a 180 degree turn. He surprises everyone. He finally surfaces from his long complacent slumber. And he eagerly jumps into the most serious fracas in philosophy for centuries.
* It sounds like Kant's the right person in the right place at the right time.
* He is. They say if God had not made an Emmanuel Kant, someone would have had to invent one. For no one is going to cut through Hume's philosophical Gordian Knot — not like Alexander had cut through the real one in ancient Phyrgia. This one will have to be methodically unravelled — step by step. Remember, Hume has shown that there is no way of proving or trusting that something is true. He has shown that most philosophical explanations of life, morals, virtue, science, and the world are absolutely bogus. So according to Hume, Harry, that means you and I may even have to throw away everything we've learned about virtues and good-leaders!
* Good heavens! But if Hume has already disproved everything, what can Emmanuel Kant do? What can we do?
* What Kant does is starts with the deductive reasoning that Galileo and Newton had applied so fruitfully to science. From there he launches a full scale frontal attack on Hume's philosophical Gordian Knot. It's all in his Critique of Pure Reason.
* Do I have to read that? It's probably difficult. Right?
* It's not only difficult. It's prolix — very long and wordy. However, what it says is important. It will later help you to more easily understand the real story

of West Point. So I'll make it easy for you. I'll <u>tell</u> you what it says.

Here's the simplified version of <u>Critique of Pure Reason</u>. David Hume had tested the two philosophical methods of proving and trusting something to be true. First, he had tried (prior) "inborn reason" [a priori] — Rationalism. Second, he had tried (post) "seeing and experience" [a posteriori] — Empiricism. He had problems with both methods. He never figured out why. Kant does! And he works out a solution to Hume's problems. It's a <u>third</u> method. What it boils down to is, he uses <u>both</u> methods — kind of a synthesis of (prior) "inborn reason" [a priori] and (post) "seeing and experience" [a posteriori]. Kant calls it a "synthetic a priori". Here's a practical example of it:

(true premiss 1) - The figure has three straight sides

(true premiss 2) - Only triangles have three straight sides

(true conclusion) - The figure is a triangle

Premiss 1 is true by "seeing and experience" [a posteriori]. We can <u>see</u> that the figure has three sides. Premiss 2 is true by "inborn reason" [a priori]. Triangles <u>must</u> have three sides, by definition of a triangle. Therefore the conclusion is absolutely guaranteed to be true. If the figure has three sides, and only triangles have three sides, then the figure has to be a triangle! It cannot be otherwise!

* That looks like the example you gave to show me Aristotle's system of logical deduction.

* It is. Aristotle called it "syllogistic" deductive reasoning. Remember? Kant calls it "transcendental" deductive reasoning [synthetic a priori] because it transcends — goes further than — both "inborn reason" [a priori] and "seeing and experience" [a posteriori]. But let's not get flustered with the fancy words. Let's keep it simple and from now on just call it — Kant's deductive reasoning! Okay?

* Sounds good to me! And do you know something, Thomas? It reminds me of a computer. Except in this case, the computer is my mind.

* That's what your mind <u>is</u>, Harry — a sophisticated computer.

* So let me get this straight, then. What I "see or experience" [a posteriori] is automatically fed into my mind-computer. My "inborn reason" [a priori] that's my built-in program processes it by, as you say, Kant's deductive reasoning. My mind-computer then spits out a conclusion about what I saw or experienced. Is that about right?

* Yes. But keep in mind, this is a monumental simplification of complex, awesome, and important thinking by Kant. And guess what's most important. It works! Emmanuel Kant pulls off the philosophical miracle of the century! He unravels the Gordian Knot that Hume had tied philosophy into! He saves philosophy! He saves his job! His reputation goes ballistic! He pulls the doubt back out, and puts the trust back into philosophy! And thanks for that! For now we can once again trust everything we have learned about virtues and leaders on our journey! That means it will all be possible to use someday at West Point![121]

Kant's deductive reasoning helps him escape from the rut he's been in for years at his University. He becomes an Enlightenment philosopher. And The Enlightenment has some nagging questions for him about God, justice, freedom, and immortality ... like, what are they? His answer is a surprise! He says, our mind is not capable of understanding what they are. They're concepts that exceed our mind's capacity to understand. But he concludes, we have the right to <u>believe</u> in all those concepts — even if they're beyond our understanding. In fact, he goes so far as to say we have a "moral necessity" to believe in them ... but not claim to know them.

Kant, the former slumbering giant of philosophy, even awakens to the romanticist parts of The Enlightenment — kind of like Rousseau. He puts out a full-blown analysis of the Arts in his work, <u>Aesthetics</u>. In it he recognizes a purpose to the Arts beyond aesthetics. He shows the Arts inspire people to think. He shows they relate to philosophy. Take the following poetic piece, for example. It's meant to inspire you to do your thing today while you are able to — for today will become the lost youth of your future years:

YOU CAN NEVER RETURN

adapted from: A.E. Housman

Into my heart an air that thrills
    From yon far homeland blows:
What are those faint remembered hills,
    What spires, what farms are those?

This is your home of lost content,
    You see it shining plain,
The happy places where you went,
    And can not come again.

The virtue is: Wisdom. Be wise enough to do things
    today while you can.

Now that Kant is shocked from his slumber, he really catches on fire! He publishes four major works in a row — all in the nine years between 1781 and 1790! That's a bunch of work — twenty-two volumes worth! Two of those works are vital to our interest, Harry. They are his <u>Critique of Practical Reason</u>, and his <u>Foundations of the Metaphysics of Morals</u>. Both are the groundwork needed to teach Virtue — morals, ethics, and character — along the way to developing good-leaders. They put Virtue on a solid, unchanging, philosophical foundation!
* So Virtue is (prior) "inborn reason" [a priori]?
* Yes! But don't ask me to give you the details. They're too complicated for now. You can study Kant's work to get the details. He fully explains how Virtue is a part of the "mind-computer's" built-in program. He also shows how "duty"

is on a level close to Virtue, above the other individual moral, ethical, and character virtues. For example, Kant shows it's a person's duty to not lie, and not cheat, and not steal, and not lust. Someday West Point will make those things part of its honor code!

* Then what about Plato's theory of "divine command"? Doesn't Kant agree with Plato that morals and ethics come from God's divine command?

* Kant does believe in God's divine command. And that's not surprising. He's a devout Lutheran Christian. Nevertheless, he is also out to justify good morals and ethics through the rigors of philosophical analysis and deduction — not merely through blind belief.

* Why does Kant say that duty is on a level above other moral, ethical, and character virtues like courage, patience, loyalty, and so on?

* Because he says your duty to acquire those virtues comes before actually aquiring them. If you first feel it's your duty to acquire the virtues, then you'll have the will to work hard at doing so. You'll work hard to do what's right, and avoid what's wrong!

* But how do I know what is right and what is wrong? How do I know what is my moral duty?

* Kant immediately recognizes that how to know the difference between right and wrong is a problem. He finds a solution. Using his new deductive reasoning, he concludes that you must "act according to a principle that can become the rule for everyone". Put simply it means that when tempted to do something, ask yourself: "what would happen to the world if everyone did this"? That's the simple guideline.

* I'm still not sure I understand what that means.

* Then let's look at a practical example. Imagine this guy named, let's say Hans, going to Kant for advice on a problem he has. This poor fellow has no inborn sense about what is right or wrong. So Kant has to give him a simple guideline:

"So Hans, you say you owe someone money? Millions? What
   have you thought about doing thus far to solve your problem?"
   "Well, if I kill him I won't have the debt anymore. That is a
      solution, isn't it Herr Kant! What do you think?"
ᵒᵒGood heavens! This man is devoid of conscience. Let me see.
   How do I get through to him? I know!ᵒᵒ "Hans. What if a rule
   said everyone must kill to solve their problems. Then everyone,
   eventually, would kill eachother. No one would be left even to
   follow that stupid rule. Would that work?"
   "I guess not. Then what if I lie to him by insisting that I
      already paid him. What about that?"
"If there was a rule that said everyone must lie, no one would
   believe anyone else. Why bother talking? We might as well
   revert back to swinging from tree to tree."
   "Then what if I actually give the money back … then steal it
      back again? That means I did, in fact, pay the debt!"

"Again, if a rule said <u>everyone</u> must steal, there could be no such thing as property. No possessions. Things would just go from person to person like the blink of an eye. It would be chaos."

"Hm. I'm stumped! It looks like I may actually have to repay my debt — or go to debtors jail?"

"It looks like it's your <u>duty</u> to repay it, Hans."[121]

So there you have an example of using Kant's guideline for determining right from wrong and knowing what your moral duty is. It may sound simple. Still, Kant says it's "categorically imperative" — an absolute obligation — that you use it to guide you on what is moral and ethical, and what isn't! For all the proofs and details, you can read Kant's masterpiece called <u>Foundations of the Metaphysics of Morals</u>. But, "act according to a principle that can be the rule for everyone," is his guideline. If there's a moral or ethical issue, ask: "what would happen if everyone did this"? Think about it, Harry!

Kant's <u>Foundations of the Metaphysics of Morals</u> is a major shift in thinking about morals, ethics, and character. It's not only that Kant studies morals, ethics, and character from the philosophical, rather than, religious basis. It's also because he proves that "duty" has a meaning far beyond a simple task-oriented individual virtue. It's on a higher level, like Trust and Honor. It's close to being (prior) "inborn reason" [a priori] — rock-solid and unchanging when everything else is changing. So when philosopher G.W.F. Hegel will someday show that "Country" is also (prior) "inborn reason" [a priori], you will have the ingredients of a famous motto — "Duty, Honor, Country".

* That's the motto of West Point!

* It's not merely a motto, Harry. It's more. It's a true rule of philosophy for leadership!

* I take it that <u>Foundations of the Metaphysics of Morals</u> is translated from German and circulated here in Europe during the 1780's?

* It certainly is! As we speak, it's likely finding its way to all corners of the Continent and England — and later, to America!

* Then every philosophy buff must surely read it — even Americans.
* Yes. In fact, there's an entourage of diplomats here in Europe from the new American nation right now. It includes Thomas Jefferson. He'll spend five years over here in Paris as America's ambassador to Europe.
* Then he must read Kant's books.
* Undoubtedly. For Kant's work is revolutionary. It becomes legendary how he saved philosophy from the stranglehold of Hume's philosophical Gordian Knot. He ranks among Plato, Aristotle, and Descartes as the greatest of philosophers. He's theoretically original, like Plato. He's encyclopedically thorough, like Aristotle. Yet, he's revolutionarily innovative, like Descartes. He's a true man of the Enlightenment. And best of all for us, Harry, he validates the philosophy of history — proves that lessons and virtues learned from history are built on bedrock, not on sand. And that's crucial. For we'll soon see that the American founders' ideologies and decisions are entirely drawn from Greek, Roman, and Enlightenment philosophy. That's why you and I are on this journey through the ages![123]

Emmanuel Kant dies in 1804. That's four years after George Washington dies. It's three years after Thomas Jefferson's Democratic Republicans wrench power for the first time from the Federalists. And it's just two years after the United States Military Academy at West Point is officially established in 1802.
* George Washington dead? What happened to all of those years? Are we going to by-pass George Washington?
* Don't worry, Harry. We'll see him.
* And who's running the United States? Did you say it's the Democratic Republicans?
* Yes. They come during Jefferson's presidency in 1801, after Washington and Adams. The Democratic Republicans are Thomas Jefferson's party.
* So is it actually Jefferson and the Democratic Republicans who will establish the United States Military Academy at West Point?
* That's right. And it will be unique … an original concept … a first.

* Oh? How so? How about those schools of Alexander the Great and the Royal Courts of Europe, and even Ignatius' Jesuit School? And what about the military academies in Europe right now?

* Europe has some academies for artillery and field studies. For example, it has the: Prussian Cadet Academy; Russian Noble Land Corps; Austrian Neustadt; French Ecole Militaire; and others in England. They're not academic institutions of higher learning, however. And many academies are little more than places to which wealthy families shunt off their sons during the difficult years of puberty. Ecole Militaire in Paris is an exception, however. It comes close to being what we call a college. Their famous graduate, Napoleon Bonaparte, went there at sixteen years old for an academic education but took a shine to the military part, instead. And you know the rest of the story. However, even the Ecole Militaire is not as unique as West Point!

* Why is that?

* Because the United States, itself, is unique and original. It's the first time an entire nation is a democratic republic. Democracies in the past — in Greece and Rome — were only city-states. They were not entire nations. The Ecole Militaire, and all the other military academies, served monarchies. Now the Ecole Militaire serves Napoleon's dictatorship of the 1800's. Our Academy at West Point is the first in history to serve a democratic republic and produce Officers that are "of the people, by the people, and for the people"!

* Then I can see how "Duty, Honor, Country" fits with a unique concept like West Point. As you say, it's not just a slogan. It's actually a description of leaders.

* And that's what General Douglas Mac Arthur will someday say in the famous speech he'll make to the Corps of Cadets at West Point during your century, Harry:

DUTY - HONOR - COUNTRY

adapted from: Gen. Mac Arthur's speech in 1962

Duty - Honor - Country, those three hallowed words,
    For a people who are free, they're freedom's great-
    est swords.
They build people's courage, when courage would fail,
    They help regain faith, when faith becomes frail;
They create new hope, when hope is forlorn,
    They build character, when character meets scorn;
They make you strong, when you're getting weak,
    They make you brave, when your fear's at peak.

They teach to be proud, when failure does stress,
    But humble remain, when you have success;
They teach to act only, when words will not do,

And comfort not seek, when challenge does sue;
They teach standing high, when the storm would call,
   But compassion yet have, when others should fall;
They teach master be, when others are meek,
   But first master self, if mast'ry you seek.

They teach you to laugh, when things become deep,
   But not forget how, when time comes to weep;
They teach to reach out, when the future is near,
   But the past not neglect, when the past was so
   dear;
They teach to be staid, when befitting to be,
   But not take yourself, too seriously;
They teach all that so, when you finish this Plan,
   An officer you'll be, and a gentleman.

The virtue is: Dedication. West Point produces dedicated
leaders for America.

* Interesting. In each pair of lines I hear Kant's simple moral guideline: "act according to a principle that can become the rule for everyone" — "what would happen if everyone did this?".
* Indeed. And, something like West Point can only happen when certain historical events bang up against certain philosophies at the same point in time!
* I hear you … but I don't quite get what you mean by that.
* I mean, for many centuries we saw things that already happened — history — drive philosophers to explain why those things happened. Then it flip-flopped. During the Renaissance, philosophers began to <u>cause</u> the things to happen — cause history. With that, a wave of "doubt and enlightenment" and opportunity — called The Enlightenment — began to build until it became a tidal wave. That tidal wave of Enlightenment crashed onto the shores of America. Enlightenment philosophy mixed with the historical circumstances in America. The result was an American Revolution. The Revolution led to many unique innovations. One of them was the military academy at West Point!
* So you're telling me the story behind West Point is a two part story. Philosophy. History.
* That's right, Harry. I've now shown you the philosophy part of the story. It's the very same stuff that America's founding fathers studied before they made their move. It's what inspired them. Now <u>you</u> know the philosophy <u>they</u> knew! Now you can better understand why they did the things they did. So, next up is history. I'm now going to show you how the history part of the story comes about in America. We'll go back again to the 1700's — the Enlightenment era. We saw what was happening over in Europe during that time. Now we'll see what was happening here in America. After that, we'll go on to put together the rest of the West Point Story![124]

5.

THE STORY BEHIND WEST POINT: THE HISTORY

To understand how and why West Point came about, you need to see the historical circumstances surrounding its founding. You are taken through America before, during, and after the Revolutionary War in a way that makes you see things with the eyes of someone who lived during that time.

CHAPTER 1: AMERICAN COLONIES

We're now back again in England's American colonies, Harry! It's around the year 1700. Remember, Enlightenment thinking in Europe is just beginning to catch on now. Locke's new empiricism in Britain is at odds with Leibnitz's rationalism in Europe. And Locke's political philosophies — life, liberty, property, rebellion — are causing a firestorm of debate in London. But here in America, that's not yet the case.

You can see that the colonists' time in America is occupied in other ways. They're making great progress carving out new communities. They've come a long way in the century since they landed at Plymouth, Massachusetts and Jamestown, Virginia. They've been cutting farms out of the raw wilderness. They've been building homes. They've been working the lands. They've been harvesting the seas. And now they're trading. So they've been self-dependent minded for a very long time. And lately, they're getting very independent minded!

* Why not. They're doing it themselves — their own way. They're living in nature and struggling to tame the wilderness.

* That's right. They're actually living the life of Rousseau's "noble savage", long before the back-to-nature bug ever buzzes in his ear. But they didn't come here to live in a raw land just to worship nature like some kind of Druids of ancient Gaul.

* I assume most come here to get away from it all — to start a new life?

* Get away from it all. Yes. They want to get away from the Old World way of thinking that believes: some people are created inferior to others; some people are the betters, others are the common herd; some people are ordinary, others are special; some people are noble and genteel, others are crude and dull; and, some are leaders by birth-right, others must never be allowed leadership.

The Old World believes your social status at birth plugs you, automatically, into a slot in the pecking order of society. But over here, if you work hard you can carve out your own slot and get ahead. In America, conscientiously working hard is a virtue. Henry Wadsworth Longfellow will talk about that virtue this way:

THE VILLAGE BLACKSMITH

excerpted from: H.W.Longfellow

Under a spreading chestnut tree
　　The village blacksmith stands;
The smith, a mighty man is he,
　　With large and sinewy hands.

His brow is wet with honest sweat,

He earns whate'er he can,
And looks the whole world in the face,
For he owes-not any man.

Toiling ... rejoicing ... sorrowing
Onward through life he goes;
Each morning sees some task begin,
Each evening sees it close.

Thanks to thee my worthy friend,
For the lesson thou hast taught!
For at the flaming forge of life,
Our fortunes must be wrought.

The virtue is: Conscientiousness. Opportunity comes to
those who conscientiously work hard.

* That's very fitting. It says people come to America for opportunity.
* Yes. For some, it's relgious opportunity. For others, it's opportunity for adventure. Some escape persecution. And some come because they hear stories of riches to be had. Then there are also those who come here to shed their chains — thieves, debtors, convicts, escaped convicts, and so on.
* Really? Criminals?
* That's right. This is open territory. You can get lost. Disappear. You can live completely free and start over again if you want to. However, everyone isn't completely free. There are black Africans who are brought here strictly to work as slaves. And guess what, Harry. There are also white Europeans who are brought here to work as, essentially, slaves! In fact, about half the total white Europeans who come over to the colonies are essentially slaves at one time or another. Except they're not called slave. They're called "indentured".
* I must have been day-dreaming the day they taught that in school. I never heard that.
* Well now you hear it! It's not commonly taught. But those debtors and criminals, as well as, religious folks and other ordinary people I mentioned are the "slaves". They have no money. Most have little more than the shirt on their back. Someone sponsors their boat passage to America. In return they're indentured. That means they legally belong to a master, usually the one who sponsored their boat passage. They're not free. They have to work for that master until he frees them.
London's docks are full of con-artists these days. They skulk around trying to fix people up with boat passages ... for a price. They lure the poor and unwary to what they call the American promised land. But they don't tell them they're signing their freedom away.
* How can they get away with that?
* There's a gimmick born every minute, Harry. This is a clever one. You can

175

picture what the victim and the con-man are each thinking as the scam is being executed :

"Come one, come all! London to America! Free!"
  "Where do I sign?" ⁰°Boy! Am I lucky!°⁰
"Just sign on the dotted line." °°Another sucker! That's ten already today!°⁰

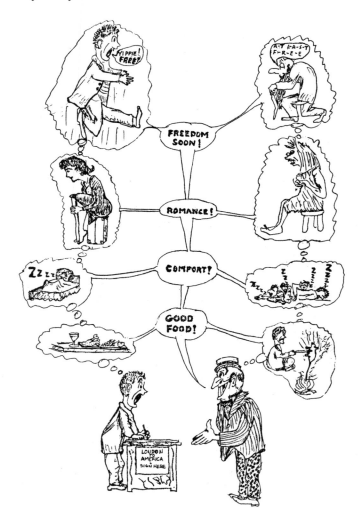

Now we'll go to Jamestown, Virginia to hear firsthand what's being said by folks just off the boat from England:

"Well, here we are! Finally, the New World — and dry land again!"

"Right you are. I'm anxious to start my new job. I'm in government work, you know — on a three year stint."

"Ohh yesss ...... The little Mrs. here and me are settling here. It took me years to save up for this trip! We'll pick up a little piece of ground to farm on. And we'll start a family. We're just on having a boy, we reckon! He'll be, Bob. Like me. He can grow up here with his head held high! No over-stuffed, flabby-faced, royalists can get up to bossing him around! That bloke in London took all our money — the last of our savings — to fix us up with this trip. So we'll not be going back!"

"All your money? I say! Sharp practice, that is! But now you're here ... all the best to you!"

"Ta! You too, gov!"

That's someone who paid his own fare. Now there's another group over there who are "sponsored", and about to get the shock of their lives. Let's hear what they have to say:

"Caw! Bloody awful trip! Awful conditions in that tub they call a ship! Nothing to eat — only occasional breast-o-rat! Or worms! And putrid water! And too crowded to sit down — much less sleep! That bloke at the London docks was a con artist! He made this sound like a holiday trip to the land of milk and honey — where everyone gets rich and respectable! Now they tell me I have to work for nothing — like a slave! They now tell me I'm to be some fat-cat's servant until they let me go! I didn't know what I was signing. I thought I was signing to learn a trade or something! And you? Where you off to?"

"Oh, I'm like you! But I'm in America five years already! I'm just unloading Master's cargo here today. And with the interest they put on my boat-fare debt, I'll not be able to pay it off in my lifetime! They'll probably hold it over my children too! I'm no different than them wretched Africans over there — on that slave ship. Poor sods. They're probably stuck for life, too! And them and me both are no different than them there horses over there. We're assets! Property! Like them horses! I'm domestic slave-labor! Them there Africans are plantation slave-labor! See them convicts and thieves from London's jails being dumped off over there? We ain't much better than them!"

"Blimey! Where am I off to, then?"

"Who knows, mate! Perhaps you're alright! Perhaps lady luck'll smile on you! I heard about one lucky bloke who got a good Master! He's practically free now ... working as an apprentice woodworker! So mate, it's the luck of the draw for you and them Africans whether you get a good master!"[1]

177

So I'll bet you didn't know there are different kinds of slavery in America at this time, Harry, did you? And I'll bet you don't know it's philosophy that will bring about the end of slavery!

* Oh? How do you figure that?

* First, take <u>moral</u> philosophy. It'll prompt many people to follow their conscience and free their African slaves. Some former African slaves even "make it" and get rich. James Forten of Philadelphia is an example. Many slaves and former slaves will be lured away by the British during the Revolutionary War. They'll "vote with their feet" and make off to the British side. But not James Forten. He'll fight for the American side. When the war is over he'll go into the sailmaking business. He had learned the trade from his father — a former slave and master sailmaker. Forten will become one of Philadelphia's richest and most distinguished citizens. Although many Africans will go over to the British side, thousands of the close to 300,000 soldiers who fought at one time or other in the Revolutionary War will be Africans ... like James Forten!

Next, take <u>scientific</u> philosophy — science. It will lead to inventions of machines. Machines will end massive labor needs. You don't need slaves if you don't need massive amounts of cheap labor!

Last, take <u>political</u> philosophy. It leads to freedom under the law. You can't have slaves forever if you're committed to freedom for all under the law!

* Then why do good, hard-working colonists allow having slaves?

* First of all, most colonists don't favor slavery ... and don't have slaves! Second, they're busy with their own families, just trying to survive. And third, slavery is still a fact of life in the world at this time. It has existed since the beginning of time. There's no means for ordinary people to kill and bury it overnight. The best way to stop it is to cut it off at the source in Africa. The problem with that is, too many Africans are making big money "trading" other Africans.

* You're telling me slavery throughout the world isn't unusual in 1700?

* That's exactly what I'm telling you. It's not moral, but not unusual. It hasn't been unusual for centuries. And slavery of all kinds is crucial in 1700's America. For instance, slaves — white and black — will someday do most of the fighting in the Revolution in order to buy their freedom. To understand a century you have to see with the eyes of that century. Sometimes it's difficult to do. But let's try right now, shall we? It's an important detour for us.

* Whatever you say, Thomas.

* Slavery began when history began! China. India. Ancient Mesopotamia. They all had slaves. And <u>not</u> black Africans! Ancient Egypt and Persia had Jews and others from the Middle East building their temples and pyramids. Aztecs and Incas used their people as slaves. And how did the unlucky ones become slaves? First, entire populations of peoples defeated in wars, raids, and conquests would be enslaved by the victors. Then, debtors and criminal offenders would sell themselves, and often their families, into slavery. It was their only way to avoid death or punishment. The rich and ruling class always had an endless appetite for slave labor. It was neither economical nor necessary to pay for labor.

* Why buy the cow or pay the farmer when you can get the milk for free? Is that how it was?

* Even worse. Slavery meant they got the cow itself for free. Even in the good democracies of Greece and Rome, slavery — white slavery — fueled their economies. Aristotle was a rare opponent of slavery. He broke with practice and tried to talk rulers into giving loyal and faithful slaves their freedom. Remember Epictetus? He was a freed slave!

* Maybe that's why Aristotle got into deep do-do with the city fathers of Athens?

* Perhaps. Later, when Christianity became powerful, the Church pushed to stamp out slavery. The Church had its moral problems in the Middle Ages. But slavery wasn't one of them. So, the rich and ruling class had to cook up another system of slavery. And they did. They called it the "feudal system"! And they gave it a new twist. They took to calling what is essentially slavery — "serfdom". But gradually, even serfdom became difficult and unrealistic to operate because of business and a money economy. So rich landlords got their lawyers to concoct clever new devices that re-packaged serfdom. One such device was called "peonage"!

Serfdom would last until well after the Middle Ages. Peonage would be legal all the way into the 1870's in some parts of Europe such as Poland, Russia, Prussia, and other Eastern European countries! Can you believe that! It's true! Unofficially, it probably even went on long after that. And all of this is only white European slavery. Then there's black African slavery.

Black African slavery arose when Arabs, and later, Europeans conquered coastal and central Africa. For centuries, Arab traders had sold the conquered black Africans to Arabs and India. Then in 1619 the first black Africans, bought from black African traders, were brought to Jamestown, Virginia by the English. At first they were put into servitude like the Indians and the indentured whites. By the time of the Revolutionary War in 1775, however, their rights would be curbed. Their only rights were: marriage; a trial; personal property; legal contracts; religious education; limited free time; and, support in sickness and old age. Contrary to general reputation, practices such as branding, chaining, or beating were forbidden. But, while not common, instances of cruelty to some slaves did occur. And the woe-be-gone practice of buying and selling black African slaves at public auction was not forbidden.

* And white European "slaves" were not bought and sold under serfdom or peonage?

* They were also bought and sold, but not often at a public auction. If a landowner sold his holdings, serfs or peons on his estate under peonage or serfdom were part of the sale. They were part of the capital assets — just like other property. But that was mostly done privately. It's kind of like your modern times, Harry. Little pieces of businesses — shares — can be sold on the open stock market at public auction, or, in a closed transaction privately. But another grim prospect for what became a majority of black Africans due to their increasing number was ... they could end up being slaves for life!

* So when the rights of black Africans are curbed here in the 1700's, that means all black Africans become slaves for life?

* No, not in all cases. Only those sold by their black African village leaders, jammed onto ships, and sent here around 1800 and after will almost always become slaves for life. But not those who are in America before that!

* How about white Europeans in serfdom, peonage, or indenture?
* Serfdom and Peonage are also usually for life. And interest on debts of indentured white's are purposely so inflated, those poor sods are also often slaves for life. But those cases are not the majority. In the case of 1800's black Africans, the majority will be slaves for life!

So, seeing slavery with the eyes of ordinary colonists here in the early 1700's, we know it's immoral but not unusual. Like the serfs and the peons of Europe at the time, black Africans are assets of their owner's business. Owners have paid for them. That cost is built into their overall business costs. Even the most compassionate owner couldn't free his slaves without losing everything. How could he convince the rest of America to do so? The Ancients started slavery! And it has gone on right up to now in the 1700's!

The Declaration of Independence will come along in 1776. It will say, "All men are <u>created</u> equal". And God not only <u>created</u> people equal, but intended everyone to <u>remain</u> equal. Therefore, by 1776, slavery will be illegal in most Northern States! The North will have freed all but 30,000 slaves! And even those 30,000 will be scheduled for freedom by 1804!

The agricultural South will have 800,000 slaves. Freeing them would wreck the economy of Southern States. So, after the Revolution, the Constitutional Convention of 1787 will not be able to get southern delegates to accept a Constitution that abolishes slavery immediately. The best it will get is a phasing out of the slave trade by 1808. But at least that vile practice will be scheduled to end. The South will have had time to re-fit its economy by then. And most delegates at the Convention will say that slavery is drying up all by itself, anyway. They predict it will completely dry up by 1808. And if it doesn't, the 1808 deadline will kick-in to finish the job!

Well, it doesn't dry up. And the 1808 deadline doesn't kick-in to finish-off slavery. In fact, nothing comes of the 1808 deadline. Why? Because the Industrial Revolution in Britain will kick-in. It will have things called "machines". These machines will have ravenous appetites for cotton.

England will bait the hook to suit the fish. Its orders to America will soar. So need for plantation labor will not dry-up. It will also soar. In the early 1800's, slavery will boil and bubble. But the Constitution also won't dry-up. Constitutional arguments will also boil and bubble — for decades. The slavery issue will rage on. That is, until a million white males will be killed and maimed in a Civil War they'll fight over slavery in the 1860's. That War will probably be partly responsible for halting Europe's peonage slavery, also. What sane European ruler in the 1860's will risk human butchery like America's Civil War in <u>his</u> country?

So when slavery ends over in Europe, folks will no longer be tied to the land or a master. They'll be allowed to emigrate to America. It's no wonder America will have a flood of imigrants from Ireland, Poland, Russia, and Eastern Europe during the late 1800's. And they're not the only ones. Asians, Mexicans, Caribbeans, and American Indians who lived under a peonage type of slavery will also be welcomed and become citizens![2] The words on the Statue of Liberty that will stand in New York harbor in the future will symbolize all of this:

MOTHER OF EXILES

excerpt: from Emma Lazarus' New Colossus,
about Bartholdi's Statue of Liberty.

"Keep, ancient lands, your storied pomp,"
  Cries she with silent lips.
"Give me your tired, your poor, Your huddled masses
  yearning to breath free, The wretched refuse of your
  teaming shore. Send these, the homeless, tempest-
  tossed to me, I lift my lamp beside the golden door!"

The virtue is: Compassion. America helps those who help
themselves.

The point I'm trying to make, Harry, is that America's heritage — including West
Point — is for all Americans! It doesn't matter how and why you and your ancestors came to be here. But it does matter that you and all Americans understand
how and why the United States came to be here. And that's what we'll get back
to now — seeing how the United States came to be.

So here in the 1700's, half the ordinary folks have felt the sting of living under
some form of slavery at one time or other. The other half have felt the sting of
prejudice and snobbery from the so called noble and genteel upper crust of society. So it's little wonder that ordinary folks deeply appreciate ideas such as freedom and liberty. It's little wonder they and their children will get fired up about
fighting for freedom and liberty — and for independence from England — later
this century in 1775. The American colonists are beginning to catch the spirit of
The Enlightenment!

* You mean the spirit of being self-sufficient and independent-minded, like you
mentioned before?

* Yes. And also the spirit of equality — the idea that ordinary folks are just as
good, competent, deserving, and valuable as the upper crust. Behavior is changing. Automatic respect for the upper crust is slipping ... especially in cities like
Boston. For instance, listen to this fine English gentleman of authority accompa-
nying his wife on a Sunday afternoon stroll:

"Just one more year now, Madame, and we may return to the gentle rolling hills and dales of our beloved England."
  "Is that your wish, Sir? May we not remain here so long as
    pleases us?"
"Of course we may, Madame. But conditions here are on the
  wane. Discipline on the decline. Respect for our caste is want-
  ing — even from the ordinary riff-raff! Here now, look at that
  peddler, or whatever, we just walked past. In other days he
  would have doffed his hat to us. No respect, I say!"

"And everything has that frightful fish-smell."

"Yes. It's those fishoil-based housepaints, you know."

"And muddy side walks. The servants are forever packing our attire off to England for cleaning."

"This provincial lot wants bringing down a peg or two. One gets the impression they think they're as good as we are."[3]

"Perhaps you shall leave that job to another generation, Sir?"

* I see what you mean, Thomas. Those two see a different attitude emerging here than in the Old World.

* It's inevitable. Look at it from the point of view of the big picture of the world — of life, what it is, and what it's all about. Civilization in the Old World is what it is — for better or for worse. There's no going back. What's done is done. Change can only be made by modifying what's there now. But this virgin continent called America is new. It gives humanity a fresh start — a second chance to do it right. It's like constructing a building. There are less problems designing and erecting a new one than making additions and alterations to an existing one. And how many times have you heard someone say, "I wish I were young again and knew what I know now"? Well, that's what Americans have here. They have the opportunity to start from scratch — but with the wisdom of the ages under their belt!

* I can see that. America is still unspoiled. And it has no "sacred cows" that cannot be changed, like Europe has.

* Correct! It's still possible in this new land to put an old soul into a young country! Ideas from the wisest men of all time can be put into action here. Ideas from the ancients — leaders like Moses, Jesus, St. Paul, Homer, Socrates, Plato, Aristotle, Cicero, Tacitus, Livy, and many others who reacted to the world and events, and proceeded to explain them. Ideas from men of the Renaissance like Machiavelli who flip-flopped philosophy — who started by telling the way it is, and finished by telling the way it ought to be. Ideas from St. Ignatius, Galileo, Montaigne, Descartes, Bacon, Coke, and other philosophers who continued to tell us the way it ought to be. And ideas from men of the Enlightenment like Newton, Locke, Rousseau, Kant, Montesquieu, Bolingbroke, and Adam Smith who caused events to happen — drove history. All of these ideas can be put into action right here. And they will be. They'll be here through the eyes and minds of future leaders in 1700's America!

St. Paul transmitted the teachings of Jesus into what became Christianity. Rome transmitted Greek culture into Roman Europe. The Arabs, and the Jews from Spain, transmitted Aristotle into Europe. Soon James Otis, Samuel Adams, Patrict Henry, Thomas Paine, and the "founding fathers" will transmit ideas from all these great philosophers to ordinary folks ... and into a new form of government. It'll be the most unique and practical implementation of philosophy ever done. It'll be the greatest philosophical experiment of all time. The work, ideas, and dedication of the giant thinkers of all time will finally be redeemed and bear fruit. They'll all be part of a new kind of civilization — embodied in the United States of America. The revolution in the hearts and minds of folks in America has already begun, Harry. Now I'll tell you how this revolution of hearts and minds turns into a shooting revolution for independence from England!

CHAPTER 2: PRE-REVOLUTION

Europe had come through centuries of wars caused by religion. We saw the wars of Reformation and Counter-Reformation between Protestant Christians and Catholic Christians. Even Cromwell's army in the English Civil War was mostly Puritan Christians. Now Europe finds something else besides religion to fight over. It's LAND. MONEY. ECONOMIC POWER. The major players in this new kind of war will be Spain, France, and England. Their fighting will chew up another hundred years. Much of the fighting will take place in and around America.

We're now in the 1750's. Spain, France, and England all have their teeth into America. But who gets what? The question begs for an answer. It can't go on this way. Take the Ohio River valley for instance. It's the gateway to westerly lands. You can slide along the Ohio River clear out to the Mississippi Valley. England claims the Ohio River is theirs. They say that they bought it from the Indians. The French, however, don't buy that claim. The Indians never owned it, they say. It wasn't theirs to sell. The French go by "catch as catch can". Possession is the law. So they build a strategically located stronghold called Fort Duquesne on the lands claimed by England. It's what will someday become Pittsburgh.

The English don't want a French fort on their lands in what's known at this time as the western Virginia territory. They muster 150 men from the Colonial branch of the British Army to kick the French out. Virginia's Governor puts a twenty-one year old commissioned Major — a land-surveyor — in charge of the expedition. They have a run-in with a French Army detachment outside of Fort Duquesne. Ten French soldiers are killed. This happens in 1754. Six years of fighting will follow! It will become known to us as the French and Indian War!

The young Major from Virginia in charge of the expedition to Fort Duquesne is someone named — George Washington. As a boy, George dreamed of military glory. Commentaries, by Caesar, is his military role model. Now he has had his first taste of action. He has fired the shot that "sets the world on fire"!

The name, George Washington, becomes an instant household word around the colonies in Boston, New York, and Philadelphia. It's even bandied about in London and Paris by the English and the French. England sends one of its crack generals, General Edward Braddock, with thousands of troops to join up with Major Washington. So, "catch as catch can" is the way France wants to play the game? Alright! Then Braddock will play it that way too! He'll catch the French with his superior force and drive them out of the Ohio Valley!

That's how it's supposed to work. But it doesn't! Braddock's army gets annihilated! Braddock is killed! Washington has two horses shot out from under him and finishes with four bullet holes in his coat! He luckily escapes death! This all happens in spite of the superior English force outnumbering their French and Indian foes by two to one!

We'll go there to see the English Army returning and hear about what happened from some of the Virginia boys:

"A massacre is what it was. Plain and simple!"

"You can't call it anything else! There we were all lined up ready to release a god-awful volley at the enemy lines. But an enemy line never appeared."

"That's right. Suddenly musket-fire came at us from all sides! We were in the middle! Surrounded! The French and Indians were hiding all around. They wore skins and bushes to blend in with the woods. We couldn't even see who to shoot at!"

"And there we were. The British in bright red. We Virginians in blue. It was a sight to behold when we were marching through the rich green forest. But we also turned out to be great targets for those cowards!"

"Then the Indians started screaming! You know, those blood-chilling war cries they like to do. That's when the British panicked!"

"That's right. They broke and ran like sheep being chased by dogs! And two out of three of our side got killed or wounded! The British Army's not as infallible as I thought!"[4]

* It sounds like the French and Indians gave the English side a clinic on guerilla warfare!

* And you'll later see that the Colonists learned something from that "clinic", too. Right now, however, they'll help the English and the Iroquois Indians go on to important victories. Six years later in 1760 the French will surrender at Montreal. Hostilities between France and England in America will come to an end.

At the Treaty of Paris, England takes all the marbles. It kicks France out of North America! England becomes the exclusive landlord. The Iroquois League — a confederation of six tribes — gets a handshake and a thin treaty that couldn't hold water. The American Colonists get experience. They experience victory in battle without the English Army's help — most notably at Lake George. They get the taste of military leadership. They experience being "united" for the first time when the Albany Congress — a meeting of the Colonies — had approved Benjamin Franklin's plan for a Union of Colonies to help England fight France. And most important, they experience how unremarkable the legendary British Army really is. All of this experience will be useful. For just fifteen years from now in 1775, you'll see them again "join" British troops on the field of battle — this time looking down the wrong end of British musket barrels!

For now though, the British troops are finally leaving. Let's watch the pomp and circumstance down at the docks of Boston as they leave. British troops wave goodbye from their ships. Colonists wave and shout goodbye from the dock:

"So long! Thanks for helping us. Have a nice trip back to
England!" ᵒᵒAnd good-riddens too!ᵒᵒ
"Yeh! Safe journey! Come again!" ᵒᵒOops! Huzzahs!
They're finally going! I thought they'd never leave!ᵒᵒ
"Goodby, God-bless!" ᵒᵒOur problems are over.ᵒᵒ [5]

Little do the Colonists know, it's only goodby till they meet again ... not forever. And it's not the end of their problems. It's the beginning of new ones. For the War drained England's Treasury. The King and his Ministers — the Crown — are strapped. And they can't squeeze more taxes out of people in England.[6]
* Why not? The King can do anything, can't he?
* That's been the most imaginative fiction written about England's monarchy, Harry. You see, taxes were already somewhat controlled way back before 1000 AD in Saxon England. There was that loose agreement between the Crown and landholding nobility known as the Ancient Constitution. Then came the Magna Carta in 1215 AD and the Glorious Revolution in 1688. Remember? All those

186

things had curbed the King's power. So he can't levy taxes in England on the people without their consent. That means Parliament has to approve them. And right now … it won't. But the people in the Colonies are 3600 miles away. They don't count … supposedly … because they're not in England. The Crown reckons it doesn't need Parliament's consent to put taxes on them. It reckons the Colonies should help pay for the French and Indian War. So the Crown jumps right in and puts new trade taxes on the Colonies![7]

Merchants, businessmen, and plantation owners in the Colonies are raking in big profits. Why should they give part of them to England? So lots of people make a mockery of the new trade taxes. They smuggle everything in … right under the noses of customs officers. Smuggling becomes so blatant that the Crown becomes frustrated. They allow what's called "general warrants". Ships, houses, or anything else can be boarded or entered or searched … and siezed! Almost anything is allowed, as long as smuggling is curbed!

Merchants in the Colonies blow their gaskets! They challenge this new "general warrants" law — the Writs of Assistance. It goes to the Massachusetts Supreme Court in Boston. And who steps up to speak for the merchants? A lawyer named **James Otis**. He was the King's Advocate General before he resigned over the Writs of Assistance — this very issue!

The case is decided in favor of the Crown, of course. But Otis becomes popular. He captured the spotlight. He had cleverly remolded the Writs of Assistance issue into a general issue on rights and liberty. He had turned both workers' and merchants' gripes into <u>philosophical causes</u>. Listen to what ordinary workers around the courthouse are saying about it:

> "Did you hear what Mr. Otis said? He said every man's house is
> his castle. Catchy phrase … isn't it. I like it!"
> "Yes. But what he means is we have rights … just like
> Englishmen over in England. He said the right to life and
> privacy comes before raising taxes. Freedom and liberty are
> inborn and come from God … not from the King!"
> "Yes, I'd like to find out more about this!"

And Listen to what merchant types leaving the courthouse say:

> "Otis has hit on something here."
> "What do you mean? We lost the case again. England and
> their upity-up ruling class puppets over here think of us as
> second class citizens. And they're holding us back. We can
> be great over here. There's fabulous potential in America.
> So what do you mean he hit on something? We're no better
> off than we were!"
> "I mean we can't get what we want by ourselves. We need sup-
> port. And who else is there? Only these ordinary workers. They
> have the same rights as we do according to Otis. So why not all
> join together?"

"Good idea! I'd like to find out more about this!"[8]

* The workers and merchants both said they want to find out more about what James Otis talked about. That's interesting!
* Indeed. They both find out they have more legal rights — even as second-class citizens — than most other people in the world. They don't have enough to keep them fat, happy, and quiet. But they have just enough freedom to get them on the road to revolution!
* Ah. I see what you mean.
* That day in Court in 1761, James Otis connected with a lot of people. He gave a philosophical lesson — the first of many — drawn from ideas of Locke, Montesquieu, Voltaire, and Rousseau. He clued people in about their liberties being trampled on. A young John Adams, future President, was there that day. Here's what he says about what he heard:

JAMES OTIS' WRITS OF ASSISTANCE SPEECH

by: John Adams

"Otis was a flame of fire! American independence was there and then born; the seeds of patriots and heroes were then and there sown. Then and there we saw the first scene of the first act of our opposition to Great Britain!"

The virtue is: Enthusiasm. It's contagious.

Otis becomes a member of the Massachusetts Colonial Assembly. That gives him time and opportunity. He has the time to write and circulate philosophical information about rights and freedom. He has the opportunity to make speeches. He knocks the monarchy — contrasts it with the justice of ancient Greece. He rouses people. The pastime in Boston becomes street demonstrations over injustice … with even some rioting. He encourages lawsuits. Law Courts are log-jammed with all kinds of Complaints. Lawyers love it. Lawyers love Otis. He's making them rich! England hates it. England hates Otis. He's defying them!

King George III calls for teaching the American "ingrates" a lesson! Those "ingrate" colonies are not just ordinary colonies of the British Empire, however. They have all the trappings of being Britain's own private third world country: cheap raw materials; captive markets; and, ready dumping ground for social undesirables.

* That sure sounds like a third world country to me.

* Sounds like it ... but it's not. Why? Because the American Colonies are prosperous. They're like diamonds in the rough. Population is exploding. It's now 2.5 million. Business is booming. The middle class is growing. An upper class — of wealth, not nobility — is appearing. Up North, this upper class is made up of merchants and businessmen. Down South, it's owners of large plantations — once those small farmers you saw struggling to clear the raw wilderness.

Since the late 1600's they've been sending their sons away to study the great philosophers. Most up North go to Yale, Harvard, or New Jersey College (now Princeton). Southerners opt for college over in England, if they don't go to William and Mary in Virginia. It takes no longer by boat to England than overland to New England during these times.

* No Southerners have been going to colleges in New England?

* Some have. But Puritanism exerts a mighty influence on the lifestyle in New England. So it depends on how a particular Southerner likes Puritanism's strict and austere lifestyle of work, thrift, charity, and worship of God. And then there's another religious consideration. There's a religious movement in the 1740's known as the "Great Awakening". It's started by a spell binding evangelist from England named George Whitefield. His fire and brimstone splits Protestant Christians! There are the "Old Lights" — Quakers and Anglicans. And there are the "New Lights" — Methodists, Presbyterians, and Baptists — begun by the new revival followers of George Whitefield. So religion does influence a college-bound young Southerner. In any event, rights, freedom, science, politics — Enlightenment philosophy — has been seeping into education at colonial colleges. That's how some men, like James Otis, know about the ideas of Plato, Aristotle, Locke, Rousseau, Newton, and other philosophers.

The Crown sees all of this: merchants' purses bulging; thriving Southern plantations; expensive travel; high-priced college educations. King George III says the whole point of having colonies is to make <u>England</u> rich, not make <u>colonists</u> rich! Most of his ministers see no merit in Otis' arguments about rights. They're minds are fixed on how to stop colonists from smuggling ... and how to teach them a lesson!

* Then I'm surprised England doesn't take more drastic action here and now.

* King George <u>III</u> is young. And he's no intellectual whiz-kid. But he's old enough and smart enough to know you shouldn't kill your cash cow just because you can't squeeze more cash out of it. He probably has been taught the ancient fable about the goose that lays the golden eggs:

THE GOOSE THAT LAID THE GOLDEN EGGS

taken from: Aesop

A man and wife had a goose that laid a golden egg every day. But they started to think they were not getting rich fast enough! They imagined the goose was made of gold inside. So, they killed it to get the whole store of gold inside all at one time! When they cut it open they found it was just like any other goose! Thus, they neither got rich fast nor got their daily golden egg! "Much" wanted "more" — and lost it all!

The virtue is: Temperance. Don't be greedy and "kill the goose that lays the golden egg".

* Then what does young King George III do?
* He appoints a new Prime Minister, George Grenville. Old George Grenville is an expert bean-counter. The more he pours over the books, the more shocked he becomes. They're in horrible shape. The Crown's been running a sloppy ship. It's time to tighten up. And there's only one way to do it. Reform the entire scheme of tariffs with the Colonies. That translates into — tighten down on them!

So old George the bean counter reports to young George the King. Here's about how it goes:

"With no disrespect to Your Majesty, it appears our country bumpkin cousins in the Colonies are not such bumpkins after all.

We're soaking them with tariffs in both directions. We're supposed to get those bumpkins coming and going. But we're getting precious little, considering the huge amount of trade."
    "I knew they were ingrates! We fight wars to protect them
    and they cheat us!"
"Here's what I propose, Your Majesty. Nail them down to the
coastal regions where we can keep track of them to collect
taxes."
    "Excellent! We'll close the western lands to them so they
    can't get us into another war with the Indians."
"I have a list of new goods to tax — the kind that are not so easy
to smuggle."
    "Good idea!"
"Now the next idea is the centerpiece! It's to get better compli-
ance on the big <u>sugar tax!</u> Ready for this? Decrease the tax a bit,
but arrest and try anyone suspected of smuggling."
    "By Jove! That's putting teeth into it!"
"And what's more Your Majesty, hold the trials in Nova Scotia."
    "Smashing old man! … Why in Nova Scotia?"
"Because they will be tried by only a judge — no jury. And those
convicted pay the costs. So it will prevent riots, by merely hold-
ing them outside the Colonies. And, it's legal outside the
Colonies."
    "Top drawer! Now we'll show them not to mess with the
    great English Crown, George!" ºº I knew I was right to pick
    you because your name is George!ºº
"With your permission, Your Majesty, I thought we might call it
… The Sugar Act!"[9]

The Sugar Act outrages Colonial businessmen — merchants and farmers alike!
It outrages James Otis! He writes and speaks against it in New England. He cir-
culates letters of protest to the other Colonies. Surprisingly, they agree with him.
He gets back letters of support from most other Colonies.

Businessmen now feel the squeeze of Grenville's taxes. The Crown is sticking
its hands into their pockets. So businessmen put the squeeze on workers. Now
workers are outraged, too! They join businessmen and rally to the cause of James
Otis and other "radical activists"!

Grenville wants to soak the Colonists further. But he fears labor's protests. So
now he comes up with a little something for the professions. It's another fabulously stupid "red-herring". The Stamp Act! Colonists now have to buy paper
from England that has a special stamp on it. The paper <u>must</u> be used for pamphlets, licenses, newspapers, legal papers, business documents, and so forth. And
it's expensive. So now Grenville has outraged the professionals — the doctors,
lawyers, clergy, publishers, and so on. They join with farmers, businessmen, and
laborers. Even highly respected English parliamentarians in London, such as
William Pitt, voice their outrage. Grenville has <u>everyone</u> outraged!

Otis proclaims, "taxation without representation is tyranny"! And that's the rub. Colonists are represented in their Colony's Assembly ... not in Parliament in London. A Colony's Assembly taxes the colonists for money needed to run the Colony. On the other hand, England gives little, and gets much. Now England wants even more. So now it's also putting taxes on the colonists directly from England. But colonists still have no representation in the Parliament! They're the only Englishmen taxed directly by Parliament that have no representation in Parliament!

Uppercrust loyalists on both sides of the Atlantic are shocked when they hear what Otis proclaimed. They call it treason. But William Pitt and others in England agree with Otis. So do some ace, radical, grass-roots agitators in Boston. Behind some of these radical agitators who I will tell you about later, the people take to the streets of Boston. They're ready to go on a rampage. Right now they're protesting outside the stamp-tax collector's house:

"You men ... listen here! You have God-given rights! Taxing
people without representation in Parliament is nothing but tyranny!
Why should our money fill King Georges's pockets?!"
　"Yeh! These uppercrust folks wear velvet suits, yet squeeze
　the last penny out of us!"
"Right! They have no compassion. They hog all the goodies for
themselves, then throw us the scraps!"
　"Yeh! We shopkeepers have a right to make a little profit
　too!"
"Yeh! And we sailors have a right to a decent wage!"
　"Yeh! And that goes for all us laborers too!"

(inside the house)

"That mob out there is after us, Andrew! See what you've done
now! I told you not to accept the job of tax collector just because
Boston's Lieutenant Governor is my brother! Now what are you
going to do? So go ahead now then Andrew. DO SOMETHING!
Say something to that rabble out there!"
　"Yes dearest. ...... Say! You out there! See here now!
　What's the meaning of this!? Who are you, anyway?" ∘∘I
　can't pick out those troublemakers, James Otis and Samuel
　Adams, with all those masks this lot is wearing. But I know
　they're out there, though.∘∘ "And you! You youngsters out
　there? Where are your parents! I shall have a word with
　them about this! Who are you the sons of?"

"Who we the sons of? We're the Sons of Liberty!"
　"Sons of Liberty! Yeh! That's catchy! I like it! Where did
　you get that from?"
"Yeh! Has a nice ring to it, doesn't it!"

192

"Ask them what they want, Andrew. Go on."

"State your business here! Otherwise, clear off!" ᵒᵒUh oh!ᵒᵒ

"Oh Yehhh! Right then! We will! You asked for it! We want to know, what's your fancy? Hanging in effigy? Tar and feathers? Trashing your house? Burning your carriage? What will it be! Take your pick!"

"See, you've made them angry now, Andrew. Do something!" ᵒᵒFirst thing would be to shut you up.ᵒᵒ "Wait! Don't do anything rash! Don't do anything — ᵒᵒI'll regretᵒᵒ — you'll regret! I'll tell you what! I quit! I hereby resign as tax collector"!

"Too late, mate! Trash the house! Hang'em in effigy! Come on, boys! Let's get this done!"[10]
(all shouting) "Yeh! Yeh! Yeh!"

The scene gets ugly, Harry. There's no need for us to see it.

* Do they hang a dummy of the collector in effigy?

* Yes. They also trash the house … along with others owned by uppercrust English loyalists in Boston. That includes the Governor's Mansion! And during the next couple of days they continue on a rampage, here and in other towns, doing more house trashings, hangings in effigy, and tar-and-featherings. By the end of 1765 Sons of Liberty groups get people to boycott and disrupt business with England all around the Colonies. By 1766 England feels the pinch. Parliament repeals the Stamp Act!

They can't repeal the colonist's interest in freedom, however! People educate themselves in political philosophy. They read pamphlets and articles circulated by a core of radicals. Agitators bring the great philosopher's ideas down to earth.

People think about political freedom and other things that haven't been done before. The following says it very well:

THINGS THAT HAVEN'T BEEN DONE

from: Edgar Guest

The things that haven't been done before,
    Those are the things to try;
Columbus dreamed of an unknown shore
    At the rim of the far-off sky.
And his heart was bold and his faith was strong
    As he ventured to dangers new,
And he paid no heed to the jeering throng
    Or fears of his doubting crew.

The things that haven't been done before,
    Are the tasks worthwhile today;
Are you one of the flock that follows,
    Or one that shall lead the way?
Are you one of the timid souls that quail
    At the jeers of a doubting crew,
Or dare you, whether you win or fail,
    Strike out for a goal that's new?

The virtue is: Initiative. Everyone respects those who
take the initiative to do something new.

Next year in 1767, England gets a new Chancellor of the Exchequer named Charles Townshend. He dreams up a new scheme of taxes to ram down the Colonists' throats. His "Townshend Act" brings the coalition of farmers, merchants, workers, and sailors back together. And they're led by those same ace agitators and Sons of Liberty. They take to the streets as they had done a couple of years before. But this time, Otis and friends are organized over a broader sweep. This time, they get Assemblies from other Colonies to formally join a boycott!

Nobody buys anything made in England. That outrages King George III. He orders the Colonial Assemblies to be disbanded. The Colonies thumb their noses at him. They knock together their own Assemblies. No problem. In fact, they love it. The Crown hates it. They're infuriated! Prime Minister North's blood boils. He threatens to send in the army. Otis blasts North. He says standing armies produce dictators like Caesar in ancient Rome, and Cromwell in England. No matter. In 1768 British troops land in Boston. They have a strict mission. Stop people from assembling. No meetings. No demonstrations. No Sons of Liberty rallies. And no sessions of the "illegal" Colonial Assembly. No nothing!

194

British troops and the people of Boston harass each other. Tension is so thick you can cut it with a knife. Everyone's on edge. On a snowy day in 1770 a British sentry is taunted by a bunch of young Boston brats. You can just imagine what happens when a bunch of kids are bent on doing a little mischief:

"I dare ya to walk up to that sentry and call'em a bloody lobster-back!"
   "Oh yehh? …… There, I did it! Now I dare <u>you</u> to throw that snowball at him. Go on. Throw it!"
"How's that for a good shot? Got'em! Now I dare <u>you</u> to walk straight up to'em and stick your tongue out at'em — right to his face. …… I double dare ya!"
   "You do, do ya? Watch this …… !"[11]

Sooner or later the sentry grabs one of the brats and smacks him! Later that evening a crowd armed with clubs confronts that lone sentry. Other British soldiers come to his rescue. One thing leads to another. There's scuffling. Somehow, a soldier's weapon discharges. The civilians swing their clubs. The soldiers fire. By the time it's all over, five civilians are dead!

Chaos reigns that night. Roving bands of angry people take to the streets. Once again the houses of pompous English loyalists and the Governor's Mansion are the targets. The Sons of Liberty call the killings an outright massacre. It becomes known all around the Colonies in every town and village as … The Boston Massacre! "Remember The Boston Massacre" becomes the sound bite and the rallying cry for every protest and demonstration! And there are lots of them!

The pressure gets too great for Lord North in England. He discusses the situation with his colleagues:

"It's one thing having British troops at frontier forts, Lord North. It's quite another having troops right in the middle of Boston. That's an incident waiting to happen. And it happened!"

"Hmm. Are you suggesting I withdraw them ... lose face in front of the world to a gang of roughnecks? I'd rather repeal the Townshend Act!"

"Perhaps we should consider doing just that ... to avoid another incident?"

"Indeed. Those taxes are more trouble than they're worth. Especially with that pack of thieves over there smuggling everything in sight anyway."

"Unfortunately we lose face over that also."

"We sha'nt repeal it then! Leave it on the books! We'll just repeal all the duties but one! Keep the tax on tea! What harm can it do?"[12]

Lord North sucks it in! He removes the Townshend duties, except for the tea tax!
* Why does he keep the tea tax? To save face?
* It's a symbol. You can't come back to fight another day if you surrender every single thing, and hand over your sword.
* I see. It makes repealing the Townshend duties a temporary — tactical — retreat on the tax issue. It's not complete surrender.

* Exactly. North is sending a message. The taxes are not gone forever. Only temporarily. The Colonists get the message. But to them the tea tax is a symbol, as well. It's a symbol of England's intention to continue suppressing their rights. Its a symbol of continuing "taxation without representation"!

During the next few years, the tea tax is the main subject of philosophical discussion that takes place between the various Colonies. It's like a little boil on the Colonists' backside that continues to fester and grow. It eventually has to be dealt with. So our agitators begin to push a complete boycott of English tea. And it works! Even down South in North Carolina, for example, the Society of Patriotic Ladies holds a big political rally. They agree not to use English tea, but to use a home brew made from rasberry leaves. Shops now cannot sell English tea. So importers don't order it. But England crams the tea, and tax, down American importers' and merchants' throats, anyway! England is using tactics that amount to little more than extortion, pure and simple!

The agitators in Boston won't sit still for extortion. So they plan a little "extortion" of their own. Fifty men will disguise themselves in Indian clothes and warpaint. They'll board the English ships in Boston Harbor that are laden with tea. They'll wait for a bright moonlit night so thay can see what they're doing. That will also allow family and friends to gather on the docks to watch the action. They consider it their legal right to avoid extortion. And they figure it's their moral right to destroy the objects of that extortion — the tea. So it's all arranged. They'll go ahead with their plan and dump all the tea into Boston Harbor!

As usual, not everyone agrees. There are always skeptics on any issue. Let's hear what a couple of them have to say:

> "It'll never work — this plan of theirs."
> "Why? What's wrong with it?"
> "It's full of holes! First off, how do fifty bumbling, stumbling, and tripping people sneak onto ships in ridiculous disguises?"
> "That's why they want a moonlit night. It's so they <u>don't</u> trip and stumble!"
> "Moonlight? That's even worse! Anyone can see them! And having a crowd of cheering relatives on shore? The whole plan sounds ridiculous! How about the British guards? They'd have to bribe the British guards — or get them drunk — or something!"
> "Now you've got the idea, mate!"
> "Ah! I see! That's different! In that case, why actually waste good British tea? As long as the British think the Indians did it — to protest shabby treatment — then we should join this little party. We can dump some tea in the harbor, but keep every second one for ourselves! Our relatives on the shore can fish them out of the harbor!"
> "That's the idea! Not such a bad plan ... eh?"[13]

They dump the tea into Boston Harbor! In the Colonies it becomes known as the big "Boston Tea Party"! In England it becomes known as the big Boston Hoax!

Parliament in London says its now beyond lawlessness. It's anarchy! King George and Parliament are now beside themselves about what to do. They're losing patience. They're losing taxes. They're losing goods. It all adds up to — they're losing control. So they take steps to regain control. They shut down Boston Harbor! And they send General Thomas Gage to set up martial law! That shuts down normal life in Boston!

The year is now 1773. The noose on the colonists is getting tighter. They now have less freedom than ever. They have less than the first settlers at Plymouth. They have less than the lowest of the low in England. It's discouraging. It's time for a gut-check. They decide to show patience and perseverance a little longer, as might be encouraged by these words drawn from McGuffey's Reader:

BE PATIENT

based on: McGuffey's Reader

The fisher who draws his net in too soon,
   Won't have any fish to sell.
The folks who give up the fight too soon,
   Haven't learned their lessons well.

If you would have your progress stay,
   Be Patient — don't go too fast,
The folks who travel a mile each day,
   May get round the world at last.

The virtue is: Patience. Your goals can be reached if you
take them a little at a time.

By 1774 the British noose begins to choke. Patience and perseverance are running out. And the colonists are split. On one side are the men of big business. They actually want a fight with the King! Their excuse is principles. Their real reason is the wealth and power that independence would bring them. On the other side are the aristocrats. They want no fight! Why should they? Life is stacked in their favor just the way it is. These "Loyalists" stick with the King. In the middle are the ordinary folks — farmers, sailors, laborers, and those slaves we talked about, both white and black. They want no fight, either! They just want to work and raise their families. But big businessmen convince them England is to blame for slavery, low wages, and joblessness — England is their enemy. Though you can't be sure about that, ordinary folks end up siding with big businessmen, anyway. But if there is a fight, ordinary folks will also end up doing all the fighting and dying ... not big businessmen! You can be sure about that!

* I know.

* So you can see why politicians and big businessmen have the least interest, and ordinary folks have the most interest, in having Good political and military leaders. If there's a fight, ordinary folks' lives, not politicians' and big businessmens' lives, depend on having Good leaders! And right now, the Colonies and those ordinary folks are, indeed, headed for a fight with England. Relations with King George and Parliament are on a slippery slope. They've been sliding downhill ever since the Writs of Assistance twelve years ago. And a few men in particular — besides James Otis — have been greasing the slope all the way. Here's the first one I'll tell you about. His name is ... **Samuel Adams**!

* He's the one mentioned by the stamp-tax collector outside his house that night, isn't he.

* Yes. And he's: a cousin of future President John Adams; an ace radical agitator; a colleague of James Otis after the Writs of Assistance; an activist; a Bostonian; a Harvard graduate; and, a political philosopher. He's also down to earth!

Sam is like Socrates of ancient Greece. He's a gadfly! Sure, he does get up on his soapbox in town. He does turn the market square into a philosophy classroom like Socrates did. But you won't see any sandals. Or beard. Or wandering. Sam's only wandering is from one pub to the next. He turns pubs into classrooms. That is, when he's not in Church. He's a Puritan!

He has a great rapport with Boston's sailors, tradesmen, dockworkers, laborers, and shopkeepers — the working class. Over a pint of beer they give him their problems and complaints. They consider him one of them. To them he's a regular guy ... for an educated, non-workingclass, Harvard grad! But, even more than that, he helps them. He has the will to help them. He has the education to help them. And he has the morals, ethics, and character to help them. He makes abstract ideas of Aristotle, Cicero, and Polybius spring to life in plain language. He says that Bostonians must have virtues like a "Christian Sparta" — valor, selflessness, and patriotism!

* I'm sure doing all of that must make him their leader.

* It does indeed, Harry. As their leader he has had his finger on the pulse of Boston for a long time. So it wasn't difficult nine years ago for him to prescribe

a new idea. That was the movement I told you about called the "Sons of Liberty". All around the Colonies, soapboxes were replaced by old elm trees as meeting places. They became known as "liberty trees". And Sam Adams with his following of agitators are the ones who had gotten ordinary folks out on the streets against the Sugar Act, Stamp Act, and Townshend Act. Remember, Harry? They're also the ones who brewed up the Boston Tea Party. Adams declared, "I think our countrymen discover the spirit of Rome and Sparta"!

* I thought the main rabble rouser was James Otis.

* It's always the first spark that's responsible for the largest fire. And James Otis did furnish the first spark that ignited firebrand Sam Adams. Then others from around the Colony joined them. Otis'earlier letters to, and replies from, other Colonies gave Sam Adams the idea of starting Committees of Correspondence. And Otis headed up the Massachusetts Committee of Correspondence. Then one day in 1769 he was delivering a fiery speech. And fiery speeches usually fire up your enemies, as well as, your friends. One fired up enemy — a commissioner of British Customs — attacked him. Otis suffered a head injury. It left him mentally incapacitated. And that was it for Otis. He was out of the struggle. But he had been a leader! He had shown others the way forward!

Sam Adams went forward. He and other firebrands that had been sparked by James Otis continued to spread the fires of patriotism far and wide. All the Colonies set up their own Committees of Correspondence. They wrote back and forth. They exchanged moral and political ideas. Locke, Hume, and Bolingbroke were probably the most quoted British philosophers. Rousseau, Montesquieu, and other "philosophes" were the most quoted French ones. The Committees distilled their ideas down to basic questions. When ... not if ... but when they rebel against England, should they still be part of the British Empire? Or, should they go for complete independence? Either way, what kind of government should they set up? Should it be one having John Locke's ideas of life, liberty, and property within the framework of a representative monarchy? Should it be Montesquieu's life, liberty, property, and representative democracy completely separate from a monarchy? Or should it be Rousseau's total participatory democracy? Whatever form of government they set up, Sam Adams and his Puritan brethren visualize it as a nearly perfect "city on a hill", similar to St. Augustine's City of God. In fact, everyone agrees that it must be heavenly, honorable, full of Virtue, and an example for all the world to follow!

Back before James Otis got his brains scrambled, he and Sam Adams had gotten the attention of the youngest rising star in Boston's shipping business. His name is ... **John Hancock**!

Hancock pushes for a government like the early republics of Greece and Rome. That means complete independence from the British Empire. England must go. That opinion makes him popular. Someday he'll become even more popular, not for his opinion, but for his signature. It will boldly be the first, largest, and clearest on a declaration of independence from England! Right now, however, he's popular with Sam Adams, but for a different reason. He provides a special kind of support. It's the kind that's needed to keep any cause going. There's no substitute for it. It's called ... money!

MONEY

A virtuous heart is precious to hold
　　More dear than money can buy,
But the greatest cause that can ever unfold
　　Without money, will wither and die.

Though money brings a measure of mirth
　　But can bring not one true friend,
In the fight for Godgiven rights here on earth
　　You need money to win in the end.

The virtue is: Humility. Don't be too proud. When virtue
　　needs help — get money!

Hancock isn't someone who gives you his umbrella while the sun shines and wants it back when it starts to rain. He's with you for better or for worse. And Sam Adams had signed up another rising star of Boston who decided to get into it for better or for worse. It's his cousin, John Adams!

John Adams is a brainy Harvard lawyer. He's ambitious. He's intellectual. And he's well read in the philosophies. So at first he was reluctant. He had told cousin Sam that belonging to a mob and living on a shoestring were not his style. But then Otis organized the Stamp Act Convention. Brainy people from all around the Colonies attended. And Sam organized Committees of Correspondence.

John Adams saw the activity wasn't just mob protests, but a real cause. Committees of Correspondence were exactly his style. For he's a philosophy "junkie", like all the other Committees of Correspondance members around the Colonies. He itches for American independence. He says a free republic is a bedrock principle ... "nature demands it" ... Plato and Aristotle, Livy and Cicero, Locke and Harrington demand it! So, John Adams joined up!

The Adams family is now well known everywhere. Sam is the rabble-rouser. John is the intellectual. In the Colonies they're known as leaders. In England they're known as troublemakers. Right now in 1774 Boston, Sam Adams is probably having a talk, and a pint of brew with the boys down at the local pub. Over in England they're probably having evening tea in the Parlimentary sitting rooms and blowing the dust off of old ideas about how to deal with rebels like those Adams cousins — especially that Sam Adams. When the dust settles, they call Sam Adams a public enemy, an outlaw, and a traitor! They're out to make an example of him. And guess how, Harry?

* By hanging him?

* Right! And right now, also in England, there's another firebrand waiting to be ignited! He lives in Thetford, Norfolk. He's an unknown, but talented writer. His name is ... **Thomas Paine**!

Tom Paine knows first hand about English white slavery! Peasant workers on the farmlands around Norfolk are "tied" to the lands by tyranny of the elite English landed gentry. He knows their tiny thatched roof "tied-cottages" and their grinding poverty. So Tom reads everything he gets his hands on about moral and political philosophy. He devotedly reads all the newspapers. And he reads about America in his local "rag". So next stop for him is the big city. London!

While in London he finagles a way to meet Benjamin Franklin! Franklin is impressed. He likes Paine's ideas. He loves his writing. He reckons Paine is made for America. Paine and patriotism are a perfect match. So Paine comes to America!

It's 1774. Thomas Paine is working as a writer and magazine editor in Philadelphia. His pamplets echo the way most people feel in their hearts about how they want to live. He has a special knack. He's able to simplify the difficult! The average Joe can understand him! And he even uses classical history to make a point! For instance, he uses Greek historian Thucydides' works to bash England's tyranny of the Colonies. He contrasts ancient Greece's benevolence toward it's Mediterranean colonies with present day England's tyranny toward it's American colonies. So his former self-education in philosophy is finally paying off!

* He must be pulling down pretty good money from his job!
* Wealth is not the beacon that guides Tom Paine's life. It's achievment. Now he can finally act upon what he believes. He can finally put his favorite philosophers' thoughts to a real cause. He can finally influence the world around him. And he can finally become a philosopher himself — a practical one!

John Locke symbolically said sixty years ago, "in the beginning, all the world was America". And Jean-Jacques Rousseau said that "unspoiled" North America can be made into the ideal society. Paine now takes these ideas closer to reality. He says that opportunity to do something great is upon us, and "we have it in our power to begin the world again"! In other words, we can put an old soul into a new Country! We're able to start from scratch with a clean slate. And isn't that exactly why Paine and thousands of others came to America?

A year from now the War will begin. Many folks will still have doubts about fighting a war with England. Freedom fighters still won't have the "numbers" supporting them. So, political activists will use the magic that Tom Paine has in his pen. They'll tell him to forget about everything else. Write about independence. That's where the action is. So, he does. He writes a pamphlet. It's a runaway bestseller that he calls Common Sense! Let's go forward to that time and hear what some Philadelphia political activists are saying about it:
"

This pamphlet, Common Sense, is explosive stuff!"
    "It is? How so?"
"You know all those farmers and frontiersmen and Southerners
    we've always had trouble reaching out to? Well, they're now all
    jumping onto our independence wagon after reading it."
    "How do you know?"
"Everywhere my business travels take me — which is far and
    wide — I hear folks talking about it. It's big! I hear city folks

speaking the unspeakable — calling for freedom from England. I hear folks down South saying the King is a jackass who we should kick out! Folks out West are questioning England's authority — asking why a small island across the ocean should rule over a whole continent. Old and young. Rich and poor. They're all out there quoting the author's words. Things like: life; liberty; independence; and so on. Everyone says they <u>do</u> make common sense! The author is right!"

"Who <u>is</u> the author, anyway?"

"A friend of a friend of Ben Franklin tells me it's a young protege of Franklin named Thomas Paine!"

"Well, Paine doesn't have his name on the book. He's making no money out of it! And I hear they'll sell 500,000 copies in the end!! That's neither common sense nor business sense! So, unless he has family connections, how does he make a living?"

"He earns it! But don't knock it. He's doing what even our Committees of Correspondance can't do. He's getting the people behind independence and revolution!"

"Yes. I must admit. Paine's a magician with the simple written word!"[14]

* Do they actually print 500,000 copies of <u>Common Sense?</u>
* They do indeed! And there are less than 3,000,000 people in the Colonies at this time, Harry.
* So almost every family must have a copy … like the <u>Bible</u>!
* That's near enough accurate. And the idea to publish <u>Common Sense</u> works. It's a great idea. It's simple. It's direct. It's convincing. And most important, it rallies people behind independence! It's many people's first introduction to the

idea of independence! It's actually like an introduction to what will later be a formal "declaration of independence"!

* It sounds like Tom Paine's on a roll. What's he write next?

* He'll first join the actual fighting! He'll sign up with the Revolutionary Army. That's when he'll write <u>The American Crises</u>. It'll be a great morale booster. During the darkest hour of the War, General Washington will see fit to read it to his troops. It will help General Washington to throw down a challenge that holds his de-moralized Army together. Paine's memorable line that will help do it is: "These are the times that try <u>men</u>'s souls"!

After the American Revolution, Paine will help in the French Revolution. He'll help to write a French Bill of Rights based on his million copy bestseller <u>The Rights of Man</u>. And he'll write another big one about religion called the <u>Age of Reason</u>. So Tom Paine is truly a practical philosopher. He's a man of deep beliefs. And he acts on them!

A young lawyer down in Virginia doesn't need to read <u>Common Sense</u> to arouse his passion for freedom. He's been ventilating that passion for ten years now. His fiery Stamp Act Speech in 1765 roasted King George <u>III</u>. He said, the king betrayed a trust, like Caesar and Charles I did. Caesar was knifed by Brutus. Charles I was beheaded by Cromwell. So what about King George? That thinly-veiled threat had drawn cries of treason from uppercrust Loyalists. So he shot back, "if this be treason, make the most of it!" In other words, as long as we're being labelled as traitors, we may as well go for the jugular by going for total sovereignty! That's when the idea of independence was implanted in this young lawyer's mind. His name is ... **Patrick Henry**!

Henry now has ten years and many such outbursts under his belt! Virginia's House of Burgesses ... shut down by England in 1774 ... is now meeting secretly. The King's noose on freedom is tighter than ever. The Burgesses barely stay one step ahead of the King's law. They now meet at a church in Richmond. The talk is about the Boston riots. They hear Massachusetts is preparing to fight. Patrick Henry delivers a speech about getting Virginia to do the same. It's his most fiery and famous speech. It is met with mixed emotions. We'll pick up his speech in the middle of his talking about the British fleets and armies that have just arrived in America:

> "Let us not deceive ourselves! These [fleets and armies] are implements of war and subjugation; the last arguments to which Kings resort! ... They are sent over to bind and rivet upon us those chains which the British ministry have been so long forging!"

And now, let's listen to what some of the Members are whispering:

> "Why does Henry hold his arms up? And he keeps them up?"
> "That's his usual bit of play-acting. He's pretending his arms are chained like a prisoner. Shh, let's listen to him."

And, Patrick Henry again:

"And what have we to oppose with? You say, try argument? I say, Sir, we have been trying that for the last ten years now! Sir, we have done everything that could be done to avert the storm which is now coming on! We have petitioned! ... Our petitions have been slighted! There is no longer any room for hope! If we wish to be free ... we must fight! I repeat it, sir, we must fight!"

And, whispering members again:

"Patrick Henry and his lunatic radical fringe are pushing us into a bloody war."
"Sounds like that."

And, Patrick Henry:

"It is too late to retire from the contest! There is no retreat but submission to slavery! Our chains are forged! Their creaking may be heard on the plains of Boston!" °°And my bloody arms are creaking from holding them up this way! °°

And, some members shouting:

"Peace! Peace! Not war! Peace, Mr. Henry!"

And, Patrick Henry again:

"Gentlemen may cry ... 'peace, peace'! But there is no peace! The war is actually begun! The next gale that sweeps from the North will bring to our ears the clash of resounding arms! Our brethren are already in the field! Why stand we here idle?"

And, members whispering again:

"Look at that. Henry's about to rupture his vocal cords. The veins and tendons are bursting out of his neck."
"Yes, he's getting louder and louder.
His voice is bouncing all around the walls of the church. He's got the walls shaking. Listen to him!"

And, Patrick Henry:

"Is life so dear, or peace so sweet, as to be purchased at the price of chains and slavery? Forbid it, Almighty God!" °°Whew! I have to put my arms down!°°

And, members:

"Look there now. Henry pretends he talks to God. He's flailing
his arms about."
   "No. No. That's not it at all, twit."
"Then what is it, Mr. Know-it-all?"
   "He's throwing off those imaginary chains, of course. "Shh!
   Hear comes his punch-line."

And finally, Patrick Henry:

"I know not what course others may take! But as for me … GIVE
ME LIBERTY, OR GIVE ME DEATH!!" [15]

* The silence is deafening! This place is stunned! He's knocked them off their
chairs!
*   Patrick Henry is a master speechmaker, Harry! He's been reading Livy,
Plutarch, Homer, Demosthenes and other classical authors since fifteen years old.
He probably lifted a few of their sound-bites. For instance, Plutarch's <u>Cato</u> has
the line "it is not now a time to talk of anything but chains or conquest, liberty or
death." Henry can speech-make as good as Homer could write! Infact, he's been
called the "forest-born Demosthenes"! Remember Demosthenes, Harry?
* Vaguely.
* Demosthenes was a statesman in 350 BC Athens. The greatest of orators in
ancient Greece, he made rousing speeches. A famous one was his "Athens
Awake" speech in which he tried to arouse Athenians to the impending threat
from King Philip of Macedon. So you can understand why they call Patrict Henry
a "forest born Demosthenes"!
* Yes. And Patrick Henry speaks directly. He's not longwinded.
* He knows that speeches measured by the hour, die with the hour. This one —
his "Virginia Awake" speech — doesn't die. It works! The speech does more

than awaken Virginia. It sweeps through the Colonies as fast as a messenger on horseback can gallop over muddy roads, ferry over rivers, and ford across streams. The post-rider — mailman — always blows his horn to announce his arrival in a town. His horn is now more than announcing his arrival. It's rallying crowds to hear what Patrick Henry said. It's bringing news of Virginia's support. That news heartens the agitators who are in and around Boston. You see, those agitators have been flirting with taking on the British "redcoats"! They've been squirelling-away guns and powder in Lexington and Concord for two years now … since 1773!

James Otis. Samuel Adams. John Hancock. Thomas Paine. Patrick Henry. Those are the "radical, extremist, agitators" who have been greasing the slippery slope that relations with mother England is on! Those are the **firebrands** who have been pushing for the rebellion that is the American colonists' natural right, according to Locke, Voltaire, and Montesquieu!

John Adams. Benjamin Franklin. George Washington. Thomas Jefferson. James Madison. Alexander Hamilton. Those are some of the big names that will someday be referred to as the "founding fathers". But up to now, in April 1775, they're doing very little that's visible to chip-in on the action. They're, basically, writing letters to eachother through their Committees of Correspondence.

* That's it? So the prime-mover for independence is Samuel Adams?
* Yes! He's the only one down on the ground in the middle of the action. He's giving a revolution it's legs. He's taking the risks. He's holding his feet to the fire. The King and Parliament want to hang him! They reckon that would cut the legs out from under the "rabble"! Sam Adams and the Sons of Liberty — Boston branch — are the ones unhappily <u>visible</u> to England! They're at the top of the King's hit-list of candidates for the hangman's noose!

On the other hand, those future "founding fathers" are happily <u>invisible</u> … for now, anyway. Here's what they've been doing during the past ten years while Sam Adams and the Sons of Liberty have been sticking their necks out. John Adams has been raking-in a bunch of money from his law practice in Boston while quietly supporting cousin Sam Adams. Ben Franklin has been into science, philosophy, and land investment in Pennsylvania. George Washington has been studying, running his farm, and investing in land in Virginia. Thomas Jefferson has been busily soaking-up history, politics, and philosophy ... and busily building his own law practice. James Madison has been growing from young Virginia schoolboy to college student. Alexander Hamilton had been living with his Aunt in the West Indies since his single-parent mother died. He's now at school in Elizabeth, New Jersey.

So, we have the so-called "radical, extremist, agitators" — called patriots. And we have their safe-distance, behind the scenes supporters — called founding fathers. Their approaches are different. They have a common goal, however. They all want to live in a Land that's not run by some distant ruler. They all want a Land that is run by Americans![16]

CHAPTER 3: REVOLUTION

About the same time that news of Patrick Henry's speech hits the streets of Boston, British General Gage's spies hear about a cache of guns and gunpowder hidden away in Concord. They learn that two of Boston's radical ringleaders, Sam Adams and John Hancock, are also hidden away in Lexington. They're enroute to an illegal meeting in Philadelphia — a Continental Congress. Now is Gage's chance. He can trash the "rabble's" stockpile of weapons. He can bag a couple of rebels. It would be a giant step. Disarm the population. Hang the leaders. Disarming the population would solve England's problem in America ... forever! And Gage can do it all in a single fifteen mile excursion west of Boston! He sets a date to secretly do it!

It's the dead of night, April 18, 1775. Seven hundred British "Redcoats", on what they think is a fun little outing, sneak across the Charles River in small boats while most of Boston sleeps. Most. Not all. For there are eyes watching British movements. Those eyes belong to a silversmith and expert horseman named Paul Revere. Revere mounts up and rides out into the countryside to alert everyone, including his good friends Sam Adams and John Hancock. He now comes tearing into Lexington:

"Someone arouse Adams and Hancock out of bed! Paul Revere's just arrived, shouting something all in a tizzy! What's that he's saying?"

"Drop your buns and grab your guns! Drop your buns and grab your guns!"

"Drop your buns and grab your guns? Paul, aren't you supposed to shout something like 'the Redcoats are coming'? Or, 'the British are coming, the British are coming'?

"I did! I did! But now that it's breakfast, this is better!"

"Oh! ... I guess so. Anyway, here come Sam Adams and John Hancock. Sam! John! I'm gathering the militia. While they're checking-in here in town, you two best be checking-out of town!" ᵒᵒAnd right now, so the Brits don't hang <u>me</u> for hiding you out!ᵒᵒ

"Yes indeed, Captain! Give us the usual minute, and we're outta here!"

"Captain, is that why we're called Minutemen ... because we <u>leave</u> on a minute's notice?"

"No. We're called Minutemen because we're supposed to <u>arrive</u> on a minute's notice! Revere said the Brits number several hundreds! But so far our numbers aren't too good! We only have several dozens!" ᵒᵒSo more guys better show, or in another minute I'm outta here too ... like Adams and Hancock!ᵒᵒ [17]

* How many more Minutemen show up?
* Seventy-five! They're only amateur militiamen — farmers. They're not much of a threat to 700 professional "Redcoats"! But, at daybreak, the "brave" Redcoats launch a full-scale frontal assault, anyway! A mounted British officer orders the farmers to disperse. The farmers see the onslaught of guns, sabres, and bayonnets bearing down on them. So that's just what they try to do — disperse and take cover. But someone's weapon discharges. That sets-off the Brits. They come in with guns blazing! It's a disaster! Lexington green fills with dust and smoke ... and shouts and groans! Suddenly, the firing stops. There's dead silence. The air clears. Eight Americans — simple farmers — lay dead on the green!

   The British troops smugly continue down the road to Concord. To them, their "fun" little outing turns out to be more fun than they expected! Ralph Waldo Emerson will later write a poem about Lexington and Concord. A part of it will go like this:

CONCORD HYMN

by: Ralph Waldo Emerson

By the rude bridge that
   arched the flood,
Their flag to April's breeze
   unfurled,
Here once the embattled
   farmers stood,
And fired the shot heard
   'round the world!

The virtue is: Initiative. The first step of great journeys
   sometimes takes great initiative.

209

* Who fired that first shot?
* It doesn't matter. That shot, like their "fun" little outing, will also turn out to be more than the British expected! That shot will be the beginning of the American Revolution — "the shot heard 'round the world"! That's right, Harry, it all begins right here today, April 19, 1775, on Lexington green!

The British now approach Concord. Luckily, Dr. Sam Prescott gets there before them to warn the townspeople. Paul Revere and friend, Billy Dawes, had both been caught by the British at Lexington. So they're out of it. Prescott happened to be on his way home to Concord. So he carried on with Revere's mission!

* At least the skirmish at Lexington gave the boys a chance to evacuate the cache of weapons they had stored at Concord.
* Right! Those Minutemen at Lexington didn't die in vain. For the weapons are gone by the time the British soldiers arrive at Concord. The British ransack through the town in disbelief. And their hysterical ransacking starts massive fires. Musket-toting farmers, approaching Concord from the north and west, see the smoke from a distance. They hussle to stop the British from trashing the town and burning it to the ground. The British hussle to the North Bridge that leads into town to block the farmers. The farmers see the fires. That won't do! They press forward! Musket fire is exchanged! Men fall ... on both sides of the bridge! The price of this little skirmish gets too high for the British! They pull out!

The Brits start making their way back toward Boston. But it's now gone too far. Too many farmers have died. The Americans can't let it end like that. They shadow the British retreat, harassing them with gunfire all the way!

The surrounding hills along Revere's and Dawe's earlier routes are finally filling with angry men. They're radical agitators, patriotic farmers, and so-called Minutemen. Many of these para-military Minutemen remember how they fought twenty years ago as young men in the French and Indian War. They remember how they won victories without the help of British regulars. And they remember how the British sometimes retreated like scared rabbits when ambushed by Indians. So they ambush the British, Indian-style. The Brits had their little massacre at Lexington. Now it's the Americans' turn. They keep the Redcoats in a crossfire all the way. They fire from behind trees and rocks and whatever cover they can find. It becomes a fifteen mile massacre!

The Redcoats' "fun" little outing has turned into a nightmare! They limp back into Boston, mauled and battered. They're numbers are decimated. The Americans have whipped them. Three British have fallen for every one American!

The roads and countryside near Boston now fill with an army of volunteers. They've come to fight for liberty. Like those "radical" agitators, they all want to live in a Country where ordinary people can enjoy freedom and independence. And right now, that isn't happening with the British in control!

* It looks to me like they're still just a mob of farmers, laborers, shopkeepers, and teenagers ... and even women!
* That's true. But what's important here is, until now, the revolution was only in people's hearts and minds. And fifty-six educated men merely <u>debated</u> revolution

210

through their Committees of Correspondence and at the Continental Congress that Adams and Hancock were headed for in Philadelphia. Now those educated men in Philadelphia have heard about Lexington and Concord. The "shot heard round the world" shocks them. Revolution is no longer a lot of hot air. It's a reality. So they rush the word back to their own Colonies. Be prepared to fight!

Most of those educated men were at the Continental Congress a year ago in 1774. They know each other. They know who stands where, regarding England. There are three factions: the radicals; the moderates; and, the reactionaries. The radicals want complete independence — no in-betweens. The moderates are undecided — sitting on the fence. The reactionaries want more rights and freedom from the British Crown and Parliament — but will still stick with the Monarchy.

The radicals, like Sam Adams, John Adams, John Hancock, Patrick Henry, and others go to work on the moderates. For example, a radical might inflame the emotions of a moderate like this:

"You've heard about the Boston Massacre?"
"Yes I have. Awful. Awful."
"We can't imagine the barbarity without being there! Five innocent people gunned down! Blood splattering all over the streets of Boston!"

"And at Lexington several days ago, a handful of merely good-time militia boys — meeting on God's own free and open town green — were brutally savaged by an entire regiment of British regulars! Eight boys dead!"
"Eight dead? God have mercy!"
"And another ten wounded and bleeding!"
"Barbaric. Barbaric!"
"And then the British were burning down the town of Concord."
"Cowardly act! Nothing less than cowardly!"
"Isaac Davis belonged to the militia. He set out to stop the town from burning to the ground — which would have left women and children homeless. Here's a note his young and pretty wife wrote:
'Isaac Davis ... was my husband: thirty years of age; four children; the youngest fifteen months old. The alarm was given in the morning, and my husband lost no time making ready to go to Concord with his Company. He said but little that morning. He seemed serious and thoughtful; but never seemed to hesitate. He only said, "take good care of the children." In the afternoon he was brought home ... a corpse!'
Sadly, there are many such stories in the ravaged countryside of Massachusetts. This is but one of them."
"Yes, that is sad. Sad and infuriating! You're right! We must not let them die in vain!"

Other radicals might pull other moderates aside to trickle out thinly veiled threats such as:

> "The people are up in arms now. It's spreading all around the Colonies. They can easily become an angry mob — like they were in Boston a few times — trashing houses of their enemies, tar and feathering, hanging their enemies in effigy! I sympathize with those who are not with us. But you have nothing to worry about, right? You're with us. Right?"
> "I'm not sure where I stand at this time."
> "Oh my! You know mob mentality, don't you? If you're not with them, you're against them! That's dangerous to your health!"
> "Yes, we must think about those things, mustn't we!"
> "Word and rumours travel fast. Your reputation will arrive home before you do. Stick with us! It will be surprisingly good for you!"

And, the radicals might quietly cut deals with moderates:

> "Throw your lot in with us. We'll run things together. Do you catch my meaning?"
> "I hear you."
> "We can divide authority up between us."
> "I'm listening. How?"
> "Well, for example, you can be head of something in purchasing, the treasury, or perhaps the army."[18]

One way or another, the radicals manage to get the moderates to vote for independence!

The Colonies are now "emerging States". Bye, bye Colonies! They unite — as an "emerging nation". The second Continental Congress appoints itself the emerging nation's "emerging government". Now the Minutemen and motley crew around Boston are their "emerging army". The Congress even kicks around the idea of writing a document that formally declares independence from England. And the Congress elects someone to be in charge of turning the "emerging army" near Boston into a real army. They commission George Washington as General and Commander-in-Chief of them ... and of all future Continental armies!

The radicals celebrate. The reactionaries grumble. George Washington sets out for Boston to take charge. Thomas Jefferson thinks about what a declaration of independence should say. The Continental Congress tries a last ditch effort for peace. They send the King an "Olive Branch Petition". It asks for peaceful change. They want something like the Glorious Revolution of 1688 England. Remember that one?

* It was a peaceful revolution ... no heads rolled. Good idea!
* It's a great idea! In hindsight, Harry, it could have altered history. But no luck. King George III tosses their Olive Branch Petition into the dust bin of history!

Meanwhile, the rag-tag volunteers near Boston decide to fortify the Bunker Hill area above Boston Harbor. With cannon they can control the Charles River from there. Maybe that'll force the Brits to leave. It's worth a try. So in the dark of night they steal up the hill. Won't General Gage be startled when he awakens next morning!

It's a good plan. Only one mistake. They scale the wrong hill! They're on a lower hump in the Bunker Hill area called Breed's Hill. No. They actually make two mistakes. The second one? They don't have any cannons! So in the morning, they find themselves looking right down the gun barrels of the British warships in the harbor. The motley crew of Americans is dumbfounded. British General Gage is delighted. So the Americans do the only thing they can, now. Dig in. They dig breast high trenches — breastworks — for cover, in order to fight like frontiersmen. Once again it's going to be the traditional British soldier verses "Hawkeye"!

* Well, firing from behind hills and rocks and trees worked during the skirmishing from Concord back to Boston, didn't it. It might work here, too.
* We'll see. We're now going up there with the Americans to see the British onslaught for ourselves.
* Whew! I can see why you call it an onslaught! Those big guns on the British warships are already pummelling the Americans ... without even any British troops!
* And speaking of troops, Harry ... look down below. There must be thousands of British marines splashing their way ashore from those warships. Here they come! That drumbeat sounds eerie! The fifes sound business-like! The roar of cannons and crash of cannonblast is getting more frequent! The marines are formed into "killing-lines"! They're slowly, steadily, relentlessly pressing up the hill toward us! They're getting closer and closer, without a sign of stopping! The men up here sound scared, based on the chatter we hear between them and their officer:

"Let's fire <u>now</u>! This is already a turkey-shoot!"

"It may be for you. You farmers and hunters shoot your muskets all the time. And some of you are in the militia. Right? So you get a chance to practice, don't you! Most of us others don't!"

"That's right! Us over here are seamen, blacksmiths, shoemakers, carpenters, shopkeepers, and plain laborers. We don't get much target practice with our guns."

(officer) "That's right men! Listen up! We don't have much gunpowder! We can't afford to miss our targets. So, don't fire 'till you see the whites of their eyes'! Don't shoot till I yell the word — FIRE! All of you got that?" ᵒᵒSome of you can't hit the broad side of a barn, otherwiseᵒᴼ.

(whispering) "I reckon I'll aim for their officers first. It'll put them in a dither without officers. Like us. We wouldn't be in this fix if we had real officers that could get us on the right hill!"

"I reckon if they get much closer, I'm not gunna even peek my head up to aim. The sheets of gunfire from their lines'll be a blizzard of musket-balls!"

"Our officer must need glasses! I saw the whites of their eyes long ago!"

(officer) "Cut the whispering! Steady now. Don't shoot 'till I yell — FIRE!

The British marines are now practically right on top of the Americans! They're a sea of red uniforms, about to swallow up everything! Bayonets pointed! Fifes playing! Cannons roaring! Cannonballs pounding! Dust thickening! Americans sweating! Faces strained with fear and pressure! The American officer is getting ready to give the order to fire.

* It's eerie, Thomas! Very eerie! Masses of soldiers getting closer and closer together, and no one firing!
* You're right! Another minute and they'll be over the top of the breastworks! But here's our officer, finally! Listen:

(shouting) "Alright, boys!

Ready!

Aim!

...

FIRE!!!"

The hill seems to explode! It's earthshaking! Deafening! Like thunder! Worse than thunder! Bullets tear through red coats on one side! Men fall on this side from the blizzard of British volleys! No more sounds of drums and fifes! Only sounds of men crying out in pain and agony! British officers go down ... a lot of Americans must have aimed at the officers! The British fall back in shock! Their ranks are halved! ...... But here comes another wave of marines again!

No need to watch any longer, Harry. This goes on and on. Wave after wave of British marines are beaten back. Finally, the Americans run out of gunpowder! ...... Suddenly, it's quiet!

Finally, the British marines get to the top of the hill. But no one is there! The Americans have vanished! The British go on to capture everything around Bunker Hill. And their bombardment sets Charlestown on fire. It burns to the ground. Still, it's a disaster for the mighty British forces. A bloodbath. Half of them — well over 1000 men — are dead. The Americans lose 440 of their 1500 comrades, friends, and family. It didn't have to be that many! For what's clear to survivors, if they had a real officer, many more would still be alive!

Two weeks later they get one! General George Washington, Commander-in-Chief of the Continental Congress' Army, arrives. Everyone has heard of him. George Washington: Colonial Officer in the French and Indian War; aide to General Braddock; whipped his weight in French at Fort Duquesne; took four bullets in his coat and lived to tell it; had two horses shot out from under him; fired the shots that started the French and Indian War.

Yes, Washington is well known. He's America's hero from the French and Indian War. He grasps European warfare. And he'll start by training his "army" that way. But he also knows guerilla warfare! He learned valuable lessons during that previous war. You'll see, Harry. They'll prove to be critical!

When Washington took this job he knew it wouldn't be easy. But he had no idea he'd have to perform a minor miracle! Up to now, all he's heard are good things. He's heard about the skirmishing back to Boston from Concord. And he's heard that 1500 of his militiamen decimated the British near Bunker Hill before running out of gunpowder. So when he arrives and sees his so-called Army, he's startled. It's not merely a raw bunch of good-time militia guys with no training. It's a rag-tag mob of assorted farmers, workers, sailors, women, and teenagers! Some have muskets. Most are "armed" with clubs, knives, and pitchforks! It's a rag-tag motley crew! But despite all that, one thing is obvious to him. They have guts! And guts is a good start!

* Their numbers have swollen! There are thousands out there!

* Other Colonies have joined in. And that causes new problems. They don't particularly like eachother. They don't trust eachother. Some think they're better than the others. And, some behave like they're campers on holiday! I'll show you what I mean, Harry. Take a look at General Washington talking to some of his "army":

> "We have a difficult challenge, men! ᵒᵒAnd boys? And even girls? God help me with this bunch!ᵒᵒ This might be the ruin of you and me! Or even the death of you and me! But I'm willing to risk it! I'm willing to sacrifice for this good cause! Are you? I'm here to turn you into an army! It takes discipline and obedience! So, work hard! Obey your Off-Off-Officers! ᵒᵒOfficers? Almost choked on my own words! These are not real Officers! They're politicians!ᵒᵒ You, uumm, Officers, may carry on now!"

And now let's listen to an Officer talking to some of the volunteers:

> "You there. <u>Yes</u> you! You hear General Washington? <u>I'm</u> the Officer around here! You have to ask me before you break ranks!"
>> "Lighten up! I only nipped across the green to visit my cousin!"

> "And you there. You ... from Pennsylvania!"
>> "Yo!"
> "Not, Yo! <u>I'm</u> Sir! You address an Officer as Sir!"
>> "Uh uh! No way do I call a guy from Boston <u>sir</u>!"

> "And <u>you</u> there! 'Buddy Buckskins'! Didn't I tell you to clean that rifle?"
>> "<u>I'll</u> be decide'n when this rifle wants a cleanin'. And I'll be decide'n when it wants a shootin' too! It's <u>my</u> rifle!"

> "Guard! That's right! You! Off your butt! On your feet! You're supposed to be on guard duty. Watching!"
>> "What's the difference? Virginia folks see just as good sittin' down. Don't Boston folks?"
> ᵒᵒHuh! Virginians! Cunning people! With slick accents!ᵒᵒ [20]

* Washington has his work cut out for him.
* True. He has problems. But sometimes problems are like forests, Harry. The best way out … is through! So, Washington far from gives up. He dives right into turning the raggedy mob of thousands into the semblance of an army!

And what a contrast across Boston! While the swearing, the hollering, the hup-hup-hup, and the clump-clump-clump goes on over here, British General Gage departs for England. His second in command, General Howe, gives him the traditional send-off. Uniforms look smart. Bugles blare. Drums beat. Bands play. Boots and rifles click with precision. The pomp and ceremony of the greatest military power in the world is on display. The latest modern rifles fire a salute. State of the art cannons bellow their farewell. And a ship of the finest navy in the world waits in the harbor to take Gage back to England. General Howe is now in command. And back across Boston: hup-hup-hup, clump-clump-clump. Washington trucks on with trying to turn his motly, rag-tag mob of civilians into an army.

Good news is about to reach Washington! Forces led by Benedict Arnold and Ethan Allen have overwhelmed the sleepy little garrison of British guarding a huge stockpile of cannons at Fort Ticonderoga near Canada. You can't fight a war without artillery. The Americans now have some. Now comes the problem. How does the Army's big, self-taught artillerist, Henry Knox, get them down to Washington in Boston? He works on it!

Meanwhile, dashing and handsome General George Montgomery leads an army into Canada. The Continental Congress had earlier sent him on a two-part mission. One, invade the British army at Quebec. Two, recruit Canadians to join the rebellion against England. After Ticonderoga, Ethan Allen also heads for Canada. His "Green Mountain Boys" will attack Montreal. And Washington orders Benedict Arnold to take another army north through Maine. He's to join forces with Montgomery in order to capture Quebec. Washington knows it would be hopeless for Montgomery alone. He remembers that General Wolf needed a huge force to wrest Quebec from the French during the French and Indian War.

The going is miserable for all of them, especially Arnold. Winter is early. They run into sub-freezing weather, torturous terrain, ice-cold rivers, treacherous swamps, and low food supplies. Early snows hinder living off the land. The men suffer greatly. They freeze. They starve. Half of them either die or stay behind. The other half barely survive. The dogged survivors finally meet up with Montgomery outside of Quebec. They're tired and weakened. A long rest before fighting is needed!

* It looks that way. But where? They have nowhere to rest but outside. Right? Can they endure the elements much longer? It's like a reverse siege. Quebec has everything ... inside. The Americans have nothing ... outside.

* Sometimes opportunity is disguised as hard work, Harry. Arnold and Montgomery figure they've already done the hard work. They figure their opportunity is now. They must attack now. But Quebec is no Ticonderoga. It's well defended up on the cliffs of the St. Lawrence River. Their best chance is the element of surprise. So they attack during a blizzard ... to catch the British off guard. It's a gallant try. But everyone soon realizes it's hopeless. Montgomery gets killed! Arnold's leg gets smashed by a musketball! They're forced into a retreat! Actually, it's more like an escape!

After all their suffering, what's left of the original three American forces leave from Canada empty handed. Arnold didn't capture Quebec. Montgomery didn't recruit any Canadians. Ethan Allen didn't capture the British at Montreal ... the British captured him and threw him in prison. And on top of all that, a diplomatic mission to Canada by Benjamin Franklin even fails. He's supposed to get Canada to join the Revolution as the fourteenth American Colony. It's a nice idea. But as you know, Harry, Canada never does join the Revolution.

So everything has failed ... even though the Americans have shown superhuman courage. And now, just to carry on, they have to do it again! They have to show courage a second time, as the following words of encouragement urge them to do:

HAVING COURAGE TWICE

Most take note of a courageous man,
Then go with the winning side.
But he who does the best he can,
Can take his loss with pride!

Beaten and down, yet still in play,
With conviction as hard as ice.
He will win some other day,
Who shows his courage twice!

The virtue is: Self-confidence. That's what it takes to be
down, yet come back.

Meanwhile, Henry Knox and his men have to show their courage twice, too. Why? First they fought to capture their massive number of cannons. Now they're suffering with trying to move that massive tonnage of cannons through the wilderness during the dead of winter. There are simply no nice convenient roads to use. First they chop their way through thick forests. Then everything gets stuck in the mud. Then it snows. Everything gets stuck in the snow. The snow melts. Everything gets stuck in the mud again. It's slow as you go. But Knox works it out! Little by little, slowly but surely, come 1776 they finally reach Washington's encampment outside Boston!

Washington also has a winter of hardship. His would-be army almost freezes. They don't have warm enough clothes. They don't have enough shoes or blankets or food. They don't even have enough guns to train with. That's because Congress says they are to "find them" out of their salaries. Trouble is, those salaries are seldom paid! So, many desert! And most sign-up for only three months. Therefore, no sooner do they start to resemble soldiers ... they go home. Many more would desert or go home were it not for their respect and confidence in Washington's leadership. So Washington can waste no time putting his newly acquired cannons to use. It's almost Spring. He knows that European generals love their Spring offensives. He figures he had better put his plan in place ... fast!

Unlike Bunker Hill, Washington does it right! He gets the cannons on the right hill. He hauls them to the top of a hill called Dorchester Heights. This time the Americans do get a commanding position over the British army below in Boston. London has been pressing Howe to level Boston — wipe out the "hornets-nest" of patriotism. Will Washington now, ironically, level the British garrison — wipe out the "hornets-nest" of Redcoats in General Howe's army?

Like the Americans on Breed's Hill, Howe's army is now looking straight into enemy gun barrels. They can't escape across the narrow neck of land leading inland. Washington will cut them to pieces. Should Howe call Washington's bluff and stay in Boston? It becomes a war of nerves!

Washington wins! Howe evacuates all the British by sea. He leaves the "hornets-nest" and heads for friendly, loyalist-rich New York City. Washington takes over Boston without spilling a drop of blood!

* Finally. Another victory. Something positive again.

* Yes. And in June 1776, something positive finally happens at Congress, too! Richard Henry Lee — radical, well-healed Virginian — makes it happen. He makes a bold proposal to send King George a declaration of all the Colonies' independence ... signed by all. The delegates in Congress know one thing for sure. If they put their name to such a declaration they become traitors to England. They'll all be hanged if captured by the British. Now they'll finally be holding their feet to the fire ... like Sam Adams and friends have been doing for years. They'll cease being behind-the-scenes philosophical supporters. Now, they are radical agitators, too!

Senior statesmen John Adams and Benjamin Franklin pick thirty three year old Thomas Jefferson to write the declaration. They tell him that something with magical powers, yet noble, will be needed to sway King George to their way of thinking. So Thomas Jefferson draws from all his former legal, historical, and

219

philosophical reading and thinking. The result is …… the **DECLARATION OF INDEPENDENCE**!

It doesn't convince King George. But that would take more than magic. That would take a miracle! For we know young King George is no mental whiz to start with. But rumour has it, he's contracting some kind of serious mental problem. Nevertheless, Thomas Jefferson gives it his best shot. He ends up writing an eloquent piece of moral and ethical and political philosophy!

In the Declaration of Independence he assembles his own views on independence, plus ideas of great philosophers, into a single document. The ideas of great philosophers are such things as Locke's rights of life, liberty, and revolt; Rousseau's democracy; Montesquieu's republicanism; Aristotle's "Happiness"; and so on. It's soaked in philosophy. It sways people toward accepting no less than complete independence!

John Adam's speech on July 1,1776 also sways people! It sways the delegates in Congress to accept the Declaration of Independence in the first place. For acceptance was not automatic. The delegates would be putting their lives on the line if they signed it. England would consider the document a declaration of treason. They would be signing their own death warrants. Adams will later say that, during his speech, he thought of Cicero and wished for Cicero's eloquence. For there was never an issue of greater importance to the entire world!

The crowd of people outside, screaming for independence, also sways Congress. So does the forest-like armada of British ships in New York harbor. They're filled with British troops … ready to stamp out the "hornets-nests" of patriotism all over America. And those troops on the ships are not even English. They're Germans — Hessians. It doesn't surprise or disappoint loyalist types. It does surprise radical patriots. It angers the "fence-sitters". Mother England is hiring outsiders to intrude in the "family" fight? That turns many undecided Americans into supporters of complete independence!

In this atmosphere of tension, delegates of the continuing Second Continental Congress adopt the Declaration of Independence on July 4, 1776! Thus, they serve notice that America forecloses England's right, forever, to rule over them! And they say why! The delegates state their firm reliance on the protection of God! And they pledge to eachother "their lives, their fortunes, and their sacred honor"!

* So now Sam Adams isn't the only one whose neck Parliament wants in the hangman's noose. He has plenty of company!

* He certainly does, Harry. I'll give you an idea of the atmosphere of tension and silence when delegates walk up to the table one at a time to sign the Declaration. It's from this letter, written afterwards, by Pennsylvania's Benjamin Rush to John Adams:

SIGNING THE DECLARATION

from: letter of Rush to Adams

"Do you recall your memorable speech upon the day on
which the vote was taken? Do you recall the awful silence

which pervaded when we were called up, one after another, to the table to subscribe to what was believed by many at that time to be our own death warrants? The silence of the morning was interrupted only for a moment by [huge] Benjamin Harrison of Virginia who said to [skinny] Elbridge Gerry of Massachusetts: 'I shall have a great advantage over you, Mr. Gerry, when we are hung for what we are now doing. From the size and weight of my body I shall die in a few minutes, but from the lightness of your body you will dance in the air an hour or two before you are dead.' This procured transient smiles, but it was soon succeeded by the solemnity with which the whole business was conducted."

The virtue is: Cooperation. It sometimes helps in handling fear.

Copies of the Declaration of Independence are sped on their way to England and all around America. On July 9th it reaches General Washington in New York. He reads it, amidst cheering and celebration, to all his troops!
* Did you say Washington is in New York? He's near that forest-like armada of British ships and troops in New York harbor? When did he go there?
* It was not long after he took Boston. He had kept Congress informed of his problems. He had advised them his rag-tag mob was progressing, but not a real army. He told them they were nowhere near ready to do battle against the world's mightiest army. Congress ordered him to New York City, anyway. Fighting General Howe's army would have been hard enough. But now ... bad luck ... the full might and power of Great Britain is in New York. And now, more than ever, it's crucial that Washington's rag-tag little army doesn't get captured. That would end the Revolution! And in Britain's eyes, the Americans wouldn't be prisoners of war. They'd be traitors!

Washington has to keep himself and his Army in the fight. He can't get knocked out in the first round. But he's facing Britain, the world champion! And his Army is amateurish, half-trained, and inexperienced at fighting. Forget Lexington and Concord, Bunker Hill, and Ticonderoga. They were only the preliminaries. Washington and his "fighter" are suddenly in the main event — the big time!

Washington approaches the fight with caution. He tries to feel-out his opponent. The British General Howe has a different strategy — go for the quick knockout. Don't fool around with these amateur colonists. So he immediately attacks with his larger, superior, professional force. He unleashes an awsome onslaught of charging, shooting, stabbing troops, and a thunderous bombardment from the warships! But just when he has the Americans trapped in a corner ... ready to hit them with the knockout punch ... Washington slips away and saves most of his so-called Army!

221

Howe's Army chases the Americans all around Long Island, Manhattan, and White Plains. They dish out terrible punishment trying to finish them off. But the startled, amateur Americans manage to stay away and keep moving. Finally Washington pulls off another sleight of hand. He gets his bruised, battered, bloodied, and wobbly Army across the Hudson River into New Jersey. The first round is over. They survive! Barely!

Now at least they have some time to lick their wounds, close their cuts, and stop the bleeding. And now Washington knows better what he can do, what he must do, what he will do. Now he's out of that geological trap and Loyalist hornets-nest they call New York City. He has favorable terrain before him. He can hit and move. Keep away from the big guns. Counterattack. Hit at the weak spots. No way can he stand toe-to-toe and trade blows with British power. He'll have to fight a guerilla war ... Indian style. They must not get knocked out of it. They must survive!

Throughout autumn and into winter Howe chases Washington's Continental army around New Jersey. The Americans hit and move. They cut up the British and bloody their noses a little at a time. The British, on the other hand, are always looking for the big blow — the knockout punch. To avoid it, Washington has to retreat across the Delaware River near Trenton. Finally, winter arrives. Bad weather changes the odds — causes upsets — according to European military thought. So part of the British army retires to the warmth of New York City for winter. They leave other parts of their army in New Jersey. General Howe figures cold weather and desertions will weaken Washington's Army over the winter. He'll finish Washington off with a crushing offensive come Spring!

* Desertion during the winter must be a problem for Washington.

* It is. But to desert, one must first belong. Many in Washington's army still feel they don't! After all, they've had promises made and broken — pay promised and not delivered! And anyone can see the British and German forces are overwhelming! People wonder how the tiny, tattered American Army can possibly win. They wonder how cold, hungry, bootless men can even survive! Wonder turns to doubt. Doubt turns to discouragement. Discouragement turns to fading support for the Revolution. Thus, the British get thousands of Americans along their route through New Jersey to New York to once again swear allegiance to the King!

* That has to be a real morale buster for the Army ... and a shock to Washington. Imagine your own people turning against you?

* It hurts! This is where Tom Paine helps. Washington has Paine's <u>American Crises</u> read to his troops. It says, "these are the times that try men's souls". This is also the time to take advantage of any kind of opportunity! And Washington's spies tell him the British's Hessian German troops are celebrating Christmas at nearby Trenton. The Hessians feel secure. They figure the Americans wouldn't be crazy enough to try crossing a treacherous ice-clogged Delaware River. But Washington does just that. They have prayers on Christmas day. Then on Christmas night ... it's back to business! Washington jockeys his men across the icy-clogged Delaware River. He launches a daring surprise attack on the celebrating Hessian Germans. It works! The half-frozen Americans drub them! They capture nearly 1000 men! The Americans finally win a round!

One week later, Washington pulls off another surprise. This time the target is an all-British force. He leaves his campfires burning to fool British spies. He quietly slips most of his army around the other side of the British at Princeton. Then, he hurls his heartened troops into another daring attack. They catch the British by surprise ... and capture Princeton! The Americans win another round! It shows that Trenton wasn't a fluke victory! And Washington shows all the skeptics that his Army has guts! In spite of what those of little faith think, he shows everyone that he and his little Army are able and willing to carry on!

CARRY ON

from: Robert Service

It's easy to fight when everythings right,
And you're mad with the thrill and the glory;
It's easy to cheer when victory's near,
And wallow in fields that are gory.
It's a different song when everythings wrong,
When you're feeling infernally mortal;
 It seems ten against one, and hope, there is none,
Buck up dear soldier, and chortle:
Carry on! Carry on!

It's so in the strife of the battle of life,
And easy to fight when you're winning;
It's easy to slave, and starve, and be brave,
When the dawn of success is beginning.
But the man who can meet despair and defeat
With a cheer, there's the man of God's choosing;
The man who can fight to Heaven's own height,
Is the man who can fight when he's losing.
Carry on, my son! Carry on!

The virtue is: Perseverance. Don't give up.

* Well, Thomas, Washington certainly shows he has perseverance! Now maybe Congress will let him run the War.
* Congress? The delegates in Philadelphia were amongst those of little faith! They had already decided Washington was doomed. They caught the first coach out of town to duck what they thought was the inevitable hangman's noose. And, they basically dumped everything into Washington's lap. So, Washington is alone. Other men would make themselves a dictator in this situation. But not Washington. He may not be an intellectual, but, he has Virtue! He knows what he wants. And dictator isn't it! He's like Caesar, the general — not Caesar, the

dictator. He sees himself as the hero of independence who will return home to his farm when it's all over.

Trenton and Princeton turn things around! They save the Revolution! They put England on notice. This Revolution will be fought on weekends and holidays — all year round. Many will die, even though incredibly, Washington lost only two men at Trenton. And those two men <u>froze</u> to death, at that.

* That <u>is</u> incredible. And we in modern America marvel at how Commander-in-chief H. Norman Schwarzkopf lost so few in the 1991 Gulf War. Although only one battle and not a war, Washington engineered an extraordinary triumph at Trenton!

* Trenton and Princeton are also important emotional victories, Harry. They bring Congress back out of hiding. They renew people's faith in the war effort. And town folks in New Jersey once again open their doors and stores to the Continental Army.

* What about that oath they took to the King?

* They say they were duped into it by being told the War was over. But let's go into a town ahead of Washington's Army and see for ourselves what town folks are saying:

> "Look! An army's approaching the town! An army's coming yet
> again!"
> "I don't see red coats. And it <u>can't</u> be Americans. It must be
> the Germans. Ah, good! We're in for another business
> bonanza here in town! Those Germans can really put the
> food and drink away. They know how to have a good time.
> And the best part — they pay! So hang up the 'Wilkommen'
> banners again, everybody! (now shouting out loud) ATTEN-
> TION EVERYONE! ALL TOWNSFOLK! LINE UP FOR
> ANOTHER PARADE! GET OUT YOUR BRITISH UNION
> JACK FLAGS AND THE 'WILKOMMEN' SIGNS!"

> "So are we on the British and German side again, mommy?"
> "Yes, of course missy. You know that from the last time!
> Now wave your little British flag. Not the one with the stars
> and stripes, honey!"
> "I get so confused, Mommy! First it's one, then the other!"

> "Look there Mrs! Here comes the advanced guard. And guess
> what? They're from <u>Washington</u>'s Army! They're talking
> about victories at Trenton and Princeton! Do you hear that,
> Mrs! I <u>knew</u> Washington could do it! Forget what every-
> one's been saying about him! I knew he was our man!"

> "Look mommy. I'm waving the British flag like you said! Aren't
> I good? Right? Right, mommy? Right?"
> "Missy! Put that flag away! Quick! Get the stars and stripes
> again! You have to wave the stars and stripes again! We're

on George Washington's side again!"
"Are we! Oh good! I like him better, anyway!"

(shouting) "GOD SAVE THE AMERICAN STATES AND THE
ARMY! LONG LIVE WASHINGTON! ... AND HURRY!
TAKE DOWN THE 'WILKOMMEN' SIGNS! EVERYONE GET
THE AMERICAN FLAGS BACK OUT!"[21]

* Even fair weather friends must look good to Washington now.
* Definitely! Friendship is like health, Harry. When you don't have it, you take
it however you can get it. And Washington now gets plenty of friendship again,
especially from folks in Morristown, New Jersey. He makes it his winter encampment. Meanwhile, General Howe parties away with his Army in New York City.
He figures he'll finish off Washington in the Spring!

Back in England, King George and all his cronies kick around various plans to
force Washington to throw in the towel. They rule out blockade because, believe
it or not, Britain is still doing brisk business with Loyalist Americans. And, they
already have plenty of troops. So they cook-up a complicated plan to divide and
conquer. They will divide the New England hornets-nest from the rest of America
by controlling the Hudson River!

England sends General John Burgoyne with his full-blown European style
army of 10,000 men and hundreds of cannons down Lake Champlain from
Montreal. General Howe is supposed to head north up the Hudson River. And a
British-Indian force is to head east from British frontier forts. They're all sup-
posed to squash the American Army up there in a three-jawed trap around Albany.
Then Howe and Burgoyne are to head south and wipe up the rest of the American
forces. Being economically interdependent, New England and the rest of
America will then beg for peace. That's how it's supposed to work. But
Commander-in-Chief, General Howe, already has cooked up his own plan. And
it's not complicated.
* Let me guess! It's to throw the knockout punch at Washington right away. End

the fight real quick.

* Exactly. And besides, he knows something London doesn't know. He knows the Americans have been working to block the Hudson River at West Point for well over a year. So why fight that battle when you don't have to? The Hudson River could be a big trap for the British. The terrain is rough. His European-style troops could be savaged by Washington's sniping, Indian-style fighters up there. Why fight a guerrilla war when you have overwhelming power on your side? He figures that Burgoyne and the Indian allies can take care of the American forces up North without his help. He plans to crush Washington, himself. He plans to personally hand-deliver Washington's sword to King George … along with a petition for peace. So Howe gets word to Burgoyne that he'll wipe-out the main part of Washington's armies at Philadelphia. Burgoyne and the army from the West are to proceed as planned — snuff out the smaller American army up there.

Burgoyne gets Indian tribes to raid American settlements. He re-captures Fort Ticonderoga. London celebrates. New England shudders. Burgoyne then takes Fort Edward without a fight. Washington calls on New Englanders to save their families. Thousands of recruits are needed. New Englanders rise to the call. The forests now become thick with American militia along Burgoyne's route south to Albany. It becomes slow and bloody for the British. They're now shadowed and harassed in a crossfire all the way. Marksmen behind trees and rocks pick off Burgoyne's troops one by one. It's a turkey shoot. It's like the British death-march from Concord to Boston in 1775!

Burgoyne finally reaches Saratoga. He's already lost hundreds of men due to the snipers. And a part of his army, foraging for food and horses, is badly whipped at Bennington, Vermont. The force from the West is also embroiled in fighting along their route. They don't make it to Albany either. The whole plan is unravelling!

Farmers and militiamen keep arriving from all over. Burgoyne is now actually outnumbered three to one! It's the European soldier verses "Hawkeye" all over again. And it's no contest. The British are slowly and methodically butchered. The slaughter goes on and on. Burgoyne runs out of supplies. Some men are too sick to fight. Others are too weak to fight. Many hundreds are wounded. And now he counts over 600 more men lost since reaching Saratoga. If this goes on, his entire army will be picked-off by American sharpshooters — one at a time. After a whole lot of soul-searching, Burgoyne decides he can't allow that to happen. This can't go on. He makes the crucial decision. He surrenders his entire Army!

The Americans suffer only 150 casualties. General Benedict Arnold is the real hero. General Horatio Gates takes all the credit. General Howe gets the blame. King George is shocked. He goes ballistic. Ben Franklin, in Paris, switches from politely pleading, to proudly pushing for aid and support from France. In the Fall of 1777, he finally gets it!

Meanwhile, Howe takes Philadelphia! He thought the Americans were daring and valiant in the face of defeat in an earlier battle at Brandywine. But they really shock him at Germantown. They take the British Army's best shots. They're knees buckle. But they fight to a standstill. Howe just can't finish them off! Washington's Army is bruised and bloodied, but it's still in there slugging it out!

It looks like Howe can't get a quick knockout, afterall!

The Fall of 1777 turns to winter. Americans get the Articles of Confederation — the first set of "federal" laws. Howe gets the warmth, comfort, and parties of Philadelphia's winter social season. He gets the hospitality of Loyalist high society. So do his men. The town fills up with uppercrust Loyalist families from around the Colonies … and their pretty daughters. The young British officers decked out in their impressive looking bright red uniforms have a ball chasing after all the eligible young ladies:

"Oh such a boring party! Slip out with me for milk and cookies, my dear Rebecca?"

"My dear Nigel, you're too, too bold. Where is your chivalry?"

"I only follow what your own Benjamin Franklin said: 'never leave till tomorrow what you can do today'."

"Mr. Franklin also says, 'make haste slowly'."

"Ah, but 'one Today is worth two Tomorrows', ma'am."

"But sir, 'he that expects nothing shall never be disappointed'."

"I do not expect rapture from you, dear ma'am. But 'being ignorant is not so much a shame, as being unwilling to learn'."

"Yet I, dear sir, must consider that 'reputation, like glass and china, is easily cracked, and never well mended'."

"Then my dear ma'am, I must take leave of our liaison. For 'early to bed and early to rise, makes a man healthy, wealthy and wise'." ᵒᵒThat should get her.ᵒᵒ

"Oh, Nigel! You're such a savage!" [22]

Scenes such as this take place all through the winter. The British and their Loyalist friends fritter away scarce food and drink with their feasts and luxury!

Washington watches them from just outside of Philadelphia in the hills of Valley Forge. These hills are windy. Snowy. Cold. Desolate. And, they become bloody. Many men don't even have shoes. Their feet leave tracks of blood in the snow!

* No shoes? That's incredible!

* Now, add hunger to the scene at Valley Forge. Add disease ... 2000 men will die from disease! Add not being paid. Add farmers returning home to their crops. Add some newcomers to America slipping back to the British side. You can begin to get an idea of how terrible this winter at Valley Forge is!

Martha Washington and George Washington suffer right along with everyone else. The men are awed with his leadership-by-example. They become endeared to her. She forages around the countryside and brings food and clothing and good spirits to the most sick and desperate of them!

The healthy are kept busy by Washington's new drill master, Baron Von Steuben, straight from the Prussian Army. He's a disciplinarian, but he's a soldiers' best friend. He's making them as good as the British soldier. They don't realize it, but that could mean life or death to them!

Even Washington's protege', the Marquis de Lafayette from France, becomes the soldiers' friend. He sets another kind of example. He's rich, but still suffers hardship right along with them for the sake of their cause! And he'll hand over much of his fortune to the American cause before it's all over!

The soldiers themselves are from the bottom of the social ladder. Many are Scotch-Irish indentured servants — part of 1/4 million "white slaves" from Northern Ireland. They've joined the Continental Army to take their chances in order to earn their freedom!

As Spring approaches, Ben Franklin in Paris gets King Louis XVI to sign an alliance with America! So ... enter France! And of immediate importance to the War ... enter Haym Solomon the Jewish financial whiz! For Solomon is trusted by France, by banks, and by the Jewish Community. He does what Congress can't do — raise money to pay for food, supplies, and wages! Washington's deputy, Nathanael Greene, tramps around the Country to find the food and supplies. Haym Solomon uses his skills, connections, and good offices — and his own money — to pay for the food and supplies. When Haym Solomon dies several years from now, he'll be penniless. He will have given everything he has to America!

So Washington does everything he can think of to hold the Army together. He even orders the play, Cato, performed for the men to shore up morale. Cato is one of Plutarch's classics. It's about the Roman general Cato, and his army, who tried to save the Roman republic. They tried to stop Caesar from forming a dictatorship. It's an example of a selfless, virtuous struggle for liberty — just the example Washington needs for morale!

By the end of Spring, misery turns to plenty at Valley Forge — plenty of food, plenty of clothing. But something more amazing happens. A metamorphosis — a change — takes place! Yes, thousands have died. But thousands survived. No

— thousands are "re-born". They're different men … and a different Army. They survived the challenge of their lives. They know what they're made of. They're proud. They're more determined than ever. Washington has enrooted his army with character! He not only has leaders of character, but followers with character! He's put old souls into young bodies the surest way — through painstakingly surviving hardship!

Valley Forge will someday be one of the models West Point follows in order to build character. Like Valley Forge, West Point will cause a metamorphesis to take place in young men and women. Like Valley Forge, hundreds will not survive the hardship at West Point. But hundreds of others will. And they also will be "re-born"! Become different people. Survive the challenge of their lives. Know what they're made of. Become leaders of character. Like the survivors at Valley Forge, they'll have old souls put into their young bodies by painstakingly surviving hardship … a different kind of hardship … but hardship, nevertheless!

* The survivors at Valley Forge aren't likely to skip-out like the others did, are they.

* You don't throw away the wheat after painstakingly separating it from the chafe, do you Harry. And General Howe, living it up in Philadelphia, likely beholds this metamorphosis of character with amazement — possibly even with horror. Washington's Army didn't freeze, crack, crumble, and disappear over the winter as he expected it to. He must now secretly conclude that he can never completely crush Washington's Army. He knows he can't sucker Washington into a European style fight. And he knows strong determination when he see's it. He's impressed. So, there will be no Spring offensive for Howe. Instead, he shocks everyone! He resigns his command and returns to England!

Howe's commander from New York City, General Henry Clinton, takes over. Unlike Howe, Clinton believes the British must master the Hudson River to master America. Therefore, he pulls the British Army out of Philadelphia and moves north. And guess what happens. Washington's newly confident and disciplined Army follows them! The momentum of the fight has changed! Now Washington chases the British, instead of the other way around! He harasses and skirmishes with Clinton's rear guard. Clinton stops moving and exchanges blows at Monmouth, New Jersey near Freehold. It's a solid round of fighting for both sides. But, when British losses mount to about 250 men, Clinton retreats. His bloodied and cut-up Army ferries across the water to New York. American losses are less than 70! Washington's Army wins another round!

During this same summer of 1778, George Rogers Clark captures forts in the Ohio Valley, including strategic Fort Vincennes. As the British fortify Hudson River strongholds, Washington moves his army to the Hudson Highlands. Like Clinton, Washington also has always advocated a master-the-Hudson strategy. And now it again looks like a British attack up the Hudson is in the cards. So the American Army gets preparations to control the Hudson at West Point up to speed!

A place called Stony Point is located several miles south of West Point. It's a granite mass jutting out into the River. The British fortify it to the teeth. General Clinton believes Stony Point is impregnable. It'll be his launching pad for the siege of West Point. For West Point is the only obstacle to his mastering the Hudson River, and thus, all of America. Washington knows Clinton is onto something there. So the Americans must do the impossible. They must capture impregnable Stony Point.

It will take a fast, daring, gutsy, surprise, well-planned, well-executed raid to overtake this impregnable stronghold. Washington gets all of that from General "Mad Anthony" Wayne! Wayne's small force of 1300 men smash their way in and capture the stronghold in July 1779! It's not a major <u>physical</u> blow to the British Army in America. But it is a <u>psychological</u> blow. It takes the champion's legs away. The British in the Hudson Highlands have nothing left with which to launch an attack on West Point! Washington waits and watches with many thousands of troops in the Hudson Highlands. England lets him. For England plans some psychological warfare of its own.

* Psychological warfare from England? How can they do that?
* Remember this, Harry. Only about one third of the people in America are revolutionaries. About one third are still loyal to England. And about one third are in between. While Washington has been out there using fancy footwork to keep his Army from getting knocked out of the fight, troubles have been brewing back home. And England knows it. So England will do everything it can to make the troubles worse. That's the psychological warfare.

We'll go around the Country and see for ourselves the troubles that are brewing. For instance, listen to this mob of people at the market in Philadelphia protesting the greed of merchants:

> "This robber baron wants two standard sacks of that new 'funny-money' in exchange for these goods! I only paid one standard sack just last week! It's outrageous. Let's throw'em in the River … with one of his standard sacks of stones for shoes! There's the scoundrel now! Let's go over and talk to him!"
>
> "What's the meaning of this? State your business!"
>
> "You're buying up all the goods! Then you're selling them to foreigners — French, Dutch, even the British — instead of to us, or to Congress for our suffering Army."
>
> "You lot can bid fair and square against foreigners."
>
> "Not when you big-wigs are colluding, hoarding, and price gouging! You're sending prices up into the cosmos, and the economy down into the toilet! Don't you know some people — especially our soldiers — are starving?"
>
> "I'm free to get as much as I can get! Now get out!"
>
> "Oh yeh! Then <u>we're</u> free to get as much as we can get, after <u>you</u> get out! Grab'm boys! Put'm on the first coach out of town!"
>
> "Help! Someone help! The mob's gone crazy! Help! It's anarchy!"
>
> "There's no one to help you now, Mister Bigshot! Your British friends have cleared off! Consider yourself lucky! You <u>could</u> be in the River wearing a sack of stones for shoes!"[23]

* So that's the trouble? Big merchants and businessmen are greedy — using underhanded methods, creating scarce supply, and running up prices? Why would they do that to their own people?

* Because greed will always be like salt-water. You know? The more you drink, the thirstier you get? It's the same for wealth. Big businesses are getting richer and richer from the misery and suffering of soldiers. By the time Congress is done paying the high prices to price-gouging businessmen for its purchases, it has no money left to pay the soldiers!

The greed and money problems split the population into three economic factions, along with the three political factions I told you about. On the one side are working people and "moral-market" backers. They care about virtues, common good, fair prices, and fair business conditions. On the other side are "free-market" backers. They're: the rich; the privileged; the big businesses; and the greedy merchants. They push laissez-faire — free trade — business conditions. Let the buyer beware. Anything goes in business ... including collusion, monopoly, price gouging, paying off officials, and using slave labor — both black and white! In the center is the new middle class — professionals, small businessmen, and government officals. Unfortunately, they side with the rich and privileged — either out of need or greed. So England schemes to widen this split between the three economic factions in America.

And money troubles are not the only troubles on the home front. Up North, some States offer slave-owners land and money for slaves they provide the Army ... both black and white ones. Slaves win their freedom if they serve out their enlistments. Down South, however, that idea is like poison. Let's listen to the talk around Charleston:

"Thay'ya puttin' slaves in the Continental ahmy up North and actually givin'em guns!"

"No! Ah wouldn't lahke to do that down heya. Mah business would go unda real fast. And ya'll can't tell. Ahm'd slaves maht just turn on us instead of on the British!"

"Ah agree. So you be careful now in town with yaw slaves! The British ah promisin' all the slaves thayr freedom if thay bolt on thay're ownas. The word's gettin 'round the plantations. But Ah he-ya that the slaves end up dead or comin back again".

"Ah know. Ah he-ya thayrs a lot in the British Ahmy. And thay're usin' some on ships, too. Thayrs a lot dyin'of small-pox and the fevah. Thay also get traded as booty or some-thin' of that sort. So thay wind up back on some other plan-tation or in the Continental Ahmy!"

"If Ah find any of mah slaves in the blue uniform, Ah'll sue the Ahmy! If thay're in the red coat, Ah'll hang'em! And if Ah catch'em escapin', or off somewhere else, thay'll be hell to pay!"

"Well, those damned British ah creatin' a holy mess around he-ya. Thay're creatin' a slave revolution raht inside of ah own revolution!"

That's happening down South. Now let's look at western New York. The British tell the Indians they can have their land back if they drive the settlers out. So Indians and Loyalists attack settlements! The town of Albany is now buzzing with fear and anger:

"Those mindless savages are on the rampage again to the west of here. I hear they're scalping women and children! That's after they burn, rape, and pillage! It's revoltin'!"

"It's that Mohawk leader, Joseph Brant. He's in tight with the British. Did you know that after he graduated from Dartmouth College he went to live in England and rubbed elbows with the elite over there? His Iroquois Confederacy has a deal going with England to get back the territory in western New York if they start an Indian uprising!"

"Word has gotten to General Washington. He's sendin' an army up here to help the frontier colonists."

"The only way to deal with those savages is savagely! Burn their villages, like they burn ours!"

"Well, I know Washington's army has to do somethin' fast and decisive up here. He's expectin' a major attack up the Hudson from New York City at any time! He can't spare those men up here for long!"[24]

General Washington does send part of his army in late 1779 to fight the Indian-Loyalist coalition. The smaller Indian forces are defeated by Washington's men. But they can't be captured. They melt into the forests. The American army burns everything in sight — food, crops, supplies, and villages. That prevents the Indians from fighting again anytime soon. But as we all know, Harry, it'll prove to be only a temporary solution to the Indian wars.

And now look at West Point. It's a bastian. It's surrounded by little fortifications called redoubts. It has hundreds of cannons. It's at the "7" in the river where ships have to stop and turn. And it has an iron chain blocking the River. That's in case anything slips by the "7" without being blown out of the water. Washington has made West Point into M.A.D. — Mutually Assured Destruction.

The British and Americans are now mutually assured anything on the river will be destroyed. It's the first American "deterrent". It's the first American "cold war", complete with tension, spying, military readiness, an iron curtain (chain), and an S.D.I. — Strategic Defense Initiative. But during the brutal winter of 1779-80, this cold war turns into cold survival for the men at West Point.

* You make it sound like that blackest of winters at Valley Forge.
* It is. And in many ways it's even worse. Survivors of both will look on it as the worst winter they've ever seen!
* In what way?
* Temperatures are sub-zero. Huts are windy. Winds are biting. Food supplies are dwindling. Clothes are raggedy. Shoes are falling apart. And it keeps snowing. Listen to what they're saying:

"I hear our commander is drawing lots, to share them huts the Massachusetts line just built."

"Is that what those stacks of timber are? Huts?"

"Yeh. And we have a choice. It's either tents, or them huts with them Massachusetts guys!"

"I'm for the tents! At least they stop the wind!"

"Yeh. And no way will I bunk with any guys from Massachusetts!"

"We'd better tell the commander, if we win the draw, we want tents!"

"Yeh. And we better tell him to draw lots for the scraps of food left in storage. I hear they're already eating birch bark, and roasted shoeleather in some other outfits."

"I heard that too. And even Officers are starving! They roasted one Officer's favorite little dog! The joke around post is that the Congress surely doesn't have a system-of-nutrition for us. It has a system-of-starvation!"

"And it doesn't have a pay system either! But, pay or no pay, when my enlistment is up ... I'm outta here! They can owe me my pay!"

"Just don't desert! The rumour is that some of those guys from Massachusetts are talking about desertion. They've been told they'll get hung if caught"

"Don't worry. I'm no quitter. Besides, things have to get better. This winter can't get any worse!"[25]

Things get worse!

* How? I don't see bloody footprints in the snow like at Valley Forge!

* No. You won't, Harry. It's so cold here, men's feet are freezing solid with gangrene <u>before</u> they can bleed! And the winter <u>does</u> get worse. Terrible blizzards of snowfall bury West Point under snow measured in feet ... not inches. It buries the firewood. It buries supply lines. It buries hope of a mild start to 1780, and an early Spring. Many will never see Spring. It buries hopes of no desertions. Desertions increase!

Massachusetts soldiers desert by the hundreds. Faithful soldiers are organized to pursue and bring them back. To keep them back they're spared the typical harsh punishments. They could have been hung or shot dead or whipped or run bare through a gauntlet of a hundred men lashing them with sticks. Now, they just get the whipping. That turns out to be a poor deterrent. A few months later, Connecticut soldiers desert!

In March the thickly frozen Hudson begins to melt. With it, melts American fear of attack from New York City. The rock-solid frozen Hudson River had become an Achilles heel. Thousands of British soldiers on sleighs, cannons included, could have made it to West Point over the frozen River in a few days. No way could weak and starving defenders have stopped them. Ironically, two feet of snow turned out to be a blessing. It prevented such a British attack. Instead, the British went to parties all winter in Loyalist New York City, as scheduled. But, like at Valley Forge, survivors of the West Point hardships will "graduate" from being ordinary men to becoming men of character. That "class" of 1780 survivors will be the first in a long and proven line of classes that will continue to graduate men and women of character through surviving hardship at West Point!

So, the Country is an array of powder-kegs. Hungry people. Unpaid soldiers. Rampaging Indians. Runaway slaves. Misery at West Point. Everyone of them threatens to explode. Every one of them threatens to blow-away the Revolution. But, ironically, the biggest threat turns out to be something caused by greed, financial bribery, and lack of character. It's called treason! And it's spelled ......

Benedict Arnold!

* So this is when Benedict Arnold commits treason at West Point.
* Yes. After this terrible winter that almost turns the "Gibralter of the Hudson" into a fortress of ghosts, Arnold gets the top command at West Point. He sells the plans of West Point to a British spy, a Major Andre. With plans in hand and Arnold in command, the British can merely walk in and take over. The Hudson River, and probably the War, will be theirs. However, Washington gets lucky. Major Andre is picked up enroute to the British command in New York. The treason is exposed. West Point is saved. America is saved. Andre is hanged. But Benedict Arnold escapes. He'll now fight against his fellow Americans!

Arnold lied to Washington. He cheated on his obligation to protect the men he was responsible for. And he stole the plans to West Point. He lied, cheated, and stole. He lacked a key moral virtue. Honesty. Someday, honesty will be the cornerstone of virtues taught at West Point! And it's no surprise that West Point's honor code will say: "you will not lie, cheat, or steal ... nor tolerate those who do!"

* It's shocking that Benedict Arnold, war hero, becomes Benedict Arnold, traitor!
* I agree, Harry. Up until now he probably was Washington's favorite General! He's smart and brave and strong willed. He was courageous at Ticonderoga, Canada, and Saratoga. But his energy and enthusiasm got channeled in the wrong direction. His strong will and courage — normally good traits — turned out to be good for England, bad for America. He's an example of the difference between people merely placed in leadership positions, even brave ones, and people who are trained to be bonafide good-leaders!

Washington, of course, is shocked out of his socks! Why did a trusted friend betray him? How does he prevent this in the future? How does he get good-leaders for the Army? How does America get good-leaders in the future? What are the answers to these questions?

Aristotle had answered these questions 2000 years ago:

FROM THE NICOMACHEAN ETHICS

by: Aristotle

Virtue, then, is of two kinds, intellectual and moral: intellectual virtue in the main owes both its birth and its growth to teaching (for which reason it requires experience and time). Moral virtue comes about as a result of habit. From this it is also plain that none of the moral virtues arise in us by nature; for nothing that exists by nature can form a habit contrary to its nature. For instance, the stone cannot be habituated to fall upward, nor can flames be habituated to flare downward. Neither by nature do the virtues [honesty] arise in us. But we are adapted to <u>receive</u> them [by nature] and they are made perfect by <u>habit</u>. For we habituate by doing, eg, become builders by building, and lyre-players by playing the lyre. So too, we become just by doing just acts, brave by doing-brave acts, [honest by honest acts]. Thus, states of character arise out of like activities — practice!

The virtue is: Wisdom. It's wiser to develope people of trust, than to trust people.

Benedict Arnold taught Washington and America a lesson. Leaders are like books. You can't tell a good one by looking at the dustcover. It's what's <u>inside</u> that counts. And by now the British know what Washington has inside. He has fought them to a stand-still. The champion British Army has not been able to knock out the amateur American upstart. The war in the North is stalemated. It's a draw. And a draw is good enough! It's a moral victory for Washington!

But now Washington has a new worry. King George and his generals have shifted the war to the South. Loyalists and slaves down there have been going over to the British side in droves. With their help, the British calculate the South will crumble. And as you're now about to see, that calculation is appearing more and more to be accurate!

Commander-in-Chief Clinton and General Cornwallis put many shiploads of troops ashore and take Savannah! Then American General Benjamin Lincoln foolishly barricades his army behind defenses in Charleston. Cornwallis surrounds them and forces him to surrender too … with 5000 men! Half those are experienced regulars of the Continental Army. Washington sends the self proclaimed hero of Saratoga, General Horatio Gates, to replace General Lincoln. Gates probably had dishonestly grabbed credit for Saratoga away from Benedict Arnold. But at least he's not a traitor like Arnold. Unfortunately, he's not a hero, either. He bungles the job, badly. He allows Cornwallis to destroy most of his army at Camden, South Carolina. Then in a panic, the "hero" of Saratoga frantically beats a chaotic retreat. Washington tells him to keep right on going. The Commander-in-Chief sends Nathanael Greene to replace him.

These have been the worst beatings of the War for the Americans. They've lost three straight rounds. Their knees are buckling. Their eyes are glazing over. Cornwallis cuts through the South like a hot knife through butter — raiding, ravaging, and destroying. Clinton tells King George the South is theirs. Leaving Cornwallis to mop up the Carolinas and Virginia, he sails with his fleet back to New York. Washington's shrinking Continental Army has now shrunk even further due to these losses down South. Clinton's next target — which he reckons to be the last — will be the Hudson River in order to finally split America in two. That means an attack on West Point. That also means Washington's northern Army is locked-in up North. It can't rescue his battered southern Army. And the problems down South are continuing. General Cornwallis' main army is marauding its way northward through the Carolinas. At the same time, British units further north are marauding their way up through Virginia. And guess who the commander of those units is? It's none other than Benedict Arnold! He's out to capture the entire rebel Virginia legislature, especially Thomas Jefferson — now the Governor of Virginia!

Thomas Jefferson is at Monticello when he gets word of the marauding British:

> "Sir! The British are in Virginia! Word's out they aim to hang you!"
>> "Oh? Have our people call out the militia. I'm reading Rousseau right now."
> "They've done that already, Governor!"

(next day)

> "Sir. The British are closer! They're ravaging Richmond! They're headed this way!"
>> "Don't worry. Our brave and glorious popular militia will protect us. Now, please allow me to continue studying my Aristotle."

(next day)

> "Sir. British dragoons are this minute a few miles from here!"
>> "Where the devil is our militia? Get someone in touch with Washington's Regulars. And, lock up my library. Hide the china and silver. Grab my diaries. And mount up my horse. I'll be leaving now … as soon as I finish breakfast."[26]

Thomas Jefferson mounts his horse and races away just in the nick of time! British dragoons arrive only a few minutes later!

* That was a close shave, Thomas. Anyone who comes that close to being hung will never forget it. I'll bet that Jefferson never forgets his "people's militia" of Virginia wasn't there when he needed them!

* No doubt! The militia is like an unfaithful marriage partner who makes a lot of promises, but lives up to little. Meanwhile, Washington up near West Point hears about the British raids in Virginia. He knows his beloved Mount Vernon is a target. He knows Benedict Arnold is involved. That makes his blood boil. He would love to capture Arnold. So he quietly peels off some troops from his Army camped near West Point. Sending them South under General Lafayette, Washington's instructions are … nail Arnold! Unfortunately, Lafayette arrives too late. Arnold slips away from the hanging noose for a second time. Lafayette finds his force in a strategic position, however. He can keep an eye on British movements. He can supply intelligence information to Washington. He's near a place called Yorktown in Virginia!

The British may think the South is theirs. But Colonel Francis Marion, the "Swamp Fox", in South Carolina has a different opinion. His army of back-woodsmen begins to cut the British up pretty good. They strike, Indian style, then melt into the swamps like foxes! Thus his name — the Swamp Fox!

Daniel Morgan and his sharp shooting guerrilla army does the same. Early in 1781, Morgan cleverly lures Cornwallis into a trap at Cowpens in South Carolina. His army badly beats up on the British. Then they disappear to fight another day. The British drive them off … but at a terrible cost in lives!

Nathanael Greene's men also wittle away at Cornwallis' army in the Carolinas using guerrilla warfare. Greene knows that Cornwallis is aching for a European style fight. So, at Guilford Court House, Greene pretends to give him one. As the cocky British "line" drives the Americans backward, the trap is sprung. Green's cavalry charges the British from all directions. The British are savagly chopped up trying to fend off the cavalry. Greene then withdraws, completely intact. So Cornwallis doesn't lose. But again, his troops are bruised and battered. They hobble and stagger northward into Virginia.

Daniel Morgan and Anthony Wayne and Lighthorse Harry Lee and Nathanael Greene and Francis Marion are winning the South back! They're stalking and trapping and cutting the British to ribbons by hit-and run attacks throughout the Carolinas and Virginia. Corwallis isn't losing the battles, but he's losing the cam-paign. We only have to listen to what his troops are saying:

> "We've six wins and no losses down 'ere mates. The rebels 'ave
> nought and six. Winning is fun, isin' it!"
>   "Ah we' avin fun Sahgent? It doesn't _feel_ like we're 'avin
>   fun! If _we_ ah winning, why do I feel so beat up?"
> "Oh. Not to worry, mate! That's only from the rebs not fight-ing
> by the rules. They don't fight fair. The cowards 'ide, instead of
> stand up and fight fair so we can 'ave a fair go at them!"
>   "Oh. Then if we ah beating them, why don't they go away?
>   They keep coming 'round again."
> "Steady on now mates. "Ere they come. They want some more,

do they? We'll give it to them! KEEP IN STRAIGH_T LINES
(shout) NOW! DON'T GE_T SLOPPY!"

"Those colonials ah shoo_ting a_t us — straigh_t away! When
do <u>we</u> shoot?"

(shout) "STEA-<u>DY</u>. KEEP MOVING FORWARD MATES. KEEP YOUR
LINES STRAIGH_T. BE ON THE READY TO FIRE NOW!"

"Fire? At what? Where ah they?"

"Blimey! They've disappeared! The cowards! They were 'ere a
momen_t ago!"

"Uh oh! Something bothers me about this se_t-up! We 'ave
done this before! …… ere they ah!"

"Bloo<u>dy</u>'ell! Look at them! Where they all come from? That
bloo<u>dy</u> lot is all 'round us! They 'ave us trapped!

(shout) AND YOU THERE! YOU TORY LOYALISTS! WHERE YOU RUN-
NING OFF TO? STOP IN THE NAME OF KING GEORGE! HE SAYS
<u>WE</u> OWN THE SOUTH! STOP!"

(shout) "KING GEORGE IS CRAZY! IF YOU OWN THE SOUTH, THEN
GOOD! YOU DON'T NEED US! WE'RE OUTTA HERE!"
ᵒᵒYou're as crazy as King George!ᵒᵒ 27

It's a long, bloody march into Virginia for Cornwallis' Army. His men need
time to rest, and lick their wounds. What better place than Yorktown? It's well
protected on a penninsula. And the British fleet is just offshore in the Chesapeake
Bay. It can deliver supplies. It can deliver troops. It can evacuate Cornwallis'
army in the highly unlikely need to retreat.

Lafayette sends Washington a report on Cornwallis' position. Washington
smells blood. Next round of fighting <u>he</u>'ll be the one on the attack, for once.

British forces are divided. Half are in New York with Clinton, half in Virginia with Cornwallis. Up North the French General de Rochambeau has finally accepted Washington's authority as the allied Commander-in-Chief. Now a joint attack is possible. Several thousand French added to the several thousand Continentals outnumber Clinton in New York. The problem is, the British still hold the wild card — the British fleet! And that means warships ... firepower ... hundreds of big cannons.

Then good news arrives. It's almost the hurricane season in the Carribean where a French fleet of ships is holed up. They're about to move North for two months. This is the opportunity Washington has been waiting for. Use the French fleet against the wild card — neutralize the British fleet. Then storm General Clinton's army with American and French troops. Trap him on Staten Island and Manhattan. Remove the threat to the Hudson River and West Point. Isolate Cornwallis' Army in Virginia. Then go get them next!

Washington's chance of landing a knockout punch soars! The plan is set. The Americans are "up" for the fight. So are the French. It sounds too good to be true. Unfortunately, it is. The French fleet commander, Admiral de Grasse, is like a school kid passing a candy store with milk money. The temptation is too great. Here he has this luscious smaller fleet of British warships — less than his twenty-eight ships — sitting right there inside of Chesapeake Bay. Why go all the way to New York? So he gets word to Washington. He'll attack the British fleet in the Chesapeake. That blows the whole plan! There goes the showdown in New York!

Washington is livid! Outraged! Finally, he decides to do the next best thing. He'll retool his showdown with the British — do it the other way around. Now he'll first get Cornwallis. Then he'll come back for Clinton later. It means a forced — hard-paced — 500 mile march to Virginia because Admiral de Grasse won't be there very long. But Washington's troops trust him. They'll follow him anywhere. If he tells them this is big, that's good enough for them!

Washington leaves 3000 men at West Point — enough to repel any attack on that citadel. He and Rochambeau set out from West Point with 7000 French and American troops. They'll join up with Lafayette's regiment, "Mad Anthony" Wayne's Southern army, Admiral de Grasse's fleet, and 3000 troops off de Grasse's ships. The total of 16,000 troops will outnumber Cornwallis' whittled down Army.

The larger French fleet of ships surprises the smaller British fleet and drives them away. That shocks Cornwallis. Now he can't escape or re-supply by sea if he has to. But he feels he shouldn't have to. Then comes another surprise. Lafayette appears with his small force. It's small, but big enough to hem Cornwallis in from one side. Still, Cornwallis feels that's not a problem either. He has another escape route ... if he even needs one!

That night, Washington arrives with his Armies. They immediately dig deep siege trenches. In the morning, Cornwallis awakens to a big shock! He has no escape route left! He's completely bottled up on the penninsula! He's surrounded — hemmed in from all sides now!

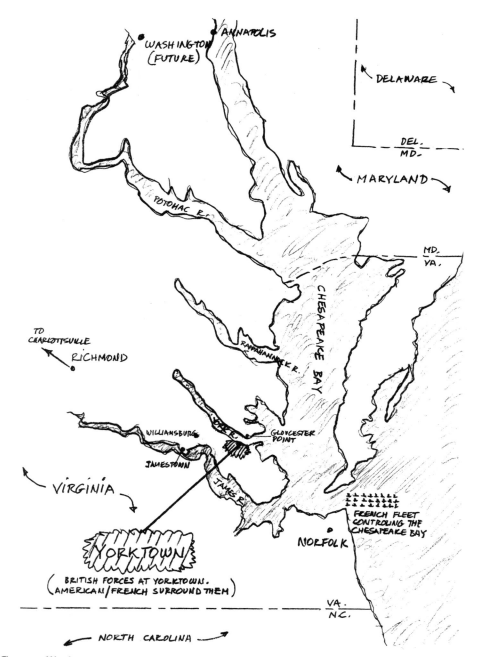

WASHINGTON
(FUTURE)

ANNAPOLIS

DELAWARE

DEL.
MD.

MARYLAND

POTOMAC R.

MD.
VA.

CHESAPEAKE BAY

TO
CHARLOTTSVILLE

RICHMOND

RAPPAHANNOCK R.

WILLIAMSBURG

YORK R.

GLOUCESTER
POINT

JAMESTOWN

VIRGINIA

JAMES R.

FRENCH FLEET
CONTROLING THE
CHESAPEAKE BAY

NORFOLK

YORKTOWN

(BRITISH FORCES AT YORKTOWN.
AMERICAN/FRENCH SURROUND THEM)

VA.
NC.

NORTH CAROLINA

Cornwallis has no way out, and no way to get supplies in, because of the huge French fleet in the Bay. He'll have to fight his way out against the larger American-French army. He's thunderstruck!

American assault forces led by Colonel Alexander Hamilton capture a major British stronghold. The French and Americans unleash withering and relentless

242

cannonading onto the trapped British army. The siege and cannonading go on and on … for twenty days! Then on 17 October 1781, Cornwallis sees that it's hopeless. He does the humane thing for his starving, battered, disease-laden men. He surrenders his entire Army!!

The surrender of Cornwallis is one of England's greatest disasters! It's one of America's greatest triumphs! General Washington's skill at coordinating many different sea and land forces is one of the great displays of leadership in history! And Cornwallis can make no excuses. No denials. No claims that guerrilla style victories are not real victories. Washington finally got his chance. He showed he can win their way — the European style way. That's what is shocking and devastating to the British back in London. It's a stunning victory for Washington … by European rules!

* Imagine the anger of King George? He must go bananas this time!

* When you're angry, you count to ten before speaking. When you're very angry, you count to one hundred. But when King George III hears the bad news from Lord North, he gets so bent out of shape, he can't even count:

> "Your majesty. I am regrettably the bearer of bad news."
> "I don't want bad news, North! Go away!"
> "Forgive me King George. It bears on our colonies with the utmost gravity. Cornwallis has lost at Yorktown!"
> "Yorktown? What the devil is Yorktown? Don't bother me with the small stuff!"
> "Yes. Yorktown is a small place. That's the good news. The bad news is … Cornwallis has surrendered his entire army! And General Clinton in New York has honored the surrender. I'm afraid we are defeated. We have lost our American colonies."

(shout) "WHAT? SURRENDERED! HE CAN'T SURRENDER! I'M THE KING! WHOSE WAR IS THIS, ANYWAY? SEND WORD HE CANNOT SURRENDER! FIGHT HARDER! CHANGE COMMANDERS! WASHINGTON'S ARMY ISN'T A REAL ARMY. JUST A BAND OF GUERRILLAS! THAT'S NOT A REAL DEFEAT! THAT'S NOT A REAL BATTLE!"

> "Forgive me Your Majesty. Washington's army fought by our rules this time."
> "THEN IT'S PARLIAMENT'S FAULT. NO, IT'S YOURS! YOUR FIRED!!" [28]

England's venture into the New World is now ending. It's ending just twenty-five miles from where it began at Jamestown 174 years ago! Washington moves his forces back up to West Point. They have thrown a knockout punch. The champ is down … for good. But, you'll see, it will be two whole years before King George reluctantly swallows a formal peace treaty. It will not be until September 1783 that he finally chokes one down.

So, that's how the philosophical revolution in the hearts and minds of people turned into a shooting revolution for independence from England. And it all began with Descartes' "doubt and enlightenment" that led to a wave of change in the 1600's. Remember? That wave of change turned into a tidal-wave that crashed down onto the shores of America during the 1700's Enlightenment. Now it has finally swallowed up England's venture in America!

* Where do the Colonies go from here?

* Good question. The shooting revolution is over. But the philosophical revolution isn't. Next up will be a philosophical revolution in government. It's like a new start for civilization — a second chance to do it right. It's being young, but having the wisdom of the wisest men God ever put on earth. Jesus. Moses. Socrates. Plato. Aristotle. Polybius. Tacitus. Cicero. Machiavelli. Bacon. Descartes. Newton. Locke. Rousseau. Montesquieu. Kant. Adam Smith. All the others. Their wisdom can be bundled together into a new Nation. The new Nation can be anchored to the virtues! It can be free from the Old World poisons of privilege and nobility. It has leaders who are able to translate philosophy into real life. So the Nation can be based on the most practical use of philosophy ever attempted. It can "begin the world again"! It can put an old soul into a young land![29]

CHAPTER 4: POST-REVOLUTION

It's 1781. A rag-tag bunch of farmers and other ordinary people have won their independence from the most powerful nation on Earth. Now comes the <u>big question</u>, Harry. Can they <u>keep</u> their independence? How do they do it? Even after Cornwallis surrenders at Yorktown, Americans are on edge about keeping their independence. So a big problem immediately rears its head. <u>Security</u>!

* I can see why. England's taking its sweet old time signing a formal peace treaty. You said they'll take two years, right? Why is that?

* To England, giving up America is like trying to swallow a lump of glue. It doesn't want to go down and leaves a bitter taste. So we can only guess what they might be up to. Perhaps they're giving America's French Alliance some time to unravel. Maybe they're waiting for Washington's Army to be discharged or to "evaporate" so they can make another military move. Maybe they're expecting chaos, mob rule, civil strife. Maybe they're giving it a little time in hope that a big problem will arise. And if one does, the British forces that are still in New York City will be right there to take control again. Remember, 1/3 of the people in America are still loyal to the King. So America is in a trial period right now. Everything could still fall apart!

On the other hand, Washington isn't about to let everything fall apart. Independence has come at too high a price in human terms. It has extracted a million cries of pain. It has raised a mountain of suffering. It has cost thousands of lives. It has "tried men's souls". It has changed men's souls. So, although Washington wants no return fight with the British Army, he's not dropping his guard, either. When he marches his Army back up to West Point after the Yorktown victory in 1781, it's business as usual until England signs the Peace Treaty.

The trouble is, it's also business as usual in the economy … monkey business! The British are right. Big problems <u>do</u> arise. Rich merchants are price-gouging, like in 1777-1779. States are printing piles of "funny money". Inflation is heating up. State legislatures are raising taxes. Ordinary folks are getting squeezed by greedy big businessmen and by new money pressures. Ordinary folks are getting mighty angry!

Washington's men — both troops and Officers — are getting mighty angry too. Congress owes them months of pay. In some cases it's years of pay. Congress owes them their bonuses for staying on after their enlistments were up. Congress owes them their pensions. But Congress isn't paying any of it. In fact, they blow off General Washington's appeals on behalf of his men. Then they flatly ignore direct appeals from the Army's Officer Corps. Army folks feel they've been forsaken — even betrayed!

* I can understand why. It seems they sacrificed the most, but got the least!

* Right! The soldiers have suffered. They often starved, while many in America got fat. They got poor, while many got rich. They're physically exhausted, while everyone else dances and celebrates. They've gone unfed, unclothed, and unsheltered. Now Congress is forcing them to go to an uncertain civilian life with empty pockets — destitute!

* I'm disappointed to hear that. And I'm surprised there's not a mutiny.
* Most of the original firebrands and patriots who pushed for revolution are no longer in Congress. There are a lot of new faces. Unfortunately, many of them are unsympathetic, and believe it or not, anti-military. So there is a mutiny! It begins with a Colonel Lewis Nicola!

Colonel Nicola commands the Corps of Invalids at West Point. They're old soldiers who have lost an arm or leg or eye in the fighting. Washington has shown them great compassion. He gave them a permanent home and a respectable job — instructing young Officer-candidates — at West Point. While commanding the Corps of Invalids, Nicola and other Officers have also been doing a lot of soul searching during fireside discussions. The result is a seven page Nicola letter that airs the Army's complaints, proclaims Congress to be useless, and plumps for another way to run the new Nation. That other way involves George Washington … specifically, King George Washington! That's right! The Army wants to make George Washington into King George I of America! Washington flatly rejects even the thought of it! He tells Nicola, you're finally getting rid of George III. You don't need a George I!

Several months pass. Then comes one of the most bazaare events in American history. The troops encamped near West Point at Newburgh finally give up on petitioning Congress. They see the only solution is to take things into their own hands. So the Army attempts a coup d'etat! Led by the Officer Corps, the Army conspires to take over everything!

For months, this "Newburgh Conspiracy" is like a complex cloak and dagger thriller. There's plotting. There's intrigue. Now finally, it's time for action. The Officers hold a final secret gathering at a meeting hall in Newburgh before the bloodshed begins. Most Officers are there. The place is buzzing with chatter. Then suddenly — unexpectedly — General Washington walks in! That gets everyone's attention. The buzz of chatter abruptly ceases. The assemblage gets tense and silent.
* They must be shocked! Their Commanding General has caught them red-handed!
* Washington begins to speak. He first sounds like one of his favorite Romans, Cato, when he faced-down the mutiny of an army, as Plutarch tells it in Lives of Cato and Caesar. He then begins to stumble over reading a passage. The room becomes impatient. Seeing that, Washington apologizes to his Officers. He explains to them that the War has not only made him grey-haired, as they can see, but also practically blind! The stir of impatience now abruptly ceases. It turns into dead silence. Washington pulls out a pair of spectacles and tries to continue.

From that point on, most Officers hear nothing else. They're stunned. They see their stoic and beloved leader is struggling. Most eyes in the room glaze over. Many men go teary eyed. Some even openly weep. They're ashamed of them-selves. The failed-eyesight part of Washington's speech is to them a symbol of the War. It's the pain! It's the wounds! It's the bloodshed! It's the suffering! It's the eight long years away from loved-ones! It's what will be a lifetime of recur-ring nightmares! It's the friends who will never return! It's the special bond with Washington that only they can ever have! The following portrays what Washington says that day in March of 1783:

DEAR COMRADE! BRAVE FIGHTER!

based on: Washington's Newburgh Speech

Dear Comrade! Brave Fighter! Your bout is almost won!
The foe who sought the mighty blow, now reaps our
        final one!
The end is near, the people cheer, they now behold
        the prize,
And they pray to know, when last the foe, shall sleep
        beneath their skies;
But, dear God! What is … this mutinous plan?
What future does it show?
Like Arnold, have my comrades now,
Joined the insidious foe?

Dear Comrade! Brave Fighter! Stand tall and hear
        them cheer,
Stand tall! Once more face the noble call, once more
        hide your fear,
Your suff'ring and your brav'ry, are all through
        mankind known,
The glory, fame, and honor won, are yours — and
        yours alone;
Dear Comrade! Brave Fighter!
With freedom nearly found,
Pray not taint your fame with blood!
Don't stain the final round!

My Comrade gives no answer, your face is firm
        and bold,
Have you forgotten Valley Forge … the hunger,
        sick, and cold?
We bore it all, we did not fall, the suff'ring now
        is done,
The cherished prize, looms 'fore our eyes, the fight
        is finally won;

So … cheer glad crowd! Guard your prize!
But I who served mankind
Pray I'm only growing grey,
Not also growing blind!

The virtue is: Loyalty. Why turn to the devil when
                you've just earned your place in heaven.

Like warm sun softens cold and solid ice, Washington's warm speech softens the cold and solid conspirators. Their coup d'etat melts away. Then it evaporates. And a breeze of emotion gently whisks it away!

Washington writes to Congress. He tells them how close it came! Congress is shaken! Their distress and anxiety gives way to awe for Washington. Awe turns into solemn deliberation on his recommendations. Then they give the Army, finally, what has been long owed and promised to them!

The affair is reported all across the Country. The Army, the Officer Corps, and George Washington see their reputations soar! The intrigue — the Newburgh Conspiracy — is submerged beneath the fortunate outcome. Few know the real story. Few know how close America came to having, not a democratic Republic, but a military dictatorship. Much of the intrigue may never be known!

That's the Newburgh Conspiracy. It's an event, intentionally kept quiet, that could have altered history. Outsiders marvel at the outcome. Insiders, such as Thomas Jefferson, know better. He had a firsthand view of the dangers of a standing army. For him, that chilling, ice-cold memory will not soon melt and evaporate and be gently whisked away. But Thomas Jefferson also saw something else he'll not soon forget. It's the "sway" that Officers who are good-leaders, such as Washington, can have on an Army. Good morals, ethics, and character — as Washington showed — can save a nation. Washington's morals, ethics, and character did save the Nation! And Thomas Jefferson will never forget it![30]

In May 1783 Washington submits a plan to Congress for a standing peacetime military setup — "Sentiments on a Peace Establishment". Those anti-military types in Congress want no part of a standing army. Congress hems and haws over it, then puts it aside.

Meanwhile, England hems and haws over evacuating New York. Finally, in November 1783 the British Army sleeps under American skies for the last time. General Sir Guy Carleton leaves with the last of his army. Redcoats have occupied New York since they captured it in 1776 when they nearly captured Washington's entire Army. Remember?
* Yes. They came real close to ending the revolution, right then and there!
* Fortunately, close only counts in darts, Harry. So now the British have packed up, turned out the lights, and closed the door behind them. Little do they know they have just permanently closed the door on 176 years in America!

Shortly after British sails disappear over the horizon, Washington leads a victory parade into New York City. The next several days bring ceremonies and celebrations. Then comes the last farewell. Washington and his Officers gather at Fraunces' Tavern in Manhattan. There are war stories. Toasts. Tears. Farewell embraces. Then Washington is gone!

The General next rides to Annapolis where Congress is meeting. The journey is slower than expected. He's mobbed by friendly, adoring crowds all along the way. Everyone wants to see him, hear him, touch him. And the people are rumour-mongering. They're asking what Washington will do next!

"Do you think we're looking at King George I of America?"
"Maybe. But I hear he turned down the Army's offer to make

him King, or Emperor — or whatever he wanted!"

"That's because he wouldn't do it by force at Newburgh. It might
be a different story if the people ask him to do it!"

"Perhaps. In fact, all of Europe expects him to take over the
Country!"

"I haven't read about that. What do they say?"

"They say it's a pipe dream to think any military leader could
give up such power and adulation."

"You mean like Caesar couldn't?"

"Right. And Cromwell. And others. I hear even King George
III said Washington will never resign his power, because he
would have to be the greatest man who ever lived in order to
do so."

"King George still does't understand what the Revolution was all
about, does he? He still doesn't get it!" [31]

* What a contrast between what the people think about Congress and what they
think about Washington.

* You're right, Harry. In fact, Congress has just been run out of Philadelphia by
an angry mob of Pennsylvania militiamen! It shows that Congress is really a
rather powerless bunch. Right now they're in Annapolis. And they're a rather
nervous bunch! They should be. The man who could be King is coming to see
them. Why? Does Washington intend to be another Julius Caesar? He has real
power. He "owns" the Army. He "owns" the people. He can easily just take over
if he so chooses. He can pick his title. King. Emperor. Dictator. Lord Protector,
like Cromwell. Whatever he wants. What can a handful of delegates in this powerless Congress do if Washington shows up with even the smallest remnants of his
Army behind him? This time Congress couldn't even skip town to save their own
necks, much less stop Washington!

Thomas Jefferson tells Congress not to worry. He assures them, all will go
well. He says that he knows George Washington. And George Washington is no

Julius Caesar or Oliver Cromwell. He's a "Cincinnatus". He says Washington actually <u>cultivates</u> his Cincinnatus image. He says Washington is proud of it.
* Cincinnatus? I don't remember him.
* Lucius Quintius Concinnatus was a Roman statesman and general. I'll tell you his story. It took place in 458 BC Rome.

CINCINNATUS

from: Livy's <u>History of Rome</u>

Cincinnatus tilled the soil of his own modest farm on the outskirts of the small 5th century BC city of Rome. He once held high office in Rome and was known to be wise, courageous, and trustworthy.

The Roman army had marched out to confront the fierce, barbarian Aequi who threatened to ransack Rome, kill all the men, and enslave all the women and children. Now messengers from the battle brought back word to the city Fathers — the Senate — that the army was trapped and faced annihilation. The people and the Senate appealed to wise and trusted Cincinnatus for help. They gave him the 'keys to the city," making him dictator of the small Roman republic, so that he would come to their rescue. Cincinnatus organized every able bodied male left in the city, no matter what his age, into another army. He marched out to the battle, cleverly reached the entrapped army, and took command. Within 16 days the Aequi were defeated and driven back into their own lands.

Cincinnatus paraded back into Rome with his army to the cheers and adulation of everyone. He could have easily remained dictator or made himself King. But, he returned power back to the people and the city Fathers, and went back again to his farm. He became the model of Roman virtues for generations to come.

The virtue is: Patriotism. John F. Kennedy once said, "ask what you can do for your Country."

Washington finally arrives in Annapolis. He meets with the Congress. The moment has come. He rises to speak. Everyone holds their breath. Is Jefferson right about Washington?

He is! Washington <u>is</u> Lucius Quintus Cincinnatus on this day in December 1783! Washington not only resigns his military Commission, but he completely retires from public life. After a short speech, he bids them all farewell. The emotion in the room brings tears to everyone's eyes. The "American Cincinnatus" leaves the building. George Washington the General, Commander-in-Chief, and possibly King or Emperor has astonished a skoffing, skeptical world. Now he's simply George Washington the farmer. He feels relief for the first time in over eight hard years. He mounts his horse and gallops south toward his beloved home at Mount Vernon … free at last![32]

The delegates also feel relief. They go home, too! And what is important to us, Harry, they never do get around to voting on Washington's "Sentiments on a Peace Establishment".

* I guess, like the Newburgh Conspiracy, Jefferson never forgets this noble deed and momentus occasion, either.

* Does one soon forget events that bear so heavily on history? I think not. Allow me to say, Thomas Jefferson was right. There was nothing to worry about when it came to George Washington's morals, ethics, and character!

There's a lot to worry about throughout the States, however. By 1786, States and settlers and Indians and frontiersman and land companies are fighting over land in the western territories. Imports are raging. Inflation is raging. Big merchants continue to price-gouge. Small merchants continue to go under. Workers continue to lose jobs. The States continue to raise taxes. And serious uprisings occur in some States!

In Massachusetts, politicians and big merchants remember mob riots in the cities, like Boston, over British taxes back in the 1760's and '70's. They don't want a sequel now because of their taxes. So they lay the heavy taxes on rural folks, not the city folks. Rural folks are those same ones — farmers — who faced down the British at Lexington and Concord and Saratoga. They're those farmers who were a big part of winning the War. They're those farmers who reeled when loved ones were killed and maimed. Now they're reeling again because of taxes and high prices! And they're also angry they never got a little piece of England's former Crown lands in America:

> "We fought the war for virtue and a better life for our children.
> But the rich city businessmen are taking all the goodies! They're getting fat — we're going broke!"
>> "Yeh. The tax loop tightens and chokes us to death! But big business falls through the loop hole!"

> "First they tax our goods. Next they tax our acres and barns.
> Now they tax our cows, pigs, and horses. Where does it end?
> Will they next tax our children — then our dogs and cats?"
>> "We can't pay our feed bills because of taxes. So they're confiscating our farms. Why don't those city folks pay their fair share of taxes?"

> "Yeh! Is this what we fought the War for?! Lose our farms?! Rot in jail?! We should petition someone! Get a hearing! Tell our side of the story!"

251

"We <u>did</u> that already, my friend! They ignored us!"

"It's those lawyers and judges and big businessmen! They're all in cahoots! <u>We're</u> the ones who fought for American land! Not them! So we want a piece of the action — some of the land! But the Courts take it all!"

"Then let's shut down the Courthouses!"
  "How do we do that?"
"Stick together! All for one and one for all! We did it before! We can do it again!"

"Yeh! Grab your muskets and pitchforks boys and follow me! I'm goin' over to join Dan Shays and his rebellion! If they won't <u>give</u> us justice — we'll <u>take</u> it!"[33]

More and more men from farms and rural towns join Dan Shays' rebellion. More than a thousand of them roust judges out of, and shut down, courthouses in western Massachusetts. Lawyers, judges, lawmakers, and big businessmen panic. They're forced to stop pulling the tricks they've been pulling on ordinary farmers. But they also get together enough cash to raise a private army. It has rifles, cannons, and thousands of men. The farmers have only muskets and pitchforks!

It's an explosive situation — businessmen vs farmers. But Shays wisely disperses his farmers after only minimum bloodshed. No need for more. He has actually gotten most concessions he wanted anyway. And there's been just enough bloodshed to "fertilize the tree of liberty". They say that liberty needs a little bit of rebellion from time to time! This is one of those times![34]

* Businessmen and politicians up and down America must be stunned by Shays' Rebellion.

* Stunned? They should be relieved! The <u>radical</u> part of Shays' Rebellion never

252

does come off. The former Crown lands never do get divied up amongst all the people who fought in the War!

* Then who gets all that land?

* One way or another, the rich and influential people end up with it! But even that doesn't relieve their shock over Shays' Rebellion . They're afraid now the "common riffraff" will reach for their muskets every time they have a complaint. So the rich and influential people demand <u>protection</u>! And they not only mean protection from mob rule. They mean: protection for the Courts; protection for free enterprise; protection from hostile Indians; protection from foreign invasion; protection from fighting between the States; protection for trade on the high seas; protection for their money and property; even protection from runaway inflation! Protection of trade, property, inflation, and free enterprise comes from laws. Protection from mobs, Indians, piracy, interstate wars, and foreign invasion comes from the Army. But all this protection takes lot's of money — money that Congress doesn't have and can't raise with the existing Articles of Confederation.

So, besides getting the land, rich and influential people also want to get stronger laws and a stronger standing Army to protect them. To them, the best way is through a government in which all States participate together. They want all States to join together — federate — into a new kind of **federal** government … with <u>them</u> running things, of course. Alexander Hamilton is their point man for pushing "federalism"! But the States already drew up their own Constitutions after the Declaration of Independence was issued. They already have the laws they want and already have State militias. So they think a federal type of government is unnecessary. Besides, it gives away the power and states-rights they fought against England to get!

Politically ambitious federalists, like Alexander Hamilton, join with rich and influential big businessmen that want all those protections. They go to work on trying to convince the States that some sort of federalism is in everyone's best interest. They point out how Shays' Rebellion scared everyone half to death. State constitutions and State militias were not good enough to stop that from happening. The "mob of riffraff" and the militia were one and the same during Shays' Rebellion. The militia just sympathetically looked-on as their buddies went on a rampage. The laws and Standing Army must be strengthened.

The States finally cave. They agree to attend a meeting to work on strengthening Congress and the Articles of Confederation. In May of 1787, fifty-five delegates drawn from all the States except Rhode Island meet in Philadelphia. They agree on one thing. The Articles of Confederation are just not good enough. They're too weak. For example, they can't levy taxes. And they're unfair. Rhode Island with its 68,000 people gets one vote, just like Virginia with its almost 750,000 people. And they don't guarantee people's rights and freedom. Each State's Constitution deals with people's rights. Some people like it that way. Others don't. So the federalists steamroll the convention into cooking-up a whole new Constitution! The meeting turns into a "Constitutional Convention"!

James Madison and Alexander Hamilton are the prime movers — organizers — of the Constitutional Convention. Madison arrives eleven days early. He wants to gather his ideas on political philosophy. He's been boning-up for the past three years on ancient governments that had some form of democracy. His mentor and good friend, Thomas Jefferson, is in France as Minister to Europe. So, Madison has been pouring over scores of books in Thomas Jefferson's library. They're about history, government, and philosophy in England, Europe, and ancient Greece and Rome. David Hume, John Locke, Montesquieu, Cicero, and Aristotle are his main sources. Thomas Jefferson also sends him a copy of Polybius. He was the historian who wrote about Greek city-state "cooperatives", for example, the Amphictyonic League (circa 400 BC) and the Achaen League (circa 200 BC). Polybius is Madison's starting point!

Madison puts together a nifty plan of government — the Virginia Plan. It's the Convention's starting point. Luckily, he also puts together notes of the convention. Otherwise history would never know what happened there. You see, the delegates vote to keep the proceedings secret! The watchful eye of press and public are kept out!

Most others at the convention are also well-read in classics, history, and political philosophy. They're some of the same men who were on the Committees of Correspondence back before the Revolution. And they've been through this before. They helped write their own State Constitutions after 1776. So although the delegates disagree on many things, they all agree that this Constitution must have three basic ideas: government by consent of the people; guaranteed freedoms and human rights; and, protection of person, property, and nation — security.

We saw philosophers, recently Rousseau, write about those ideas. But no nation has ever used them before. England has come closest. But England has a King — and no written constitution. This Convention is the first time since the world began that free people are sitting down and kicking around ideas on how to govern themselves. It's totally new. Totally unique. There are no previous guidelines to follow. It's the first time a plan of government will be hashed-out, written down, and voted on by all the people. The plan will be called **The Constitution of the United States of America**!

This Constitution solves the English problem when sometimes the King had too much power, sometimes Parliament had too much power. The Constitution itself is more powerful than anything or anybody. It's the supreme law. No one is allowed to break its rules — not a President, not a Congress, not an Army, not a court of law. That's what England doesn't have. That's what no English army nor any army or officer corps ever before had as its "master". Keep that in mind, Harry. It's important on our journey toward answering the question — **why West Point**!

All summer the delegates — in secret — bicker over every point. It's as if a ghost is there with them. The ghost is Machiavelli. For the squabbles are all about power! Finally in September they emerge with seven short statements, called Articles. And that's it! **The Constitution**!

Benjamin Franklin's friend from the Pennsylvania delegation, Gouverneur Morris, offically writes the whole thing up. And he takes it upon himself to dash off a Preamble — an introduction — while he's at it. It starts with the words "we the people". These are the very words that Native Americans like the Iroquois have for years begun treaties with. The rest of the Preamble says the things people worried about after Shays' Rebellion. Here it is:

THE PREAMBLE

from: The Constitution of the U.S.A.

WE THE PEOPLE of the United States, in order to form
a more perfect union, establish justice, insure domestic
tranquility, provide for the common defence, promote the
general welfare, and secure the blessings of liberty to ourselves and our posterity, do ordain and establish this
Constitution for the United States of America.

The virtue is: Cooperation. America is built on cooperation
between WE THE PEOPLE.

Now the <u>States</u> have to approve the Constitution. And it doesn't look good for
Virginia, New York, and Massachusetts. Virginia's popular governor, Edmund
Randolph, refuses to sign. He walks out. Co-author of Virginia's State Bill of
Rights, George Mason, does the same. So does the delegate from Massachusetts
and pre-War radical ally of Samuel Adams, Elbridge Gerry. In fact, nineteen other
delegates snub the convention completely. They never show up. And the only
one to sign from New York is Alexander Hamilton.
* It's not unanimously popular then. Why is that?
* Why? Most people have a bill of rights in their State. The Constitution does-
n't. Should they trust that the Constitution will later have one? A bill of rights is
one of the things the "little guy" fought and died for. And do you think there
should be an unlimited standing army? Some fear another Caesar or Cromwell
might emerge. Others remember the Boston Massacre and British Army occupation. Most remember the recent Newburgh Conspiracy.
* How do the firebrands who originated the Revolution feel about it? For
instance, James Otis?
* You'll remember he dropped out of sight after he went mad from that clunk on
the head? Well lightning struck a second time, Harry ... literally. He died back
in 1783 when his house was hit by lightning! At least before he died he knew
America had won its independence!
* How about Sam Adams? And John Hancock?
* Hancock spent just about his entire fortune on the War. And he's against this
Constitution — unless it gets its own bill of rights. Sam Adams feels the same.
And he wants something else he started it all for — <u>direct</u> democracy, rather than
indirect democracy through representatives!
* And Patrick Henry?
* Henry's already delivering fiery speeches against federal domination. He's a
states-righter, and one of those delegates who didn't even bother to show up in
Philadelphia. He said he "smelled a rat"!
* That leaves Thomas Paine.
* Tom Paine's over in Europe. He's agitating his heart out for Frenchmen to

255

emulate the American Revolution. But he had always pushed for total direct democracy, also.

* So <u>none</u> of the old radical firebrands are happy?

* When you've bled a full cup of blood and get only half a cup back, is the cup half full or half empty? I say, so long as there's a chance for the cup to be topped up, it's half full. And there <u>is</u> a way to top up — make additions to — the Constitution. It's called <u>amendments</u>!

Due to public outrage, the big issue — a bill of rights — is nimbly promised by James Madison. He says he'll put in a bill of rights at the very first session of Congress. He pledges his word! And his word is as solid as gold! He's a man of Stoic honor — a lifelong fan of Cicero and Seneca. So, with trust in Madison, a lot more folks jump onto the bandwagon favoring the Constitution!

Remember all the bickering the delegates did for months when writing the Constitution, Harry? Well, it's now repeated by ordinary people all around the country. Let's listen to the man-in-the-street. First in Philadelphia:

> "I am authorized to hand out these copies of the Constitution."
> "This is it?" ᵒᵒAfter all of that?ᵒᵒ
> "Best solutions are simplest!" ᵒᵒEspecially for <u>your</u> simple mind.ᵒᵒ
> "Where's our bill of rights? Don't we get a bill of rights?
> That's what we fought the War for!"
> "I have a list of things here. Let's see. Freedom of speech.
> Freedom of the press. Freedom of religion. Freedom of assem-
> bly. The right to bear arms. Freedom from search. The right to
> a trial. Are those the things you're talking about?"
> "Yeh! That's them! That's the stuff we fought the War for!"
> "I am authorized to tell you they will be put into law at the <u>first</u>
> session if there's a new Congress." ᵒᵒSo go get your representa-
> tive to ratify!ᵒᵒ
> "Oh! Smashing! Sounds alright then!"

In Boston:

> "Yes indeed. This is the stuff we need. Laws to keep the rabble
> under control. Congress can raise an army. Collect taxes.
> Protect our businesses. Protect our money."
> "Right! <u>That's</u> the kind of protection we want."
> "And the kind of opportunity, too. That's what we fought England
> for. The chance to get rich — step in and take their place! Why
> should they have all the goodies? Now <u>we'll</u> get rich instead of
> them!"
> "That's alright for you big businesses. But what about us
> small businessmen?" ᵒᵒWe did the fighting, not you. And not
> just to get rich!ᵒᵒ
> "You entrepreneurs and small merchants throw your lot in with us.
> You'll get rich hanging on to our coat tails."

"What about virtue?"

"Virtue's fine. But what comes first — profit or virtue?"

In western Massachusetts:

"Seen that new Constitution?"

"Yep."

"What do you think of it?"

"What do you think of it?"

"I like it."

"Oh? …. I hate it."

"Why's that?"

"We threw out the British 'cause they reckoned they were a
higher authority to us. Now another higher authority's back
on us again. We're settin' up another authority that'll swallow up our State's rights. That's no good."

"But it's a way to solve our money problems. And everyone gets
to pay taxes! Not only us!"

"Hmm. I have to see that to believe it."

And in Virginia:

"Ya'll look here. No 'bill of rahts' in this here Constitution!"

"What's the difference? We already have one in Virginia."

"But Ahm thinkin' we fought the War so us folk would be runnin'
things. Now we all can't even vote directly for a President or
Senate — only for this here House of Representatives. And who
knows what that is. Will they do what we all tell them to do? Or
will they do their own thang — like elected aristocracy? Will
they actually represent us folk? Or do they represent the rich fat
cats that put them in office — the big businessmen?"

"How ya'll thinkin' they represent big businessmen? What's
big businessmen got to do with it?"

"The same thang big businessmen had to do with Shays' Rebellion
up north there in Massachusetts. Remember how big businessmen bought and controlled thay own ahmy for thay own purposes? Well don't ya'll thenk they can buy and control representatives in Congress for thay own purposes too?"

"Ah. Ahm catchin yo drift. It's lookin' lahk it'll take a faya
bit of money to get elected, isn't it! ∘∘And we ain't got it.∘∘

"Ah thought we all fought the War fowa direct democratic participation, not fowa professional politicians. If Tom Jefferson was
he-ya, Ah thank it'd be different. But thaya conveniently packed
him off to France. Jefferson said we-ya all supposed to be small,
rural, virtuous, pastoral, farming communities. We-ya supposed
to have small wards of a few hundred folks votin' on everythang,

257

and passin' <u>ahr</u> decisions up via <u>ahr</u> representative who votes <u>ahr</u> way. Where's that all gone to? <u>True</u> democracy, Ah mean?"

"Ah could't say. But in this here setup ahr representatives vote how <u>they</u> all want to, not how <u>we</u> all want to!"

"And maybe thay'll vote the way big businessmen want to. Who thay all represent, anyway?" ᵒᵒPatrick Henry's right. Ah smell a rat, here!ᵒᵒ

"Well, when Tom Jefferson comes home maybe he'll change some thangs usin' them amendments?"

"Maybe." ᵒᵒBut y'all don't be holdin your breath. He's only one man.ᵒᵒ

"Well <u>nothins</u> perfect! And this he-ya Constitution's better than anything in all history. Isn't that part of what we fought the War for? And we all can have a full time ahmy so them redcoats and them Indians don't get at us again!"

"Ah must say, it <u>does</u> indeed give us all security. We don't want everythang we fought for slippin' away from us again some day!"[35]

* I'm surprised. A lot of people are less than satisfied with the Constitution.
* That's what happens when you're forced to buy the cow in order to get the milk. Probably the majority of people don't want another "Leviathan" — a huge and colossal layer of government to replace the British one they just got rid of. So the people and their State legislatures take a lot of time debating. They're being asked to just give away the independence so many fought so hard to get!

Federalists, like Alexander Hamilton, keep right on pushing. They write the <u>Federalist Papers</u>. This collection of essays uses a lot of ancient wisdom to gar-ner support for Federalism. It explains, describes, and clarifies. It deflects criti-cism. It sells the Constitution. After almost a year, most of the States have slowly but surely signed on. Finally in July 1788 the Constitution is adopted! It becomes the law of the land! The States are now officially **The United States of America**!

Early in 1789 George Washington will be the first President. And James Madison's Bill of Rights will be passed, as promised, by the First Congress. They're the first ten Amendments to the Constitution. They're what most people fought the Revolution for. Much of them are actually Thomas Jefferson's ideas and words! Now he also has a stake in The Constitution!

The Revolutionary Era is ending. Educated, ambitious men have aroused ordinary people with philosophical ideals. They've led ordinary people to victory. Now they've put the new Nation on a regimen to become a world-class superstar — a world champion. And the new Nation also has "teeth" to fight any challenger. That's because the Constitution allows Congress to raise an Army!

The day in September 1787 that the Constitutional Convention had completed its work, Ben Franklin was met outside by friends. The Philadelphia mayor's wife had asked him what kind of a government America will have. He had replied, "a Republic madam — if you can keep it"! Well, Harry, those words were not just meant for his friends that day. They were meant for you — and for your time — and for all times!

So that's how The United States comes about. Now to understand how West Point comes about we'll next have to see how the Military Establishment of The United States comes about. To understand the Military Establishment we'll look at what happens in America after George Washington's inauguration in 1789. And what happens, Harry, is the first test of the words Ben Franklin uttered that day: "IF YOU CAN <u>KEEP</u> IT."[36]

CHAPTER 5: FEDERALIST PERIOD

Endings. Beginnings. You remember important days in history as either one or the other. But some days are <u>both</u> endings <u>and</u> beginnings. Today is that kind of day, Harry. It's April 30, 1789. We're at Federal Hall overlooking Broad and Wall Streets in New York City. It's inauguration day. That's George Washington you see, taking the new oath of office:

OATH OF THE PRESIDENT OF THE UNITED STATES

"I do solemnly swear that I will faithfully execute the
Office of President of the United States, and will to the
best of my Ability, PRESERVE, PROTECT, AND
DEFEND the Constitution of the United States".

The virtue is: Responsibility. This oath clearly states a
President's first responsibilities.

It's short and simple. But the words are powerful and explosive. They're explosive enough to blow anyone out of the water — even George Washington. For "President" is an unknown and totally new job. It's being the leader of a totally new kind of government. So the challenge President Washington faces today is awesome. Yes, today you're seeing both an ending and a beginning. Today is the end of Revolutionary America and the beginning of Federalist America!
* And just how do you "preserve, protect, and defend" the Constitution?
* You start by uniting people, not dividing them. You get their confidence, not suspicion. Then, you tackle the problems that made a national Constitution necessary, like: justice; taxes; inflation; the courts; the economy; foreign relations; national security; and, the Indian frontier. It's called nation building!

One person could never do all that. So, Washington rounds-up some help — a "Cabinet"! Attorney General goes to Edmund Randolf. Chief Justice goes to John Jay. Secretary of Treasury to Alexander Hamilton. Secretary of State to Thomas Jefferson. Secretary of War to Henry Knox. And Advisor (Chief of Staff) to James Madison. John Adams is the Vice President.

During 1789, Washington focuses on the "preserving" part of his oath. He hammers away at uniting the Nation and building confidence. He pushes economic programs that hit folks where it helps — in their pocketbooks. Business becomes good. Crops are abundant. People are optimistic. He mostly ignores the "protect and defend" parts of the oath. But not for long!

Indian relations west of Pittsburgh, at this time called the Northwest Territory, are worsening. Washington has been aware of this for several months now. Just a few days after inauguration the Territorial Governor, Arthur St.Clair, had presented him with all the cruel, bitter, unvarnished facts. Efforts toward peace treaties had broken down. Prospects look bleak!

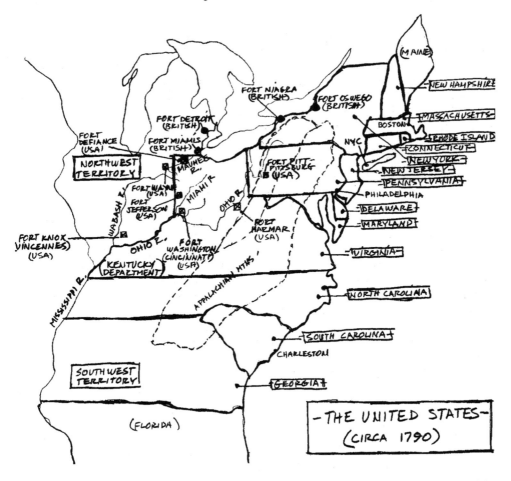

- THE UNITED STATES -
(CIRCA 1790)

Indians and frontiersmen murder, torture, pillage, and scalp eachother. One side is as brutal as the other. Onto the scene come families of settlers. They're peaceful and innocent. The Indians savagely massacre them anyway. So expeditions of frontiersmen retaliate. They wipe out whole Indian villages — sometimes even relatively peaceful ones. That turns friendly tribes into hardcore enemies.
* Who started all this in the first place?
* That's harder to say than trying to say who started the Boston Massacre, or who fired the first shots at Lexington and Concord. We know that even in the 1600's, white settlers moving West were frightened off by Indians who said the settlers were trying to take over their land. But going way back to the beginning of civilization, Harry, advanced societies justified taking over backward societies through the principle called "inevitability of progress". The question of who lived on what land was settled by who took it by force and kept it … the principle called "right of conquest".

* It comes down to power — like Machiavelli said.
* Right. America defeated Britain and its Indian allies. So American settlers want to cash in on their newly won "right of conquest". They want to move straight into those territories that are presently lived on by Britain's Indian allies. But the British don't want to evacuate their forts, as required by the Peace Treaty. They don't want Americans. Nor do the Indians. So, backed by British weapons and British encouragement, the Indians are butchering innocent white families! In a way, the War hasn't completely ended. The British haven't discharged their last obligation under the Treaty of Paris. And their Indian Allies don't care about some Treaty of Paris. This all makes Western frontiersmen fume with anger. They had helped to fight the British and Indians in Western New York and the Carolinas during the War. Now their new government's Army can't help them to protect their rights as citizens?

Land speculators also fume! Three companies have sewed up large chunks of the Northwest Territory. The shareholder lists read like "Who's Who in America." And almost every higher ranking Army Officer also owns shares in one or another of them. That includes the commander of America's lone regiment of regulars, General Josiah Harmar, and the Northwest Territory's Governor, Arthur St.Clair. So, speculators have huge clout. They stir frontiersmen into action against the Indians. Speculators and frontiersmen get the President's and Congress' attention.

President Washington is still swamped with nation building. He can't get personally involved yet. The "protect and defend" part of his oath will still have to wait. But he gets his Secretary of War, Henry Knox, to ask Congress to increase the puny little American Army. Knox asks that the Army be raised from 840 regulars to over 2000. Knox, St.Clair, and Harmar think that 1200 more regulars are needed to "neutralize" the Indians and protect the settlers. Congress gives them less than 400! It's not nearly enough!

Governor St.Clair is able to scare up an extra 1500 militia from Kentucky and Pennsylvania. So in 1790, General Harmar leads 2000 troops into Ohio in the Northwest Territory. Little Turtle, battle chieftain of the Miami Tribe, traps them! The militia is spooked off! The remaining outnumbered regulars get overrun! Little Turtle metes out a bloody defeat. We'll listen to what the demoralized regulars are saying as they limp back into the safety of Fort Washington:

> "It was shameful. Just shameful. They have to give us more regulars. Did you see how them militiamen panicked!"
> "They ditched their guns, left the wounded, and bolted as fast as their legs could carry them."
> "It was horrible. I never want to fight alongside them militiamen again. And their ragamuffin officers were not much better! They practically led their men in panic! They have no discipline!"
> "It wasn't only horrible. It was cowardice. That's what I say. I could hear my captured buddies that the militia ran out on . They were screaming from being tortured by those blood thirsty Indians. Then the screaming stopped! But I'll hear it the rest of my life!"[37]

262

* It sounds disgraceful. Yet, I can understand the militiamen, Thomas. When death stared them in the face, I'm sure the faces of their wives and children and mothers and fathers flashed through their minds. They didn't want to die! They're not real professional soldiers, just civilian militia. It's not really what they chose to do. They didn't really want to be out there. So a lot of them panicked. I'm sure they didn't stop to think they would cause the death of others.

* That is the nature of militia, Harry. It cannot be otherwise. They didn't know what they had done. Just like President Washington doesn't know what his deputies have done. He doesn't know they've just set off a savage Indian war! The hacked and burned and tortured body of a white speculator has just been found ... with two crossed warclubs on it! Crossed warclubs are the Indian declaration of war!

Knox, Washington, and Congress are alarmed by the bumbling disgrace of General Harmar's defeat. Governor St. Clair and Knox now recommend an army of 3000 men. And not militia! The Army must be under federal control, training, and discipline! But Congress won't authorize more than about 800 new regulars. So Knox proposes "levied" federal troops. Not regulars. Not militia. Something in between. They'd be federal troops called to active duty only when needed. Otherwise, most would be held as "Reserves". It's cheaper than regulars. And it's not the "standing army" concept so feared by Congress.

Congress approves! They also approve St. Clair becoming Major General St. Clair to take personal command. Knox and St. Clair bring in militia and frontiersmen from Kentucky. They keep the Indians occupied while St. Clair's invasion force is put together. Mounted Kentuckians burn and ravage Indian villages! Indians burn and ravage whites! As always occurs, innocents are killed in the crossfire — including women and children! By the time St. Clair gets going, frontier hatred and atrocities are rampant!

St. Clair can't get up enough new "levies." Grudgingly, he resorts to using some militia again to build up the numbers. He departs Fort Washington with 2300 troops. His goal — invasion and occupation to secure the Indian heartland. But Little Turtle isn't about to sit in that Indian heartland and wait for him. He heads south toward the American force with 1000 warriors. His goal this time is not just ambush and guerrilla warfare. It's complete annihilation!

During the American march both militia and "levies" desert in droves! St. Clair ends up with only 1400 troops by the time the Indians attack! He gets only halfway to the Indian heartland before being attacked. Little Turtle gets all the way to his goal. In November 1791 he annihilates the American force!

Perhaps 400 of the 1400 Americans escape and straggle back to the safety of Fort Jefferson. They talk about how lucky they are. They could have all been wiped out. But the Indians stopped to rape, torture, and pillage the captured, instead of pursuing others fleeing or retreating! Some survivors here in Fort Jefferson are being interviewed by the press:

(press) "What happened up there? How far north were you?"

> "The whole thing was a complete surprise! We were told that Little Turtle was at least 75 miles north of us. I figured we'd run into him in a week. But a couple days later he attacked us! He must've covered fifty miles like it was nothing!"
> "Yeh. It was dawn. Their war cries scared off the militia and a lot of "levies". Chaos erupted! Men dropped their weapons and ran for cover! But there <u>was</u> no cover! We were surrounded!"
> "The camp turned into a slaughter house! We fought our best for a while. But, wide open, we stopped being an army and became cattle! It was no longer a battle! It was a slaughter!"
> "And surrender is worthless. You just get tortured and killed! So some of us tried to break out. The only reason we made it is them Indians got involved in scalping. I saw hundreds of scalped heads steaming and smoking like chimneys in the cold mornin' air!"
> "And them there poor womenfolk … I saw some chopped nearly in half! And some with their breasts cut off, besides being scalped! And women were being thrown right into blazing fires along with the Officers!"

(press) "Gruesome. And did the Army inflict any damage on the Indians?"

> "I didn't see more than a few dozen Indians killed."
> "Me neither. Then again, we was busy scidaddeling by that time!" [38]

* That's sick! What are the actual casualties, Thomas?
* Little Turtle's are only twenty-one! St. Clair's approach one thousand! But St. Clair himself survived to tell his version of the story! It turns out to be a story of the most humbling, one-sided Indian victory in all of American history! Custer's last stand and the massacre of Braddock's army during the French and Indian War can't touch it for how few Indians were killed!
* Washington must have blown a gasket.

264

I WANT TO REPORT, SIR, THAT THE WAR-CRIES FIRST SCARED OFF THOSE POOR MILITIA FOLKS. THEN I SAW SCALPED HEADS STEAMIN' AND SMOKIN' LIKE CHIMNEYS IN THE COLD MORNIN' AIR !

* Disasters always hurt the most when they're partly self-inflicted. And President Washington had carefully lectured — ordered — St.Clair to "beware of surprise". He said to "act at all times as if preparing for surprise attack". Then St.Clair goes and gets his army annihilated ... due to a surprise attack! I think anyone would "blow a gasket" under those circumstances.

Pressures on President Washington, and on Secretary of State Thomas Jefferson, build up in other places besides the Northwest Territory. In the Southwest Territory the 5000-warrior Creek Indians led by educated "half-blood", Alexander McGillivray, clash with settlers from Georgia and South Carolina. They're headed for open warfare! In Western Pennsylvania the hated Whiskey Tax causes open lawlessness that reminds everyone of Shays' Rebellion. That's headed for civil war! Abroad, Americans are held for ransom in Algerian prisons! And Barbary Coast pirates raid American shipping in the Atlantic around North Africa!

Even revolutionary France's war with Spain, Britain, and the rest of Europe is spilling over to America. Britain siezes American vessels trading in the French West Indies! French ambassador, Charles Genet, sabotages American policy by prodding Americans to raid British shipping and to attack Louisiana and Spanish Florida! British captains kidnap American sailors to serve on their warships! Spain bribes Creek Indians and renegade whites to ally against America! And, agents of Spain and Britain push for a coordinated Indian war throughout the Northwest and Southwest Territories!

Time, money, treaties, diplomacy, and Thomas Jefferson iron out most of that menu of problems. Most. Not all. For, money and treaties and diplomacy mean nothing to the Indians of the Northwest Territory — nor to the Whiskey Tax protestors in Western Pennsylvania. The Indians refuse to budge one inch toward a peace treaty. Why should they? They're winning! The Whiskey Tax protestors refuse to budge one inch toward curbing their lawlessness. And why should they? Congress has already "caved" on some of the Whiskey Tax regulations. Lawlessness is paying off!

Unfortunately, Washington's personal attention has had to be elsewhere. He's been working like a dog to engineer a completely new kind of government, and to win the population's loyalty to that government, and to wax international respect for that government. But how much respect can his government get if it allows its American citizens to be murdered, and its Army to be crushed by a bunch of savage-like Indians?

So St.Clair's annihilation and the Whiskey Tax lawlessness finally get Washington's attention! In Philadelphia, now the seat of government since late 1790, he puts his head together with Henry Knox, Alexander Hamilton, and Thomas Jefferson. They unanimously decide on what's needed to win in the Northwest. It boils down to: good leadership based upon talent and character, not political connections; regular soldiers based upon training and discipline, not the false economy of militia or reserve levies; and, a real General to be in charge, not a political appointee. So they come up with a 5000 man "legion". And they pick "Mad" Anthony Wayne as its General. They wrap it up into a new "Military Act of 1792". After hot debate in Congress, the Act finally passes ... narrowly!

* "Legion"? Why do they call it a "legion"?
* Washington and Knox said they got the "legion" concept from Steuben. Legion was the name the ancient Romans gave a division of their army that was self-contained.
* Interesting. And it's better because of — ?
* It's tailored toward wilderness campaigns against guerilla warriors like the Indians. In this case, they divide their Legionary Army into four sub-legions, each of 1250 men. Each sub-legion has its own share of infantry, cavalry, and artillery. Each is, in effect, a little army itself. Each is self-contained and able to stand and fight alone, if necessary.
* I see. Greater flexibility. Sounds reasonable!
* In 1794, Canadian Governor Lord Dorchester (formerly known as British General Guy Carleton who was the one who vacated New York City in 1783) tells the Indians that England will soon join them if they wage war against the United States. That torpedoes last ditch hopes Americans had for an Indian peace treaty. Now the United States faces military encirclement. It has the British in the north in Canada, Miami and Shawnee tribes in the Northwest, Spain in the south in Florida, Creek Indians in the Southwest, and Spain's and Britain's navies on the east in the Atlantic!

In America, fear of war now rages. Congress even approves building a Navy. And it passes an Act that will be important for you and I to remember, Harry. It's the "Corps of Artillerists and Engineers Act of 1794". In that Act is something that's little known by most people, and long forgotten by most historians. It's an official school for training officers for the United States Army ... a **West Point School**!

America is tense. Suddenly, the British brazenly build a fort on American Soil. To Washington, that's the last straw. That's invasion! He orders Anthony Wayne and his Legion to move on the encroaching British fort. Little Turtle of the Miamis and Blue Jacket of the Shawnee spring their usual clever trap. This time it doesn't work. The Indians immediately see that this army is different. It has discipline and leadership. This time the Indians are shocked. The shoe is on the other foot. Their 1000-warrior force gets crushed. Routed. They break and run to avoid repeated bayonnet charges. Hundreds of Indians scatter like deer in all directions and melt into the thick forests. The legionaires pursue them. Then the Legion pens-up the British in their illegal fort. The British are captive. Wayne is now free to "clean out" every Indian and British crop, town, village, and storehouse he can find. And he does just that. In the end, less than fifty Americans are killed. The Miami and Shawnee lose many hundreds! The legion's ninety-seven day campaign thoroughly defeats and humiliates both the British and the Indians!

Meanwhile, lawlessness in Western Pennsylvania over the whiskey tax grows into full scale rebellion. It's like the 1000-man Shays' Rebellion. But the "Whiskey Rebellion" has 15,000 men! It's out of control! Anarchy reigns! The rebels torch homes, hijack the mail, terrorize citizens, and occupy all of Pittsburgh! Whatsmore, they seek British support!

President Washington — political efforts exhausted — resorts to radical measures. He mobilizes a force of 15,000 militiamen from Virginia, Maryland, New Jersey, and Eastern Pennsylvania. Now a commanding general is needed.
* That's a large force at someone's personal disposal. It's the size of the American Army at the end of the Revolution, isn't it?
* Just about. And a large army — a potential for tyranny — has always been watched with a suspicious eye. So who might be trusted in charge of such a large force of armed men? Who is the only proven "American Cincinnatus"? ..... George Washington! So President Washington personally leads the army of 15,000 into Western Pennsylvania. The rebels hear of this large force coming their way with Washington himself in command. It's a wake-up call for the ringleaders who are out there firing-up people:

"Who's that whacko riding in and disrupting this rally?"
   "I think you should listen to him, man!"

"THE BLUECOATS ARE COMING! THE BLUECOATS ARE
   COMING!"
   "Bluecoats? We're the bluecoats! We're the militia!"
"These militia are from other States!"
   "Other States? Are they paying the whiskey tax in other
   States? Those danged traitors!"
 "They're ready to come across the mountains at us."
   "Nonsense man! Hannibal himself would sooner cross the
   Alps rather than these mountains!"
"There's tens and tens of thousands of militiamen. And
 Washington himself has taken personal command!"
   "Tens of thousands? Washington? Right then! That's it for
   me! Drink up men! It's the last of this stuff you'll be havin'.
   (shouting) LOOKS LIKE YOU FOLKS OUT THERE WILL
   HAVE TO PAY THE TAX AFTER ALL! WASHINGTON'S
   COMIN'!"

"What about the British help you said we're getting?"

"Forget the British! Washington already whipped them, didn't he! As for me, I'm the firebrand, not the fire! I'll leave the fighting to you! I'm gettin' outta here!

"Yeh. Where's the nearest polling place? I'm goin' down to sign that oath of loyalty to the United States they've been pushin' us to do ... before Washington gets here! [39]

Their "revolution" falls apart! The ringleaders flee westward! The Whiskey Rebellion is put down without spilling a drop of blood ... or whiskey!

* Incredible! It never became a civil war! And, can you believe what that British government is doing, Thomas? They're trying to take back America by sneaking through the back door, using Indians and insurgents! It's like they're trying to undo what's been done ... trying to bring back the "good old days"!

* All the kings horses and all the kings men, will not bring the "good old days" back again. So the British would be better off forgetting about the "good old days" when they were the masters of America. They should bear up and heed words to the wise, like the following ones:

THE INEVITABLE

by: Dr. Reinhold Niebuhr

God grant me: the serenity
To accept the things I cannot change;
The courage to change the things I can;
And the wisdom to know the difference.

The virtue is: Faith. Accept the inevitable, have faith, and
go on from there.

But the British don't. Thus far, they have gone out of their way to make President Washington's life difficult. Nonetheless, Washington has answered that Inauguration Day question ... "just how does one preserve, protect, and defend the Constitution?". He has silenced Europeans, cynical of American independence, who had skoffed: "can they <u>keep</u> their independence?" And he has proven the foresight in Franklin's comment: "you have a republic ... IF YOU CAN KEEP IT!".

* So it looks like Washington is holding the Republic together by a shoestring here in 1794. And he's probably the only one who can do it! Aren't half the Congressmen still States-righters who are anti-Constitution?

* Harry, 1/5 of people are anti-<u>anything</u> ... all the time! And Washington never forgot that domestic and foreign cynics are watching his every move — waiting for the American experiment to fail. But it hasn't ... for now. He has waxed America's reputation ... for now. He has won respect for the government from Americans in the West ... for now. He has justified a regular army and military establishment ... for now. He has sent a loud and clear message about America's resolve to all enemies, foreign and domestic ...for now. And of special interest to you and me, Harry, he has shown that virtuous and competent leaders are invaluable in defending the nation!

It's now 1795 . The Jay Treaty, hotly debated in Congress here in Philadelphia, finally gets the British out of North American forts ... but in exchange for unpopular trade agreements and concessions. Next year Washington chooses not to stand for President again. He retires! John Adams, a Federalist, is elected President. Thomas Jefferson gets just three less electoral votes than Adams. So he's Vice-President ... even though he's not a Federalist.

France takes the Jay Treaty as American betrayal — as an alliance with England against them. Therefore, they maraud American shipping. They plot an invasion from the South. And perhaps they even plot to overthrow the government from within. So French intrigues with anti-Federalists, those who would like to have a different Constitution, cause Federalists' suspicions to soar. There's a war with France in all but a declaration. It's called a Quasi-War!

The Nation clamors for an increase in protection. That means an increase in the Army. Congress, with its usual paranoia over large standing armies, hysterically debates it for months. Finally, in 1798 a "New Army" — 12,000 men — is approved. President Adams must decide who he can trust to head it. He admires Washington. He contrasts Washington's patriotism with Caesar's and Alexander's ambition. He says Washington is the only one he trusts to head such a threatening force. So he asks Washington to accept the role. Washington accepts — but on the condition that he doesn't have to come out of retirement. He'll only minister broad control and guidance. In turn, he looks for a right-hand-man. His old aide, Alexander Hamilton, bugs him so much for the job, he finally turns day-to-day command over to him. He gives Hamilton the rank of Major-General!

Adams and Jefferson never saw eye-to-eye with Hamilton. Washington's retirement and Adams' election at last had Hamilton on the outside looking in.

Now he's back! And nothing has changed! They still don't see eye-to-eye with him! For instance, Adams says the New Army is strictly meant to deter or fight French aggression. It must then be disbanded. Adams wants no new Cromwell or Caesar with a standing army. Hamilton, on the other hand, says that's the problem. France <u>does</u> want another Caesar. They want to mimick ancient Rome. They're looking for a <u>French</u> Caesar to come along. They want to run the world! And it's just when America is on the verge of greatness, itself!

So Hamilton says the New Army must be permanent. It's the only deterrent to France. It's also the instrument needed to fulfill America's destiny to be a world leader among nations. So he advises Adams to forget standing army paranoia. The New Army is necessary for westward expansion, national destiny, and protection from foreign invasion!

Hamilton and other Federalists can squabble all they want to over the the New Army. Adams is about to pull a surprise. He mimics his lifelong idol, Cicero, and plays the self-sacrificing hero. He sacrifices popularity for virtue by suing for peace with Napoleon Bonaparte of France! His own Federalists are thunderstruck! They think it's Quasi-War surrender. Adams thinks it's a stroke of genius. Jefferson thinks it's dynamite. And why wouldn't he. He's a Democratic-Republican. His opposition, the Federalist Party, is being torn apart. It's disintegrating. Adams is at war with Hamilton, with his own Cabinet, and with other Federalists in Congress. And Thomas Jefferson will be running for President against Adams and his disintegrating Federalist Party in the upcoming election!

The Federalist Party comes unstuck. <u>Hamilton</u> Federalists say they'd sooner have Thomas Jefferson as President than John Adams. <u>Adams</u> Federalists say they'd sooner have Thomas Jefferson than any Hamilton Federalist. They will both get their wish. Thomas Jefferson will be elected President in 1800! Adams, Hamilton, and other Federalists' squabbling amongst eachother will kill the Federalist Party forever! And standing army paranoia will have been the root cause of its death!

* George Washington doesn't rescue the Federalists, as usual?
* Not this time. It's true, Washington still enjoys a fountain of affection with the people. The Federalists well know that's where he always drew his water — his support. For years the Federalists have used Washington's fountain of affection with the people to fill their own buckets. And that's been their chief strength — the colossus of Washington's merits with the people. Now it's their weakness. For they never got to build their own fountain of support with the people while they were drawing from Washington's well. No, Harry, Washington doesn't come to the rescue this time. He never sees the Federalist Party's death in 1800. He never sees Jefferson's election in 1800. In fact, he never sees 1800. He's destined to be a man of the 1700's. Just a few days before the turn of the century, the fountain's spigot is turned off. George Washington dies! With him dies the Federalist Party. But, putting paranoia and politics aside, now everyone gives the Federalists their due credit for being the entrepreneurs of a new nation and a new kind of government. George Washington was their leader, architect, and guiding light!
* You might say that George Washington honorably "captained" the ship of State.

He navigated a unified group of individual States through uncharted waters. America sorely misses him!

* Well said, Harry. America <u>does</u> sorely miss him. And your words remind me of the famous words in "<u>Oh Captain! My Captain!</u>" by Walt Whitman. That poem can as accurately be applied to George Washington as it later will be to Abraham Lincoln. For the colossus of Washington's virtuous leadership first won independence, then <u>guided</u> it!

OH CAPTAIN! MY CAPTAIN!

by: Walt Whitman

O Captain! My Captain! Our fearful trip is done,
The ship has weather'd every rack, the prize
    we sought is won,
The port is near, the bells I hear, the people all
    exulting,
While follow eyes the steady keel, the vessel
    grim and daring;
But O heart! heart! heart!
O the bleeding drops of red,
Where on the deck my Captain lies,
Fallen cold and dead.

O Captain! My Captain! Rise up and hear the
    bells;
Rise up — for you the flag is flung — for you the
    bugle trills,
For you bouquets and ribbon'd wreaths — for
    you the shores a-crowding,
For you they call, the swaying mass, their eager
    faces turning;
Here Captain! Dear father!
This arm beneath your head!
It is some dream that on the deck,
You've fallen cold and dead.

My Captain does not answer, his lips are pale
    and still,
My father does not feel my arm, he has no
    pulse nor will,
The ship is anchor'd safe and sound, its voyage
    closed and done,
From fearful trip the victor ship comes in with
    object won;

271

Exult O shores and ring O bells!
But I with mournful tread,
Walk the deck my Captain lies,
  Fallen cold and dead.

The virtue is: Respect. Show respect for sacrifice and accomplish-
        ment of predecessors.

Once again leaving aside paranoia over standing armies, we must admit that the
Federalists were not only the builders of a new Nation, but also the creators of its
Military Establishment. A Continental Army was necessary to win independence.
A Military Establishment will be necessary, as Benjamin Franklin said, to <u>keep</u>
it![40]

6.

THE STORY BEHIND WEST POINT: THE FOUNDING - HOW?

You see how West Point goes from being
strictly a Revolutionary War stronghold,
to being a place to train army officers,
and finally to being the place to locate
the United States Military Academy.

CHAPTER 1: THE MILITARY ESTABLISHMENT

It's now 1800. Thomas Jefferson is President-elect. The seat of government is moving from Philadelphia. It's home will be the new District of Columbia — Washington D.C. George Washington's chair-back in Philadelphia's Convention Hall has a half-sun decoration. Is it a rising or a setting sun? Benjamin Franklin symbolically decided at the end of the Constitutional Convention in 1787 that it was a <u>rising</u> sun. And for the Democratic-Republicans, it's still a rising sun. But for the Federalists … it's setting!

The 1700's belonged to the Federalists. Now the 1800's belong to the Democratic-Republicans. And so does the Federalist's forever badgered Military Establishment!

* And the Military Establishment still has no military academy?

* No, but we're getting the scent, Harry! We'll first have to find out how that peacetime Military Establishment itself came about before we can find out how a military academy arises out of it. So we'll go back twenty years to the beginning of the peacetime Military Establishment. But this time we'll view those twenty years from the <u>military</u> point of view. And we'll begin with Washington's "Sentiments on a Peace Establishment" in 1783.

* I remember that, Thomas. The Continental Congress discussed it, but never voted on it.

* That's right. The Continental Congress thought it was too ambitious. Washington considered it bare bones. Historians call it one of the great State papers in American history! In it, Washington pushed for a Regular Army of only 2600 Officers and men; an umbrella of frontier and coastal forts; enough Officer - leaders to quickly expand the Army if necessary; arsenals and magazines to store munitions and equipment; State militias reorganized under a national format; and … a military academy!

Alexander Hamilton headed the committee that reported on Washington's plan in 1783. Standing army paranoiacs in Congress fought it every inch of the way. It never got off the ground. In fact, it got buried. Neither Hamilton nor Washington nor anyone else brought it up again with the Continental Congress. The next time it surfaced was four years later during the Constitutional Convention in 1787.

Military debate at that Constitutional Convention was deep and fierce! The term, "standing army" had become infamous. It had become another name for a system of terror. Anti-Federalist States-righters — mostly future Democratic-Republicans — said "regular army" equals "standing army". Federalists — backers of big central government — rounded up all the usual arguments favoring a regular army: preparedness; deterrence; security; strength through central control; and so forth. All of these would be targeted against Indian Wars, European invasion, and internal civil disorder.

The two sides compromised. A regular army, and a military establishment, was not chiseled in stone into the Constitution. But the Constitution gave a two-house Congress power to vote them into law at its own pleasure. Thus, it allowed a regular <u>peacetime</u> army — a "standing army" as anti-Federalists called it. This whipped-up a storm of controversy. It's one of the reasons some delegates walked out and others snubbed the Constitutional Convention to start with. In the end, only Congress was empowered to: create military "institutions"; make the rules and standards; control forts, arsenals, shipyards, and other needed infrastructure; use troops to check invasion or crush rebellion; and, declare war. The President, with George Washington in mind, was made the Commander-in-Chief. He was empowered to wage a declared war, direct military operations, and appoint the Army's Officers, with Senate approval. Washington's "Sentiments on a Peace Establishment" was not specifically written into the Constitution. But the Constitution made some kind of military establishment completely legal. Now Congress had military teeth!

* And a military academy?
* Many Democratic-Republicans asked: is a military academy not un-Constitutional? It isn't specifically mentioned in the Constitution. On the other hand, the Constitution says Congress can create any national military institutions it wants to. And a military academy would be a national military institution. So it was a gray area for argument. You could take any side that suited your political or philosophical situation.
* Spin it to meet your own purposes, in other words.
* Every era, as you say, "spins" its laws to suit its purposes, Harry. By 1790, however, Congress had not even used the military teeth given to it by the Constitution's laws. The Military Establishment was still merely the First Regiment — a mere 840 Officers and men. Congress had only approved those to "awe" the Indians. That's when the Indians awed General Harmar, instead. Remember the returning survivors' stories? We can just imagine what pro-Army Representatives must have said to anti-Army Representatives in the halls of Congress when they heard those stories:

> "Harmar and St.Clair requested 1200 more regulars. Of course,
>   you anti-Army paranoics gave them less than 400!"
>   "They had a total of 1200 regulars. That should have been
>   enough to awe the Indians."
> "Awe the Indians, you say? Ha! I'm told that the Indians are not
>   'awed' by the puny amount of men in our puny little Army.
>   They're awed by the comic spectacle of our political imbecility
>   and by the puny amount of grey-matter we must have in our
>   brains! They must have laughed themselves silly all the way
>   back to their wigwams!" [1]

It's true that Congress approved only a measly 400 more troops. But it was the first movement off dead-center. It moved the Army a notch closer to Washington's "Peace Establishment".

The drubbing that General Harmer's army took brought about the next change. That's when Congress increased the Regular Army again. Another regiment of 800 men brought it to about 2000. Congress also authorized 3000 "levies" — reserves. Remember? All this was to now "over awe" the Indians. The "levies" turned out to be a disaster during General St.Clair's annihilation in December 1791. The Indians weren't "over awed". But the Army's size had been ratcheted-up another notch!

St. Clair's annihilation, which meant virtual disappearance of an American Army, sent shock waves across the Nation. The press raged-on about it. Pro-army Federalists and anti-army Democratic-Republicans lambasted eachother in Congress. After weeks of venomous argument, Congress passed the "1792 Act for Protection of the Frontiers" — the "Legion Act". This is the one, Harry, that created the 5000-man Legion under Anthony Wayne. It was a major military reform. It was the largest-yet troop increase. It ratcheted-up the Military Establishment several notches all at one time!

* And it gave Anthony Wayne the tools to crush the Indians and humble the British "invasion".

* Right. It turned the Army around; erased the stain of defeat; rebuilt pride; and, restored morale and confidence. The 1792 "Legion Act" propelled the Army far into the future!

Then came 1794. Wayne routed the Indians. Washington crushed the Whiskey Rebellion. But war with Britain was also on the horizon. So Congress passed the "Act to Provide Naval Armament" in March 1794 — the seed of a U.S. Navy. It also passed the "Act for a Corps of Artillerists and Engineers" in May 1794. This 1000-man Corps would build and run forts, arsenals, armories, and coastal defenses. Its headquarters at West Point included the **West Point School** to train Officers — the seed of a formal military academy. West Pointers were in Wayne's victorious "Legion"!

War with Britain never came. Instead came ugly debates over the Jay Treaty. Those debates overshadowed the "Military Establishment Act of 1796" — the most crucial in the history of creating an American military establishment!

* Interesting! I never heard of it.

* You're not alone. And it was hugely important! Why? Because it passed <u>during peacetime</u>! It was the true start of a peacetime Army! It wasn't just "spun" for the 1790's era. It was the outline of American military security for the next century to come! Even George Washington wrote his "Sentiments" during times of Indian hostilities, domestic strife, and British frontier occupation ... not during peacetime. And even then, he couldn't get a decision out of Congress on it. The "Act of 1796" did get a decision out of Congress. That was: to keep the Army basically the same as it was during all the hostilities of 1794 ... even though there were no hostilities in 1796!

After the Jay Treaty with England, the special relationship between France and America went down the toilet. Storm clouds of the undeclared war — the Quasi War — gathered. A frenzy of Federalist military proposals gushed forth. Anti-militarists fought them tooth and nail. All the old standing army paranoia, fear of invasion, and drain on federal revenues were screened and shaken through the debating process. What came through was no less than <u>five</u> armies!

* Five? That's going from one extreme to the other!

* And all paid for with a new land tax.

* Uh oh! A tax? Not debt creation? No borrowing?

* No. Just a <u>tax</u>, Harry! And you're correct in saying, uh oh. For the nation exploded in anger over it! A rebellion called "Fries' Rebellion" erupted — again in Pennsylvania. You can just imagine what the man on the street in Pennsylvania was saying this time:

> "Here we go again! First the Whiskey Tax. Now this tax. And
>   for what? Armies — with no war to fight?"
>   "That's what I say. There's no more likelihood of our seeing
>   the French Army on American soil than our seeing Heaven
>   right now!"
> "And have you read about the 'garbage' of society this Army is
>   digging up? Marines are fighting dockhands! Privates are knif-
>   ing tavern-owners! Soldiers are beating up Constables! They're
>   nothing but villainous cut-throats! No better than the British sol-
>   diers used to be!"
>   "Yeh. But we didn't have to pay the British! These bloody

ragamuffins in the New Army are nothing but loungers living off our taxes! And where are the Officers who are supposed to be their leaders?"[2]

* Sounds like getting good men for the Army, including Officers, wasn't easy.
* Can you get cream — good men — without allowing enough time for the cream to rise? I think not. Especially now, when a lot of "cream" is needed — enough for five armies!
* I can't imagine five armies. What in the world were they?
* First was the "old Army" of 1794 — Wayne's Legion, including the Corps of Engineers and Artillerists — about 5000 men. Second was the "New Army" of 12,000 men voted in by Congress in July 1798. Those two were the regular Army. Third was the Volunteer corps approved specifically in May 1798 for the Quasi-War. Fourth, a 10,000-man "Provisional Army" — reserves — also authorized in May 1798. And fifth, an "Eventual Army" of 25,000 to be raised as needed.
* The Military Establishment became byzantine.
* Indeed. That's four new armies, besides the Legion! Were they really just created for a possible war with France? Or, were they really for Alexander Hamilton, their prime mover and commander? Either way, they were political armies — the most political armies in American history. And two years later, by June of 1800 — they were gone! President Adams made nice with Napoleon Bonaparte. Alexander Hamilton's new armies got the ax!

Democratic-Republicans were jubilant! They had massive celebrations! It was like the Fourth of July!

"What's all the bells, canons, and festivities?"
"Independence day. They're celebrating all around the Country."

"Independence Day? How can that be? It's not July 4th yet for two more weeks! Are those folks daft? Who are they?"

"Oh, they're only the Democratic-Republicans ... celebrating the 'death' of Hamilton's New Army. They say any day <u>that</u> happens is independence day to them!"

"Oh, well. I guess any excuse is good enough when it comes to celebrating. Let's grab a tankard of brew and join in the toasting!"[3]

John Adams gets the credit. He avoided an all out war with Napoleon. And thus, he was also able to kill off the only political army in American history.

* So. It was <u>Adams</u> who prevented America being dragged into the Napoleonic Wars. <u>That</u>'s how America stayed out of the fray!

* Yes. And that's how President-elect Jefferson got the 5000 man Army he inherited in the year 1801 when he moved his new government to Washington D.C. The Army was now back to 1794 levels — the levels endorsed by that history-making Act of 1796 that created a peacetime Army.

We've now looked at how the Military Establishment came about in post-Revolution America. Now, we'll focus-in even closer. We'll see how a <u>military academy</u> comes about as a part of that Military Establishment. So we'll not be making the trip with the President-elect Jefferson government to Washington D.C., Harry. Instead, we'll be visiting West Point again. We'll be going twenty-five years back in time again to the Revolutionary era. And this time we'll be looking at those twenty-five years strictly from the standpoint of a military academy for America![4]

CHAPTER 2: WEST POINT: PRE-1794

We're now back in 1775 again, Harry. The Revolutionary War has just begun. George Washington pushes to turn West Point into the "Gibralter of America". He also pushes for a military academy to turn Officers into leaders. Henry Knox slams the Continental Army's amateur Officers. Like Washington, he also pushes for an academy. John Adams takes up their cause at the Continental Congress in Philadelphia. In October 1776 he proposes a military academy. Congress agrees. They form a committee to cook-up a plan for one. But the plan gets shoved onto the back burner ... simmers ... and evaporates!

Washington keeps up a steady drum-beat for what's called "officers and gentlemen" ... and for a military academy to develope them. Back here in this century there's more to the word "gentleman" than you think. It's not just the word used for a person who does the Sir Walter Raleigh routine — not just courtesy. To George Washington, "gentleman" is Stoic virtues and character. It's the ideas of Seneca he read about during his youth. It's the virtues and character of the Stoic, Marcus Aurelius, that guided him all during his life. In fact, the chapter headings in Marcus Aurelius' book are the very maxims Washington cited in his own book, the Maxims of Washington. So when Washington pleads for Officers who are "gentlemen", he means men with morals, ethics, and character! But men like that are rare birds — hard to come by. The best way to get them is to develop them at a military academy set up just for that purpose. For example, he writes the following letter to the Continental Congress and to John Hancock, its President, during the War:

WASHINGTON ON GOOD-LEADERS

from: Washington's War letters to Congress

"As the War must be carried on systematically, and to do
it, you must have good Officers — induce Gentlemen and
Men of Character to engage. 'Till the bulk of your
Officers are composed of such persons as are actuated by
Principles of Honour, you have little to expect from them.
No instance has yet happened of good or bad behavior in a
corps of our service that has not originated with the
Officer — the Man who puts life in his hands, hazards his
health, and forsakes the Sweets of domestic enjoyments.
If encouragement then is given as will induce Gentlemen
and Men of Character to engage, we should in a little time
have an Army able to cope with any that can be opposed
to it: but, if the only merit an Officer possesses is to raise
[boss around] Men, no order, nor no discipline can prevail;
nor will the Officer ever meet with that respect which is

essentially necessary. I have never been witness to a single instance that can justify a different opinion. The firmness requisite is only to be obtained by a <u>constant course</u> of discipline and service. And to bring men to a proper degree — is not the work of a day, a Month, or even a Year."

The virtue is: Dedication. Good-leaders need not only backbone but background, gotten by dedicated effort

Washington's words fall on deaf ears. The Revolutionary War wears on ... and there's no formal military academy yet at West Point. Instead, Officers learn discipline at the "school of hard knocks" during those hard winter campaigns. Canada! Trenton! Valley Forge! Morristown! West Point! They're the "schools"! And their teachers are those twin taskmasters of discipline ... hardship and hardwork!
* Like "gentleman", I suspect there's also more meaning to the word "discipline" back during these times than in my time.
* Indeed there is. Back here, "discipline" is not just self-control. It's another word for character! Not until American Officers learned "discipline" — character — at those schools of hard knocks did they stand a chance against the British pros. Before that, they got crushed! Thanks to Washington's magic, they survived. But Washington knows that's no way to run an Army. That's why he'll never stop pushing for a proper military academy!
    The Corps of Invalids gets to West Point in 1781. Do you remember them, Harry? They're disabled vets. Now they serve as a "school" for indoctrinating young apprentice Officers. They teach mathematics, military arts, and of course, "discipline". The school is crude. It's unofficial. It's not a formal school. But, it's the first stab at one at West Point.
* It looks kind of ... rough!
* It's not only rough. It's shaky. Here's the situation in 1783 after Yorktown. Washington sends his "Sentiments on a Peace Establishment" down to the Congress. In it he wants Congress to formally establish a military academy. Meanwhile, he also wants the Corps of Invalids to carry on with their instructing. But they're discouraged. The "school" is not just winding down after Yorktown, but evaporating before their eyes! Thus, many of the Invalids turn to hard drink for lack of nothing better to do. They revert to sitting around and firing off old war stories — like already well known Margaret "Molly" Corbin over there does.
* You mean the one screeching at those privates to salute? Ah, I suspected that was a woman.
* We'll eavesdrop on what they say when she leaves:

"Whew! Thank goodness she's gone! That Molly Corbin's a bonafide battle-ax. She curses like the worst of them. She swills down grog with the hardest drinkers. Screams like a crow. And God knows what else. Then she expects us to <u>salute</u> her? How'd she ever get in this man's Army, anyway?"

"'Tar true. All those things she do. But a bonafide hero she also be ... by Act of Congress! 'Twer 1776 when she be helpin' her husband work an artillery piece. He be killed! She be takin' over ... breast cut to ribbons, arm half severed off by grapeshot! She be carryin' on with the battle for him!"

"Hmm. And now she's officially a soldier ... with the Corps of Invalids?"

"Aye. That she be. But 'tar true. Yon Molly can be a shrill and nasty woman!" [5]

After the Peace Treaty in 1783, the Army empties its ranks. Molly has few privates left to haze now. The troops are back home. That is, except for eighty men shared by West Point and Fort Pitt. They're the entire Continental Army. In 1784 America has eighty soldiers to guard three million people!

From 1784 to 1793 West Point is a sleepy little garrison. Meanwhile: settlers fight indians; Massachusetts has Shays' Rebellion; States ratify the Constitution; Little Turtle routs General Harmer; Blue Jacket and Little Turtle annihilate General St.Clair.

Now we come to 1793. Men for "Mad" Anthony Wayne's Legion come to West Point for training. The place begins to bustle again with training activities. President Washington's office bustles with preparing another proposal for a military academy. It's the ideal time to hit on Congress again for one. It's ten years since he formally proposed his "Sentiments on a Peace Establishment" back in 1783. But in between he had lost no opportunity to keep up a steady drumbeat for an academy. And he's not the only one. Quartermaster-General, Thomas Pickering, had a plan. Chief Engineer, Louis Du Portail — a Frenchman, had one. So did Secretary of War Benjamin Lincoln. Henry Knox was so enthusiastic about it, he tried to set one up unofficially down in New Jersey during the War. And he actually had a military school in his 1790 Bill — the one that gave St.Clair a few more troops. The idea was gutted by Congress, along with the troops. But the most philosophical plan was General Steuben's, probably because of his special background.

FREDERICK WILHELM VON STEUBEN – (1730 - 1794)

from: Horst Ueberhorst's biography

George Washington and Frederick von Steuben shared the same military philosophy, including the need to develope "officers and gentlemen" at a military academy.

Born in Magdeburg, Germany in 1730, von Steuben was a Prussian Officer like his father before him. He had served for twenty years in the army under the King of Prussia before meeting Benjamin Franklin in Paris. Franklin recommended von Steuben to General Washington and in February 1778 von Steuben arrived at Washington's winter headquarters in Valley Forge, Pennsylvania.

Washington closely observed von Steuben. He saw that Steuben's tough and meticulous training regimen was borrowed heavily from drill, custom, and discipline of the Prussian Army, but tailored to America's democratic Army. Washington was so impressed he wrote to the Continental Congress about this "gentleman" — this educated man trained throughout life in the virtues of honor, courage, loyalty, courtesy, and "gentlemanly" traits of character. Congress appointed von Steuben Inspector-General, Major General, with responsibility for supply and for discipline and for training troops and for instructing officers.

Steuben devised his "Regulations for the Order and Discipline of the Troops of the United States" based on experience and observation at Valley Forge. Known as the "Blue Book" after the color of its cover, it was used for training and regulation of both troops and Officers. Congress approved it as the American Army's official regulations, and it became the most valued book of its time.

One of Steuben's many memoranda on the military establishment was "Concept of National Defense" in 1784, heavily based on the Swiss military system. There would be three regional military departments in the United States, each having its own military academy to develope

Officers. The "Blue Book" was one of his bedrocks for an academy. The other bedrock was his Concept of Education.

The "Blue Book" had Prussian and ancient military tradition running through it. But it was a clear rejection of the "old world" method of training ordinary soldiers by brutally transforming them into machines that perform specific functions. The soldier's safety and well-being were now an Officer's obligation and responsibility. Steuben recognized the American soldier was different from the European for the very reasons that the Revolution was fought — for respect and individual freedoms. The American Officer was to be a new breed of leader in step with a State that was a new breed of nation.

Steuben's Concept of Education had some parallels to the Prussian Cadet Academy. It retained classical Officer's "gentlemanly" virtues of honor, courage, and loyalty. But, it added a critical new virtue. Trust! It added others such as compassion and responsibility. And, appreciation for American democracy became paramount. All of these were in his Concept of Education using professors and masters of the arts of morals, history, and philosophy. There would be senior Officers assigned to drill, order, and discipline.

He visualized a military academy developing Leaders, not just Engineers. It would take a total of three years. America was to require neither ancestry nor wealth for those in its Officer Corps. But an academy would be expensive, so, he suggested that each cadet be required to pay 300 dollars per year. That was an amount only the most well-to-do families could afford. Those who would be career Army Officers might be relieved of that cost!

Much of what Frederick Wilhelm von Steuben proposed was ultimately adopted by the [unofficial] West Point Officer School in 1794 and the [official] U.S. Military Academy at West Point in 1802. West Point's roots reach back to Europe via Steuben, and all the way back to Ancient times via Europe!

The virtue is: Responsibility. It's the responsibility of government to provide soldiers with good-leaders.

* So how does Washington's latest "military academy" request do?
* Congress does it again in 1793! They reject Washington's military academy!

284

They deny him his dream! There will be no U.S. Military Academy again this year![6]

CHAPTER 3: WEST POINT OFFICER TRAINING SCHOOL

So, Harry, Congress pruned the military academy out of Washington's 1793 Bill! Thomas Jefferson had said a military academy might be unconstitutional. It has to be a standing institution. It creates a standing officer corps. That's the framework of a standing army. And the framework — an officer corps — is the army. The army only does what its officer corps tells it to do. As an officer corps goes, so goes an army. If it is loyal and trustworthy, so is an army. If not, watch out!

Not only are standing armies not specifically provided for in the Constitution, they are infamous for having been the scourge of Europe's troubled history. On the other hand, Steuben, as an ex-European Officer, sees things differently than Thomas Jefferson. He speaks from experience, and he advises Congress that an American Standing Army would be different than traditional European standing armies:

STEUBEN ON AN AMERICAN STANDING ARMY AND ACADEMY[7]

"All armies mirror the local situation of the Country, the spirit of government, the character of the Nation. Yes Fellow Citizens I admit it — it is a Standing Army, but composed of your brothers and your sons. Can you require or conceive a better security? Are they not your natural guardians?"

The virtue is: Loyalty. There is nothing to fear if leaders are loyal to the "People".

Now comes May 1794. Congress comes up with a compromise between what Washington and Steuben want, and what Thomas Jefferson warns against. Congress allows an officer training "school" — the West Point School. It's to have books, instruments, apparatus, and three French military engineers as instructors. The 1794 "Act for a Corps of Artillerists and Engineers" establishes vacancies for cadets within regular Army companies stationed at West Point.

The first cadets arrive at West Point in 1794. Lieutenant Colonel Stephen Rochefontaine designs the courses. The technical part uses books on engineering drawing and fortifications. The leadership part is a tribute to Steuben. It uses his Blue Book. This all happens none too soon as far as Steuben is concerned. For 1794 is the year he dies! At least he lived to see the seeds of a bonafide military academy being planted!

Next comes the "Military Establishment Act of 1796". That's the landmark Act which created a peacetime Army for the first time by keeping the wartime setup of 1794. It's also the Act that, for the last time as President, Washington uses to take another crack at getting a military academy. And for the last time it's nice try … but no cigar! The Act, nevertheless, retains the **West Point School** for training officers.

Then bad luck strikes. A fire! It brings instruction to an abrupt halt! Books, apparatus, and the building are snuffed out! Rochefontaine scrounges up what's left and reorganizes. He makes the best of it. The **West Point School** limps on with what's left!

Now comes 1798. That's when storm clouds of the Quasi-War with France begin to appear. That's when that embattled Bill in Congress gives Alexander Hamilton his "New Army". That same Bill also breaths new life into the **West Point School**. Congress gives its blessing to four new teachers. And they're for the arts and sciences, not just technology!

* So more than drawing, artillery, and fortifications classes are now allowed … at least by law.

* Yes. And Congress also doubles the number of cadets allowed. The school inches closer to Washington's vision, again at least by law …… but not in reality!

By 1799 Hamilton is on a roll! Among his pet projects, he works on plans for a <u>formal</u> military academy. It's the most comprehensive plan to date — a General Military Academy having four Schools. In his plan every cadet would first attend the Fundamental School for two years. It's curriculum would have: math; design; philosophy; geography; and chemistry. Then cadets would attend one of the other three Advanced Schools for another two years. Those three Schools would be: the School of Engineers and Artillerists; the School of Infantry and Cavalry; and, the School of the Navy.

Now retired, Washington backs Hamilton's plan. But several Adams Federalists join forces with Democratic-Republicans against it. They label Hamilton "America's would-be Alexander I". They remind everyone it isn't Washington's plan. It's Hamilton's. And Hamilton Federalists are bitterly challenging Adams in the coming election. So Hamilton's military academy plan goes nowhere! Next year in 1800 Congress permanently kills it … right along with his New Army!

CHAPTER 4: THE UNITED STATES MILITARY ACADEMY

Let's go back again to December 12, 1799 when George Washington is grave-ly ill. It's then that he puts his wishes for a formal military academy into writing for the last time. Here's an excerpt from that letter:

WASHINGTON: A LAST WISH[9]

"The establishment of an institution of this kind, upon a respectable and extensive basis, has ever been considered by me as an object of primary importance to this Country; and while I was in the Chair of Government, I omitted no proper opportunity of recommending it to the Legislature."

The virtue is: Sincerity. The most sincere statements are from the death-bed.

And I'll tell you a little known fact. This is the last public letter George Washington ever writes! For just two days after he writes it …… he dies.
* His wishes for a military academy were in his thoughts right to the end of his life — like a Last Wish!
* And Destiny has its way of granting a Last Wish gradually and at an appointed hour. Yes, Harry, you could call this a dying man's Last Wish. It's practically a death-bed wish. You would think that men of good will should make an effort to grant this beloved American his Last Wish. After all, here was a man who could have easily taken over the Country at the end of the War. Instead, he squashed the only United States Army coup-de-etat in history — the Newburgh Conspiracy. Here was a man who railed against his Officers who wanted to make him King. Here was a man who opposed a constitutional monarchy — with him as monarch for life — when it was discussed at the Constitutional Convention. Anyone would have to be convinced Washington's motives for a military academy couldn't be sin-ister. His motives had to be entirely noble and honorable. If the "American Cincinnatus" didn't fear an academy after decades of hashing and rehashing it, need America fear one?[10]
George Washington's death is now followed by a flourish of people pushing for a military academy. It seems like everyone is keen to get into the game of full-filling the great man's Last Wish.
* They're probably struck by the loss and feel they owe him something. And they do. Everything!
* Harry, I'm pleasantly surprised you appreciate that. It may be too late to close the barn door after the horses are out. But it's never to late to know you should have! I know it's hard to see things with the eyes of another era … even though you're here on the spot. And I know this may sound corny to a person from your

288

era. But "civility" — such as granting a Last Wish — is taken seriously back here. It's valued and esteemed in 1800 America!

* Then who's all going to bat for Washington's academy wish?

* President John Adams. Secretary Samuel Dexter. Alexander Hamilton. They're the most visible. And Vice President Thomas Jefferson is the most visibly not opposed. He remains silent on the issue ... for the first time ever!

* Interesting. But I wouldn't say that's a <u>flourish</u> of people.

STEADY ON THERE! I DIDN'T SAY A MILITARY ACADEMY WASN'T A GOOD IDEA. I ONLY SAID IT'S NOT CONSTITUTIONAL!

* Oh-h-h, there are others — Congressmen, newspapers, and so on. Still, the very first one who goes to bat for a military academy after Washington dies is President Adams. On January 14, 1800, exactly one month after Washington's death, Adams asks Congress to establish a permanent military academy. Now, I ask you, why would he wait for this particular moment in time if not to be the one who fulfills Washington's Last Wish?

* Isn't 1800 an election year?

* It's true that the next election is coming up. But can he win votes doing this? Look at the facts. On one side are <u>Hamilton</u> Federalists. Adams lost their support long ago. That's why there's a Hamilton Federalist faction. So he won't likely win votes under any circumstances from the hard core Hamilton Federalist camp, will he Harry!

* No, I guess he won't!

* On the other side are the Democratic-Republicans. They were strongly against the Bills containing the New Armies, a military academy, and everything else military. They're solidly in Thomas Jefferson's camp, are they not?

* I would think so.

* In the middle are his own <u>Adams</u> Federalists. Even many of them are against a military academy. Wouldn't he risk losing some of them by proposing a military academy?

* I would think that's possible.

* So Adams has little to gain, politically, by supporting a military academy. Don't you agree?
* Yes, It sounds like he would lose votes.
* He <u>does</u>. He never musters enough votes in Congress for an academy![11]

Next up to bat, Secretary of War James McHenry. He petitions Congress to establish a military academy. And, speaking of newspapers going to bat for Washington's Last Wish, McHenry's petition is published by major newspapers all around the Country. Here's a digest from one of them:

ESTABLISHMENT OF A MILITARY ACADEMY

by: Secretary James McHenry
From the <u>New York Spectator</u> paper,
February 22, 1800.

"George Washington urged a Military Academy for years. During the War he said that he had 'an Army of men, but few (real) Officers or soldiers in that Army; Time and Instructors are required — to enable the Army, to meet the enemy upon anything like Equal Terms.' The Officers are to be instructed in <u>moral, mechanical, geometrical, and physical</u> rules; it calls for profound study; does it consist with humane and enlightened policy to march men imperfectly instructed and disciplined against veteran troops commanded by skillful and scientific Officers?

The secret of discipline (character) and military science were well known to those ancient governments whose generals and troops have filled the world with the splendor of their victories. According to (the Roman) Scipio, nothing contributed to military success so much as skill in the individual Officers. Livy told of the importance of severity of Roman discipline and training under Caesar; Machiavelli placed it (success) most dependent on long practiced discipline (character) and military science. Writers of all ages emphasized the importance of discipline and military science."

The virtue is: Duty. We have a duty to provide troops
with good-leaders.

McHenry's petition creates a stir. But political in-fighting becomes vicious in this election year. His support in Congress for an academy sputters and conks out. In fact, the opposition even tries to shut down what's left of the **West Point School**!

Next up, Alexander Hamilton. His academy proposal has already been rejected. But "Alexander I" doesn't give up easily. He presses the issue again during the summer of 1800.

* Of course. Isn't a military academy part of his New Army and his grand military scheme?

* That scheme is dead. President Adams began dismantling the New Army months ago and finished the job in June 1800. Remember the Democratic-Republican celebrations we went to? Now Hamilton is wrapped up in this nasty election fight. So, does once again plumping for an academy make good political sense to you? The Adams vs. Hamilton vendetta is raging full blast. Adams supporters are attacking Hamilton's militarism. Hamilton has to dump his militaristic image. Do you dump a militaristic image by openly plumping for a military academy? Of course not. But, he's doing it anyway. He's shooting himself in the foot! Why would a clever Alexander Hamilton intentionally shoot himself in the foot? Why would he plump for a military academy amid a blizzard of attacks on his militarism? Is it loyalty to his old boss, George Washington? Does he think that sympathy for anything to do with George Washington will gain him votes, even if it has to do with the military? Or is he just trying to grant an old friend's Last Wish?[12]

* It could be any of those. It could be all of those.

* Then, like Adams, an academy doesn't politically help him either, does it?

* No. I guess not.

* Meanwhile, Samuel Dexter comes on board as Adams' Secretary of War. Dexter is keen on a military academy. He comes up with a new twist on how to get one. It's low profile. It skirts around Congress. It's politically unassailable. And it uses what's already in place — the 1794 and 1798 Artillerists and Engineers Acts. Dexter springs his new idea on Adams.

> "Mr. President, a completely new academy would be poison to you at this time."
>
> "Yes, I know, Sam. Congress has an angry look. It's the coming elections." °°Not to mention I've been playing the old standing army and warmonger game to bash Hamilton.°°
>
> "But there is a way Sir. You can use the existing **West Point School!**"
>
> "I am not ready to travel that road again. That has been done. I want to give Washington his military academy. Nothing less." °°And I want that feather in my cap for doing it.°°
>
> "A few well targeted appointments can't hurt your election prospects, Sir. And you have several in hand for the already existing **West Point School!**"
>
> "Is that true? .... In such case, I am ready to appoint both cadets and teachers. You are to take the earliest measures — quietly — toward finding the proper characters!" °°I guess Washington will have to wait!°° [13]

Dexter's list of "proper characters" is "well targeted"! An example is Jonathan Williams — Benjamin Franklin's nephew! Williams knows mathematics, philosophy, and military engineering. However, he's not a teacher. He's not a soldier, either. But, he's a well connected Federalist. So he gets an offer to teach at the **West Point School** and be direct commissioned to the rank of Major. At the same time, Dexter tips Williams off that he'll be the top dog of any future military academy. Williams accepts the commission. He can only hope for an academy!

It's now November 1800. The presidential campaign is finished. So is John Adams! He does better than expected everywhere … except Alexander Hamilton's New York. There he gets buried. Hamilton sees to it. That also buries Adams' dream of re-election. Democratic-Republicans take over, for the first time ever!

* So Adams is finished. What a strange twist of fate. Hamilton ironically handed the Presidency to Thomas Jefferson!

* Yes. But Adams isn't quite finished. He still has "markers" to redeem to those who supported him. So during his last days in Office he makes a ton of appointments, including for the Army. However, Jonathan Williams is left dangling. The future of both Williams and the West Point School now appears bleak![14]

Thomas Jefferson is inaugurated on March 4, 1801. Democratic-Republicans are on cloud nine over their success. Then out of the clear blue sky comes the shock of their lives! Thomas Jefferson tells them he's establishing a military academy!

* Whew! The only sounds must have been jaws hitting the table and guys falling off their chairs!

* That's right. And it's only April 1801 — barely a month after inauguration. That month the President and Secretary of War, Henry Dearborn, select a top-dog

for their academy-to-be. It's none other than Adams' "well-targeted" appointment — Federalist, Jonathan Williams!

* Whew! That must be another shock! A Federalist!
* Within another month, other teachers are sorted out. Facilities are made ready at West Point. Cadets arrive. New life is breathed into the existing school at West Point. New classes begin in September 1801. Meanwhile, the President and Dearborn quietly work on new legislation — a military peace establishment law. It will legalize a bonafide military academy!

In March 1802, Congress passes "An Act Fixing the Military Peace Establishment of the United States". Tucked between other things in the Act is a new Corps of Engineers for West Point. And it says this Corps of Engineers shall "constitute" — which in the early 1800's means to setup or establish — a military academy! The President signs the Bill into law on March 16, 1802. It offically creates the United States Military Academy at West Point — "Mr. Jefferson's Academy"!

* That's ironic. Thomas Jefferson is the one who finally fulfills George Washington's "Last Wish"! And Jefferson was always opposed to a military academy!
* That's right, Harry. Whatsmore, the Federalists had burned themselves out over military issues, including an academy. And Thomas Jefferson's Democratic-Republicans had poured fuel onto those fiery military issues to cleverly help the Federalists destroy themselves. The Democratic-Republicans rose to power out of the ashes. Now they see the wisdom in "Sentiments on a Peace Establishment" that George Washington had proposed nineteen years ago. Their "Act Fixing The Military Peace Establishment of the United States" is "broadly" the same as Washington's "Sentiments" — including a military academy. I say, "broadly", because there is a difference between them. That difference is in the details. You'll see later, Harry, those details make all the difference! But, anyway, that's how the Military Academy at West Point came about![15]
* I have to ask you an obvious question, Thomas. As Thomas Jefferson was always cool on a military academy, why did he lock right onto establishing one when he became President? Why did he of all people found a military academy!
* That's the mystery, Harry! In order for you to know why he founded the Military Academy, you have to get to know him. Sound impossible? Well, it isn't! For that's just what you shall do next! You shall get to know Thomas Jefferson!

7.

THE STORY BEHIND WEST POINT: THE FOUNDING - WHY?

To discover what West Point is really all about and why it took Thomas Jefferson to found it, you need to get to know Thomas Jefferson! You get inside his head and heart by seeing what happened in his life that made him be the man he was, and made him do the things he did. Once you get to understand Thomas Jefferson, you understand why he founded West Point. And why he founded it is proven, once and for all, by true and validly deductible reasoning.

CHAPTER 1: THOMAS JEFFERSON

So, Harry, President Thomas Jefferson's announcement of an official United States Military Academy floored everyone!
* And he never gave his reasons?
* Does the fox let the hound know which way he's headed? No, Thomas Jefferson never made a proclamation such as, "I shall establish a military academy … for this and this and this reason". But then, Thomas Jefferson purposely didn't give reasons for many things he did. That was his nature!
* Are you saying he wasn't exactly the great communicator?
* He was not the great speechmaker that Patrick Henry was. But he was a great philosopher! And he always put his philosophies to good practical use … as leader, lawyer, artist, architect, scientist, inventor, musician, educator, engineer, librarian, politician, and agriculturalist! Allow me to say that many consider Thomas Jefferson to be the philosophical father — intellectual father — of the United States! That includes John F. Kennedy in your modern era, Harry. Here's what Kennedy said on one occasion:

J.F.K. ON THOMAS JEFFERSON

It happened one evening at the White House. President Kennedy was having a special dinner party for America's Nobel Prize winners. At this celebration Kennedy made the following pronouncement:

"This is the most extraordinary collection of talents that has ever been gathered together at this White House … with the possible exception of when Thomas Jefferson dined alone!"

It was the ultimate compliment.

The virtue is: Sincerity. Flattery by others is the most sincere compliment.

Thomas Jefferson was talented, alright. His talent's were already making him famous long before the Revolution. But his privacy began to suffer. And he loved his privacy. So he put up an imaginary wall. He guarded himself from the inquiring public.
* Ah. Privacy was a problem, even back then?
* Yes. And Thomas Jefferson also liked to guard the privacy of his thoughts. He didn't often tell people around him what he was thinking. As a result, he made a lot of cloak-and-dagger type of decisions. And when he did tell people what he

was thinking, he was always careful about what he said and who he said it to. So the real story from Thomas Jefferson on many issues is often skanty — even non-existent. West Point is one of those issues! Cold, hard, objective information about West Point is thin!

* Then how can we know why he established West Point?

* Thomas Jefferson erected a wall of privacy. But there's still a huge amount of knowledge about him. Who he was. Where he came from. What he wrote. What he did. What he said. His library offers a picture of what he read and studied. And there are an immense number of documents written by Thomas Jefferson himself. Take letters, for example. Historians know of maybe 75,000! All of these sources reveal who Thomas Jefferson was and how he thought. They get you inside his head and his heart. They help you get to know him. Once you do, you'll understand <u>why</u> he founded the United States Military Academy. So I'll not only show you what he does. Through his writings, I'll show you what he felt and thought![1]

However, I'm getting ahead of the story. Let's back-up again and journey back to the year 1743 — thirty-two years before the Revolution began. Let's see Thomas Jefferson, and start to learn about him, first hand!

* I assume that's the year he's born?

* That's right. Thomas Jefferson's father, Peter Jefferson, is of Welsh origin. His mother, Jane Randolph Jefferson's ancestors are from Scotland. But they actually lived in, and emigrated from, England. Peter Jefferson is a hearty, self-made farmer who carves a modest farm out of the raw wilderness. He calls it Shadwell, after the English town his wife, Jane, was born in. The hard working Jeffersons are trying to turn their farm into a thriving plantation. So that's the scene in which we find young Thomas Jefferson: born on the wild frontier; experiencing the naked wilderness with a sturdy father — his best pal; learning words and penmanship from a self-educated father — his first mentor; growing from frontier lad to Virginia gentry because of a hardworking father — his lifelong idol!

* So Thomas Jefferson actually knows both "worlds" — first the hearty frontier farm world, and second, the Virginia plantation gentry world.

* Yes. And that's important to remember. For both worlds make him what he is!

First, the frontier brings him close to nature. So, botany, biology, and geology are in his bones. They tweak his curiosity. He seeks answers — enlightenment. That will eventually tweak his interest in all 1700's Enlightenment. Nature. Science. Law. Government. Mathematics. Almost everything. He will some-day be America's legendary Enlightenment philosopher!

Second, As Peter Jefferson turns their frontier farm into a thriving plantation, the Jeffersons turn into landed gentry. And Virginia landed gentry not only cultivate their land. They also cultivate their children into a culture of their own. They "till" the best codes of conduct, using the English gentry as their earthly model. They "plant" morals, ethics, and character, using Greek, Roman, and Judao-Christian philosophies as their "seeds". Their "product" is the "Virginia Gentleman".

Being a Virginia Gentleman means having good moral, ethical, and character traits such as trust, honor, courage, respect, kindness, loyalty, responsibility, and so on. It also means being a good-leader both in public and private life. That takes training. So young Thomas does more than learn from a loving father to catch fish and hunt deer and ride horses and paddle canoes and shoot wild turkeys. Peter Jefferson does more than teach him to say his prayers and to read the Bible. He does more than show him life. He shows him education! He sends him to the Latin School ... at nine years old!

Young Thomas is learning Latin, Greek, and French. He's so dedicated, he even reads his Homer and Vergil to his father during canoe trips.

* Interesting. But why learn Latin and Greek and French?
* Because to learn about the virtues, you have to read the Classics from ancient Greece and Rome. Some of the Classics have been translated into French, but none into English. Therefore, you have to learn how to read Greek and Latin, or at least French. If you don't, you can't get into higher education. All college entrance tests involve translating Classical works to and from Greek and Latin. So even pre-teenagers have to read certain Classical masters such as poet Homer, historian Xenophon, orator Demosthenes, philosopher Cicero, and parts of the New Testament ... and all in Greek and Latin!
* That sounds difficult.
* It's not only the work that's difficult. In these times it's also the teachers that are difficult. Some are very strict. And some have an unkind, severe, brutal, terrifying, or even sadistic sense of humor. For instance, something akin to the following student gossip has probably taken place hundreds of times:

"Do we have a new teacher this year? The young teachers never
    seem to stay. Then they say we read Latin horribly, and translate
    it worse. Whose fault is it? I reckon their diplomas, written in
    Latin, contain more Latin then they know!"
    "No, we may be in for it. We may have that Mr. Jones again!"
"Oh no! That slave-driver ... with his rattan cane? He unmerci-
    fully whips his students into shame and silent tears. That thing
    hurts!"
    "I know. And it's never his poor teaching methods at fault,
        either!"
"No. It's always us. ... Last year in class he called on me to do
    something or other with an active verb. But he never taught us!
    So he said to me, 'alright muttonhead, give me the answer!' I
    couldn't, of course. So he whacks me on the rear-end. He asks
    another plaguey (troublesome) question about verbs. I couldn't
    answer, so he says, 'then I'll tell you ... an active verb passes an
    action (and whacks me) to you the object (whacks me again)
    from I the actor (and whacks me again). Now do you get it?'"
    "He gave me a lashing also. A merciless tongue-lashing. It
        drew tears. So he called me up to him. I was about ready to
        get down on my knees and beg his forgiveness. I've seen
        that work with him! But he asked me, 'do you know Mr. (so
        and so)?' I said, 'yes sir'! Of course, I didn't have a clue
        who he was. And he asked, 'do you know Mr. (somebody

else)?' I said, 'yes sir', again. 'I whipped them both', he said. 'And they are now bloody great men, are they not?' I said, 'yes sir'. 'Then what say you to that', he asked me. I said, 'you mean to make a bloody great man out of me, also?' The class roared. And I couldn't believe it … even Mr. Jones smiled. He said, 'go to your seat you rascal, I shall not touch you again'. And guess what? He never did!"

"Well, we'll see if your luck holds up. He's your teacher again! Here he comes!"

"Shh, let's hear what he says. Quiet! Shhh."

"Well class, what kind of students are you this year? A bunch of little marble players? Or, scholars? Well … we shall see!"[2]

Young Thomas is lucky. He seldom gets "caned" by his teachers. He mostly gets inspired. And he's <u>lucky</u> his teachers are inspiring disciplinarians. He'll need them. For, catastrophe suddenly strikes. Young Thomas' father — his pal, idol, and inspiration …….. dies!

Fourteen year old Thomas would sooner be struck by lightning! Suddenly, he has no role model. He has no father to be with. It looks like his world will crumble. But even in death his father won't let anything happen to his son. He has written down his Last Wish. It is that Thomas continue on in schooling to get a full blown Classical education … no matter what happens!

Thomas' mother is crushed and grief-stricken! So she has guardians looking after Thomas' best interests. They send him off to a boarding school. It's the Classical school run by the strict and pushy Reverend Maury. Young Thomas' training and education to become a "Virginia Gentleman" surges forward!

All through his life Thomas Jefferson will often speak with great love and fondness of his father whose legacy to him was that Last Wish. As time goes by, he will come more and more to realize the great love and Virtue that inspired his father to leave that Last Wish. And what's important to us, Harry, Peter Jefferson's Last Wish will inspire a lifetime belief in the power of Virtue in young Thomas!

That lifetime belief in the power of Virtue starts to surface immediately at Reverend Maury's boarding school. Young Thomas keeps up a diary of what he reads in Greek, Latin, history, and philosophy. It has his own notes and comments, and is really like a book of virtues. He'll eventually make entries up to when he's thirty years old. This diary is his <u>Literary Commonplace Book</u>. It will be part of his secret family treasures which will not become public until the 20th century, Harry!

* That's fascinating. And what does he mean by "Commonplace"?

* A commonplace book is a special diary. It's a collection of notes, passages, and quotation's from what you <u>read</u> — not what you <u>do</u>.

* I see. It's not Jefferson's regular diary.

* No. And it's like a filter. It doesn't have <u>everything</u> he reads. It has what he considers important, and leaves out the rest. It has what he wants to remember. If you read it, you see Thomas Jefferson's philosophy taking shape right before your eyes. It's a deep personal gauge of his philosophical beliefs. It's like a window to his heart and mind. It's the array of moral, ethical, and character virtues that guide his life. It's actually kind of his bible of philosophy!

Thomas Jefferson will someday have other commonplace books, as well ... like his legal commonplace book. They could all be put together and titled "The Real Jefferson, Self-Revealed", because they paint a picture of him that's not painted by historians. For example, his early entries into the <u>Literary Commonplace Book</u> are Stoic philosophy. They help him to deal with his father's death. He writes this in Greek from Euripides' work, Orestes: "nothing is so terrible, be it pain or death, that man cannot bear"; from Horaces' <u>Satires</u>: "the free man is one who handles life with discipline and without fear of death"; and in Latin from Cicero's <u>Tusculan Disputations</u>: "those afraid of death live with souls not at peace, while others live happy lives". Cicero, the Roman, wrote that last quotation in the shadow of his daughter's death. Thomas, the Virginian, copied it into his <u>Commonplace Book</u> in the shadow of his father's death. Stoic philosophy is a sturdy shoulder to lean on. And right now, Thomas needs one!

* None of that surprises me, knowing how close he was to his father. It sounds like he begins turning to the philosophers for the guidance his father used to give him.

* Where better to turn? And Stoicism will help him to bear up to many other deaths during his lifetime. You'll see, he'll have much more than his share of them. His <u>Commonplace Book</u> will overflow with philosophical entries on death and immortality. They'll help him maintain a Stoic view toward death — one he'll maintain all his life. The following quotation is taken from his favorite Classic poet, Homer, and entered into his <u>Commonplace Book</u>:

DEATH SERVING ONE'S COUNTRY

from: Homer

Death is the worst, a Fate which all must try,
And for our Country, it is a Bliss to die,

The gallant Man, though slain in Fight he be,
Yet leaves his Nation safe, his children free,
Entails a debt on all the grateful State,
His own brave Friends shall glory in his Fate,
His wife live Honoured, his Race succeed,
And late Posterity, enjoy the Deed.

The virtue is: Honor. Even death is a form of honor when
serving Country.

This bit of Homer is Stoic philosophy ... 500 years before Stoicism! Thomas will one day display Stoicism when he decides to risk his life to rebel against England. So it's no surprise that a book by the Stoic philosopher, Seneca, will be on his bed-table many years from now when he dies. But death and immortality are not the only subjects in his Commonplace Book. There are moralizing speeches by Euripides. There is satirical humor from Samuel Butler's Hudibras in which young Thomas finds honor and integrity. Then there's Fenelon's Telemaque — just great tales filled with examples of virtues! The Commonplace Book has more than four hundred entries! There are thirty different authors!

Thomas is not only interested in philosophy of the heart! He's also interested in the philosophy of science. He loves logic and mathematics. He's a math whiz! It plays a key role in developing many of Thomas Jefferson's virtues. For math demands accuracy, dedication, perseverance, and attention to details. And it builds discipline. They're the reasons why math will someday be a tool used at West Point to mold those character traits in future Army Officers, Harry![3]

At seventeen, Thomas' guardians enroll him in the College of William and Mary at Williamsburg, Virginia. From fourteen to seventeen years old he had been forced to be the "man of the house". Now he's finally headed for college to fulfill his father's Last Wish. So in 1760, he leaves his mother, six sisters, and three year old brother at Shadwell. He's heard that the chaos called the French and Indian War has just ended. He hasn't heard that the chaos at William and Mary has just begun!

* Chaos? I don't get you!
* Most students at William and Mary come from wealthy families. Many of the students are those former little "marble-playing rascals". They still manage to find chaotic diversions from their studies! The discussion going on over there tells you what I mean:

"Did you hear what happened to our philosophy professor and
friend, the Reverend Owen?"
"You mean after our recent brawl in town? No, I didn't."
"They gave the Reverend the push! They forced him to resign!
President Dawson said that the Reverend has been setting a bad
example by leading us students in brawls against the townsmen."
"President Dawson! Why that blackguard! That hypocrite!"

301

That double-dealer! He's the pan calling the kettle black! What kind of an example does <u>he</u> set: getting drunk in the local taverns; betting on the horses and cockfights; gambling with cardplaying?"

"True! He'll continue to have <u>his</u> fun. But what do <u>we</u> do for fun … now that there will be no more town brawls? Study? These studies are no fun. They're little beyond grammar school level!"

"What do you say about following President Dawson's example! We can go down and bet on the horses and the cockfights! Or play cards!"

"A game of cards sounds like just the thing. I'm in!"[4]

* William and Mary College doesn't sound too clever, Thomas. Idle time? Town brawls? I thought it was a more serious place.

* Every college has its deadbeats, Harry. But you get out of a college what you put into it. And young Thomas Jefferson puts a lot into it. No town brawling, or card playing, or horse betting, or tobacco smoking … or even much drinking for him. This lean, rough-hewn, broad-shouldered, square-jawed, reddish-haired, hazel-eyed, now over six-foot tall young man likes music, dancing, and flirting with all the girls. He longs for the sports he used to play with his father. But he now has to settle for getting in a one or two mile run each day. In his spare time he also finds about fifteen hours a day to read and study! Yes, he <u>is</u> different! And his professors, William Small and George Wythe, recognize that!

* Are you exaggerating? Does he really hit the books that hard?

* It's true. He's quite keen to learn — and learn fast! He does put about fifteen hours daily into his studies and outside reading. His Professors, Small and Wythe, are greatly impressed with him. He's a proud feather in their cap. So they show him off. They bring Thomas along with them to dine with a Francis Fauquier, a fellow intellectual of Williamsburg. It doesn't hurt that he happens to also be the

Governor of Virginia!

Fauquier is, like Small and Wythe, also impressed with young Thomas. After that, the four of them frequently philosophize over a dinner. Imagine. Thomas Jefferson at only twenty years old is already rubbing elbows with the famous and influential.

Mathematics is Thomas Jefferson's number one passion. Next is science. But he's becoming an ace at Greek and Roman history and philosophy as well. And he <u>learns</u> from history. He's practical. Being practical, he next weighs up all the practical reasons to go on to study law for a profession. He concludes that law is at minimum a career springboard. So he decides to stay on at William and Mary to study law under Professor Wythe. It will take him five more years. He will start another commonplace book. This one is a legal and political diary.

Thomas goes home to Shadwell during school breaks. He and his best friend, Dabney Carr, always study together. They have a special place beneath an oak tree that's on top of the little mountain near Shadwell. It's out of earshot from everyone. They can pretend they're giving speeches. They can argue mock cases out loud. They can even rehearse, without being embarrassed, how to chat up the girls! To their surprise it's the latter that bears the first fruit. Dabney Carr chat's up, falls in love, and marries Thomas' nineteen year old sister, Martha!

Thomas and — now brother-in-law — Dabney Carr become attached to that spot on the little mountain. They make a pact — a kind of last wish! They agree that the survivor of them will look after the affairs of the first of them to die, and bury him there. That day seems so far away. Little do they know that Thomas will out-live Dabney by fifty years! Still, true to their pact, the two men <u>will</u> someday be buried on top of that little mountain where they studied in their youth! So too will their families!

Thomas will also someday build a home on that little mountain. He'll be inspired to do so by Cato, Pliny, and other Romans who bragged about mansions high up on hills in their writings. He'll also be inspired by his knowledge of Latin when he names his home. He'll call it ... Monticello! It means "little mountain"!

Thomas, Dabney, and Martha spend many happy days on their little mountain. But those happy days don't last very long. Just three months after Dabney marries Martha, grief strikes. Thomas' two years older sister, Jane, dies! Jane was as close a sister to Thomas as Dabney Carr is a friend. But their thing together wasn't studies. It was music. They had always teamed up together at social gatherings. Jane sang, Thomas played the violin. They were a big hit! Even in church, they did the Psalm-tunes together at weekly services!

So Jane's death leaves a large ache in Thomas' heart. It drives him into an early return back to Williamsburg to submerge himself in his law books. That's his way of trying to forget — trying to ease the pain of loss and sorrow — like he did after his father died. He drowns his sorrow in work. He reads and writes ... making notes in his <u>Literary Commonplace Book</u>. He reads and writes ... making notes in his legal commonplace diary. He even learns enough of the Anglo-Saxon language to read old books [written in Anglo Saxon] on England's Ancient Constitution. Remember the Ancient Constitution, Harry? They were the "laws" used back in the Saxon Age of England, prior to William the Conqueror's inva-

sion from France in 1066 AD. The Saxon Age was England's golden age of liberty. There was only loose monarchism … and little in the way of feudal slavery.
* I never knew there was an actual Anglo-Saxon language. That's what I call really getting at the primary sources of English law!
* To examine the teeth of a horse you go straight to the horses mouth, don't you! Well, Thomas wants to get to the teeth of English law. Why? He's working out a philosophy on the way people in a society should live together. And he doesn't only read old Anglo-Saxon books on the Ancient Constitution to do it. His legal and literary commonplace diaries show that he reads everything on English law. That includes famous but difficult stuff such as: Sir Edward Coke's Institutes; Lord Kames' Historical Law Tracts; William Somner's Treatise of Gavelkind; and, Sir William Blackstone's Commentaries on the Laws of England. Have you heard of them? They're the backbone of English, and now, American law. He also reads political philosophy by Locke, Hume, and Montesquieu … and of course, by Henry St. John Bolingbroke who is one of his favorites for ancient and English philosophy.

Those law studies turn out to be very timely. For, it's 1765. That's when Virginia's House of Burgesses passes a Resolution to oppose the fabulously stupid Stamp Act. Patrick Henry's famous Stamp Act Speech is what inflames them to do so. The day Patrick Henry delivers that speech the young law student, Thomas Jefferson, listens intently to the whole thing. Thomas watches from the doorway of the House of Burgesses chamber. He sees Patrick Henry reel off his famous quotation, "if this be treason, then make the most of it". Young Thomas sees he's no match for Patrick Henry's passion at legal oratory. But he also sees he's more than a match for Patrick Henry's knowledge on English law. Thomas is probably more than a match for anyone there that day! After studying all those old books, his knowledge on the subject is, like they say, more rare than hens teeth!

Patrick Henry shocked everyone that day. Townsfolk, legal experts, and law students are buzzing with gossip. A discussion between young Thomas and a fellow law student who is a monarchist would have gone something like this:

> "Patrick Henry's speech was pure treason, would you not agree Mr. Jefferson?"
>> "If there is no allegiance to something [England], there can be no treason. Therefore in our case, it is not treason! We are merely reclaiming our long absent historic liberties given to us by the Ancient Constitution. We have no allegiance to Crown laws."
> "The Ancient Constitution? From Saxon times? Hah! How, sir, has that relevance? Only the numerous common laws have relevance."
>> "Our ancestors were defrauded of their liberties by the art and finesse of William the Conqueror's lawyers! Like Tacitus said, the more numerous the laws, the more corrupt the commonwealth!"

"Our ancestors, Mr. Jefferson? The Saxons? Hah! They were merely crowds of rude, barely humanized beggars. They were ..." (then he does a half hour recital, dumping on the Anglo-Saxons).[5]

"You shall be worthy of being called 'lawyer' some day, sir."

"Yes, of that I am sure. But why does Tom Jefferson admit that to me?"

"Because it is the lawyer's trade to know little, question everything, yield nothing, and talk for hours, like you just did!"[6]

* That's quite a knock on lawyers by someone who chose law for his profession.
* To Thomas Jefferson it's merely the old roast, "yesterday I knock lawyers, today I are one"! He doesn't say lawyering is a bad idea. He just says it's not being done right. For come 1767 young Thomas is one! He's introduced to law practice at the General Court of Virginia by his mentor, George Wythe. And he also still has good political connections. They're good enough to get him elected to the House of Burgesses. It's there he first meets George Washington — seemingly, everyone's hero. Washington's the strong silent type like Thomas' father was!

At twenty-six, Thomas is a man of property — 1900 acres at Shadwell that he inherited from the father he greatly misses. He begins to level the top of his little mountain — 580 feet in elevation. It's the first step toward creating his estate, Monticello. He throws up a one-room, red-brick wing to live in. Now, there's no rush to complete the house. He can work on his plan. He'll be architect, construction foreman, and landscape artist all in one. He'll fabricate his own bricks, forge his own nails, and cut his own lumber. He'll make almost everything right there on the plantation.

Thomas finishes his one room, red brick wing just in time! Shortly afterward, Shadwell burns to the ground! The fire consumes his library of books and papers. He immediately begins replacing them and putting together a new library. Decades later it'll become the Library of Congress with 6700 books .. less just a few! He'll always keep a few favorites on classics, mathematics, and philosophy. What better way will there be to fool the weariness of old age than with the virtues of classics, the truth of mathematics, and the soundness of philosophy?[7]

In 1770 Thomas hears about the Boston Massacre. He also hears about a pretty, twenty-one year old widow named Martha Wayles! Her deceased young husband had been at William and Mary with him. Her father, John Wayles, owns a large plantation. He's also an influential lawyer in Williamsburg. Thomas begins to visit with Martha.

Thomas Jefferson always thinks long-term. But he also likes to get the ball rolling on things right away. And Martha Wayles is practically a replica of the girl of his dreams. She has taller than average height, expressive hazel eyes, shining lush auburn hair, trim and graceful figure, and is described as easy to both look at and talk to. She enjoys riding, dancing, singing, reading, playing the harpsicord, and keeping meticulous accounts. She shares his religious faith, and is sweet tempered, affectionate to his interests, and attentive to what pleases him. She's willingly devoted and socially able to help him further his career. In many ways she's just like him. And, like him, she loves kids. Their courtship from 1770 to 1772 is long enough for Thomas. They get married on New Years Day, 1772!

Thomas is twenty-nine, Martha twenty-three. The next ten years will show he made the right choice. He'll need all of her qualities and support. For the 1770's will be politically stormy years. However, there's a lull in the political storm with England for the moment. Thomas spends April and October in Williamsburg. The rest of that year he's on his hill ... cutting roads, building fences, starting on Monticello, and experimenting with trees, shrubs, fruits, grains, and vegetables. He also reads abundantly. And companionable wife, Martha Wayles Jefferson, gives him their first child. They name her Martha, also. In future years young Martha will be one of the jewels of Thomas Jefferson's life!

Between 1772 and 1782 Martha Wayles Jefferson will give birth to six children. Only two, Martha and Maria, will survive. The other four will not live beyond childhood. Thomas and wife Martha, grief-stricken for long periods over each death, will desperately cling to eachother. They will exchange hundreds of love letters when he has to be away serving in government. Few of those letters will ever be read by anyone else. Only mention of them will be found. That's typical Thomas Jefferson. He'll retain a lifelong desire to keep many things private, or secret, or off-the-record!

Thomas Jefferson's absences from Monticello and his beloved wife Martha begin when problems heat up with England in early 1773. For instance, just a few months after little Martha's birth is when Bostonites pull off the famous Boston Tea Party. That's when the British react by closing the port of Boston. Now Thomas reacts, too! He sponsors a resolution in the House of Burgesses to unite with the other Colonies. His best friend and new delegate, Dabney Carr, moves the resolution in the House. When it passes, Crown Governor Dunmore dissolves the House of Burgesses once again. But it's too late. Virginia is officially united in anger with the other Colonies!

Dabney Carr's speech is magnificent. It's his first speech as a delegate. It will also be his last. A month later in Charlottesville he has an attack of typhoid fever. Suddenly, at just twenty-nine years of age, Dabney is dead. Thomas is true to Dabney's last wish and their pact of ten years ago. He buries his friend beneath that oak tree on the little mountain, Monticello, where they studied as young law students. And he takes his distraught sister, Martha Carr — Dabney's wife — and her six children into his house! From that day forward, he and loving wife Martha Wayles Jefferson will raise and educate those six children as their own!

Meanwhile, the Committees of Correspondence of all colonies agree to hold a big Continental Congress at Philadelphia in June 1774. Virginia's Burgesses hold a convention to select their delegates to that Congress. Thomas is one of them. But he can't make it. Wife Martha is sick. He's sick. And they now have a house full of kids to look after![8]

Nine years ago, everyone had heard about Patrict Henry's Stamp Act speech. Everyone knew what he said. No one knew what the real whiz-kid on the subject, Thomas Jefferson, could have said. Now they'll know! To make up for his absence, Thomas sends the Convention a manuscript of his views on the Colonies' legal arguments against England. It's his <u>Summary View of the Rights of British America</u>. Most of it comes from his legal commonplace diary and includes: The Ancient Constitution; John Locke's political philosophies; the French philosophes; and, English Common Law as written by Sir Edward Coke, William Somner, Lord Kames, and Sir William Blackstone.

* It appears that his <u>Summary View</u> is inspired mostly by British authors.
* And much of those British authors' writings on English Common Law stems from ancient Romans like Tacitus and Caesar. Some of their writings tell us that Tacitus and Caesar saw republican methods actually being used by Germanic "tribes" as far back as the first century AD. For instance, Lord Kames drew on Tacitus' writings to show Germanic people held land freely and privately. William Somner used both Tacitus and Julius Caesar to illustrate there was Germanic republicanism way back then. So Thomas draws from these sources in his <u>Summary View</u>. And why not! The home land of those Germanic "tribes" described by Tacitus and Caesar was Saxony. That's exactly where the Saxons of England migrated from and took their name from. And they brought their republican traditions with them. Even more important, they brought the idea that they did <u>not</u> owe obedience to the Prince of Saxony, even though they came from Saxony! So Thomas says, likewise, the American colonists do <u>not</u> owe obedience to the King of England, even though they came from England! Thomas Jefferson's <u>Summary View</u> turns out to be kind of a declaration of independence … two years before the real **DECLARATION OF INDEPENDENCE**!

Next year in early 1775 another convention of Virginians meets in Richmond. They select delegates to a second Continental Congress to be held in June 1775, again in Philadelphia. That's when Patrick Henry delivers his fiery "give me liberty, or give me death" speech. With Patrick Henry, Thomas again makes it onto the Virginia delegation. And when he makes it to Philadelphia this time, his reputation precedes him. His <u>Summary View of the Rights of British America</u> had been embraced with great enthusiasm by the first Continental Congress the year before. So, in spite of his relative youth, the delegates elect him president of this second Congress!

What also precedes him — and everyone else — is the "shot heard round the world". Fighting had broken out at Lexington and Concord in April 1775. Last year, his <u>Summary View</u> defended American rights. This year he submits a <u>Declaration of the Causes and Necessity for Taking Up Arms</u> which defends the Massachusetts farmers' right to have resorted to violence. In it he gives both the King and Parliament a lesson on English history and philosophy!

* You mean <u>his</u> version of English history and philosophy.

* Yes. But it's the version of many British historians as well. The bone of contention between historians of English history is the Ancient English Constitution. Anti-monarchy types — Whigs — date it from 800's AD Anglo-Saxon England or earlier, as Jefferson does. Pro-monarchy types — Tories — date it <u>after</u> William the Conqueror's invasion from Normandy in 1066 AD.

* What difference does the Ancient Constitution's date make?

* If it dates before William the Conqueror's invasion in 1066, it has precedence over laws made by the present line of British Kings! Thus, Thomas can legally claim back the rights and independence given to Englishmen by the Ancient Constitution, in addition to God-given rights! He tells the Crown that England should leave America's colonists from England alone, just as the Prince of Saxony had left England's colonists from Saxony alone. Otherwise, Americans will do what's necessary for independence.

* It sounds like Jefferson considers the Ancient Constitution and English history just as important to Americans as American history.

* He does! Every American should know something about ancient English history. Here's a short version of it:

A SHORT HISTORY OF ANCIENT ENGLAND

Greek navigator, Pytheas, explored the coast of Britain about 325 BC! Sometime during the next century the Celts from Europe overran aborigines of Britain and Ireland, as they had most of Europe. The inhabitants of Britain became known as Britons. In 55 BC Julius Caesar arrived. Britain was ruled by Romans. Roman law, politics, engineering, and even Christianity migrated there. Four centuries later, the Romans pulled out as the Roman Empire went into decline. It was 410 AD. That opened the way for the Angles and the Saxons who had been raiding from Denmark and Saxony for decades. Part of Britain became known as Angle-land, or England. A Briton called Arthur won a legendary battle that temporarily halted the invaders. However, during the 500's AD, the newcomers collectively known as Anglo-Saxons controlled England. They killed, enslaved, or drove Britons west toward what is now Wales. Few Celtic sounding places survived. Christianity faded. Britain filled up with people of the Germanic tribes from Saxony ... bringing their traditions of rudimentary republicanism with them.

During the 600's AD, Britain became divided into several kingdoms. But Christianity returned. It came from two directions — Latin Rome and Celtic Ireland. Latin and Celtic scholarship came together to produce a flowering of culture unequaled in the Dark Ages of Europe. That's when Bede The Venerable wrote his history of the English people, and Alcuin was commissioned by Charlemagne of Europe to head his palace school.

Warfare gradually turned England into one kingdom. Still, for decades the Danish Vikings raided and plundered eastern England. They sought conquest of all England. King Alfred was all that stood in their way. Alfred built the first English navy. He organized the Anglo-Saxon 'fyrd' — militia — giving militiamen land, and allowing them to take turns alternating between farming and fighting. He, thus, halted the Danish advance. Alfred also turned his attention to civil matters. He combined the existing legal and government systems and issued his own set of "dooms" — laws. And, he promoted scholarship: translated Latin works; secured the services of philosopher John Scotus Erigena; and, compiled a history of the English people, The Anglo-Saxon Chronicle, so as to update Bede The Venerable's older history.

England had the most advanced government in western Europe: a council of wise men — "witenagemot", the forerunner of Parliament — to advise the King; forty "shires" — counties — with law courts and delegates that met twice a year; and, smaller units of about 100 people for taxation, military, and administration — called "hundreds" — that met every four weeks. That was only around 900 AD!

A new round of Danish invasions came in about 1010 AD. Decades of turbulence followed. That led to William the Conqueror of Normandy [the coast of France] invading across the Channel and defeating the Saxon King Harold II at Hastings in 1066 AD. It was the turning point in English history. Norman feudalism replaced Saxon liberty and the land was divided-up amongst the nobility of the Norman Conquerors. England's ancient "dooms" and government — the Ancient Constitution — was replaced with a new legal, social, and political structure.[9]

The virtue is: Responsibility. There will always be predators. Each must take the responsibility to defend themselves.

You can understand why Cromwell in 1649 claimed they were merely restoring the Ancient Constitution and the Saxon rights that William the Conqueror illegally took away in 1066 AD! In 1776, Thomas Jefferson will claim a legal right to do the same! He will cleverly merge English history, Colonial history, Saxon rights, the Ancient Constitution, and John Locke's political philosophy, and come up with a unique, American, moral sense philosophy … tailor made to American independence!

At the second Continental Congress, Thomas backs George Washington over John Hancock for commander-in-chief of a Continental Army. Washington gets the job and heads off to the rag-tag "army" near Boston. Thomas returns to Virginia. His second child, Jane, has died at eighteen months old. And his mother, Jane Randolph Jefferson, is seriously ill. In early 1776 — she dies too.

* Oh my! How much grief can one person take?

* As usual, Thomas keeps his innermost thoughts and feelings to himself. Philosophy and literature help him through. They can help anyone through sad times, as the following poem tries to do:

THE RAINY DAY

from: Henry Wadsworth Longfellow

My life is cold, and dark, and dreary;
It rains, and the wind is never weary;
My thoughts still cling to the moldering Past,
But the hopes of youth fall thick in the blast,
    And the days are dark and dreary.

Be still, sad heart! cease repining;
Behind those clouds the sun is shining;
Thy fate is the common fate of all,
For into each life some rain must fall,
    Some days are dark and dreary.

The virtue is: Courage. Facing life's difficulties can be
the hardest kind of courage:

Thomas is finally able to return to Philadelphia in May of 1776. In June he gets on a committee to prepare a declaration of the Colonies' independence from England. In turn, he gets the job of actually writing it. When he finishes his **DECLARATION OF INDEPENDENCE** the gathering doesn't exactly embrace him with open arms. Quite the opposite. Many delegates are openly hostile toward him! Perhaps it's jealousy. Perhaps they're afraid to sign such a document. Who knows? During debate over it, they accuse him of sounding too much like John Locke. They rip him on originality. That stuns him! Did they absurdly expect him to construct a whole new philosophy in a few days? He thought he did something good. Now suddenly, great pressure and stinging criticism are brought to bear on him. Suddenly he's alone. Even his ally and father-figure, George Washington, is no longer there in Philadelphia to help him. Thomas asks himself, why do they attack me? Who needs this?

Thomas is now in a pressure cooker. He's forced to do what he never dreamed he would have to do amongst supposed colleagues — <u>defend</u> himself! Here's what he says:

IN DEFENSE OF THE DECLARATION OF INDEPENDENCE

from: Thomas Jefferson

"I know only that I turned to neither book nor pamphlet while writing it. I did not consider it as any part of my charge to invent <u>new</u> ideas altogether and to offer no senti-ment which had been expressed before.

The essential thing was not to find out new principles, or new arguments, never before thought of, not merely to say things which had never been said before; but to place before mankind the common sense of the subject, in terms so plain and firm as to command their assent. Neither aiming at original principles or sentiments, nor copied from any particular and previous writing, it was intended as an expression of the American mind. All its authority rests on the harmonizing sentiments of the day, whether expressed in conversation, in letters, and in printed essays in the elementary books of public right — from Aristotle, Cicero, Locke, and Sidney".

The virtue is: Truth. Tell the facts clearly and honestly.

Those are Thomas Jefferson's words. No false pride, bravado, or "gloriola". He says he wrote what he had thought about for years. He says he simply com-bined the best ideas of the all-time masters and engineered them to legally and philosophically fit America. He says he hopes this clears up the situation. And it does! His "defense" ends the criticism. Finally after three days, on the evening of July 4, 1776, Thomas Jeferson's **DECLARATION OF INDEPENDENCE** is signed!
* They actually knitpicked it for three days? That's strange. You would think everyone was ready to go, as far as a declaration was concerned. They had already accepted such a declaration when they accepted Thomas' <u>Summary View of the Rights of British America</u> and his <u>Declaration of the Causes of Taking Up</u>

Arms! He just refined the wording of those two documents and combined them into one document, right?

* Yes. The knitpicking <u>was</u> strange. And it might have gone on even longer had it not been for the flies!

* Flies?

* Yes. Hot weather, open windows, nearby horse stables, and nasty-biting horse-flies came together that day as though heaven was looking down upon that gathering. The flies drove everyone nuts! They hastened the vote. Even in ripe old age, Thomas Jefferson will often tell the story about the "flies" with great merriment ... and with great relief!

Thomas is also under other kinds of pressure again. He has problems back home. Wife Martha is ailing. His business affairs are also ailing. And he has the pressing duty to write the State Constitution for Virginia. He resigns from Congress and returns home. But his stint in Philadelphia has been an education. The unexpected ordeal of defending his **DECLARATION OF INDEPEN-DENCE** taught him a lesson. We know he's already privately cautious. From now on he'll be <u>publicly</u> cautious and have all his ducks lined up — have support — before doing anything that may be the least bit controversial!

* Well, maybe it was a lot of pressure. But his **DECLARATION OF INDE-PENDENCE** assures he'll be famous for all time.

* Only because the Revolution will be successful. Only because George Washington will miraculously keep the Army from falling apart. Otherwise, the **DECLARATION** could have merely ended up in the dustbin of history. So, at this point in time, nobody knows what will happen. On his sacred honor Thomas Jefferson pledged his life and fortune. He could easily lose them both! He spends the next four years during the Revolution trying to hold on to them![10]

As George Washington guides The Revolutionary War, Thomas works on guiding and reforming his State. He begins to construct a new republic for Virginia. His Virginia Republic draws on complex philosophical ideas from Aristotle, Montesquieu, Harrington, Locke, and the Scottish "moral sense" philosophers. His goal is simple, however. He wants a virtuous Republic. Period! He knows he'll have to be progressive and visionary ... and thick-skinned. He is. And it gets him into hot water. Why? Because, many of his Bills are severe blows to the privileged class! They're Bills such as: disestablishing the Anglican Church as the only religion; revising the land and property inheritance laws; establishing religious freedom; promoting education for everyone with his <u>More General Diffusion of Knowledge</u>; making the criminal code more humanitarian; and, proposing a real democratic Constitution for Virginia. His "reformation" earns him bitter hatred from the privileged class. His lifelong breach with the privileged class is already opening up here in 1779!

* But he does succeed in reforming Virginia?

* He does indeed! And for ordinary Virginians it's as easy as throwing off an old and putting on a new suit of clothes. It's a chaste — uncorrupt and virtuous — reformation! And the privileged class will now have something else to groan about. Their critic, Thomas Jefferson, is elected governor of Virginia in 1779! At thirty-six years old he's top dog of the largest and foremost "Nation-State" in

North America. Did you know, at this time, Virginia is what will someday be Ohio, Illinois, Indiana, Kentucky, West Virginia, and Virginia all put together?

It's also at this time that King George's masterplan for conquering the South is about to go into full swing. For two years Governor Jefferson gives General Washington unwavering support. When the Continental armies are starving ... he sends food. When they're deserting ... he recruits men. When bankrupt ... he sends money. He tirelessly helps the Commander-in-Chief to keep the American Army together. Governor Jefferson is the one who sends supplies to Generals Greene, Morgan, Wayne, Lafayette, and Steuben — Washington's commanders in the South — when British forces slash and burn their way northward into Virginia!

When the British hit town — outside Richmond — Thomas ends up alone. His entire government flees. But Richmond is stacked with vital war materials. They must not fall into British hands. They must be smuggled out of Richmond. With no one else left, Thomas mounts his horse and personally takes command of that mission!

He spends forty-eight straight hours in the saddle of his horse, evacuating the crucial war materials. The mission is progressing nicely. Then, suddenly, his horse keels over and dies under him from exhaustion! Now he needs a horse to save the mission ... and Virginia! His predicament is what Shakespeare told us King Richard III faced at the battle of Bosworth:

MY KINGDOM FOR A HORSE

from: Shakespeare's <u>King Richard III</u>

It was before the Battle of Bosworth Field in 1485.
King Richard's blacksmith had one more shoe to put on
Richard's horse when he ran out of horseshoe nails. He
made due with something else. He hoped it would hold!
But he wasn't certain!
Later that day, that very shoe flew off during the thick
of battle. King Richard's horse stumbled and fell.
Richard was thrown to the ground. For a brief moment he
was stunned. During that moment his horse bolted off.
Richard saw Henry the Tudor's soldiers closing in on him.
He waved his sword and shouted these now immortalized
words, "A horse! A horse! My kingdom for a horse!"
But there would be no horse for him. His army had crum-
bled. His men had fled. All around him were only
Henry's men, eager to be the ones to capture a King! And
it all happened for want of a simple horseshoe nail.
Because:
    For want of a nail, a shoe was lost,
    For want of a shoe, a horse was lost,

For want of a horse, a battle was lost,
For want of a battle, a kingdom was lost,
And all for the want of a nail.

The virtue is: Duty. Neglecting the smallest duty can lead
to dire results.

No way is Thomas Jefferson about to risk a result such as:

For want of a horse, a mission is lost,
For want of a mission, Virginia is lost,
For want of Virginia, America is lost,
And all for the want of a horse.

Far from neglecting small duties, Thomas always goes the extra mile. And this time he does so — literally! He slings the bridle and saddle on his back. He humps them the extra mile, or so, to the next farmhouse in order to get another horse.
* He probably tells the farmer: "A horse. A horse. Your country for a horse!" Right?
* More than likely. But, unlike King Richard III, Thomas Jefferson does get a horse! He succeeds in his mission! He helps to save Virginia! That helps to save America! He's there when General Washington needs him!

Thomas' wife, Martha Wayles Jefferson also needs him! Her state of health is becoming a shambles! So she makes him promise he will not run for Office after this term as Governor — that he will not leave her again. He keeps his promise. He never leaves her again!

In the midst of it all, his infant son — his only son — dies! It's a shocking blow! And little does he know life at home will deal him another blow. He has a near-fatal horseback riding accident! It confines him to the house for what seems to be forever. Not a time-waster, Thomas begins to write. The result will turn out to be his Notes on Virginia!
* I never heard of it.
* It's about life in America in 1781, as seen through the eyes of a Virginian. Little does Thomas know it will later become a big thing. But that's later. Right now in 1781 the big thing is the battle at Yorktown, Virginia. General Washington has just forced British General Cornwallis to surrender! More than half the British Army has been disarmed! The rest — in New York — therefore can't carry on. They honor Cornwallis' surrender! The War is over! [11]

All Virginia rejoices! Life is returning to normal. But not for Thomas Jefferson. For some reason wife Martha continues to ail. Her health goes from bad to worse. The suspense over her condition during the coming months has him worried sick. But the suspense ends sooner than expected. In September 1782 at just thirty-three years old ... she dies.

Martha Wayles Jefferson and Thomas Jefferson had ten idyllic years of unchequered happiness together. To the end, she was his trim, sweet, graceful, personable, true love and best friend. During their final days together they had desperately clung to eachother — as if to hold back the darkness. The following love poem written by Martha Wayles Jefferson during her final days will later be discovered. It alludes to <u>Tristram Shandy</u> which, along with the ancient Gaelic poems of Ossian, they likely read together by firelight one cold night while snowbound during their honeymoon, ten years ago. Begun by Martha in her own handwriting, it ends in his handwriting — when she had become too weak to even hold a quill pen to write:

PRELUDE TO FAREWELL

From: Martha Wayles Jefferson
To: Thomas Jefferson

Time wastes too fast: ... every letter
I trace tells me with what rapidity
life follows my pen. The days and hours
of it are flying over our heads like
clouds of a windy day ... never to return.
More of everything presses on ... and every
time I kiss your hand to bid farewell,
every absence which follows it, are
preludes to that eternal separation
which we are shortly to make!

The virtue is: Dedication. Love is a form of dedication.

She was the cherished companion of Thomas Jefferson's life. Now she's gone.

Thomas buries Martha Wayles Jefferson under the oak tree at Monticello with other loved ones. On her gravestone he has two lines from Homer's Iliad about the next life [called Hades] inscribed in Greek letters that say:

"Though someday dead in the grave and in Hades, Even there I
shall remember my sweet friend."

At the funeral, Thomas Jefferson is crushed. He's shaken. He's drowning in grief. He's so weakened and unsteady he has to be helped into his study, completely withdrawn from reality. He never leaves that room for three weeks. He just paces back and forth, thinking day and night, sleeping only when collapsing from exhaustion.

Finally, he regains enough strength to at least leave the house. He rides out on horseback around their little mountain. Then he takes to riding out almost daily, rambling along the trails he and Martha Wayles Jefferson had always loved.

There are melancholy remembrances. There are outbursts of tears and grief. He's one who takes the marriage vows seriously. He truly believes that God joins man and woman into one. Now he's half. How does half a person go on? He will have to learn.

For most of three months Thomas is beside himself. Ten year old daughter, Martha, is also beside him. She's his faithful little companion. She witnesses, and records, his grief. She keeps him going. She helps him learn how to go on. With her love and help, he slowly comes out of his stupor and deep depression.[12]

He now decides to take his seat at Congress in Annapolis. That's the time he assures everyone that General Washington will not take over America and become a dictator — that Washington is Cincinnatus, not Caesar. That's when <u>General</u> George Washington, Commander-in-Chief, resigns and becomes <u>citizen</u> George Washington, farmer. Remember, Harry?
* Yes. And now I realize why Jefferson knew Washington would resign. He simply knows Washington too well to think otherwise.
* And by now, perhaps you're getting to know Thomas Jefferson too well to be surprised that he once again buries himself in work in order to forget. Work and philosophy have always been his therapies for sorrow. So he accepts being the head of almost every committee in Congress. He proceeds to convert the currency to dollars, apportion the Continental debt, make the Old Northwest a part of the Confederation, and so on. And make no mistake, it's a great accomplishment to do those things. For Congress is a real quarrelsome bunch during these times. Days on end are wasted on petty bickering over unimportant questions. But he's basically a quiet person and a good listener. So he always welcomes other people's views. However, he'll later comment with great sadness about the many occasions of petty bickering, raucous debate, and useless discussion in Congress over trivial matters. And even <u>he</u> had been drawn into a useless discussion on one occasion. It went like this:

"Mr. Jefferson. How can you sit here in Congress and allow such
imperfect reasoning to pass your ears unchallenged — unsilenced?"
"My good man, to challenge is easy, to silence would be
impossible".
"But silence belongs to you, Sir. You sit there and say nothing."
"If delegates talk too much, can it be otherwise in a Congress to
which the people send 150 lawyers as delegates? That
150 lawyers should get any business done ought not to be
expected."
"That smacks of an excuse, Sir, to avoid the heat of argument".
(looking down) "I once knew a fellow law student. He knew
little. Said much. Antagonized everyone. Yielded on nothing.
And talked by the hour. I was overjoyed with the prospect of
never seeing him again. But my mentor, Professor Wythe,
warned me that this fellow would someday return. Professor
Wythe was right! (now looking up) …….. You're back!"[13]

316

In May 1784, Congress appoints Thomas Jefferson foreign minister with full powers. He joins John Adams and Benjamin Franklin in Paris. They spend two years drafting treaties with twenty foreign nations. Then Thomas' position as minister is extended for three additional years. When Franklin returns to America, Thomas takes on his job. He also takes on Franklin's popularity. The French get to love this "Virginia Gentleman". They admire his intellectual and philosophical bent.

Diplomatic duties keep him busy. But he never forgets who he is and where he comes from. He arranges to have a statue of his hero and father-figure, General Washington, sculpted and put on a pedestal. He makes time to personally monitor its progress, step by step. When completed, he sends it home to Richmond. It's an omen of how he thinks American Army Officers must be — like American Cincinnatus' of honor and character!

Thomas Jefferson lives and works in France five years! But it's not all work. He travels, observes, and learns. To him learning is rest and relaxation. He sees England — and learns. He absorbs France, Italy, Holland, and Germany — and learns. Everywhere he goes he's a notetaking, enquiring tourist. He jots down specifications as if designing a machine shop. He goes out of his way to see a new machine rather than see an old painting. He sees old paintings too. But he even studies those with a kind of mathematical eye. Everywhere, he calculates how the things he observes and likes can benefit America. There's much he observes and likes.

There's also much he observes and hates! He observes squalor and corruption in cities. Great masses of people are poor. Factory workers are exploited. Living conditions are miserable. Corrupt and powerful big-businessmen are controlling supposedly free men. He's also shocked at the moral depravity! Adulterous intrigues are not at all uncommon. Marital love and domestic happiness are less than sacrosanct. Lust — for both sex and luxury — is becoming destructive to health.

Thomas is concerned that America might catch these social ills! He writes to George Washington about them. In his letters to Washington you can see he clearly blames industrialization that requires people to live close together in cities. He says that an agrarian — agricultural — citizenry is America's best hedge against this European style of moral and economic lust, corruption, and depravity. On the other hand, he recognizes that manufacturing generates wealth and power for a nation. So he admits America will eventually also have to jump on the manufacturing bandwagon. But he says America must take care to do it limitedly and reluctantly.

* Why limitedly? Why limit wealth and power?
* Because you don't bite at the bait until you see there's no hook beneath it. And from his firsthand knowledge of Europe, Thomas sees a big hook! Europe is class-ridden. As Voltaire said, people are either hammers or anvils — either privileged or poverty-stricken. There's mischief at the top and misery at the bottom. The number of middle class people may be increasing, but the number of poverty-stricken laborers are increasing even faster. So the hook that Thomas foresees with manufacturing is the rise of a whole new underclass of poor people crowded together in cities. He thinks it can wreck American dreams of freedom, liberty, and democracy!

Despite Europe's social ills, Thomas soaks-up Paris' social life. He has a following of female admirers. To them, he's different. He's not upity-up, despite the fact he's world-renowned. They're flattered that he would befriend them, both socially and intellectually. And he has a youthful crush on one admirer in particular. Her name is Maria Cosway. She's twenty-seven, English, coquettish, and lovely-looking. This forty-three year old widower is impressed with her. He even breaks his wrist childishly showing-off, jumping over a fence. He loses his heart to her ... and almost his head!

The lovely Maria Cosway can never be his! She turns out to be married! But, luckily, Mr. Cosway is a practical man. He's an artist who's immersed in his paintings. So he's actually happy to have this trusted American to befriend his neglected wife in order to keep the "wolves" of Paris out of her boudoir. And he knows that Thomas Jefferson will befriend her discreetly and honorably!

So Thomas is socially active once again. But, he's still lonely inside. His letters tell us he misses home, and children, and deceased wife Martha. And it gets worse. His sister-in-law back in Virginia gets word to him that his youngest child, Lucy, has just died. Now Thomas has only two children left — young Martha, and younger Maria. He allows all his feelings to hang out in his letters to them. Only to them would this shy and quiet man do so. You can read hundreds of his letters. In them, you can see he's warm and affectionate. But you can see he's also fatherly. He pours out much of his philosophy on life in his fatherly advice to them. Here's some of what flows from those letters to his "two jewels", as he calls them:

SOME THOMAS JEFFERSON PHILOSOPHY ON LIFE

from: Thomas Jefferson's private letters to his children

"Of all the cancers of human happiness, none corrodes

with so silent yet so destructive a tooth as laziness."

"Idleness begets boredom, boredom begets depression, and depression begets a diseased body".

"If at any moment you catch yourself in idleness, start from it — draw back from it — as if from the edge of a cliff."

"My expectations from you are high. Resolve and hard work are all you need to attain them".

"Nothing in this world can make me so happy or so miserable as you — my children."

"To your sister and yourself I look to give the evening of my life, serene and contented. Its morning has been clouded by loss after loss, till I have nothing left but you."

"Youth is a time when great exertions are necessary but you have little time left to make them."

"Be industrious. Think nothing unsurmountable by resolve and hard work, and you will be all we wish you to be."

"It is part of the American character to consider nothing hopeless. Surmount every difficulty by resolve and inventiveness."

"Above all things be Good — because without that, we can neither be valued by others, nor set any value on ourselves."

"Always be truthful; no vice is so mean and useless as the want of truth."

"Anger only serves to torment ourselves, turn others away, and turn off their esteem."

"When you teach good traits you will be more fixed in them yourself."

"The true secret — grand recipe — for happiness is to be always engaged in activity. The idle are the only unhappy ones."

"Try to let everybody's faults be forgotten, as you would wish yours to be."

"The Almighty has never made known when he created life and when he will put an end to it. You can only prepare for that event by never saying or doing a bad thing. Follow your conscience, that faithful internal monitor which our Maker has given all of us."

The virtue is: Conscientiousness. It is the first part of achievement.

Meanwhile, in 1787 Paris, there are rumblings of a bloody revolution that will tear France apart come 1789. In 1787 Philadelphia, there are rumblings of a written Constitution that will put The United States of America together come 1789. The author of America's **DECLARATION OF INDEPENDENCE** surely should be with the fifty-five men writing a Constitution. But, he's in Paris. In future, many will say the Constitution shows Thomas Jefferson was absent.

Though absent, Thomas Jefferson receives a draft copy of the Constitution from his protege', James Madison. His reaction? It's like his thoughts on Europe. There's a lot he likes. There's a lot he dislikes. There are things he feels must be in it that are not, like: a bill of rights; limits on federal power; direct democratic participation; restrictions on monopolies; and, term limits for everyone. He thinks the Constitution is too vague. It lacks detail and definition. As a lawyer he knows that the less Constitutional law left for lawyers to interpret, the better it will be!

Some suggestions that Thomas sends back to Madison do pay off! For instance, Madison uses his suggestions for a Bill of Rights! But the Constitution of the United States will still end up being too general. Little do they know, that will create problems — like a resurgence of monarchism, like "factions" called political parties, and like controversy, especially between Thomas Jefferson and Alexander Hamilton. However, the solutions to these problems will fortunately lead to some unique American inventions and institutions. One of them will be the United States Military Academy — West Point!

It's now 1789. Back home the Constitution goes into effect on March 4th. That gets The United States of America going. In Paris the mobs storm the Bastille prison on July 14th. That gets the French Revolution going. Thomas feels his work in Europe is finished. He's ready to leave. He will leave with mixed feelings. He likes England, especially the English garden. He says, "it's the article in which England surpasses all the earth". But England's rulers dislike Americans — even more than they did during the War. When in England, Thomas was treated shabbily by the King and his government. Not so in France, however. France loves Americans. In spite of some moral disappointments, Thomas pays tribute to France, the place that has been his home for the past five years. Of course he prefers family, friends, and the land of his birth and youth. America is number one. But France will always be number two!

In the autumn of 1789 Thomas Jefferson sails for Virginia. So ends an important chapter in his life ... and in his evolving philosophy. He never returns to France again![15]

Thomas is welcomed home by hundreds of friends and family and well-wishers. What a tearfully happy occasion it is! He's also greeted with a letter awaiting his arrival. It's from President Washington. The President has appointed him Secretary of State! At this point, all Thomas wants is peace and quiet and home and family and farming ...... and time to finish building his beloved Monticello. But it's not to be. For, the letter of appointment is also a personal plea from Washington. It's gently persuasive. It's sincerely friendly. It's flattering ... and by no less than the person he admires the most, and had in Paris virtually "put on a pedestal".

* How can Thomas Jefferson not answer the call, then? How can he turn down, as you say, his father-figure?

* He can't! So, he's now off to the seat of government in New York. He joins Hamilton and others in Washington's Cabinet. The good news for everyone is — he's unique. He's the only one in the Cabinet who has seen life on both sides of the Atlantic. His experiences in Europe have shown him what <u>not</u> to do and what people would <u>not</u> want for America. It's like seeing a land-mine ahead and being able to avoid it before it explodes under you. The bad news is — he's actually <u>too</u> unique. No others have experienced what he has. So how can they fully understand him? They can't. It will bring him future problems. His political philosophy coupled with his real-life experiences will open up a wide gulf between him and Hamilton Federalists on how America should be run!

In New York, Thomas is treated like the conquering hero come home. He's the toast of the town. Like in Paris, he's in hot demand. He's the guest of honor at umpteen dinner parties during the first few months. But he's also shocked! It almost feels like he's in England! He's awe-struck by anti-democratic and pro-monarchist sentiments! He realizes that New York is still a hot bed of monarchism!

Politics is the hot topic at dinner parties. He's usually the only one who supports republicanism and grass-roots democracy. He feels like a stranger in his own Country! Bits of dinner-party banter would most likely sound like this:

"How do you like the Constitution, Mr. Jefferson?"

"It's a good start."

"That's what we say. Good start, but doesn't go far enough. We
need to come closer to Britain's monarchy model. After all, they
have centuries of experience with these things".

°°Hmm …… not what I meant.°° "I mean we need more direct
democratic participation. I mean those who fought the War
need to get more of what they fought for."

"Oh! Right! No harm throwing a few crumbs of freedom to the
rabble … so long as we don't go too far. Besides, didn't you
once say the tree of liberty is watered with the blood of patriots,
Mr. Secretary?"

"Yes I did. But make sure the patriots get to eat the fruit of
the tree afterwards! Those patriots, my dear Madam, are
what you refer to as 'rabble'! °°Huh! Rabble! Easy for you
Tories to say! Your kind didn't spill any of your own blood.
Worse yet, you Tory wives and your daughters were here
flirting with the dashing British officers, the very same ones
that were killing Americans!°° You say, go too far? How far
is too far, if we don't wish to forsake those who gave their
lives for this?"

"How far? We can give them their liberties, as we have. Why
not! But not land or wealth … or, God forbid, <u>real</u> democratic
power. The rabble could not handle real democratic power!"

321

"Hmm. On a lighter note, madam. I am sincerely flattered by this wonderful hospitality toward me in New York."

"We're quite happy to do it, Mr. Secretary. We look for excuses these days to roll out the red carpet. We used to wine and dine the nobility, aristocrats, and British Officers on a regular basis, you know. Now that's all gone."

"Indeed." ∞And I'm sure your kind would like to bring it all back, too!∞ 16

Thomas is up against Constitutional monarchists. And Alexander Hamilton — Secretary of the Treasury — is their darling!

The Constitution is like a political football. Thomas pushes it toward the more democratic goal, Hamilton toward the more monarchist goal.

* I don't understand. Explain that for me, will you?

* It's very simple. Thomas Jefferson is for a real democratic Republic with people voting on laws directly at the grass-roots level. Alexander Hamilton is for a strong centralized Republic with a king or lifetime president and elite representatives from the upper-class. The Constitution has something in between. Jefferson and Hamilton both see the Constitution of 1787 as a good start. But both have designs on "improving" it their own way. And each knows the other wants to move the political football in the opposite direction!

* I see. And the Army? And a military academy? How do they fit into this picture?

* Armies and military academies have always been "tools". Kings, emperors, and dictators have used them merely to gain wealth and power. That's why Thomas Jefferson is leery of the Army. That's why Alexander Hamilton loves it! The Army is actually a big part of Hamilton's game plan. To him the Army is not just for defense. It's also for what's called political persuasion — sort of non-violent power. He's a Constitutional monarchist. So he would love to re-tool the Constitution. The military, and a military academy, are the main tools in his toolbox. That scares Thomas Jefferson! The battle lines are drawn!

* Battle lines? My history lessons always said that Washington, Jefferson, and Hamilton were buddy-buddy nation builders.

* Washington has been Hamilton's mentor and father-figure — the father Hamilton never had. But Washington has also been Thomas' father-figure — the father he lost at fourteen years old. So Hamilton and Thomas are kind of like two brothers who live with eachother every day but don't get along real well!

* They don't get along? They're both in Washington's Cabinet. That must be a problem.

* It is. They're similar in that they both seek Washington's "blessing". But that's where the similarity ends. Otherwise, they mix like oil and water. They're on opposite sides of the fence on most things. Thomas Jefferson is quiet and steady — long term in his thinking. Alexander Hamilton is outspoken and explosive — unpredictable in his thinking. Thomas at 6'-2" is a tower of Virginia gentlemanly caution. Hamilton at 5'-7" is a social-climbing, aggressive-minded bantam. Thomas trusts simple country virtues. Hamilton coddles big-city financial moguls. Thomas is a brilliant intellectual. Hamilton is a brilliant wheeler-dealer. Thomas is interested in education and democracy. Hamilton is interested in money and power. Hamilton quickly inflates his department to seventy bureaucrats. Thomas makes due with five. Thomas says his thinking has been most influenced by Locke, Newton, and Bacon. Hamilton says his has been most influenced by warrior-come-dictator Julius Caesar. Thomas, like Rousseau, believes ordinary people can govern themselves. Hamilton, like Hobbes, scoffs at such a notion. He believes people can't govern hemselves, and, America is best governed by the elite of society, like in England.

For the next four years they rub along together. And they clash. And they rub along. And they clash. It's endless. But it's not due to lack of mutual respect. Thomas calls Hamilton a collossus at finances. Hamilton calls Thomas an intellectual genius. So they clash. But it's strictly over each of their strong political convictions!

* Still, there must be a lot of friction in Washington's Cabinet.

* Well Harry, you're not transported from Colonies to Country on a feather bed. But despite the friction, Thomas and Alexander Hamilton both get their jobs done. As we know, Thomas deals effectively with Creek Indians, Barbary Coast pirates, Algerians holding Americans hostage, British siezing American ships, British kidnapping American sailors, Spain and Britain stirring-up the Indians, and French Ambassador Genet sabotaging American neutrality. Hamilton works out America's financial problems. His policies lead to prosperity.

Business grows stronger. So do businessmen. Hamilton is their fair-haired boy. Backed by big-business — and their Congressmen — Hamilton's star is on the rise. He becomes more and more cocky inside of Washington's government. Thomas, in turn, becomes more and more concerned that big-business will control the government. Money and profits for the few become more important than morals, ethics, democracy, and opportunity for the many. Finally, Thomas openly voices his concerns in public. That outrages Hamilton's backers.

Controversey now rages! The Hamilton faction uses the press to attack Thomas Jefferson. Their mouthpiece is the newspaper, Gazette of the United States. It's bitter. It stoops to slander and innuendo and personal attack. As is his nature, Thomas refuses to stoop to the Gazette's level of gutter politics. Luckily, another newspaper named the National Gazette comes to his rescue. It shows how he and other republicans are not the troublemakers Hamiltonians make them out to be. They're merely opposed to kingly government! Thomas will later tell President Washington that the National Gazette deserves credit for helping save the nation from a British-style constitutional monarchy!

All the political hot air causes the Hamilton Federalist's balloon to rise higher than ever. It also causes the rise of a new political Party called the Democratic-Republican Party that pushes for true democracy. Thomas Jefferson is the philosophical leader. But James Madison will have to be the practical leader. For Thomas' time in politics is up. He had promised Washington four years of service. He gave it. He withstood years of endless attacks by Hamilton's cronies — the wealthy aristocrats and big businessmen closely connected with England. Now he just wants to go home to family, friends, and farm. He looks forward to Monticello, Montaigne, and mathematics — peace and tranquility, books and philosophy, and science and agriculture. He needs a rest from politics, the powerful, and the newspapers!

* I can understand him taking a rest from politics. But from newspapers? I can't imagine Jefferson not knowing what's going on in America.

* Ignorance is the safest pillow upon which a man can rest his head, Harry. And that's all Thomas Jefferson wants to do now — rest his head, read the local news, and avoid the big political newspapers. So he asks Washington to understand why he'll depart on schedule. The President does understand. Little does everyone know, Alexander Hamilton understands too! He's also burned out! He'll soon afterward also tell Washington he's leaving!

It's 1794. Wayne's "Legion" crushes the Indians. Washington snuffs out the Whiskey Rebellion. Thomas Jefferson bids the President a fond farewell. And, finally back home, Thomas breathes new life into Monticello.[17] He calculates a six year crop rotation plan. Six year plan! That's typical Thomas Jefferson, Harry! He believes you should always think long term when doing something! You may not get it all done today. Or next month. Or next year. But get started. Take the first step. Get it off the ground. He knows that some things take patience, perseverance, and hard work. Few will say that better than poet, Longfellow, does in this excerpt:

THE LADDER OF ST. AUGUSTINE

from: Henry Wadsworth Longfellow

We have not wings, we cannot soar;
    But we have feet to scale and climb
By slow degrees, by more and more,
    The cloudy summits of our time.

The mighty pyramids of stone
    Like wedges in the desert airs,
When nearer seen, and better known,
    Are but gigantic flights of stairs.

The heights by great men reached and kept
    Were not attained by sudden flight,
But they, while their companions slept,
    Were toiling upward in the night.

The virtue is: Patience. Learn to get started, then continue patiently.

Thomas lives the farmer's life for three years. He also works on his house. He forms and fires every brick, forges and hardens every nail, and teaches his African farmhands everything from carpentry, bricklaying, blacksmithing, and cabinet-making, to cloth-spinning and clothes-making. And he does find time to write a few letters.

During this time in his life, he doesn't keep in real close touch with friends. But, his few letters are effective. His political ideas leak out from them and touch some of the current hot issues of the day. He talks about monarchical Hamiltonian Federalists being on the rise. He says aristocratic British-style government is their goal. The average American doesn't want that again. But the Hamiltonian Federalist faction doesn't care what average Americans want. They're geared to what rich Americans want. And they're the ones who are capturing most levers of power. So Thomas Jefferson may be out of sight. But he's not out of mind. He's on the mind of his Democratic-Republican friends. They want to draft him for President in 1796 ... in his absence ... like it or not! He doesn't like it!

This all happens when George Washington decides to retire. Vice President John Adams becomes the Federalist's nominee. He wants the job badly. He campaigns hard. On the other hand, Thomas Jefferson hardly campaigns. He has little interest in campaigning. So Adams squeeks in. He gets just three more electoral votes than Thomas Jefferson. That makes John Adams the President. And in these times, it makes Thomas Jefferson the Vice-President!

An interesting thing happens to Thomas Jefferson on the way to the inauguration. He's met by a large delegation of military people — led by Officers and ex-

Officers. They stick a huge banner in front of him.
* Probably blasting him for being against a regular standing Army. Right?
* No. Quite the contrary! It says: JEFFERSON THE FRIEND OF THE PEO-PLE! He's thrilled that military types realize that. For he is the friend of the people. As Steuben said, the American Army is the people — America's sons and brothers and husbands. You'll see later, Harry, that Thomas Jefferson will never forget this touching tribute to him!

You'll see right now that Hamiltonian Federalists will never forget Thomas' past ties with the people of France, either. Do you remember that tidal-wave of philosophical change I told you about, Harry? It struck down onto American shores in the 1760's and touched-off the American Revolution. Well, it touched-off another revolution too — the French Revolution. But now that Revolution has turned into a full-scale European War! And its shock-waves are reaching America! Neither France nor England is respecting America's neutrality. They're both ravaging American ships and trade. But France is doing it better. So France looks like the bad guy. And Hamiltonians blame Thomas Jefferson!
* How can they blame him?
* Easy. Many of the people he knew and advised in France became revolutionaries. And now he's against war with France. So the Hamilton Federalists put two and two together and say he must be involved. They tell him to prove otherwise. As usual, Thomas says not a word in self-defense. He says the accusation is too ridiculous to be worthy of the time and effort it takes to reply. He'll leave it to the American public to judge such slander.

Passions rise. The political heat is turned up. That's when "Quasi-War" with France leads to the "New Army". Remember? Alexander Hamilton is its commander. Then comes the political intrigue and military manipulation and international conspiracy. It strikes fear into the hearts of people. It threatens the ideals Americans fought and died for. And it deeply alarms Thomas Jefferson!

Thomas had always viewed the second Office, Vice President, as easy and honorable. And he had always thought the first Office, President, to be a hard and miserable splendor. But the easy way doesn't always work when something needs to be fixed. You have to do whatever it takes, no matter how hard and miserable, if there's a job to be done. So should he make a run for President? Is there a job that can be done? Is it his responsibility if there is one to be done? The following passages give the answer to these questions:

THE BRIDGE BUILDER

from: Will Allen Dromgoole

An old man, going a lone highway,
Came, in the evening, cold and gray,
To a chasm — vast, and deep, and wide,
Through which was flowing a sullen tide.

326

The old man crossed in the twilight dim,
The sullen stream had no fears for him,
But he turned when safe on the other side,
And was building a bridge to span the tide.

"Old man", said a fellow pilgrim near,
"You waste scarce strength with building here,
  Your journey must now end one day,
  You never again will pass this way,
  Having crossed the chasm, deep and wide,
  Why build you a bridge to the other side?"

The builder lifted his old gray head,
"In the path over which I've come," he said,
"There follows behind a youth one day,
  Whose feet must also pass this way,
  He, too, must cross in the twilight dim,
  This bridge I'm building will be for him!"

The virtue is: Duty. Each generation has a duty to prepare the next generation.

Thomas now sees there is a job to be done. The job goes back to the basic question George Washington long ago had to deal with. How do you "preserve, protect, and defend" the Constitution? Washington's colossal reputation allowed him to do it. But that died when he died. Now, once and for all, how do you "preserve, protect, and defend" the Constitution permanently ... no matter who is the President? The job of finding a way will not be easy. But it will be next to impossible for Thomas if he isn't the President. So at fifty-five, he makes the big decision. Family, friends, and farming — the peace and tranquility of Monticello — will have to wait once again. The government is fractured. It needs mending ... permanently. The first object of his heart at this time will have to be America. Formerly dead set against running, he changes his mind. He makes it known he will be the Democratic-Republican candidate for President in the 1800 election![18]

During 1799 and early 1800, Thomas spends a lot of time telling the American people about his political philosophy and his "vision for America".

* I would think they know what he stands for by now.
* Not really. Hamilton Federalists have muddied and slandered him ... they've already dumped the pigs into the trough and muddied the water, so to speak. He has to clear it up. And he'll never clear it up unless he separates the pigs from the trough — separates the slander from the truth — and makes his political philosophy and vision for America clear to the people once and for all. That will be the guts of his Presidential Campaign. And for you, Harry, that will be the guts of you're being able to understand why he later establishes the United States Military Academy ... West Point!

* I see. Run it by me then!
* I'll start by asking you what the difference is between a Hamilton Federalist and a Democratic-Republican — between a Hamiltonian and a Jeffersonian.
* Is that a trick question?
* No trick question. In fact, that difference is the cause of most problems around the turn of the century! And it has to do with philosophy. A Hamiltonian and a Jeffersonian would argue their differences this way:

> "The reason we Hamiltonians fought the Revolution was merely to kick the British out and step into their shoes — take their place running everything! Didn't you Democratic Republicans know that?"
>
> "No. Folks who did the <u>real</u> fighting and bleeding and dying did it for a complete change, with them sharing things and <u>them</u> running things."
>
> "You don't understand. Think of America as a shop. It still operates the same way. It sells the same things. It's the same shop, merely under American management!"
>
> "Yes, we Jeffersonians agree it's a shop under American management. But it <u>doesn't</u> sell the same things. It's a <u>different</u> shop. We've shut the old shop down — put it out of business. Our new one is supposed to sell something better than the old one, and for <u>all</u> the people. It's called — Democracy!"[19]

* So let me get this straight. The Hamilton Federalists want to modify the Constitution to have a setup similar to what the British have ... except without the British. But the Democratic-Republicans want to modify the Constitution in the

opposite direction. They want to have a real democratic setup ... with the <u>people</u> running things. But how would the people run things?

* Thomas pictures the Revolutionary War and independence and the Constitution as stepping-stones to the ultimate dream. That ultimate dream is nothing less for America than a virtuous democracy in a republic. He says <u>that</u> was the whole object of the Revolution. Anything less wasn't worth the lives, the blood, the risk, and the expense that was suffered![20] He has a "vision for America" — for the most perfect nation and political setup ever known to mankind. And it's based on what he calls God's "natural law"!

* What's "natural law"?

* Plato said "natural law" is something eternal. It boils down to God somehow getting his message to us about the right way to live. Aristotle said it's inborn ability to reason-out the right way to live based on mankind's past experiences.[21] Cicero, Seneca, and Epictetus — the Stoics — agree with both Plato and Aristotle. What it boils down to, Harry, is this: God's "natural law" gives us a bunch of "natural rights", which are things like: <u>life</u> — the right to live and stay alive; <u>liberty</u> — the right to freedom to live how you choose; <u>happiness</u> — the right to enjoy the fruits of your labor; and <u>change</u> — the right to remove unjust government, by force if necessary. So, life, liberty, happiness, and change ... as Thomas Jefferson said in the **DECLARATION OF INDEPENDENCE** ... are inalienable God-given natural rights that come from God's natural law![22]

* So, natural law says that the natural rights of life, liberty, happiness, and change are what God wants people to have?

* Right. But you also have to rub along in society with <u>other</u> people. You're not just tucked away by yourself in some private cocoon with your own natural rights. Other people have natural rights of life, liberty, happiness, and change. You have to respect <u>their</u> natural rights if you want them to respect <u>yours</u>.[23]

* But what is it that would make other people bother to respect my natural rights?

* Aristotle, Rousseau, and Bolingbroke said people are born with a "fitness for society" — fitness to live with other people and respect their rights.[24] Kant's <u>Foundations of the Metaphysics of Morals</u> boiled down respect for other people's rights to the plain language question, "what would happen if <u>everyone</u> did this". Thomas Jefferson, with Epicurean Simplicity, puts these together and simply calls respect for other people's rights ..... "moral sense".

Unfortunately, history, Hobbes, and Machiavelli have all shown that kings and rulers choose to ignore their "moral sense". The rulers don't allow the ruled to have natural rights of life, liberty, happiness, and change. So, like Aristotle, Rousseau, and Bolingbroke, Thomas Jefferson says it's only the ruled — you and I — who care about our natural rights. And the only way you and I can guarantee our natural rights is with true self-government — <u>true total participatory democracy</u>! Elected representation is a good start. But it's not good enough!

* Why isn't elected representation good enough?

* Because, as Rousseau said, it becomes "elected aristocracy"! Is the flock not happier by themselves than under the care of wolves?

* I see what you mean. Then how would true total participatory democracy actually work?

* In total participatory democracy the "ruled" — you and I — would vote directly on all the laws. The centerpiece of Thomas Jefferson's idea of true total participatory democracy is what he calls — "ward-democracy"!

In ward-democracy, towns and counties would be divided into "wards" of however many people allow for orderly, individual discussion. Thomas calls them "little republics". They can have 100 people, like the ancient English "100's". Or, they can have considerably more, so long as you the individual can debate and vote on all the laws and issues firsthand. When your ward votes on an issue, its decision would be passed via a "representative" to the next larger "republic", such as a town or a county. When the votes of all the different wards are counted, that town or county's tally of wards for and against the issue would be passed along by someone to the next-larger "republic", such as a State assembly or federal congressional district. Their tally would be in turn passed along by someone for the final federal or State tally on the issue. And that's how laws would be voted on!

* So "wards" are the basic building blocks of what Thomas Jefferson says would be the first-ever truly democratic, federal-type of Republic? It sounds good ... if the people are competent to make intelligent votes.

* That's the challenge, of course. Thomas says people have that innate moral sense. Yes. But he recognises that the moral sense, like the sense of seeing and hearing or the strength of an arm or leg, is unevenly distributed among people. People are not all the same. No one is born with perfect moral sense or perfect competence to make intelligent choices.

* I can see that would be the problem with ward-democracy.

* Yes. But Thomas Jefferson has the solution! He says the key to making ward-democracy work is education! Granted, people may have deficits in their moral sense and intellectual competence. But moral sense and intellectual competence can be developed and strengthened through the right kind of training and education — like sight and hearing and arms and legs can be developed.

Following in the footsteps of Aristotle's Nicomachean Ethics, Rousseau's Emile, Montesquieu's Spirit of the Laws, and James Harrington's Oceana, Thomas Jefferson's first step for training and education is to develope the moral sense. The second step is to teach reading, writing, arithmetic, and the basics of government to qualify people to vote intelligently within their wards. Total participatory democracy doesn't work if it's a totally ignorant democracy![25] You can give a cow wings, Harry, but it still can't fly! That's basically what Thomas says in his:

A BILL FOR THE MORE GENERAL DIFFUSION
OF KNOWLEDGE

by: Thomas Jefferson

"Every government degenerates when entrusted to the rulers. The people themselves are its only safe depositories. And to render even them safe, their minds must be improved.

Those persons who nature hath endowed with genius and virtue should be rendered, by education, worthy to receive and able to guard the sacred deposit of the rights and liberties of their fellow citizens. They should be called to that charge without regard to wealth, birth, or other accidental condition or circumstance."

The virtue is: Justice. Allow people fair treatment according to their ability.

And that also brings us to his third step for education — justly identifying and developing leadership. Thomas says, like the moral sense and strength of limbs, the natural intellectual capacity — what he calls "genius" — is also unevenly distributed among people. If you have natural "genius", and the desire, you should be able to continue your education at a more advanced educational institution — a college, academy, or university — to further develope your wisdom and virtues. Like Plato's "Guardians" and Rousseau's "Legislators", you would then return as a teacher or advisor to your "little republic" — your ward. You could intelligently and convincingly lay out the issues to the people of your ward, and carry you're ward's decisions to the next higher level of government. And the best part, you wouldn't have to be from the old aristocracy of birth and privilege, or from the emerging aristocracy of money. You wouldn't be a wolf in care of the flock! You could be a member of the flock in care of other members of the flock! You would be a kind of new "aristocracy" based only on Virtue and Knowledge, not on money. Thomas calls it, from God's natural law, the "natural aristocracy". We've been calling it good-leaders! And speaking of money, I'll touch on the role economics plays.[26]

Like Aristotle, Rousseau, Montesquieu, and James Harrington, Thomas Jefferson says you shouldn't have to devote your entire time and energy just to staying alive. You need a "satisfactory economic situation". Then you'll be free to participate directly and personally in your ward "republic". You'll have the time for self-government. You'll have a stake in self-government. You'll have a stake in law and order. And, you'll have a hand in your own future! [27] So, where Thomas sees an economic policy that would free you to participate in ward-democracy, he backs it. Where he sees an economic policy that would hinder you from full democratic participation, he opposes it. That's why he opposes Hamilton and his crowd. They: push for a big Federal government that concentrates economic decision-making in the "few"; give economic opportunity only to wealthy merchants and big business; and, back an "aristocracy" based strictly on wealth, or even on birth![28]

So. There you have it, Harry! That's Thomas Jefferson's presidential campaign of 1800! He finally separates the pigs from the trough and clears-up the political water. Now you know his political philosophy and vision for America.

To sum up, Americans have God-given natural rights of life, liberty, happiness, change, and participatory ward-democracy that come from God's natural law. Participatory ward-democracy is what protects the rights of life, liberty, happiness, and change. Moral sense education, intellectual education, and leadership education — Thomas Jefferson's three goals for education — are needed in order to make participatory ward-democracy work. Now everyone knows the truth about what Thomas Jefferson stands for!

* So, in addition to monarchists, Thomas Jefferson also sees the "pseudo-aristocracy" and powerful big-business as obstructions to his vision for America.

* Yes. That's why he sees participatory ward-democracy, through which you can truly "vote the bums out", as the best insurance against political tyranny of the rich and powerful over the people. True democracy removes fear of political tyranny! It also removes an old philosophical dilemma that even Democratic-Republicans have been groping with. Some want to base America on John Locke's natural "liberal" rights. Others think it should be based on classical republican democracy. Now they can have both! With Thomas Jefferson's participatory ward democracy, natural rights and classical republican democracy are perfect together!

* What insurance is there against the masses turning real democracy into raging anarchy — mob rule — before education, economics, and ward-democracy have a chance to kick-in?

* In Thomas Jefferson's vision for America that's where the Army kicks-in!

* What if the Army kicks-in on the side of the anarchists?

* We'll be getting to that problem later, Harry. But right now, let's continue with learning about Thomas Jefferson. It's the year 1800. The ballots are cast. The election is over. America is deeply split. The two Democratic-Republicans, Thomas Jefferson and Aaron Burr, are tied — 73 electoral votes each! The Federalists, John Adams and Charles Pinckney, have 65 and 64. The so called people's House of Representatives votes to break the tie, as prescribed by the Constitution. Finally, in February 1801 Thomas Jefferson becomes the third President of the United States! On March 4th he's sworn in at his inauguration. And almost immediately in April is when he tells insiders about his plans for a military academy! On March 16, 1802 he signs the "Act" into law that legally and officially creates the United States Military Academy at West Point!

Looking forward from where we are in 1802, Thomas Jefferson will live another twenty four years! He will reach eighty-three! His life will have been one of love of philosophy; of privacy and secrecy; of genius and invention; of duty and self-discipline; of quiet reserve and immense energy; of great accomplishments and enormous intellectual activity; of tender fatherly affection but lifelong need of his own father; and, of heartache after heartache on the death of many loved ones. By the winter of his life he will have accomplished all he can. In a sense he will not have much more to live for. He will be less and less tethered to this world. But he is blessed with a caring family. He will not be put out to pasture as so often happens to many still-viable old people, just because they're old — like the one in the following story:

BUILDING-BLOCKS OF LIFE

from: The Brothers Grimm

Once upon a time there was a nice old woman whose husband died and left her all alone. As the years passed she grew more feeble. She thought her son, for whom she had lovingly worked her fingers to the bone to take good care of, would now take good care of <u>her.</u> But she trembled so badly she would sometimes drop her peas or spill her drink all over the table during dinner. The son and his wife became too annoyed with her to take care of her.

They put her in a nice home for old people, with a nice little room, with a nice little table in one corner just for her to eat her meals on. Each day, while sitting alone eating, she would look up lovingly with tear-filled eyes at the picture of her son hanging on her wall. Others in the home who had no children would ask why she was there when she had a son? But she would brag about him nevertheless. For her, he could do no wrong!

One evening the son and his wife called their small child for dinner, but the little boy didn't want any just yet. He was too busy playing on the floor with his building-blocks. The father asked him what he was so busy making. He looked up smiling proudly! He said, "I'm making a nice home, with a nice little room, and a nice little table in the corner that you or Mommy can eat on by yourself someday when I get big!" The parents put down their forks. They gazed at their little boy for a few minutes. Their eyes glazed over ... then filled with tears. Then they both quietly began to weep.

The next day they led the old mother out of the old people's home. On the way out, she proudly bragged to everyone that they passed: "this is my son .... and he's taking me home"!

The virtue is: Compassion. As you sow, so shall you
              reap.

The love and care and compassion that Thomas Jefferson gave to his family and loved ones all his life will be returned by them in his old age. He will spend his remaining days peacefully living with them under their loving care at his own beloved Monticello. Near the end he will be able to share thoughts such as this with his young grandson:

TO THOMAS JEFFERSON RANDOLPH ABOUT DEATH

from: Thomas Jefferson - 83 years old

"Do not imagine for a moment that I feel the smallest solicitude about the result (death). I am like an old watch, with a pinion worn out here, and a wheel there, until it can go no longer."[29]

The virtue is: Fortitude. Mental fortitude is needed to face pain, peril ... and death.

* So Jefferson will someday face death as he has always faced life — guided by philosophy.
* Philosophy doesn't merely <u>guide</u> his life, Harry. As we have seen throughout, he actually uses philosophy to micro-manage his life — in fact, micro-manage everything he does. So it will be no coincidence that books on philosophy will someday be found at his bedside in death ... as they were in life.
At eighty-three years old on the Fourth of July in 1826, Thomas Jefferson's eyes will close in their final slumber. ..... His oldest pen-pal, friendly competitor, and other Revolutionary War survivor, John Adams, at ninety-three years old will also succumb in Massachusetts ... on the same day! That day, the last words John Adams will mumble with his last breath are: "Thomas Jefferson still survives". Little will he know, however, that just a few hours before in Virginia ... on the same day ... Thomas Jefferson <u>did not</u> "still survive"! Both men will die on Independence Day, within a few hours of eachother! It will be exactly the 50th anniversary of the day both of these "giants" thumbed their noses at King George's hangman and put their signatures on the **DECLARATION OF INDE-PENDENCE!**
* That's eerie!

* So, Harry! That will be Thomas Jefferson's life! That's how it will end, come 1826. However, 1826 is still twenty four years down the road from where we are right now in 1802! I've jumped ahead on our journey. Now we'll pick it up again where we left off before I started our detour to look at his life. You'll remember, we were in Washington D.C. He has been "Mr. President Jefferson" for over a year now. He's still far from being that old worn-out watch! At fifty-nine, he's ticking along nicely! And in the quiet, cautious, low-profile, almost secret way that experience has taught him to be prudent, he's ticking along nicely in that new job as President ...... with his new military academy quietly tucked away up along the Hudson River at West Point!
* Interesting. Despite Jefferson and others often having said America <u>can't</u> have

334

a standing army and <u>can't</u> have a military academy …… now they have both!

* Yes. But now you know the head and heart of Thomas Jefferson. Now you know what makes him tick. So you should be able to understand why he thinks that America can now have a standing army and a military academy. You should be able to understand why he officially establishes a military college for America — the United States Military Academy — West Point!

CHAPTER 2 : MR. JEFFERSON'S ACADEMY

It's 1802. A peacetime Standing Army and a United States Military Academy for the Standing Army are now real … thanks to President Jefferson and "An Act Fixing the Military Peace Establishment of the United States". From now on we'll just call it the "1802 Military Act".

* Is Jefferson really the founder of the United States Military Academy? Or is it Congress, or his Secretary of War, or some others I've heard mentioned?

* Let me put it to you this way, Harry. We know Thomas Jefferson is the President in 1802, don't we.

* Yes.

* And we know that an Act the President's people writes and gets approved by Congress is credited to that President. Right?

* Of course.

* Then President Jefferson certainly gets credit for the "1802 Military Act". And in this case, he did more than just take credit for it. He personally <u>created</u> it! He was ably assisted by his Secretary of War, Henry Dearborn. But everyone knew it was really his baby![30] So we know for sure, the following premiss is a true, documented, historical fact:

> (premiss) - President Jefferson is credited with the "1802
> Military Act"

In the "1802 Military Act" President Jefferson set up what he called a Corps of Engineers. The Act assigned this Corps the job of founding and operating a military academy to educate and train Officers for a Standing Army. So we also know for sure that I'm telling you a true, documented, historical fact when I say:

> (premiss) - the "1802 Military Act" founded the United States
> Military Academy

When we put these two premisses together, we have no choice but the conclusion that follows them:

> (premiss) - President Jefferson is credited with the "1802
> Military Act"
> (premiss) - The "1802 Military Act" founded the United States
> Military Academy
> _____
>
> (conclusion) - President Jefferson is credited with founding the
> United States Military Academy

That is known in logic as a "true and valid deductive proof".

* It sounds right … I guess.

* It cannot be otherwise, Harry. In a <u>true</u> and <u>valid</u> deductive proof, true pre-

misses are an absolute guarantee that the conclusion is true! The <u>truth</u> of the premisses springs from facts, experiences, observations, and so on [a posteriori]. The <u>validity</u> emerges from our innate sense of reason and logic [a priori]. Let me give you an easy illustration:

If we show it's a true premiss that:	A equals B
And show it's a true premiss that:	A equals C
	—————————
We conclude from reason and logic:	B equals C

There is no way in the world this conclusion can be wrong.

* I see it helps to remember how Emmanuel Kant put experience and observation [a posteriori] together with our innate logic and reason [a priori] to arrive at conclusions [synthetic a priori].

* It does! But credit has to go to Aristotle and his syllogism as the first to prove conclusions by logic. Remember? Anyway, when we use the logic called deductive proof [true and valid], we know conclusions are <u>absolutely guaranteed</u> to be true! We shall use deductive proof from here on in to prove <u>why</u> President Jefferson did or did not intend to do something.

* I see. So we have proven that the United States Military Academy at West Point is truly Mr. Jefferson's Academy. Now I have to ask you the next logical question. In fact, it's the <u>big</u> question! **WHY?** <u>Why</u> did he found the U.S. Military Academy? He always said a bonafide military academy is unconstitutional!

* Harry, you play the violin by the letter of the music when you can. But sometimes you have to wing it, and play by ear. In this case, the exact letter of the Constitution says you can have needed military "institutions". It doesn't say, specifically, a military academy is one of them. That's true. But, it doesn't say it <u>isn't</u>, either! So President Jefferson played by ear. He founded the U.S. Military Academy. And he'll defend his playing by ear regarding the U.S. Military Academy, the same way he'll defend his Embargo and his Louisiana Purchase, in this letter: [31]

A LAW BEYOND THE CONSTITUTION

from: Thomas Jefferson, written
to John Colvin, 9/20/1810

The question you propose, whether circumstances do not sometimes occur which make it a duty to assume authority <u>beyond what is specified</u> by the law, is easy in principle but sometimes embarassing in practice. Even a strict observance of the written law, doubtless one of the highest duties, is not the highest. The laws of **necessity**, of **self-preservation**, of **saving our country** when in danger are of higher obligation!

> These principles ... <u>do not</u> authorize persons to take
> such cases out of the written law. So the line of discrimi-
> nation between cases may be difficult, but the good officer
> of government is bound to draw a line at his own peril,
> and throw himself on the justice of his country and recti-
> tude of his motives.

> The virtue is: Courage. It takes courage to do the harder
> right than the easier wrong.

* Jefferson's opinion regarding what is un-Constitutional has changed!
* If it's not specifically prohibited by the Constitution, it's not specifically un-Constitutional, is it! Take a peacetime standing army, for example. It's not specifically in the Constitution. But it's not specifically prohibited. Thomas Jefferson sees a big role for state militias. However, he didn't actively oppose the 1796 Military Act that, for the first time, allowed a peacetime Standing Army.[32]
* But I still have to ask the same question. **WHY**? <u>Why</u> did he found a U.S. Military Academy?
* A person usually has two reasons for doing something. One is the noble, good sounding reason. The other is the real reason! The noble, good sounding reason for founding a Military Academy might be to do what all those other guys couldn't do — be the one who fulfills George Washington's "last wish". We have neither direct nor deductive proof of that reason, however.
* And the real reason?
* One thing for sure, he obviously thinks America needs one!
* <u>Why</u> does he think America needs one? Has he now joined others in thinking America must preserve its Revolutionary War military experience by teaching warfare, weaponry, and fortifications —the "military arts"? That's it, isn't it! It's obvious! That's why he founded the U.S. Military Academy!
* True. It wouldn't be called a military academy if it didn't do military things. But you're saying President Jefferson took on the considerable financial, political, and Constitutional risk of statutorally founding a bonafide U.S. Military Academy solely and specifically to teach the "military arts"?
* Yes. As I said, it's the obvious conclusion!
* Then let's examine that. Here's what our deductive proof would have to look like <u>if</u> your "obvious" conclusion is true:

> (premiss) - President Jefferson founded the U.S. Military
>   Academy
> (premiss) - the U.S. Military Academy is <u>needed</u> to teach,
>   and <u>does</u> solely and specifically teach, the
>   "military arts"

_____

(conclusion) - President Jefferson founded the U.S. Military

Academy solely and specifically to teach the "military arts"

Unfortunately, the second premiss would not be true, Harry. We know they're teaching a number of college subjects at the U.S. Military Academy that have little to do with warfare, weaponry, and fortifications — the "military arts". Besides, President Jefferson did <u>not</u> need a statutorally formal, bonafide, U.S. Military Academy just to teach the "military arts"! They had already been doing that for a long time at the existing West Point school, informally, since the Corps of Invalids during the Revolution, and formally, since the 1794 Military Statute! Besides, in <u>A Law Beyond the Constitution</u>, Thomas Jefferson said the only reasons he would skirt around the letter of the Constitution would be out of **necessity, self-preservation**, or **saving our country**. Skirting around the Constitution by founding a statutorally formal, bonafide military academy solely and specifically to teach the "military arts" sure doesn't fulfill any of those reasons ... especially since the "military arts" are already being taught. So here's what our deductive proof regarding the "military arts" really looks like:

(premiss) - President Jefferson founded the U.S. Military Academy

(premiss) - the U.S. Military Academy <u>was not</u> needed to teach, and <u>does not</u> solely and specifically teach, the "military arts"

(conclusion) - President Jefferson <u>did not</u> found the U.S. Military Academy solely and specifically to teach the "military arts"

No matter what President Jefferson's real reason is for founding the U.S. Military Academy it <u>will</u>, of course, teach warfare, weaponry, and fortifications — the "military arts". Otherwise, it wouldn't be called a military academy. But that cannot be, and is not, the reason he founded it!

* You're right. And, the U.S. Military Academy was founded under the Corps of Engineers. So Jefferson obviously had engineering in mind. He probably remembers how Washington had to hire foreign engineers to handle his artillery and fortifications during the Revolution. Are there any engineering colleges yet in America in 1802?

* Not yet. They've been teaching artillery and fortifications at the West Point school. That doesn't make it an engineering college, though.

* Perhaps Jefferson figured he could beef up the existing school with a bunch of engineering courses. And bingo! He'd have the first engineering college! Maybe that's it. Maybe he founded the Military Academy to be, academically, an engineering college!

* That would be a good reason. Here's what that deductive proof would have to look like <u>if</u> it were an engineering college:

> (premiss) - an engineering college has to have an engineering
> curriculum
> (premiss) - the U.S. Military Academy has an engineering
> curriculum
> _____
> (conclusion) - the U.S. Military Academy is an engineering
> college

That's a true and valid conclusion, <u>if</u> the Academy has a bonafide engineering curriculum. So let's see what science and engineering subjects they're teaching. They have: surveying; drawing; artillery; fortifications; simple algebra; and elementary geometry.
* That's it? Even a former liberal arts student like me knows that's not a bonafide engineering curriculum.
* No. Those subjects can only give cadets enough practical skills to draw maps, lay artillery, and construct fortifications. In fact, they're about the same subjects that Lt. Colonel Rochfontaine already had at the West Point school back in 1794. So here's what is actually true and validly deductible when it comes to engineering:

> (premiss) - an engineering college has to have an engineering
> curriculum
> (premiss) - the U.S. Military Academy <u>does not</u> have an
> engineering curriculum
> _____
> (conclusion) - therefore, the U.S. Military Academy <u>is not</u> an
> engineering college

President Jefferson certainly did not found the U.S. Military Academy as an engineering college! About twenty years from now, they will have a bonafide engineering curriculum at the Academy. An appointee of President Jefferson named Sylvanus Thayer will see to that. But that's another story. For now, and for many years to come, it's simply not an engineering college! [33]
And guess what, Harry? It's not even strictly for the Corps of Engineers. Listen to these facts. President Jefferson will eventually hand out over one hundred appointments to West Point. About fifty will graduate. Only fourteen will end up in the Corps of Engineers. Fourteen! That's a telling statistic! [34]
* And he couldn't have founded it as a college that promotes his passion for Enlightenment science by substituting the sciences for the classics. The curriculum of subjects has little science!
* Correct! Besides, like George Washington and others, Thomas Jefferson has been pushing awfully hard for a national university where they would do that — teach more science, less classics. But, he's had no luck. He's now working on a university in Virginia, not far from Monticello. You'll someday know it as the University of Virginia! [35]
So, Harry, ... Military Arts ... Engineering ... Science. They're all good reasons to found a bonafide military academy. But as reasons, we just can't square

them with the facts! And we just can't square them with the way many early cadets at West Point tell it:

> "But for its chaos and rioting, I now might be reading the classics at that Virginia 'grammar school', William and Mary College!"
>> "Oh? I looked for technology. My <u>father</u> looked for discipline. West Point was a happy joining of both … and better than being with rich monarchists at Yale!"
> "You two should have taken the classics and Yale. I can see that here at West Point, receiving a qualified engineering education is a fiction, excepting doing so by our own extra industry".
>> "We're not here for engineering or the Classics, are we! We're here to become bonafide Army Officers to serve our Nation. As far as I'm concerned, getting a college education along the way makes me forever thankful to Thomas Jefferson for the opportunity". °°And also thankful this is an academy type of college having tutoring from the advanced down to <u>my</u> basic academic level, or I'd never make it through!°° [36]

* I see what you mean, Thomas. Then why would President Jefferson go out of his way to commit what in the eyes of his own supporters is a cardinal sin — found a military academy? Those very same supporters back in 1800 attempted to kill off even the West Point school.[37] Why buck his own Democratic-Republican supporters head-on? Even I now know those guys hate military academies. As you said, military academies have too often been used for sinister purposes. Kings

and tyrants have used them as a tool to back up their political shenanigans. ...
Maybe Jefferson is doing the same thing? Maybe he's playing Party politics?
Perhaps he founded the U.S. Military Academy strictly for Party political reasons?

* I'm surprised to hear you say that, Harry, now that you know Thomas Jefferson.
* Why? Having disproved and disposed of the "military arts", engineering, and
science as reasons, what else is there? In fact, can you just put yourself in
Jefferson's predicament?
* Yes. Go on.
* It looks to me like his Presidency is starting out on a shoestring. He only got
about 25% of the electoral votes. He had to be voted in by the House of
Representatives. I imagine lots of people have a problem with that. And I imag-
ine the outgoing Federalists had loaded-up most parts of the government with
their friends. Right?
* They certainly did! Federalists still control most parts of the civil service, the
law courts, and the Army. They could get what is still a very monarchistic
"Hamiltonian Army" to rise up against Jefferson. Democratic-Republicans could
be denied the victory they won at the polls![38]
* So his support is weak.
* Perhaps. It's true that some Federalist guys — Hamiltonian types — are as
monarchistic as British Torys. But a lot of other Federalist guys are as "republi-
can" as Democratic-Republicans! In fact, President Jefferson refers to them as his
"republican Federalists!"[39]   Besides, Aaron Burr's electoral votes bring the
Democratic-Republican total to 53%! And they did break the tie by a vote in the
House of Representatives, as they were supposed to do.
* So Jefferson does have political support in the Congress?
* Yes. And can you tell me how a military academy can possibly help President
Jefferson politically? It sure can't do anything about the Federalists still running
things. It can't do anything to help him weed out corruption and incompetence.
It can't stop entrenched monarchists, or anyone, from trying to oust him or overthrow the government. He certainly has to do something to remove fear of those
problems. But he can only do that if he reforms things and "cleans house". And
that means he would have to reform a lot of things, and hire and fire a lot of people in the civil service, the law Courts, and the Army!
* That's true.
* And that's exactly what he does! He reforms things. He hires and fires people
in the civil service, the law Courts, and the Army to remove fear of what they
might get up to. But the way he does it shows he's <u>not</u> playing Party politics!
* How can you say he's not playing Party politics? It's always Party politics
when politicians hire and fire and clean house.
* I can see in order to prove his reforming things is not for strictly Party political reasons, I'll have to show you how he does it.
* To convince me he's not playing politics ... yes ... you will.
* Well to start with, we know by now that Thomas Jefferson has no intention of
being a career politician in the first place, don't we. He said he sees public office
as a duty to Country ... not a duty to Party ... not a career. He believes everyone

342

should see it that way. He believes people should do a stretch in government only for philosophical reasons. So he has very little patience with entrenched bureaucratic incompetents or the dishonest of any political Party or faction, including his own! He plans to go back home to Monticello when the work he has to do is done. And he told us during the Presidential Campaign what that work is: stop America's <u>current</u> slide back toward a British-style monarchistic setup; do something to stop it <u>permanently</u>; and, complete the revolution of 1775 by finally giving the people <u>real</u> democracy.[40] True, that means he has to reform a lot of things. And that reformation has to include hiring and firing in the civil service, law Courts, and Army. But he intends his reformation to be a "Chaste Reformation".[41]

* Chaste Reformation! Great label! But, what's it mean?

* We know Thomas Jefferson always thinks long term and does things gradually. And I think you would agree he's a kind person. He couldn't reform things or hire and fire ruthlessly. In fact, he basically promised he wouldn't do so in his First Inauguration Address. So that's why he uses the word "chaste". By "chaste" he means: pure; uncorrupt; virtuous; and, "unmarried", as in, not "married" to any political Party! Now I'll show you that his "chaste" reforms and hiring and firing are based on very specific, non-partisan, philosophic and special principles — <u>not</u> strict Party politics! [42]

President Jefferson's philosophic and special principles are his ground-rules. He practically jumps through hoops in letter after letter to explain them to people. He has to explain them to his Democratic-Republicans who want a ruthless purge of all Federalists ... which he will not do! He even explains them to Federalists who expect to be hunted down like wild beasts ... which he also will not do![43] And he can explain them to you too, Harry. Go through his papers. Read but a fraction of his letters on the subject. Take the trouble to look at what he actually does. You'll see what I mean. They're all documented and historical facts. He uses the following <u>specific</u> philosophic and special principles as his rules for reforms and hiring and firing:

JEFFERSON ON HIS CHASTE REFORMATION

from: letters by Thomas Jefferson

"No good man should be disturbed for mere difference of opinion."[44]

"Removals are on fixed rules, applied to every case without passion or partiality."[45]

"Removals must be as few as possible, that they must be made gradually, and be bottomed on some malversation — evil or corrupt misconduct. Or on some inherent disqualification, like Adams' hurried 'midnight appointments' before he left office."[46]

"The majority as well as the minority each have its rights, including a proportionate share of public office."[47]

343

"The only questions concerning a candidate shall be: Is he honest? Is he capable? Is he faithful to the Constitution?"[48]

"Nobody knows better the formidable phalanx [the Macedonian battle formation] opposed to the republican features of our Constitution. To bear up against this, the talents and virtues of our Country must be formed into a phalanx also."[49]

"Good principles, wisely and honestly administered, cannot fail to attach our fellow citizens to the order of things we espouse."[50]

"To appoint a "monarchist" to office in the United States is like appointing an athiest to the priesthood!"[51]

The virtue is: Temperance. The middle way may be the wise way.

* I guess that says it all, Thomas. It shows his reforms are not intended to be strict Party politics. He says so in his own words … over and over again!
* Good. Then I'm sure you agree this premiss is true:

> (premiss) - President Jefferson's Chaste Reformation of the civil
> service, law Courts, and Army is intended to be based
> on philosophic and special principles

* Sure. I have no problem with that.
* And I have no problem showing you Thomas Jefferson's deeds don't remain in the shadow of his words very long, either. He wastes no time turning the nice words of his <u>Chaste Reformation</u> into real deeds. And he creates quite a stir in Congress. In fact, he upsets a lot of people in his own Party who expected Federalist's heads to roll. For example: Federalist, Rufus King, is hired to be minister to England; Federalist, James Marbury, of the future watershed case known as Marbury vs Madison, is re-hired as a Supreme Court justice; Federalist, Army Brigadier General James Wilkinson, is retained as America's #1soldier; Federalist, Charles Pinckney, is hired as minister to Spain; Federalist, Calab Swan, is retained on the Army General Staff; Federalist, Allen McLane, Collector of the Port of Wilmington, Delaware (next to President, one of the highest paid jobs) is re-hired despite pressure and petitions from Democratic-Republicans; Federalist, John Steele, is re-hired as controller of the Treasury. Even monarchic Hamilton Federalist, Lieutenant Colonel Thomas Cushing, is retained on the Army General Staff. And monarchic Hamilton Federalist, Army Staff Officer Edward Turner, is transfered to a non-staff position — but not fired! I can show you dozens of other documented cases in which President Jefferson turns his nice words into deeds.[52]
* The last two are actually Hamilton Federalists? That's the faction that "ripped" Jefferson, personally, for years!

* And the firebrand Democratic-Republican Congressman, Elbridge Gerry of Massachusetts, says that most Hamilton Federalists are still ripping him. Gerry is one of the guys who wanted to see Federalist's heads roll. Instead he gets a shock. His zealous Democratic-Republican brother's head rolls instead! His brother gets fired from his high paid government post because of official misconduct! And so does a Randolph from Virginia, David Randolph! Both cases are embarrassments to Thomas Jefferson![53]
* So why would Jefferson keep any monarchistic Hamilton Federalist, and yet fire some Democratic-Republicans he knows?
* Because he believes there are good and upright people in every faction. He judges a person on his merits and says, "a moral and good man is worthy of esteem, no matter his politics". He does keep some monarchists who have a special talent. But he takes care to also keep them isolated and powerless. So, as you can see, President Jefferson sticks to specific philosophic and special principles when hiring and firing and reforming things. He first, gives monarchists the ax … excluding the exceptions that have a special talent. Next, anyone from any Party who is dishonest or incompetent gets the ax!
* So Federalists who are honest and competent have nothing to fear?
* Thomas Jefferson says he will respect honesty and competence wherever he finds it.[54] Again, read his intentions. Look at documented examples of his actual deeds, like the ones I just showed you. Look at other examples in the public records. They all prove:

> (premiss) - the philosophic and special principles are strictly intended to weed out monarchists, incompetents, and the dishonest

* I have no problem seeing that's true, also. Jefferson's deeds prove his words and intentions! First we heard his words and intentions in all his letters — his philosophic and special principles in <u>Jefferson on His Chaste Reformation</u>. Then, we saw how his actual deeds carried out all those words and intentions!
* Good. So here's our conclusion … and it's absolutely guaranteed to be true and valid by our deductive proof:

> (premiss) - President Jefferson's Chaste Reformation of the civil service, law Courts, and Army is intended to be based on philosophic and special principles
> (premiss) - the philosophic and special principles are strictly intended to weed out monarchists, incompetents, and the dishonest
> _____
> (conclusion) - President Jefferson's Chaste Reformation of the civil service, law Courts, and Army is strictly intended to weed out monarchists, incompetents, and the dishonest.

In other words, Harry, Thomas Jefferson's Chaste Reformation is purposely intended <u>not</u> to be Party politics!

Now let's look at the Army in more detail. Prior to June 1802 they had 230 Officers in the Army. That's thanks to more than 80 last minute "midnight appointments" that President Adams made during his last weeks in Office. Those 230 Officers are the most allowed by law for an Army of 5000 men. But right now the Army doesn't have 5000 men. They only have 3600. So guess what? That's President Jefferson's excuse to get rid of monarchistic Hamilton Federalists in the Officer Corps. Adams thought he was sticking it to the Democratic-Republicans with his midnight appointments. So, you can imagine the pleasure President Jefferson and Secretary Dearborn must have taken with the excuse Adams handed them to cook up something new!

"John Adams thought he slipped us a rotten apple with his midnight appointments to the Officer corps, Mr. President!"
"Indeed. How little <u>he</u> knows! He has handed us a juicy opportunity! We can slice it, rearrange it, cut out the bad parts, and spice it up. We'll make that apple into a palatable apple pie!"
"I can cook up something quite good. I shall make it something easy for Congress and the Officer Corps to swallow, Sir!"
"Good! I've hired Captain Meriwether Lewis to assist us. Thanks to Mr. Adams, the Officer Corps is over-staffed by 1/3. Mr. Adams has unwittingly saved us embarassment. He has handed us the excuse to cut out 80 or so monarchists and incompetents with little note or fanfare. So cook up something good, Mr. Secretary. You know the recipe!"
"I do indeed — the same principles you're applying to the civil service and the law courts, I presume?"
"Precisely. And my assistant, Captain Meriwether Lewis, has a roster of the 230 Officers, coded as to their individual ability and Virtue. You and he are to use it as your guide. He knows the code."
"With your permission, I shall slice out and rearrange regiments to lawfully eliminate slots now held by monarchists and incompetents. And I shall cook up a new Corps of Artillerists, Corps of Engineers, and a few new ranks so as to retain <u>non</u>-monarchic Officers."
"And don't forget my military academy! When we are finished we shall bring our apple pie to the table as 'An Act Fixing the Military Peace Establishment of the United States'". °°And, I shall grant George Washington his last wish. He shall finally have his military academy! That will top-off our apple pie very nicely!°° 55

"An Act Fixing the Military Peace Establishment of the United States" — the "1802 Military Act" — finishes with an Army of 3300. That's just 300 less than President Jefferson inherited! But his Army of 3300 now has the correct Officer strength. Secretary Dearborn lawfully "fired" 88 Officers. From the Roster of Officers, here's the story on the ones he fired": 14 current Officers who are positively monarchistic ; 11 current ones who are likely monarchistic; 27 new "midnight appointments" who are likely monarchistic; and, 36 new and current Officers, including Jefferson supporters, who are considered unworthy or incompetent!

Now the Army Officer Corps has 142 Officers: about 23 are politically neutral — independent; only 9 are Democratic-Republicans; 106 are Federalists — the kind favoring a Republic as provided in the Constitution; and, there are still 4 hardcore monarchists, retained only because of some exceptional talent or ability.[56]

* Most of the Officers are actually still Federalists!
* Correct! So here's another conclusion I absolutely guarantee is true and valid because we know the two premises are true documented facts:

> (premiss) - President Jefferson's Chaste Reformation of the civil
> service, law courts, and Army is strictly intended to
> weed out monarchists, incompetents, and the dis-
> honest
> (premiss) - Chaste Reformation of the Army is part of President
> Jefferson's Chaste Reformation
>
> ---
>
> (conclusion) - President Jefferson's Chaste Reformation of the
> Army is strictly intended to weed out monarchists,
> incompetents, and the dishonest

He's not playing Party politics with the Army, Harry. The people he fires are from all Parties and factions, including his own!

* But, does that hold true for the U.S. Military Academy, also?

* Of course! The Military Academy is the Army! But you can also look at it this way, if you'd like to:

> (premiss) - the "1802 Military Act" is, in fact, President Jefferson's Chaste Reformation of the Army
> (premiss) - the Military Academy is part of that "1802 Military Act"
> _____
> (conclusion) - the Military Academy is part of President Jefferson's Chaste Reformation of the Army

And:

> (premiss) - the Military Academy is part of President Jefferson's Chaste Reformation of the Army
> (premiss) - President Jefferson's Chaste Reformation of the Army weeds out monarchists, incompetents, and the dishonest
> _____
> (conclusion) - the Military Academy weeds out monarchists, incompetents, and the dishonest

As the Academy is part of President Jefferson's Chaste Reformation of the Army, he's not playing Party politics there, either. He did not found the U.S. Military Academy for Party political reasons!

* I guess not.

* You don't sound completely convinced. ...... Well, I'm sure you agree the following premiss is true and valid:

> (premiss) - President Jefferson's reason for founding the Academy was not for Party political purposes _if_ his deeds, appointments, and rejections there were not for Party political purposes

* Yes. That's obvious.

* Then we'll look at his deeds, appointments, and rejections specifically at the Military Academy if you like. We know from the archives that all the information available shows three things about guys who enter the Academy as cadets. One: most are sons of soldiers or patriots from the Revolution — they're not monarchists. Two: most have already had some education — they're not incompetent. Three: all are certified to possess good moral character — they're not dishonest. Not monarchist, not incompetent, and not dishonest. Sound familiar? They're the three criteria used in Thomas Jefferson's Chaste Reformation! So it's no surprise they pop-up again here![57]

* What about their family's political Party?

* The archives also show that Academy appointees are sons of soldiers or patriots from both Parties ... but not monarchists! Who knows, maybe they're the ones who wildly greeted Thomas at John Adams' 1797 presidential inauguration in the military throng carrying signs saying, "Jefferson, The Friend Of The People". Do you remember that? Perhaps early cadet appointee Joseph Totten, son of General J.G. Totten, was there with his father that day; maybe cadet Hannibal Allen, son of Colonel Ethan Allen remembers; or, cadet William Gates, son of Captain Samuel Gates; or, cadet Louis Loramier, son of Colonel Loramier; or, cadet Edward deRussey, future Academy superintendent and son of a naval officer; or, Satterlee Clarke, son of General Isaac Clarke; or, cadet Thomas Beall, son of Captain Lloyd Beall; or, cadet Henry Jackson, son of Major Jackson; or, cadet Alexander Williams, son of first West Point Superintendent Major Jonathan Williams. These and other early cadets are from families of both political Parties ... not just the Democratic-Republican Party.

Just eight out of over fourty applicants' letters requesting appointments mention the republican philosophy of government. And only a few of those eight specifically mention the Democratic-Republican Party. One letter that does is for a Moses Elliot. But it doesn't matter. For some unknown reason he never makes it into West Point. Neither does Erasmus Thompson who is recommended by a Democratic-Republican professor at West Point, Jared Mansfield. Nor does Democratic-Republican, John Reed. And a D.B. Heil has a big political backer, but little education. He never gets appointed, either. Nor does Bray Brunch who's "backed by every Republican in Congress". Nor does John Donnelly who's "family are good Whigs and firm friends of the Government". Yet John Heilmann, son of Dr. H. Heilmann, British General Burgoyne's physician in the Revolution, is appointed and enters. So is Frederick Lewis who was educated in France at his "psuedo-aristocratic" family's expense, and was at the French military academy. So are London educated Sam Noah and John Wyndham. But not Horatio Lord Viscount Roberts. And a letter from one Sylvester Roberts says he's a twenty-two year old who formerly "conducted" the Republican Fountain newspaper in Hudson, N.Y. He talks republicanism. That's good. But he admits to playing politics, anyway, and doesn't consider it dishonest. That's bad. He wrote his own recommendation letter. That's disrespectful! He's another Democratic-Republican who doesn't get an appointment to West Point! [58]

* Well, that shows me cadet appointments are not based strictly on Party politics. How about teaching staff appointments?

* There are five early academic staff members: Federalist, Major Jonathan Williams, as the first West Point superintendent; Federalist, Captain William Amhurst Barron, as a professor; Federalist, Lieutenant Joseph G. Swift, as an instructor; Democratic-Republican, George Baron, as a professor; and, Democratic-Republican, Jared Mansfied, as a professor.

Jonathan Williams was secretary to his Federalist uncle, Benjamin Franklin, and was an outstanding scientific figure in America. Captain William Amhurst Barron taught at aristocratic Harvard. George Baron taught at the Royal Military

Academy in Woolwich, England. Jared Mansfield taught at aristocratic Yale. There are no Party politics in those resumes either, are there!

* No. Only two out of five are Democratic-Republicans!

* And, ironically, it's not long before they fire one of those two Democratic-Republicans. George Baron gets the push because they find his moral and character traits are not suitable for a Military Academy![59] So, we have now proven the following premiss regarding the Academy to be true:

> (premiss) - President Jefferson's deeds, appointments, and rejections were not for Party political purposes.

I've shown you lots of appointments and rejections from both Parties. I've shown you that his criteria for the Academy are the same as for the rest of the Army, the civil service, and the law Courts, namely, to weed out monarchists, incompetents, and the dishonest. Furthermore, if he wanted to play Party politics, he wouldn't need an Academy to politically stack his Officer Corps. He could simply dole out <u>Direct Commissions</u> to Party zealots. After all, he's the Commander-in-chief! So the following true and valid premisses guarantee the conclusion that flows from them to be true:

> (premiss) - President Jefferson's reason for founding the
> Academy was not for Party political purposes <u>if</u> his
> deeds, appointments, and rejections there were not
> for Party political purposes
>
> (premiss) - President Jefferson's deeds, appointments, and rejections <u>were not</u> for Party political purposes
>
> ---
>
> (conclusion) - President Jefferson's reason for founding the
> Academy <u>was not</u> for Party political purposes

Neither his intentions nor deeds when it comes to the Military Academy were for Party political purposes. He hired and fired in all parts of his government painstakingly and conscientiously. We have volumes of records to prove it. They show that, under pressure and criticism from his own political Party, he followed a reasoned, patient, moderate, and consistent course of action. He stuck to his philosophic principles. And would you expect anything different from Thomas Jefferson ... now that you know him, Harry?[60]

* Not really. So the reason Jefferson founded the U.S. Military Academy is not for the military arts, or engineering, or science, or Party politics. Then what is the reason? **WHY**, did he found it? Do <u>you</u> even know? .... We know he's big on philosophy. Could the reason possibly have something to do with his philosophy?[61]

* Well, he <u>is</u> called America's philosophical father. So let's explore that possiblity. We'll see if the reason he founded the Academy has something to do with his philosophy.

I'll start by telling you Thomas Jefferson's philosophy begins <u>outside</u> of space and time with what you call God in Heaven. God imposes something called "natural law" on everything, including you here <u>inside</u> of space and time on Earth, Harry. And God's "natural law" puts a "natural obligation" on you to pursue Virtue — those moral, ethical, and character virtues we've been talking about — what Aristotle and Epicurus broadly referred to as Happiness.[62] As a reward for pursuing Virtue, God's "natural law" gives you something in return called "natural rights". Presidential candidate Thomas Jefferson told you about them during the 1800 campaign. Remember? They're things like: the right to life; the right to liberty; the right to property; the right to change governments; and, the right to <u>real</u> self-government. But Thomas Jefferson is a natural born engineer. I mean, he's not just good at the new philosophy of engineering ... he's good at engineering his philosophy. And he always engineers his philosophy toward some <u>practical</u> goal in life. So he engineered all those natural rights into a practical philosophy called his "vision for America".

* I remember.

* The generation of 1776 had a revolution to get the natural rights of life, liberty, property, change, and real self-government. Thomas Jefferson says they still don't <u>fully</u> have all of them. And they don't have <u>real</u> self-government <u>at all</u>! Without real self-government, he says the revolution still isn't finished — even though the shooting part is over![63] So, he wants to engineer his philosophy to give the generation of 1776 the rest of what they bled for during the shooting part of the revolution. He wants to finally give them and future generations real self-government — true direct participatory democracy. He calls it "ward-democracy"! That would finish what he considers to be "the Constitution's interesting first effort". That would complete his "vision for America". It would finish the "unfinished revolution"! [64]

* Then does he jump right in and push for true participatory democracy — ward-democracy — with his colleagues, like he jumped right in and pushed the "1802 Military Act" with Secretary Dearborn?

* Not yet. But this is how he discusses the "unfinished revolution" with his stable of colleagues:

> "Gentlemen. We ditched George <u>III</u> for virtuous self-government. But this is not it!"
>> "No. We have recently seen but a grotesque imitation of it, Mr. President!"
> "It has been a travesty! Now, all factions must come together in the spirit of 1776!"
>> "That was the point in your Inaugural Address, was it not Mr. President?"
> "Indeed it was, Mr. Madison! °°And whether Party zealots like it or not, it shall be in my First Annual Address, also.°° We know where we are, and where we wish to go. The question is, what is the best way to get there? What is the best way to give our fellow Americans all the 'goodies' they've been waiting for?"[65]

By "goodies" Thomas Jefferson means ward-democracy — the <u>final</u> part of his "vision for America". But he can't push for ward-democracy before he takes care of two other parts of his "vision for America" that are urgent! The <u>first</u> part is to stop America's <u>current</u> slide back to a British-style monarchistic setup. That means "cleaning house" — cleaning out monarchists, incompetents, and the dishonest from the civil service, law courts, and the Army! The <u>second</u> part is to find a way to keep them out and to "preserve, protect, and defend" America's Republic and its Constitution, <u>permanently</u>! That means finding a way to <u>permanently</u> prevent anyone, domestic or foreign, from overthrowing the government or conquering the United States of America!

The <u>first</u> part of his "vision for America", cleaning out monarchists, incompetents, and the dishonest using his Chaste Reformation, has been coming along nicely. Now comes the <u>second</u> part. He has to find a way to <u>keep</u> them out, and to "preserve, protect, and defend" the Republic and Constitution against all other threats, <u>permanently</u>! If he can do those things, he'll at least preserve what America has already achieved. He'll preserve the Constitution's "interesting first effort".

* "Cleaning house" using his Chaste Reformation doesn't do those things?

* A little rain doesn't wash away the stripes of the tiger, does it Harry. Thomas Jefferson's "cleaning house" doesn't reform anyone, as in wash away their old ideas and convert them to his way of thinking. Rich, monarchistic, big-business, pseudo-aristocrats might still resort to force, like they did during Shays' Rebellion, in order to squash any movement toward a real participatory ward-democracy. Or they might even challenge the Republic as it now stands. In other words, he must beware of a counter-reformation by all those people who still dream of taking over and re-organizing America into a British-style setup. He also must find a way to permanently guard America from being conquered by some foreign army such as Spain's, France's, or England's. Then there are the hostile Indians on the frontiers. Who knows what they'll get up to next? And

before America can finally have true participatory democracy, he needs a way to prevent even democracy from becoming mobocracy — militant anarchy. He said America has to "beware a military force, even of citizens"! So he needs a way for Americans to <u>permanently</u> protect their Republic and Constitution, not only from foreigners, but even from other Americans!

* How could other Americans, or anyone, take over?

* Remember how they did it in Boston in the 1770's to get the revolution against England going? Well, that's one way. But you don't need to know all the ways of overthrowing governments. The most important thing for you to know is, when push comes to shove, everything comes down to raw physical power. And that means everything comes down to the Army!

For instance, someone could work his way into controlling the existing Standing Army. He could use the Army's raw physical power to grab political power, as the Roman generals used to do, and as Cromwell did. He could scrap the Constitution and the Republic ... make himself dictator. It only takes someone clever and ambitious with the Army behind him. A Caesar. A Cromwell. A Napoleon. John Adams and Thomas Jefferson both believed ... even feared ... Alexander Hamilton might do that in America with the New Army!

And how about anarchy? We already witnessed near-misses of anarchy — mobocracy — taking over in America. Shays' Rebellion. The Whiskey Rebellion. Fries' Rebellion. We saw how the Revolution over in France started off in 1789 as a good thing for the people, then turned into bloody chaos and anarchy and dictatorship by Napoleon and his army.

No, Harry. Before President Jefferson can push laws to give the people <u>real</u> self-government — true participatory democracy — he has to find how to "preserve, protect, and defend" for all time — permanently — what America has already earned! That has to be his top priority. Now he appreciates the wisdom in Benjamin Franklin's statement, "you have a Republic, if you can <u>keep</u> it"![66]

* So Washington found a way to win independence. Now it's up to Jefferson to find a way to secure it, permanently. Is that it?

* That's it. Whether the threat to America is from tyrants or anarchists, civil or military, foreign or domestic, Thomas Jefferson now believes the ultimate insurance against invasion from the outside, or overthrow from the inside, is a regular and permanent Standing Army! He now sees a crucial role for a Standing Army in his philosophy and "vision for America"!

* How do we know that? Wasn't he always in favor of militias? Don't he and other Democratic-Republicans, and even "republican" Federalists, still fear standing armies? Didn't everyone expect him to completely scrap the existing Standing Army?

* Everything you say is true. He and others do still fear the traditional standing army. Alexander Hamilton's New Army, and other incidents, certainly dredged up that fear all over again. And he still sees a role for militias. However, he's not as much against standing armies as people think. As far back as 1784 he actually had a plan of defense that would use a regular standing army on America's borders! And now the Indian Wars, Anthony Wayne's successful "Legion", the Genet Affair, the Quasi War with France, his disappointments over militias, and his urgent priority to permanently guard against all foreign or domestic enemies were enough to convince him an American Standing Army is needed. Witness, he did-n't ditch the existing Standing Army in his 1802 Military Act and rely on militias, as many of his Democratic-Republican colleagues expected him to. In fact, the 1802 Military Act basically "says" America needs a regular Standing Army, does-n't it! We don't need to prove that premiss. It's self-evident … or there would-n't be an 1802 Military Act in the first place! So self-evident, also, is the follow-ing true and valid deductive proof that President Jefferson is for a Standing Army:

> (premiss) - President Jefferson created the 1802 Military Act
> (premiss) - the 1802 Military Act "says" America needs a
> Standing Army
> _____
> (conclusion) - President Jefferson "says" America needs a
> Standing Army

Keeping a Standing Army is the only way President Jefferson can have America permanently guard against all enemies domestic or foreign. Therefore he needs a Standing Army that he and America can permanently trust! He needs a Standing Army that will be permanently loyal to the Constitution and Republic! It needs to be a new special American kind of Standing Army — a <u>Good</u> Standing Army … yes, as in the philosophical "Good"! And that, my friend, is a completely dif-ferent kettle of fish than ever before in history, as far as standing armies are con-cerned!

* I can see it is! It just takes one guy like Caesar, Napoleon, or Cromwell, and a bunch of bad-leaders in the Officer Corps to follow him … and poof … all of America's hard work and sacrifice goes up in smoke!

* That's right. And you've just put your finger on it. As an officer corps goes, so goes an army! Alexander the Great understood that. He indoctrinated sons of elite families at his Royal Pages officer school to bind their loyalty to him, per-sonally. Roman Generals, including Caesar, understood it. They could not have come to power without their officer corps' backing. Kings throughout history understood it. They held on to power by making their friends the officers in their armies. Washington understood it. He prevented the Army from overthrowing Congress by dissolving his Officer Corps' Newburgh Conspiracy. He wrote, "no instance has yet happened of good or bad behavior in a corps of our service that has not originated with the Officer". Napoleon understood it. He used his offi-cer corps, and thereby the army, to make himself the dictator of all Europe! And Thomas Jefferson understands it. He said, "the militia were heroes only when they had heroes to lead them". So logic [a priori] and historical facts [a posteri-ori] prove that the key to any army's trust and loyalty is its officer corps!

* Of course. My era would call that common knowledge.

* So does President Jefferson! He knows the key to removing fear of a Standing Army and creating a Good Standing Army is his Officer Corps! Witness … we previously proved from documented facts that President Jefferson's Chaste Reformation of the Army specifically removes monarchistic, incompetent, or dis-

honest Officers in order to end up with the right kind of Officer Corps. So the following premiss is true and valid:

> (premiss) - President Jefferson's Chaste Reformation of the
> Army is to have the right kind of Officer Corps

And witness also, the reason for his Chaste Reformation in the first place was to <u>remove fear</u> of the civil service, law courts, and Standing Army. Remember? So we know the following premiss is also true and valid:

> (premiss) - President Jefferson's Chaste Reformation of the
> Army is to remove fear of a Standing Army

Putting these true and valid premisses together gives us:

> (premiss) - President Jefferson's Chaste Reformation of the
> Army is to have the right kind of Officer Corps
> (premiss) - President Jefferson's Chaste Reformation of the
> Army is to remove fear of a Standing Army
> _____
> (conclusion) - the right kind of Officer Corps removes fear of a
> Standing Army

He'll later also say this: "in raising standing armies, while our functionaries [Officers] are honest and vigilant and wise [the right kind], we have nothing to fear".[67] In other words, he'll essentially say what we just took the trouble to prove, namely:

> - the right kind of Officer Corps removes fear of a
> Standing Army

* I agree. He confirms our conclusion ... straight from his own lips. But now that leads me straight to two other questions:

> 1. How do you get the right kind of Officers?
> 2. What <u>are</u> the right kind of Officers?

* You've hit on the key questions. And, I'll now show you that President Jefferson's answer to both those questions is what his father, Peter Jefferson, once willed to a young Tom Jefferson .... EDUCATION!
* Education? You're telling me <u>education</u> is Jefferson's answer to what are, and how we get, the right kind of Officers?
* Yes. And that in turn will clear the way for him to give the generation of 1776 and future generations the last part of his "vision for America" — true participatory ward-democracy! You see, education is not only his answer to what are, and how to get, the right kind of Officers. It's <u>also</u> at the heart of true participatory

ward-democracy. For he always said the Constitution with its indirect and "electoral" voting is an interesting first effort toward some form of democracy. But ward-democracy, with an educated citizenry, is the best political insurance against monarchism and political tyranny. It's the ultimate check on the Constitution's checks and balances. He was originally putting his ideas on education to practical use in order to make ward-democracy work. Now, ironically, he can also put them to use in order to make a Standing Army work! And here are the nuts and bolts of how he does that!

Back in 1778 when he was reforming education in Virginia, Thomas Jefferson said that everyone must get a "basic education" in order to make ward-democracy work. He had sponsored a law, his Bill 79, that provided a "basic education" for everyone. There would be "basic schools" in all local wards. Everyone would learn to read, to write, to judge morally, and to vote understandingly on the issues. Therefore, "basic education" would be kind of like a conduit that connects all generations of Americans. America's core values and heritage of democracy would flow from generation to generation through the conduit of "basic education".

* I remember that. And I would say that's crucial!
* Absolutely crucial, Harry. In another law called Bill 80, Thomas Jefferson said there's also another reason for education. He tells us to look at past democracies such as in Rome and in ancient Greece. They show us that, under morally decayed and politically corrupt leaders, a democracy can decay as easily as iron rusts. So, besides basic education, he had put a kind of "rust and decay preventative" in Bills 79 and 80. It was "advanced education" ... at "advanced schools"!
* What are "advanced schools"?
* Colleges, academies, or universities. After basic schools, the "more worthy and fitly formed" students would be sent to regional "portal schools", then on to "advanced schools".[68] On not just one occasion, but on many occasions to many people, he gave his reasons for "advanced schools". His reasons are actually his definition of what "advanced schools" are. Here's what he said, in his own words:

DEFINITION OF ADVANCED SCHOOLS

from: Thomas Jefferson's own writings

– GENERALLY, the purpose of "advanced schools" is:

"to breed Aristotle's Happiness — namely, virtues, knowledge, and a sense of public service."[69]
"to have the means for government to make the core principle of a republic — Virtue — the main object of education", as also Montesquieu said in his Spirit of the Laws.[70]
"to allow those persons who are able to guard the sacred deposit of the rights and liberties of fellow citizens

to be called to that service **to leadership** without regard to their wealth, birth, or other accidental condition or circumstance".[71]

– SPECIFICALLY, "advanced schools" are intended to:

"teach national and individual morals, ethics, and character", as also John Locke advised in his Politics and Education.[72]

"point out the relationship between the fall of past empires and the lack of virtues in their **leaders**."[73]

"imprint 'amor patriae' — love of Country — on student's minds while young, instead of trying to compel their loyalty at some later date", as also Cicero said in the Tusculan Disputations.[74]

"imbed in students a disregard of [great] wealth, an unfaltering devotion to right and wrong, an inflexibility in the face of danger, and a Stoic's conception of duty and service", as also Roman historian, Tacitus, advised in The Histories.[75]

"practice and condition moral behavior — exercise the 'moral spring'— and develope a habit of thinking and acting virtuously", as also Aristotle advised in his Nicomachean Ethics.[76]

"provide talented **leadership** — (good-leaders) — from amongst the people themselves" like Lycurgus did in Sparta, as Plato in The Republic and Rousseau in Emile both also advised.[77]

"endow these future guardian **leaders** of America with 'science and virtue' in order to watch and preserve that sacred deposit of the people's rights."[78]

"teach the curriculum of subjects in the light of a democracy in a republic".[79]

"adapt studies to technical and professional goals, not just liesurely, aristocratic, cultural fancies".[80]

The virtue is: Service. Leaders with a will to serve the nation need to have Virtue and Knowledge.

So, Harry, lay aside so-called expert opinion and intellectual speculation. Read what Thomas Jefferson says himself, here and in many other writings, about "advanced schools". He flat-out tells us his reason for "advanced schools" is to produce the right kind of leaders! Therefore:

(premiss) - President Jefferson's reason for "advanced schools" is to produce the right kind of leaders

357

I'm sure you can agree with that?

* I have no choice but to agree. That's what he says here in his own words, and in his Bills 79 and 80.

* Let me say, however, he's not talking about just any educated guys to be leaders. All through his writings he says the idea is to produce leaders having Virtue and Knowledge — having "<u>honest</u> hearts and <u>knowing</u> heads". He says such leaders would be able to "pursue the interests of our Country with the purest integrity, the most chaste honor". That's what we've been calling good-leaders! And there's a lifetime of letters between him and education pundits, Joel Barlow and Pierre DuPont, about what "advanced education" to him boils down to. We have tons of documented proof showing:[81]

>(premiss) - President Jefferson's reason for "advanced schools"
>is to produce **leaders of Virtue and Knowledge**

If we put the last two premisses together, we have:

>(premiss) - President Jefferson's reason for "advanced schools"
>is to produce **leaders of Virtue and Knowledge**
>(premiss) - President Jefferson's reason for "advanced schools"
>is to produce the right kind of leaders
>
>_____
>
>(conclusion) - **leaders of Virtue and Knowledge** are the right
>kind of leaders

In the Army, the leaders are the Officers. Therefore:

>(premiss) - **leaders of Virtue and Knowledge** are the right kind
>of <u>Officers</u>

Let's put this together with our previous true premiss about removing fear of a Standing Army. We come up with a simple, but true and valid, conclusion about leaders of Virtue and Knowledge:

>(premiss) - **leaders of Virtue and Knowledge** are the right kind
>of Officers
>(premiss) - the right kind of Officers remove fear of a Standing
>Army
>
>_____
>
>(conclusion) - **leaders of Virtue and Knowledge** remove fear of a
>Standing Army

And that, Harry, is the nuts and bolts of how President Jefferson makes education work to make a Standing Army work, and how it answers the two questions you previously asked:

1. How do you get the right kind of Officers?
2. What are the right kind of Officers?

You get the right kind of Officers by developing them at an "advanced school". And, the right kind of Officers are **leaders of Virtue and Knowledge**. They are: apolitical and politically inactive; loyal to only the Constitution and its democratic Republic; possessed with the moral, ethical, and character virtues that have to be practiced daily to become habit … as Thomas Jefferson, Washington, Steuben, Plato, Aristotle, Epictetus, and Epicurus preached; able to function under stress to protect their young soldiers' lives, as Washington did in the Revolution and Wayne did at "Fallen Timbers"; and, able to win!

* So, tell me if I have this right? Jefferson says the right kind of Officers for a Good Standing Army are leaders of Virtue and Knowledge? We can develope those leaders at what he calls an "advanced school"? Therefore, you're telling me, he founded the U.S. Military Academy as an "advanced school" to produce Officers who are leaders of Virtue and Knowledge?

* That's right, Harry.

* But, is the Military Academy really an "advanced school"? Does it measure up to Jefferson's own Definition of Advanced Schools? It doesn't seem to be like Oxford, Cambridge, Yale, Harvard, or any of those other advanced schools.

* At this early stage you can't expect it to compare with long established colleges. But does it have to? Does Thomas Jefferson even want it to? Remember, his "advanced school" is purposely different than existing traditional advanced schools!

* True. But I still ask you, does it meet his own definition of an "advanced school"?

* Let's take a look! We can zoom-in closer to see what he says about "advanced schools" with respect to coursework. Here goes!

Back in 1779 Virginia, Thomas Jefferson was bent on making big changes in coursework at "advanced schools" using his Bill 80. He was changing William and Mary College, for instance, from offering only the musty old classics for aristocrats, to teaching "science and virtue" for the technical and professional needs of a growing Nation. He was the first to push specialization. And he was the first to push remedial "portal-school" subjects right at William and Mary for students who needed more background! He boldly abandoned the old straight-laced, four-year progression of subjects![82] He made sure a student's needs and professional goals, not tradition, would dictate which subjects to take, and for how long![83]

In the late 1790's and early 1800's, Thomas Jefferson had to update some ideas from his Bill 80 that was bent on liberating "advanced schools".[84] For instance, he always said society would have two intellectual classes — the "laboring" class and the "learned" class. If you're in the laboring class, you would only attend the "basic schools". If you're in the learned class, you would go on to "advanced schools". You would become one of the traditional professionals in law, medicine, ministry, or the arts.[85] But now, a changing Nation has forced Thomas Jefferson to change, also! He now says society needs a third intellectual class — the technological professionals! So he gets some ideas on technological education from scholarly friends Joseph Priestly and Pierre DuPont DeNemours. He borrows a few things from the technical side of Benjamin Franklin's Philadelphia Academy. He even uses some suggestions from a French philosopher friend, Destutt de Tracy. Combining their ideas with his own, he engineers a new plan to change "advanced schools"![86] To his Bill 80 for changing an "advanced school" like William and Mary, he: adds a track of study in technology alongside the traditional tracks in pre-law, pre-medicine, and so on; cuts out or modifies many traditional classical subjects; has "portal schools" grafted onto the early years of college-work for people who need more preparation; and, gives artisans a chance to study their technological specialty in more detail . It's a typical utilitarian engineered Thomas Jefferson plan![87]

Examples of new "advanced schools" are Albemarle Academy and Central College in Virginia. They're both portal school and college! Typically, Thomas Jefferson has his friend and teacher, Thomas Cooper, double as an instructor on the portal-school side and as a professor on the regular college side. Students aged 16-19 have their "advanced education" tailored to meet their needs. They get a general education, and a track of subjects leading to one of the professions — now to include a technological profession — for as long or short a time as they need.[88]

* I see. So by the time Jefferson founds the Military Academy, he has a tried and proven track record with "advanced schools" and knows exactly what he wants. And it looks to me like he wants "advanced schools" to be <u>hybrids</u> ... part portal-school ... part college, academy, or university ... part professional school.

* That's right. He's for any mix of those three that meets a student's needs.[89]

* Then is that what the Military Academy is — one of Thomas Jefferson's new hybrid type of "advanced schools"?

* We'll have a look inside the Academy to see. Let's eavesdrop on a few cadets to get their slant on what they do here:

> "What's cookin'?"
> "The ranks of our small corps are further thinned by one."
> "I know. Cadet Lillie, the foolish little twit, packed it in. But he was only here because his father, the former West Point commander, died. He had nowhere to go. So Dearborn and Jefferson took pity on him. There have been a few other special cadets who don't belong here!"
> "That's a few too many! ᵒᵒAnd probably not the last of them.ᵒᵒ However, I wasn't referring to Lillie. I was talking about my mess mate."
> "Oh! Right! Your mess mate told me, a while back, he didn't like it here! Pity. He cuts a smart appearance in these expensive uniforms we have. Our long tailed, single breasted, high collared, blue coat with our shining eagle buttons suits him."
> "<u>Suited</u> him!"
> ᵒᵒHe's history?ᵒᵒ "Oh, right! <u>Suited</u> him! Well, I know the discipline <u>didn't</u> suit him! He couldn't cut the duties, military drills, punishments, confinements...."

"He'll do fine in civilian life. The military just wasn't his cup of tea. I don't like discipline either. But, I'll stick it out. It's part of the deal."

"You're not supposed to like it. You're supposed to be able to take it. It's now the American way of becoming an Officer. That's why Jefferson established this place ... so Officers won't be like they used to be. It's something entirely new. Like America is entirely new. You have to be able to <u>take</u> orders before you can <u>give</u> orders ... like General Washington said. You know the drill! You've heard it a dozen times!"

°°At <u>least</u> that many!°° "And I don't mind the late afternoon classes on duty. Or Steuben's reg.'s. Or the sermons and moral lectures at the tables. It's all that other knit-picking bothers me. It's no wonder close to half the cadets don't stop here — pack it in! They call us 'gentlemen cadets'? I don't feel that way. Do you?"

"Don't we have enlisted men waiting on us ... one to a mess of four? Don't we have these prestigious uniforms? Aren't we taking turns leading real companies of soldiers? Aren't we learning character? Aren't we learning a profession?"

"I guess your right."

"Besides. Being styled 'gentleman Officer' now means being an Officer having character and virtues! It's not being a pampered aristocrat ... like those officers back in '96 who resisted being trained!" °°And probably burnt down the classroom building to get out of training and discipline!°°

"They must have thought they were above it all ... like Tories do. Well, at least the Academy's not a Tory school. Politics aren't even discussed here!"

"But we <u>do</u> get newspapers of both Parties, don't we!"

"Yes. But no Tory one, thank heavens."

"It's more like thanks to President Jefferson!"[90]

361

* That gives me some idea of life at West Point. But they're only talking about Virtue and Leadership ... not academics!

* Ah! But at Mr. Jefferson's Academy, Virtue and Leadership are part of the academics! He's forging a whole new kind of Officer Corps, Harry. He's working toward a time when America's Army Officers will no longer be merely appointed and put in charge of men straight away. They'll have to earn their Commissions! They'll have to learn through books and instruction to be the right kind of Officers. They'll have to live and practice being the right kind of Officers. They'll have to be professional leaders having Virtue and Knowledge: moral, ethical, and character Virtue; military, intellectual, and technical Knowledge. The Military Academy's curriculum has to be a new synthesis of Virtue, technology, and the military arts!

Back in December 1802 Superintendent Jonathan Williams talked about some of his own and President Jefferson's thinking on the Academy. He lets in some additional light on the subject.[91]

STATEMENT RELATIVE TO THE MILITARY ACADEMY

from: Superintendent Jonathan Williams
December 14, 1802

Even instruction in science, mathematics, and the art of war and fortifications cannot fullfill the objective we contemplate. Efficient military [leadership] requires a wider scale. President Jefferson founded a military academy for that certain wider objective [leadership].

The first requisite in composing such a body of men is Character.

The virtue is: Obligation. Government is obliged to provide good-leaders for the military.

America's military Officers need to be rare birds! And that's why we need to look at every kind of instruction cadets get. We're comparing the Academy with Thomas Jefferson's Definition of Advanced Schools. We're not comparing it with the well known traditional colleges — the ones he wants to change! He typically starts modestly, like he did with Monticello and with his five-year agricultural plan. Remember? He keeps himself low profile ... has Dearborn write all the letters. However, he keeps a watchful eye over everything!

* He keeps a low profile? Why? Don't you find that curious?

* No. The fox doesn't announce he's found a back door to the hen house, does he! Nor does he try to get all the hens at once! Thomas Jefferson's low profile is why information on academics at the Academy is sparse. However, we have records, notations in the margins of books, and so forth. From those sources we

know the following books and subjects, and most likely others, are studied at the Academy in the early years:[92]

EARLY STUDIES AT WEST POINT

from: (see notes)

I – <u>CLASSROOM STUDIES</u> –

1.) <u>Technical</u> –

C.H. Hutton, <u>Mathematics</u>, London (1800) – You have to know math for technology. But like Rene Descartes and Baruch Spinoza, Thomas Jefferson always said math is also a tool for developing character traits like mental discipline, perseverence, and so forth.[93]

Professor George Baron was C.H.Hutton's colleague in London. He knew the Hutton book, he had mathematical discipline, and was not a monarchist. Yet, he lacked moral standards. He was fired for "conduct unworthy an Officer, setting an example injurious to the morals of cadets and disgraceful to the Institution". This episode reveals the Academy's intentions concerning morals, ethics, and character.[94]

W. Enfield, <u>Natural Philosophy</u> – You have to know science for technology. But science also develops mental discipline and ability to reason. Professor Jared Mansfield gave this course. It's an introduction to the physics of technical subjects like statics, mechanics, structures, motion, hydraulics, hydrostatics, and so on. While teaching at Yale he had published a book, <u>Essays Mathematical and Physical</u>. President Jefferson has purchased a number of copies. It's hard to believe Mansfield doesn't lecture from his own book at the Academy, besides the Enfield book.

S. de Vauban, Treatise of Fortifications, France – Superintendent and Professor, Jonathan Williams, must have also used his own book, <u>Elements of Fortifications</u> (1801) to teach cadets how to apply their math, drawing, and natural philosophy toward

363

designing and constructing roads, buildings, and fortifications.[95]

H.O. de Scheel, <u>Treatise of Artillery</u>, France – Williams did a published translation from French. Again, it's hard to believe his translation is not used at least for lectures on Artillery.

Drawing – There are drawing instruments so there must be a book, or perhaps lectures with notetaking.

Surveying – There are field instruments so again there must be a book, or perhaps just lectures with notetaking.[96]

2.) <u>Virtue</u> –

Francois Desiree Masson, <u>Masson's Grammar and Reader</u>, France (1797) – The French language is also a tool. It will allow cadets to read books on technology, as well as, books about morals and history that are in French.[97] Masson was appointed Professor of French in 1803. Thomas Jefferson likes books that give moral lessons while teaching a language. Greek and Latin classics that taught <u>him</u> individual and national morals are now being translated into French. Even the "French method" of math and natural philosophy is still in French in Bezout's <u>Mathematics</u> and Muschenbroek's <u>Physics</u>. And Thomas leans toward these French textbooks for those able to go beyond Hutton's <u>Mathematics</u>.[98] Masson used his own book. But he also used the following book that taught morals and French at the same time.

Francois Fenelon, <u>Adventures of Telemachus, Son of Ulysses</u>, Boston (1797) – This isn't surprising! The "fingerprints" of Thomas Jefferson — lifelong education mentor — are all over this one! <u>Telemachus</u> is one of his alltime favorites as a teaching tool: he read it in <u>his</u> youth; with Don Quixote, it's one of his favorite "works of imagination"; he always required it for the dozens of students he privately tutored; like his other teaching favorites, Defoe's <u>Robinson Crusoe</u> and Rousseau's <u>Emile</u>, it

portrays the mentor system he favors for teaching ...
like Professors Small and Wythe mentored him.
<u>Telemachus</u> tells about the virtues and pitfalls of
republics, monarchies, and tyrannies that son,
Telemachus, encountered while searching the ancient
world for father, Ulysses. The novel merges together
epic, history, and fantasy to encourage moral imitation. It teaches love of Country. It shows students
how to live and practice good morals and character
in order to learn them.[99]

Michael Martel, <u>Martel's Elements in Three
Volumes</u>, New York (1796) – Vol.I is "Essays on
History and Moral Philosophy"; Vol.II is, "French
Language"; Vol.III is "Anecdotes". Thomas
Jefferson believed that learning languages and his-
tory also serves as training in morals and leader-
ship.

Baron Von Steuben's, <u>Regulations and Drill</u>, as
updated – Lectures on drill, duties, and regulations
have been given during the late afternoon hours
ever since there was a school at West Point. We
know that lectures on "discipline" and "gentlemanly" conduct are meant to build moral, ethical, and
character virtues. Any of the non-technical aspects
of the "military arts" — tactics, military history,
and so forth — would be covered during this
time.[100]

II – <u>FIELD STUDIES</u> –

1.) <u>Technical</u> –

During the mid-afternoon hours cadets take to
the outdoors. They do practical field surveying.
They sketch-out topographical drawings. They
learn practical construction and construction management. They do practical artillery exercises. In
short, they do experimentation and get hands-on
experience.[101]

2.) <u>Leadership</u>–

During late afternoons cadets do individual and
Company level military drill and discipline. They

act as non-comissioned and comissioned Officers. They get hands-on leadership training by often commanding real Companies.[102] Jonathan Williams said this in December 1802 when he wrote he has "two Captains employed as academic professors, therefore two other Captains are required to perform the military duties, along with the two 1st Lieutenants, two 2nd Lieutenants, and 4 cadets for the management (leadership) of the troops."[103] Physical fitness is achieved through the military drills and through afternoon field sports.[104]

III – EXTRA-CURRICULAR ACTIVITIES –

Cadets have two unique opportunities for extra activities of an academic nature. They are:

1.) <u>Library</u> – Secretary Dearborn, always under President Jefferson's instructions, told Jonathan Williams to set up a library. Williams has a personal library, given to him by his uncle Benjamin Franklin. He makes it available to cadets. Those wishing to "render themselves more serviceable by their own industry" can become more advanced through independent study. As nephew and secretary to Benjamin Franklin who founded the American Philosophical Society, and himself an officer of the Society, Williams' library is unique. It's a valuable opportunity for cadets to enrich their knowledge.[105]

2.) <u>American Military Philosophical Society</u> – Jonathan Williams initiated this Society as a "valuable adjunct" to the Academy. It "promotes intellectual discourse" in technology and natural philosophy. It's a golden opportunity for cadets at West Point that students at other colleges do not have available to them. That's because it meets here at West Point! It's membership has distinguished men like Thomas Jefferson, James Madison, James Monroe, John Quincy Adams, Robert Fulton, Eli Whitney, and over 200 others, both foreign and domestic.[106]

The virtue is: Patience. The longest journey starts with the first small steps ... even in education.

These <u>Early Studies</u> are vintage utilitarian engineered Jefferson thinking. What it boils down to, he kills two birds with one stone throughout. For instance, he uses math for technological studies <u>and</u> for mental discipline. And he teaches the French language for being able to study technological books <u>and</u> for reading books that teach morals, ethics, and character.

* You didn't mention how many years cadets have to be at the Military Academy.
* They put in more time than first meets the eye, Harry. Cadets have 4 hours of classroom instruction in the mornings and about 3 hours of field and classroom instruction in the afternoons.[107] That goes on 6 days a week, 36 weeks a year. That's about 7 hours per day x 6 days per week = 42 hours per week; about 42 hours x 36 weeks = about 1500 hours per school year.[108] A student on 15 credits per semester at the typical college or university during your modern era, Harry, has about 15 hours of instruction per week. The school year during your modern era is only about 30 weeks. So, that's 15 hours x 30 weeks = about 450 hours per year. That's not much! Compare 1500 hours and 450 hours. It means a cadet back here in the early years of West Point has as many hours of instruction in one year as a student in your modern era has in about three years. A cadet's informal military instruction, training, practice, and discipline would add even many more hours!

Now for study-time. We'll be more than fair. We'll add just 1/2 hr. study-time for each of those 1500 hrs. instruction a cadet gets. That means the total time he puts in is 2250 hours. We'll add 1-1/2 hours study time for each of the 450 hours instruction your modern student gets. That makes the total 1125 hours. Compare 2250 and 1125 hours. Excluding military things, a cadet back here puts in as much time in one year as your modern student does in two years. And even back here at William and Mary, for example, they have only math, language, and natural philosophy during the first couple of years. Some even just attend the portal-school. That's similar to the Academy![109] In that respect the Military Academy is not much different than a college like William and Mary during many students' early years.

* Yes. I can see that. And, although it's not a school of engineering, or science, or the classics, the Academy has a little of them all. That's different! The biggest difference, though, is what you told me about the schedule. It's very compressed! It's too difficult! They need to spread it out!
* President Jefferson and Dearborn are working within very narrow limits. It's a constant juggling act. They need Army Officers when current ones resign, retire, or are run out for various reasons. They designed the "1802 Military Act" to fill that need. And within the Act, the Military Academy itself is designed to fill that need. The Act gives the President exceptional powers to fill that need. He can promote Officers of his new [Engineers and Artillerists] Corps at West Point straight up to higher ranks. He's not bound by the rules of rank and seniority as in the rest of the Army. The guys he promotes to higher ranks in his new Corps can be moved into other units outside of that Corps ... but keep their higher rank! He then refills his Corps with new graduates from the Military Academy. Soon his West Point leaders of Virtue and Knowledge should be running the Army! And that, after all, is the whole idea!

So, President Jefferson and Secretary Dearborn have to juggle three things: one, how many Military Academy cadets they need to commission into the Standing Army, and when; two, how much time they need to "mold" cadets at the Military Academy; and three, how much education their new cadets had before coming to the Military Academy.[110]

* Then I can see that the program in the early years of the Military Academy has to be very flexible.

* And it is. For example, President Jefferson often has to commission Officers out of the Academy in about one year. That's why so many early appointees to the Academy have already been to "advanced schools" — colleges — before coming to West Point. Take, for example: Sylvanus Thayer who graduated from Dartmouth, first in his class; Alden Partridge and William Partridge who both graduated from Dartmouth; Satterlee Clark who graduated from Burlington College; Luther Dyer from Norwich Academy; Luther Hitchcock from Middlebury College; John Wyndham from college in London; Thomas Beall from Washington Academy; Alpheus Roberts from Dartmouth College; Richard Ashley from Williams; George Hight from Washington College; Federick Lewis from the Academy in Paris; Erastus Roberts who was in Law School; Cobb and Sawyer from Burlington College; Chandler and Herman from Washington College; Kingsbury, Greenwood, Walcott, and Burton from Dartmouth; and many others.[111] These are cadets who already had "advanced school" — college — studies in the mathematics, moral philosophy, and natural philosophy parts of the Academy's curriculum. They only need the professional part. That is, they only need studies and practice in: leadership; technology; American military indoctrination; and, morals, ethics, and character.[112] You'll ask, how can they become leaders of Virtue and Knowledge so soon? Is one year enough time? According to Plato, Aristotle, Epictetus, and Locke it isn't! But to get the Academy into the business of helping keep the Army a Good Standing Army, it will have to do … for now![113]

So, a lot of guys who already have college education make it through West Point in about one year. That's broadly the same as two years in your modern era, Harry. In fact, thirty-seven of fifty who graduate during Thomas Jefferson's presidency make it in less than two years. That's broadly the same as less than four years in your modern era. The guys who are not full college graduates had at least some college work before coming to the Academy. Therefore, all thirty-seven begin instruction at either the college or professional level at the Academy. The remaining thirteen of the fifty will take more than two years to make it through. Those thirteen attended only "basic schools" before the Academy. Therefore they need Thomas Jefferson's complete hybrid type "advanced school" treatment — portal-level, college-level, and, finally, professional track.[114]

Some college graduate appointees are cadets who can actually also assist with instruction of other cadets! For example, Satterlee Clark's letter of recommendation from Burlington College certifies that he is "qualified to teach".[115]

* I see. Then the bottom line of all this is that Jefferson had "basic schools" and "advanced schools" in his philosophy of education. The U.S. Military Academy is <u>not</u> a "basic school". <u>Early Studies at West Point</u> tell me that. Besides, all cadets who entered already had "basic school" education. Most of them even had at least some college work. So the Academy <u>has</u> to be what Jefferson calls an "advanced school".

* The Academy is actually a good example of one! It meets all the criteria in his <u>Definition of Advanced Schools</u>! Yes, the Academy is an "advanced school". Thomas Jefferson tells you that himself in his own words!

* And it doesn't matter that he uses the word "academy" in the title, instead of the word "college"?

* No. In fact, Thomas Jefferson also tells you in his own words why he uses the word "academy". He says: "an academy is an <u>advanced school</u> that can offer many disciplines".[116] And, "many disciplines", describes the Military Academy perfectly. It's a portal school, a college, and a professional school all in one. They teach math, science, humanities, technology, the military arts, and leadership. It's a prototype of his new hybrid type of "advanced school"! So I'm sure you'll agree that both logic [a priori] and fact [a posteriori] prove:

> (premiss) - the United States Military Academy is an "advanced school"

* I agree! The proof is abundant. As you said, Jefferson tells me that in his own words!

* Then guess what else he tells you, Harry! He finally tells you the reason **WHY** he founded the United States Military Academy! The two premisses that we have just proven to be true and valid absolutely guarantees the conclusion as to **WHY** he founded it is also true and valid:

> (premiss) - President Jefferson's reason for "advanced schools" is to produce **leaders of Virtue and Knowledge**
>
> (premiss) - the United States Military Academy is an "advanced school"
>
> _____
>
> (conclusion) - President Jefferson's reason for the United States Military Academy is to produce **leaders of Virtue and Knowledge**

In fact, we can even widen that conclusion, using what we have now proven!

> (premiss) - President Jefferson's reason for the United States Military Academy is to produce **leaders of Virtue and Knowledge**
>
> (premiss) - **leaders of Virtue and Knowledge** remove fear of a Standing Army
>
> _____
>
> (conclusion) - President Jefferson's reason for the United States Military Academy is to produce **leaders of Virtue and Knowledge** to remove fear of a Standing Army

So now you know **WHY** President Jefferson founded the United States Military Academy, Harry! It wasn't strictly for the military arts, although the military arts are, of course, taught. It wasn't as an engineering college, although construction and artillery and fortifications are also taught. It wasn't a school of Enlightenment science, although there is some math and science taught. And it wasn't for Party politics, although political monarchists are not welcome. It's what you guessed at, a while back. It basically boils down to **PHILOSOPHY**! Thomas Jefferson engineered his philosophy of education to produce the **leaders of Virtue and Knowledge** that are needed to remove fear of a Standing Army and create a Good Standing Army in order to permanently preserve, protect, and defend the Republic and Constitution from all threats. And that in turn will clear the way for him to finally give the generation of 1776 and future generations the last part of his "vision for America" — true participatory ward-democracy!

President Jefferson finally gets Congress in 1808 to allow him to fully "endeavor to procure a good plan", as he had put it.[117] He actually has to deliver a Special Message to Congress to bring them around:

SPECIAL MESSAGE TO CONGRESS
18 MARCH 1808 – [118]

from: President Thomas Jefferson

"The scale on which the Military Academy at West
Point was originally established is become too limited to
furnish the number of well instructed subjects — Officers
— which the public service calls for. The want of such
characters is already sensibly felt and will be increased
with the enlargment of our plan".

The virtue is: Temperance. First test the water with a toe,
as Jefferson did, before jumping-in!

Thomas Jefferson has been "testing the water with a toe" in his usual cautious manner during the past few years . Now he's ready to jump in with both feet! He gets Congress' blessing for 156 additional cadets. The Academy can now have 200 at any one time. That year, 1808, 56 Thomas Jefferson appointees enter West Point. Now he and Dearborn have bigger numbers to work with. That means more flexibly. Therefore, not as many new cadets need to have had college work before coming to the Academy. Most can study at the Academy for three years or more.

There will be additional books used. For example, one of Thomas Jefferson's favorites on law, Principles of Natural and Political Law by J.J. Burlamaqui (Cambridge, 1807) turns up as a textbook. And Captain Joseph G. Swift puts in his own pitch to upgrade things. It includes new Professors for: Mathematics;

Geography; Ethics and Morality; Ancient and Modern History; and, Astronomy and Natural Philosophy! He ties down what's needed to get into the Academy … and what's needed to stay in. And President Jefferson gives new recommendations on books to use. Most of Swift's proposal becomes Law. Morse's History, Plutarch's Lives, and Morse's Geography will be added as textbooks to be used. And Polybius and Caesar, whose writings about republicanism in ancient Saxony run all through Thomas Jefferson's revolutionary writings, will be read.[119]

Looking forward from here, Harry, Swift becomes the Academy's Superintendent under fourth President James Madison. But, with the approaching War of 1812, the new Secretary of War immediately puts the Swift Law on ice![120] Still, Thomas Jefferson's West Point graduates walk off with a lot of the big praise and credit for victory in the War of 1812. They're even helped by some of the recent West Point grads who were intensively put through the Academy in less than two years because of the War. After the War, new Superintendent Alden Partridge resurrects the Swift Law and uses it![121]

In 1817 Thomas Jefferson's prize catch of 1807, Sylvanus Thayer, becomes Superintendent. The Military Academy continues to produce leaders of Virtue and Knowledge. It's already the foremost institution in the world for producing leaders of Virtue. But now, for the first time, Sylvanus Thayer makes sure that Knowledge includes a real engineering curriculum. West Point boasts the first ever full, bonafide American college engineering program! He will make it the premier engineering force in America for a century to come. And that sort of excellence doesn't come easily. Getting to the top of the heap comes at a high price![122]

* I know. It always does.

* Thayer knows too. He gets West Point to the top by being a tough taskmaster … but fair! The percentage of cadets who graduate in his sixteen years as Superintendent is only 28-38% of those who enter! He sets tough standards of discipline, organization, and teaching methods that they still use at West Point in your modern era, Harry. And for rearing West Point to the top of the heap of "advanced schools" they name him "The Father of the Military Academy".[123]

A statue will eventually be raised to permanently honor Sylvanus Thayer as "The Father of the Military Academy". It's not far from the old graves of Revolutionary War heroes that Dr. Vangilder, a New York physician, reminisced about in a poem he wrote after visiting West Point back in the early 1800's:[124]

REMINISCENCE OF WEST POINT

written by: Dr. Vangilder

But where are the heroes whose home was once here,
    Who here raised the standard of freedom so dear,
When the legions of tyranny ravaged our shore,
    They guarded their homes mid the battles' fierce
    roar.
They sleep in yon vale, their rude fortress below,

> While shrill through the valley the mountain winds
> blow,
> And darkly the shade of the cedar is spread,
> Where lowly they lie in the sleep of the dead.

The virtue is: Appreciation. Loyalty and dedication begin
by appreciation of past heroes.

* Sylvanus Thayer will be called "The Father of the Military Academy"? I have to wonder how Jefferson would feel about that.
* How about George Washington? He, in fact, proposed a military academy seven times during his life! Remember? And a total of fourteen other men also proposed an Academy, Harry!
* Still. Jefferson made it happen. Not Thayer.
* True. But Thomas Jefferson believes that the man who rears a child is the true father. He thinks you don't deserve to be called "parent" or "father" unless you've earned it over time. He says the brief act of creation doesn't do it. Just being the natural father isn't good enough. Not that our natural father doesn't give us genetic characteristics. But he agrees with John Locke and others that nurture and education give us our ultimate characteristics … including our character! And that's the way it is with his "child" — the Military Academy — that he created. He's responsible for its legal creation. Certainly, he's the "genetic father". He even "nursed" it along for a while during its infancy. And when he created a bonafide Military Academy he was even able to finally fulfill the last wish of his longtime father-figure, George Washington — the Academy's "spiritual grandfather". But I know Thomas Jefferson would agree that Sylvanus Thayer is "The Father of the Military Academy". Thayer is the one who, through years of "nurture", gives West Point its ultimate practical character.
* I see. I never thought of it that way.
* Still, crises being the father of creation, it was President Jefferson who created the Academy's unique genetic character. And that's what we're interested in, Harry![125]
* I'm not sure what you mean by the Academy's genetic character.
* I mean that, throughout history, the cement of monarchies was the one virtue called loyalty. Military academies bred officers loyal to the monarch. Period. Now, Thomas Jefferson has come along and made all the virtues — Virtue and Knowledge — the cement of America's Republic. He says education for Virtue and Knowledge is continually needed to renew the spirit of 1776 in the leaders who are produced at the Military Academy. Every new generation of Officers needs to feel the pain the Revolutionary generation suffered.[126] So it isn't surprising he listened to what Lord Chesterfield said in Letters To His Son, namely: "men are what they are made by education and company between the ages of 15 and 25 years old." And no surprise he used the advice of his friend, Benjamin Rush, who said: "I find it possible — through the right kind of educational institution — to convert men".[127] President Jefferson founded his Military Academy

to "convert men" ... into Officers who are leaders of Virtue and Knowledge!
* Yes. And now I see why it was necessary for us to prove it. As you pointed out, records show Jefferson said very little about his Academy. He kept it low-profile.
* My guess is, if he didn't, it might have been purged from his "1802 Military Act" like military academy proposals had been purged in the past!

So that's it, Harry. You now know the role Mr. Jefferson's Academy plays in his "vision for America", and how it fits into his philosophy on life. You now know **WHY** he founded the United States Military Academy!
* Tell me if I get the whole picture:

- Jefferson's "vision for America" comes out of his overall philosophy.
- His "vision for America" is to; <u>immediately</u> save America from monarchy; <u>permanently</u> guard America and the Constitution; and, <u>finally</u> give the people true participatory ward democracy.
- He believes a Standing Army is the only way to save America, and permanently guard America and the Constitution.
- But, there's a historical fear of standing armies.
- His solution to overcoming that fear is to have Army Officers who are leaders of Virtue and Knowledge.
- So, using his philosophy of education, he founded the Military Academy to produce Officers who are leaders of Virtue and Knowledge ... create a Good Standing Army ... to remove fear of the Standing Army.

Do I have it right?
* You've got it! And think about this, Harry. For the first time in history a military academy is used to keep the <u>people</u> in power, not to keep a monarch in power. That means it's a whole new thing. It's a whole new kind of military academy. It's completely different. It's geared to supply Officers who for the first time in history will not be the tools of political power. Philosophical differences between "factions" in government can be peacefully debated without influence of the Army's power. That's different. For remember, the Army that President Jefferson inherited had a bunch of monarchistic, aristocratic, Hamiltonian Officers openly opposed to the Constitution's democracy in a Republic. Now that's all changed. The Officer Corps is now and forever non-monarchist, non-aristocratic, and non-political. It's now drawn from every corner of America. It comes from every social class in America ... not just the priviliged social caste that officer corps' throughout history had come from. Never again does America have to fear that its Officer Corps will use an American Standing Army's raw power to topple civilian liberty. The Officer Corps' loyalty is with the people ... through the Constitution. The United States Military Academy — West Point — is the key to keeping it that way. It will continue to keep the Officer Corps that

way as long as it continues to produce leaders of Virtue and Knowledge — continues to "put old souls into young bodies" ... and "old heads" on top of those bodies. West Point is the only place in the world that truly does that!

CHAPTER 3: EPITAPH

Thomas Jefferson was the last witness, with John Adams, to a glorious and tumultuous past. He died believing they never properly completed the American revolution. To him, it remained an unfinished revolution. For he never got the last part of his "vision for America" — true participatory ward-democracy. But he saw to it that future generations would have a shot at it. To do that, he had to pull off the first and second parts of his "vision for America". The first part saved the Republic by halting America's slide back toward a British-style monarchistic setup. The second part permanently preserved, protected, and defended the Republic and Constitution against monarchists and all other foreign or domestic threats, for all time. He saved America! He kept it safe for democracy!

Spain, France, and England ... I guess all Europe ... always considered America's democracy in a Republic to be an experiment. President Washington was able to preserve, protect, and defend the American "experiment" pretty much because of his towering image. When he left office in the late 1790's, however, they all figured the "experiment" would finally fall apart. They were all licking their chops, ready to pounce, if and when it did. And it almost did ... until Thomas Jefferson became the President.

President Jefferson showed them all. He reformed America ... forever. His chaste reformation of America created two unique new institutions — West Point and a Good Standing Army. West Point would produce Army Officers who are leaders of Virtue and Knowledge in order to create a Good Standing Army and remove the historical fear of standing armies. In turn, America's Good Standing Army would be the solution to the problem of how to preserve, protect, and defend the Republic and Constitution, permanently. The Nation would never again have to depend on someone's towering image to do that. The American "experiment" would change from experiment to fact. And future generations would have a shot at getting true participatory ward-democracy.

Thomas Jefferson always hoped the University of Virginia, his "lifelong favorite" creation — his high profile project — could have come along in time to play a role in helping him save America. It didn't! But at least West Point, his "other creation" — his low profile project — did! And he never lived to see whether his University of Virginia would truly bridge past and present, as he hoped it would. But he did live to see his other creation, West Point, renew the spirit of 1776, make the young understand what the Revolutionary generation accomplished, and allow rising generations to continue what their forefathers began. He saw West Point bridge past and present under his former appointee, Sylvanus Thayer!

* Jefferson's saving America is not big in history books though, is it!

* No. Historians don't treat it as a "cause-celebre", Harry. That's because Thomas Jefferson had to engineer it in such a chaste, subtle, low profile way. However, it is actually one of his most brilliant accomplishments. Saving America for democracy is quietly at the top of the heap, along with the Declaration of Independence and Louisiana Purchase, as the most important things Thomas Jefferson did for America. And West Point played a key role in helping him do it!

Money was raised for a monument — a West Point memorial to Thomas Jefferson, its philosophical father. Only a portrait was commissioned. It remains the sole tribute to the founder of the United States Military Academy at West Point.[128]

8.

EPILOGUE

You get an exclusive look inside the West
Point of today to witness what cadets go
through on a daily basis, two hundred years
after its founding. Are Thomas Jefferson's
Virtue and Knowledge, and Thayer's methods,
still employed? You see the way it is today!
And you see Harry tell Congress how he feels
it ought to be!

CHAPTER 1: WEST POINT: THE WAY IT IS

That's the story behind West Point. It's an epic journey through civilization. And you were there, Harry. You walked amongst the gods and the greats. How many people have done that?

* Certainly no one I know! You said it would be a fantastic journey! And it was! Now, somehow, the world looks different to me ... especially here at West Point!

* That's because you're now seeing West Point through the eyes of history and philosophy.

* Yes. But I have to wonder as I look at the <u>outside</u> of these granite walls, are Jefferson's philosophical reasons for founding West Point still alive <u>inside</u> the walls? And I have to wonder, is Thayer's "nurture" still alive and well in there?

* Inside these walls, they still do meet Thomas Jefferson's <u>Definition of Advanced Schools</u> and fulfill his philosophical aim to produce leaders of Virtue and Knowledge. Those are still the most important things they do here. In fact, West Point's curriculum is just what Thomas Jefferson ordered. It has his equal balance of culture and the sciences — now called Arts and Sciences. It has his technology track, now called an engineering track. It has the leadership and professional military track. It has his belief in using courses and activities to teach subject-matter and Virtue at the same time. And Cadets have to learn time management because they still put in a lot more hours than students at other colleges. In fact, West Point is probably the only college left that measures up to Thomas Jefferson's philosophy of what "advanced education" should be like! But when you ask about Thayer's nurture, what do you mean? <u>How</u>? <u>How</u> they mold cadets ... now?

* In other words, say I were a young cadet at modern West Point. Give me some idea of what I would have to do.[1]

* Okay! To start with, Thayer's nurture is still alive and well. However, we all know society and "raw" Cadets are always changing. So the folks at the Academy are continually refining how they develop leaders. They've gotten better and better at it! I'll show you what they get up to inside these granite walls. We'll look at some typical situations. Then you'll see for yourself what you would have to do and the way it's done now — the way it is!

* You might begin by telling me how it is those baldheaded guys over there have come to be dressed so funny! The T-shirts and shorts aren't bad. But check out those funny looking socks and shoes. Who are those guys?

* Let's listen to what that Cadet in the perfectly tailored gray uniform and red sash around his waist is telling them:

"Welcome to Beast Barracks ... °°oops°° ... Cadet Basic Training.
This isn't college yet! If you're still around come the end of
August, <u>then</u> you become college students. Where did you all come
from?"
°°I better be friendly°° "Hi! I'm Jeff!"
"<u>I</u> don't care <u>what</u> your name is, °°smackhead°°! I <u>asked</u>, where did
you all come from!"

"Oh! I couldn't tell ya where they'all come from, your honor. But I hail from Texas!". ᵒᵒWhy does he sound so mad at me?ᵒᵒ "Texas! I hear only two things come from Texas! ... ᵒᵒI better not say it.ᵒᵒ ... Well, never mind. I don't care what <u>State</u> you're from, <u>either</u>! What <u>station</u> did you come from just now? Post over here candidate! Let's have a look at your travel tag!" ᵒᵒGod help this guy's squad leader.ᵒᵒ ²

The ones in shorts are new cadets — "Plebes". It's their first day. Reception Day. R-Day. It's July 1st — the first day of their new life. They'll be hassled, hustled, and harassed every minute. Later in life they'll all agree ... it was the longest day of their lives!

On R-Day their lives change for good. <u>They</u> will change for good. They'll never again be the same. Little do parents know, they're seeing what to them has always been their "little kid" — <u>their</u> boy or girl — for the last time!

* Last time? I don't get you!

* That last tearful hug and kiss at home or at West Point's Reception area ... that's truly good-bye. They'll never again hug <u>their</u> kid. What I mean is, their kid will never again be the one they knew before. It'll never be the same!

Parents will get to see their kid one last time, but only: from a distance; dressed in Cadet gray; marching onto the "Plain"; at the swearing-in ceremony; at the end of R-Day. Then the kid that belonged to them — the one only <u>they</u> knew — will disappear inside the massive gray granite walls of West Point!

All around this very same Plain during coming months, Plebes will work their young souls and bodies and hearts out. And the Academy picks Plebes with out-standing young souls and bodies to start with! They'll gradually have "<u>old</u> souls put into their young bodies". And while that's happening, they'll gradually leave their young souls — their youth — right here on this Plain at West Point, forever! Their young souls will join the "long gray line" of thousands left here since 1802!

WHEN TOMORROW STARTS WITHOUT ME
(A message to Mom)

When Tomorrow Starts Without Me
And I'm Not There To See
If The Sun Should Rise And Find Your Eyes
All Filled With Tears For Me;
I Wish So Much You Wouldn't Cry
The Way You Did Today
While Thinking Of The Many Things
We Didn't Get To Say.

I Know How Much You Love Me,
As Much As I Love You,
And Each Time That You Think Of Me
I Know You'll Miss Me, Too;
But When Tomorrow Starts Without Me,
Please Try To Understand
That An Angel Came And Called My Name,
And Took Me By The Hand.

There Was So Much Before Me
And So Much I Could Do
It Seemed Almost Impossible
That I'd Be Leaving You;
I Thought Of All The Yesterdays
The Good Times And The Bad
I Thought Of All The Love We Shared
And All The Fun We Had.

If I Could Relive Yesterday
I Thought Just For A While
I'd Say Goodbye And Kiss You
And Maybe Make You Smile;
So When Tomorrow Starts Without Me
Don't Think We're Far Apart
For Every Time You Think Of Me
I'm Right There In Your Heart.[2]

* You make it sound like, if I'm a Cadet, I'm now "lost" inside of West Point.
* That's a good way of putting it, Harry. Essentially, you are. And for good reason. It's the first step on a long, tough road toward learning, and living by, moral, ethical, and character virtues. You have to be isolated from the outside world in order to do that. You're going to become a rare bird. That isn't easy!

You begin by learning about the ethical virtues — Justice, Freedom, Privacy,

380

Liberty, Independence, Individuality, and all those things. They're the things John Locke and Thomas Jefferson called "natural rights"! Remember? For the first time in your life you'll get to know what they really mean! And do you know how you'll do that? By not having them!

It all starts on R-Day. You "start life again" with bald head, short pants, knee socks, and black shoes. Why? Because you have no choice! That's the first message to you that your independence is being wiped out. You'll get a lot of messages like that. All your independence will be wiped out for a while. So that's Independence! Like the Revolutionary generation, you'll know what it is by not having it. That's why the Revolution was about Independence, not about a penny tax on tea.

You're now dressed the same as everyone else — in uniform. You're individuality is gone. You're being "reborn" at West Point. And everyone is reborn equal. That's Individuality! You'll know better what's meant by "all men are created equal".

Next, you're forbidden to have snacks or phones or money or jewelry or appliances or televisions. You're subject to search and inspection at any time. You have little to no freedom or privacy for a while. Freedom and Privacy! You'll understand a lot better why James Otis railed against search and siezure.

You can't do what you want to. You can't go where you want to. You can't talk when you want to. You lose your liberty. Liberty! That's what Patrick Henry railed on about in his "give me liberty or give me death" speech.

You don't have the freedom of speech to say what you want to say. You can't even explain yourself or defend your actions. There's no justice for you. You're allowed only four responses: yes sir; no sir; no excuse sir; and, sir I do not understand. You learn about justice by living with injustice! So that's Justice! It was the fuel for Samuel Adams' speeches and Thomas Paine's Common Sense.

* If I'm a Cadet, I can't even talk in my own room?
* Only to other Plebes. Let's peek into this room of three Plebes just before lights out at the end of R-Day:

"Heh, heads up guys!"
"Yeh! Here comes our squad-leader again!"

"You plebes rappin' away when it still looks like the black hole of Calcutta in here?"
(All) "Yes sir!"
"Why isn't this room A.M.I.'d, Mister Moore?"
"No excuse, Sir!"
"It's almost lights out! Climb into your racks! Get it done at dawn!"
(All) "Yes sir!"

"Can you believe our squad leader? We work at it all night and he calls our room the black hole of Calcutta? And what's A.M.I., anyway?"

"Shhh. We better sleep. …… What the heck is that crunching sound?"

"I'm biting into my apple, Moore. I carried it around since lunch, till I had a minute to eat it. Now is my first chance!" ……
(plunk)

"Did you drop it?!" ᵒᵒNo answer. He dropped it! He fell asleep after one bite?! (Looking up) Oh Mister Ceiling up there, what have I gotten myself into?ᵒᵒ [3]

You'll learn ethical virtues and natural rights by <u>living without them</u>!

Learning ethical virtues teaches another important virtue. Appreciation! You can't help but appreciate James Otis, Sam Adams, Patrick Henry, and Tom Paine … and understand what George Washington and Thomas Jefferson were all about. You can step into the shoes of the generation of 1776. You will appreciate what the Revolutionary War accomplished. You will learn to better understand and appreciate America. Yes, you'll have to endure hardship and sacrifice to learn Appreciation and to win back some Justice and Freedom and Liberty. But at least you won't have to bleed and suffer and die to do it — like the Revolutionary generation did — like the men that Dr. Vangilder's poem talked about — like the men during that terrible West Point winter of 1780 — like the men who suffered at Valley Forge — like the men on that death march to Canada — like the men at Lexington and Concord and Bunker Hill! Still, like them, you'll appreciate what it's like to live without Justice and Freedom and Liberty — to live without natural rights. And as you gradually earn back your natural rights, it will be done one by one. That way you'll truly savor and appreciate each one!

Appreciation is also a "root-virtue". Did you know that other virtues like Loyalty and Dedication and Patriotism … to America and The Constitution … can only become habit if you have true Appreciation? Think about it! When you have true Appreciation for America you know it's worth helping to "preserve, protect, and defend". You know it's worth your Loyalty. It's worth your Dedication. It's worth fighting for. And not just because you need to give back services for your scholarship. Not just because you signed your name on the dotted line and you're stuck!

It's because you want to ….
* You want to fight? Nobody wants to ….
* I was starting to say, you want to do what's necessary for America. One of the greatest generals, Douglas MacArthur, said it best in a special address to the "Corps" at West Point:

THE NATION'S DESTINY IN YOUR HANDS

taken from: Douglas MacArthur's 1962
speech to West Point Cadets

From your ranks come the great captains who hold the nation's destiny in their hands the moment the war tocsin (war alarm) sounds. This does not mean that you are war mongers. On the contrary, soldiers (military Officers) above all other people, pray for peace. For they must suffer and bear the deepest wounds and scars of war. However, always in our ears ring the ominous words of Plato, that wisest of philosophers: "Only the dead have seen the end of war"!

The virtue is: Appreciation. It's the binder that holds
together a winning Officer Corps.

So that's the "root-virtue" — Appreciation! Thomas Jefferson and Montesquieu both said that in order to preserve a government we must appreciate it (love it).[4]

Two other "root" type of moral, ethical, and character virtues smack you right between the eyes the very minute you step foot onto West Point as a new Cadet — Obedience and Fortitude (Stress)! And you start to learn about a fourth "root-virtue" almost immediately. That one is — Honor! If you were a Cadet, Harry, you would learn and practice all four of these "root-virtues" in everything you do at West Point. That's why I call them root-virtues. You would do little missions in order to learn and practice the other moral, ethical, and character virtues. But in each mission you would be learning Appreciation, Obedience, Fortitude (Stress), and Honor … at the same time!

* In other words, I'm under stress and on my honor and learning to obey in everything I do? That's hard!

* That's "followership"! You need to learn followership before you can learn leadership! Obedience is the "root-virtue" that followership grows from. So you first learn Obedience, then followership, then leadership!

* Followership. That's an interesting concept. It must be something new — and something unique to West Point.

* It's not new Harry. Even Benjamin Franklin, way back in the 1700's said: "he that cannot obey, cannot command". He that cannot follow, cannot lead. "Let the first lesson be obedience, and the rest may be what you wish".[5] No matter how big

your job as a leader, you'll always have to answer to someone. You may become a great leader ... but you'll always be a follower, also! Unless, of course, you become an absolute dictator. And even then, you would still have to follow the laws of mankind, and of your Maker. So that's Obedience. Like the Ten Commandments maintains order in regular life, Obedience is necessary for maintaining order in military life!

* In other words, everyone has a boss! Except God!
* That's exactly my point, Harry.
* And Fortitude? How is Fortitude a "root-virtue"?
* Fortitude is at the root of being able to withstand Stress! In the military it's the difference between life and death! Officers must not fold up in a stressful situation, be it on the battlefield, in the air, or at the operating table in surgery. Otherwise, how can they protect the lives of America's young sons and daughters who are entrusted to them? So, above all, Officers must learn to function under stress. It takes a lot of time to learn. West Point gives it four years. Some never learn. But West Point has a duty to sort out who can and who can't. Those who probably can never function well under stress shouldn't be Officers! They may be super-smart. They may have the potential to be big-shots in civilian life. But they shouldn't be pilots, surgeons, or combat leaders if they don't function well under stress! They shouldn't be put into a position of holding people's lives in their hands! Many sons and daughters have died unnecessarily in wars because of their officers!
* I agree. In fact, shouldn't that be the most important thing West Point does? Isn't that the most important thing it does? Doesn't West Point sort out people who, ultimately, just cannot handle stress? I wouldn't want my kid taking orders from someone who is not stress-tested! Would you?
* Who would, Harry? Who would? And yes, that is probably the most important difference West Point makes. It's one of the ways the Officer's Commission through West Point is different from others. West Point produces Officers who have proven they can withstand many different kinds of stress put on them for four years! No one can predict what any person will do when someone starts shooting at them in war. And granted, except for the odd "live ammo" drill, no one tests West Point cadets by shooting at them! But short of being shot at, Cadets are stressed in every other way. They learn to manage fear and stress — both the mental and physical kinds. It would be surprising, and the exception, if they folded when the chaos and shooting began!
* That's what I thought! That alone makes West Point worth it! If you're the parent of an enlisted kid, it may save your kid's life!
* So that's Fortitude — Stress. It's the top priority for a military officer according to the Spartans and St. Ignatius and Washington and Thayer and many others! Even St.Paul in Romans 5:1-5 said: "hardship makes leaders (able to) function under stress"!

Fortitude is also the "root-virtue" of other character virtues such as Perseverance and Courage. For example, we're now in an early morning of what's nicknamed "Beast Barracks", the 6-1/2 weeks of Cadet Basic Training that begins on R-Day. The term, "beast" symbolizes that Plebes, like beasts, have little to no natural rights. This group running toward us isn't just saying "yes sir", or "no sir", and so on — the four responses they're allowed. They can also be given permission to say something

384

other than those four responses. As they come closer, you'll hear that they're all shouting a little "cadence" for spirit, as they run in formation:

> "Crusaders hit the beach at dawn!
> Fighting till the last is gone!
> Keeping enemies at bay!
> Crusaders always lead the way!
> Hooooooo!"

That would be C-Company, nicknamed Crusaders. They've been running for ... well ... a long time. They're being pushed to their limits. They're building physical endurance. But the main purpose is to build the character virtue — Perseverance. As you can see, some of them are beginning to fall out:

(whispering Plebes) "How long we been running?"
                 "It seems, forever. I'm tired, and it isn't even breakfast-time yet!"

(shouting Leader)   "Who's yackin' back there! You stragglers ... pick up the pace! You two ... grab that smack who's falling down and drag him along with you!"[6]

That's Perseverance. It's the trait that got Washington's Army from West Point to Virginia on foot ... and in time to trap Cornwallis at Yorktown and win the Revolutionary War!

And now let's go and look at another outgrowth of the "root-virtue" Fortitude. This one is: Courage.
* I see what you mean by Courage! That cliff they're repelling down has to be 100 feet high! That does take Courage!
* It's just one example of the many ways West Point teaches and monitors Courage. The real test comes next, however. It's the cliff-climbing back up with only a safety rope!

> "Good job coming down cadets! But that's the easy part. Now
> for the hard part! Climbing back up! Just do it the way we
> taught you. And remember! That cliff's wet this morning! If

you slip, hang onto that safety rope for dear life! You'll swing out off the cliff, but it'll bring you back in! <u>You</u>! You did good coming down. <u>You</u> go first!

"Yes sir". °°That's what I get for doing good!°°

"There goes Kahl. °°Better him than me.°° He's half way up. ...... Ooops! Oh man! He slipped! He's danglin'out off the cliff! He's got the safety rope!"

"Thank God! That was close!"

"Too close!" °°This isn't for me!°°

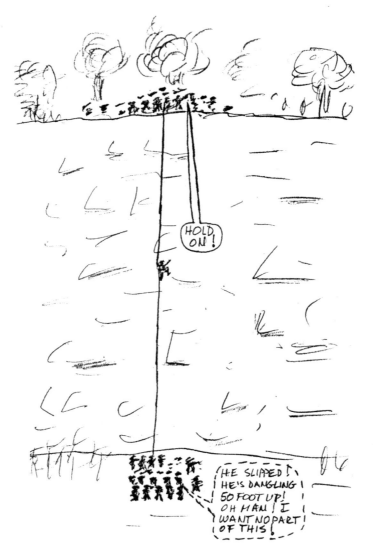

"Okay! Who's next!"
   (whispering) "Not me, man. Kahl's the athlete. If that hap-
   pens to him, I want no part of this!"
"Who said that!? What chicken-smack said that!? It was <u>you</u>,
   wasn't it mister! What's your problem?!"
   "Yes, sir. No excuse, sir!"
"You're right! You have no excuse! Come on! You're next up!"
   "Yes, sir!"

There he goes, Harry. That Cadet must conquer his fear of danger. If he does-
n't ... he's out! And so that's Courage. That Cadet's danger isn't the kind of dan-
ger Thomas Jefferson, for instance, faced as Governor of Virginia during the
Revolution — namely, certain death if captured doing what he had to do. But, it
is grave danger, nonetheless.
Our fourth "root-virtue" — Honor — is at the heart of <u>everything</u> West Point
does!
* What do you call Honor, Thomas? What is Honor at West Point?
*   Honor? First, take the moral philosophies of Plato, Aristotle, Epicurus,
Epictetus, Kant, and others. Add Thomas Jefferson's "moral sense" philosophy.
Then, add a bit of what boys and girls are taught in "Sunday School" about the
Ten Commandments. Put it all together. The result is a simple West Point Honor
Code. It connects with Truth and Integrity and Trust. And it goes like this:

A Cadet will not lie!   [will tell the Truth]
A Cadet will not cheat! [must have the Integrity to stick to the
                        rules, codes, and regulations]
A Cadet will not steal! [can be Trusted]

* That's simple enough!
* But that's not all! What's in the interest of the bee, must also be in the interest
of the hive. Right? Thomas Jefferson, like Aristotle before him, said that morals
are not just a <u>private</u> concern. They're also a <u>public</u> concern. True moral virtue
— Honor — shows how Good you are, privately. But it also shows how Good
society is, publicly. So Honor has a <u>social</u> dimension to it. This social dimension
starts with individual Truth, Integrity, and Trust. Then it says that <u>every</u> individual in society has to be that way to make it work! Those who don't live honorably can easily take advantage of those who do.
* That's a problem!
* Dishonor is more than a problem. It's a sickness! A cancer! It slowly kills society, morally ... like in ancient Rome! Remember? Society must not tolerate that
sickness. And society starts with each person! That means each person must not
tolerate dishonor!
* What's the practical remedy for that sickness — dishonor? Is there one?
* Yes. It's called ... prevention! Each person must oppose and expose anyone
who acts without Honor — without Truth, Trust, and Integrity. And from that
"preventive medicine" we get the last part of West Point's Honor Code. It says:

A Cadet <u>will not tolerate</u> those who lie or cheat or steal.
* I see! Then I take it the complete West Point Honor Code is:

A Cadet will not lie, cheat, or steal … nor <u>tolerate</u> those who do.

* Exactly right! The toleration part forbids covering up what you know someone has done wrong. It's the "self-policing" part of the code. It's the deterrent — the preventative medicine!
* I see! Actually, I can't see an Honor Code working very well without it!
* Cadets say it's the hardest part! All your life you learn to never "rat" on your buddies. You stick up for them. You cover for them. Now you're told you have to report them if they do something wrong. You're told that your loyalty to the greater good — Honor, West Point, the Army, America — has to be greater than loyalty to a buddy!
* That <u>does</u> sound like the hardest part. It must be a real dilemma for them as cadets, and later, as Officers.
* It is! It's choosing the harder right, rather than the easier wrong. But if everyone did so, we'd have an ever-rising upward spiral of morals in society!
* That would be nice. For once something that feeds on itself would do so for "good", not for "bad". And what happens to me as a Cadet if I violate the Honor Code?
* Intentional violation? You're out! You get expelled! And that brings us to our next look at life inside West Point. I see an expulsion waiting to happen over there! Do you see that Cadet, a Sophomore (Yearling), sneaking into his room after taps and lights out? That's a breach of regulations. He thinks no one sees him. But they do:

"Uh Oh! See that? Williams is breaking the regs. If he doesn't
turn himself in … I'll have to!"
"How can you do <u>that</u>. <u>You're</u> only a Plebe. You'll get in
trouble!"
"I'll have to! It's the toleration clause! If I don't, then you have
to turn <u>me</u> in! And <u>I</u> get kicked out!"
"You're right! If <u>I</u> cover up, <u>I'm</u> in trouble too."
"And how about his roommate? Is he away on leave? Or did he
see it, too? Yes, I'd better report this."

* That sounds less like Honor, Thomas, and more like self-interest.
* You're right. The first stage of Honor is partly self-interest. You want to stay out of trouble. You don't want to be kicked out. That's why the toleration clause is so important. But that leads to the second stage of Honor. It kind of grows on you. Let's get what the Sophomore, Williams, who breached the regulations is thinking:

ooOh well. This is a breach of the reg's. If I don't turn myself in,
it could be an Honor violation. I don't think anyone saw me. So

388

I'm alright that way. But that's not what we're taught to do here, I'm not gonna waste all that … and embarass West Point. I'll turn myself in first thing in the morning![oO]

Now that's the second stage of Honor. The Sophomore isn't turning himself in out of self-interest — out of fear of getting kicked out. He thinks no one saw him. So he thinks he can get away with it if he wants to. But he's turning himself in anyway. He now puts the values of his institution ahead of covering up for himself — the harder right above the easier wrong. He doesn't want to undermine the purpose and foundation of West Point, the Army, and fellow Cadets. He took an oath!

Little does this Sophomore know that he was seen by, not only those Plebes, but by a Senior (Firstie):

[oO]Oh no! I wish Williams hadn't snuck in late. He's a good guy. But I <u>have</u> to report him. Honor is honor. Truth is truth. I'll give him a chance to turn himself in first. If he doesn't, then that's it![oO 8]

That's the third level of Honor. It's the highest level — a philosophical level. With that Senior, Honor has now become habit. He has "internalized" Honor! That's the ultimate goal of the Honor program!
* If I'm a Cadet at West Point, I don't know if I can do that! Isn't that third level

a bit too difficult and philosophical?
* Harry. The Academy isn't asking anyone to drink the poison hemlock like Socrates did or slit their wrists like Seneca did to show their Honor. The Academy boils Honor down to two steps. The first is to learn <u>what</u> Honor is. The second is to have the <u>will</u> to make it habit — to internalize it! There are, no doubt, some who will <u>never</u> make Honor a habit. But you can rest assured, West Point does

all it can to help them try! If you have the <u>will</u> to try, West Point gives you four years to turn Honor into habit — to practice internalizing it — by living every single day that way.

* I see. At other colleges I might learn <u>about</u> Honor. Here at West Point I not only learn <u>about</u> Honor, I do it! I <u>practice</u> it! I <u>live</u> it ... every day! That makes a big difference!

* That's what Honor boils down to, Harry. As Aristotle and Epictetus and Seneca and St.Paul said, it takes time, practice, and the will to turn it into habit!

* Is that what the noise is in the hallways this morning — Cadets practicing Honor?

* Not quite! That's the Upperclass Cadets checking out their Plebes' "knowledge" and appearance!. Listen to what this first Upper-class Cadet is saying to the Plebe:

> "Recite the last paragraph of the Code of Conduct, mister!"
> "Yes sir! Paragraph VI of the Code of Conduct says, 'I will never forget that I am an American, fighting for freedom, responsible for my actions, and dedicated to the principles which made my Country free. I will trust in my God and in the United States of America', Sir!"

Now let's go down the hallway and listen to other Upperclass Cadets and Plebes:

> "What did President Theodore Roosevelt say at West Point's first Centennial?"
> "Sir, he said, 'during the century, no other institution in the land has contributed so many names as West Point to the honor roll of the Nation's greatest citizens', Sir!"

> "What's the organ in Cadet Chapel noted for, Smith?"
> "It's the largest chapel organ in the world, Sir!"

> "Mister! Tell me what the Sheridan Memorial is and what it says!"
> "Sir, it was dedicated to sportsmanship after a cadet was fatally injured in football against Yale. It says, 'Life is the greatest of all games. Play it with courage, wisdom, and loyalty'."

> "Tell me the ranks of Army and Navy Officers, 0-1 to 0-10!"
> "Sir, 0-1 Army is 2nd Lieutenant; 0-1 Navy is Ensign; 0-2 Army is ...."

> "Who invented baseball, Harris?"
> "Abner Doubleday, Class of 1842, Sir!"

"Beanhead! Describe the insignias of rank in the enlisted Army!"
"Sir, to start with is ————".

"Who built the Panama Canal, mister?"
"Sir, Major General George Washington Goethals, Class of 1880."

"What's the Silver Star awarded for, Cadet Lee?"
"Sir, the Silver Star is awarded for conspicuous gallantry in action, not quite the level of the Medal of Honor."

"Name the only Five-star Generals, Mr. Jones!"
"Sir, they are: Air Force — Henry "Hap" Arnold, USMA 1907; Army — Omar Bradley, USMA 1915; Army — Dwight Eisenhower, USMA 1915; Army — Douglas MacArthur, USMA 1903; and Army — George Marshall, VMI 1901."

"Mister, let's have 'Scott's Fixed Opinion'!"
"Sir, General Winfield Scott said, 'I give it as my fixed opin- ion that but for our graduated cadets the war with Mexico might have lasted some four or five years ... ; whereas, in less than two campaigns, we conquered a great Country'."
"Not perfect, but you've got enough of it to 'save' you for now. In the future, get everything perfect! Lee and Grant and Sherman did! MacArthur and Eisenhower did! Schwarzkopf did! Now it's your turn. That is, unless you think you're better than them. Do you?
"No, sir!" [9]

391

As you can see, Harry, the Plebes are firing-off various pieces of military and leadership "knowledge". This goes on every day! Besides the courses that they take in History and Leadership, this is the principal way of fostering the virtues of Loyalty, Dedication, and Patriotism. This "knowledge" is in the cadet handbook called <u>The Bugle Notes</u>. It binds together today's Cadets in a "shared culture", and links them with Cadets of years gone by!

* I can see how that's effective. If I'm a Cadet, I'm doing the same things Lee, Grant, Pershing, Arnold, MacArthur, Eisenhower, and more recently, Schwarzkopf did.

* And like them you have to learn the 300-page Bugle Notes … cover-to-cover! You get "qualified", page by page, by your Cadet Leader.

* "Shared culture" … an interesting way to imbed Loyalty, Dedication, and Patriotism.

* It's nothing new. It's a technique used by military academies ever since Alexander the Great's Royal Pages military academy. And if you're a Plebe in that hallway, Harry, you also get checked out for appearance — polished brass, shined shoes, and many other little details concerning your uniform. We'll check out what's happening with that Plebe over there. I notice he's run in and out of his room two or three times now:

(hallway)   "Mister Scott! Your brass is better. But what's that label doing peeking out of your shirt?"

(looking down)   "Oh! Yes … no … I mean, no excuse Sir!"

           "I didn't tell you to look down! Did I? Don't 'spaz'! Head up! Eyes forward! Post to your room and fix it, mister! You have one minute!"

              "Yes, sir!"

(in the room)	"You guys didn't see my label? Some roommates!" "Sorry, Scott. There you go. Let's have a look. You'll make it this time."

(hallway)	"Mister. You got the label. But not good enough! Now you missed something else! I want you perfect! Find out what's wrong! You have one minute!" "Yes, Sir!"

(in the room)	"<u>Now</u> what's wrong? He told <u>me</u> to find it this time. "Oh! Shute! We missed it! Your bottom shirt-button is undone! There. You're good <u>now</u>. Hold it! White thread on your back. OK. Good luck!"

(hallway)	"Let's have another look, Scott! ——— Finally! You're squared away! You wasted my good time. Get it right <u>first time</u> next time! And it better not be this way at SAMI tomorrow!" "Yes, sir!" [10]

* It took that Cadet, Scott, five trips back and forth from his room before he finally got it right, Thomas. What's the point of that? And what in the world is SAMI?
* As a Cadet, you're purposely held to a high standard with every little thing you do. <u>Nothing</u> is made easy. It makes you try and try again until you get it right and succeed in reaching your goal. It builds the character virtue ... Determination!

So that's Determination! West Point takes a page out of Epictetus' <u>Encheiridion</u>. If you remember, Harry, Epictetus was a slave who earned freedom through hard work and Determination. Therefore, Determination as a virtue loomed big throughout his Stoic philosophy. He pushed it! And so does West Point! And you asked what SAMI is? That's Saturday A.M. (morning) Inspection, of course. The dreaded "SAMI"!
* And what's that all about?
* We'll go forward in time to that right now. Let's go into this Plebe room. The Upperclass Cadet is talking to the Plebes:

"You better get squared-away, Plebe, or you're gonna have big trouble!"
"Yes sir!" °°He must be busting my chops!°°
"See my white glove here? It's dirty! You have to clean the <u>edges</u> of your desk, not just the top! And you! Did your Momma teach you to be that sloppy? Your dresser drawers are a shambles! I'm now gonna do you a favor. I'm gonna dump them all out onto the floor so you can start fresh! Fold your underwear and socks the way you're supposed to ... perfectly! We want perfection around here! You don't have your Momma to wipe your nose anymore! <u>You</u> have to do it yourself!"

ºº Mom would be proud at how good my room looks!ºº

"And Beanheads! Next time get this floor <u>spotless</u>! See those scuff marks? And look at your glass, mister. It's dirty! See those drying stains? Do you see them?"

"Yes sir." ºº He calls that dirty?ºº

"Any questions?"

"Permission to speak, Sir?"

"You have permission to speak, Cadet!"

"Sir, why is it so important to have everything so perfect? I thought we did a pretty good job, Sir."

"If you're on the front lines, don't you want the rear artillery fire control Officer to get the enemy's position coordinates on the map <u>perfect</u> — so you don't get blown up by your own artillery? Or do you just want him to do a <u>pretty</u> good job?"

"Yes, Sir! No, Sir!"

"If you're a helicopter pilot, don't you want to be sure that you're identified as 'friendly', not 'enemy' aircraft — so you don't become a 'friendly fire' fatality?"

"Yes, Sir!"

"If you're wounded and in surgery, don't you want the Army Surgeon to be <u>perfect</u> enough to cut every last little bit of metal out of you so you don't get infection — and maybe die?!"

"Yes, Sir!"

"That's why everything you do, no matter how small, has to be done as perfectly as possible. It has to become second nature."

"Permission to speak, Sir?" You mean perfection has to become a habit?"

"That's it exactly, Mister! You need Conscientiousness to make perfection a habit!" [11]

So, this virtue is — Conscientiousness! Remember how King Richard III lost a kingdom for want of conscientious attention to a detail — a simple horseshoe nail?

* Now I see why those Upperclass Cadets have perfect uniforms. It's become second nature to them! There aren't many of them here, though.

* The Cadets you see here in the perfect looking uniforms are Seniors (Firsties) and Juniors (Cows). They're practicing leadership by training the new cadets. Other Seniors and Juniors are out in the regular Army — on the wing of Army drill sergeants — helping to train new enlisted recruits. And others are several miles from here at Camp Buckner. They're in charge of new Sophomores (Yearlings) who have to do Cadet Field Training before starting their second academic year.

* What's Cadet Field Training?

* Sophomores pick up where they left off last summer when they were Plebes in Cadet Basic Training. If and when they make it through their Plebe year, they get more military training. They also get a taste of the various Branches of the Army. They, of course, continue to practice the root moral, ethical, and character virtues — Appreciation, Obedience, Fortitude (Stress), and Honor. And they work on other virtues like Courage and Responsibility ... and Cooperation!

As Plebes they had learned about "cooperate and graduate". For example, they had certain "duties" to do every day like: cleaning; delivering various things; knowing what's in the newspaper every day and "discussing" it with Upperclass Cadets; knowing what's in the menu for the day in order to "brief" Upperclass Cadets on it; knowing the "poop" — what's going on at West Point and keeping Upperclass Cadets informed; and, doing "chores" at the tables during meals.

Up to this point it sounds more like Responsibility than Cooperation. And it is. And at this point, it's Responsibility for little things. In future years it'll be for big things — like people's lives! But here's where Cooperation comes in. It comes in because there's just not enough time for Plebes to complete all their Responsibilities themselves. They need help. So, they learn to be creative, imaginative, and innovative. And they learn to cooperate with eachother ... "cooperate and graduate". Now, as Sophomores at Camp Buckner in Cadet Field training, they continue to learn about Cooperation! Let's look at this team of six Sophomores on the Leadership Obstacle Course. They're at the "four level platform". Each level is made of logs. The levels are nine feet apart! Cadets have to climb up one side and down the other.

* Nine feet apart? That's higher than the ceiling of a room! They need a ladder for that!

* They can't use anything! They can only use eachother. They must cooperate to make it. Watch how they boost and hoist and pull and support and stand on eachother. In the end they all make it up and down!

The four level platform teaches Cooperation! It's one of many "missions" they have that does so. The missions are geared so Cadets learn that their success and destiny is linked to their fellow soldiers. During the eight weeks at Buckner they do everything from cooperate at pulling a "disabled" heavy truck uphill, to cooperate at constructing a portable pontoon bridge having sections that weigh in the tons!

* And you said the Sophomores at Buckner are made to do things to test and strengthen their courage again?
* Yes. But not only to test their courage. Also to build … Self-confidence. For example, they do "combatives". They "beat" eachother around with pugil sticks — long sticks with pads on each end. They do the feared Confidence Course. It includes that ten story log tower over there. Cadets climb up, over the top, and down again. Trouble is, when you're at the top you feel it swaying in the wind. And it comes to sort of a point at the top. When you swing your body over that top point to the other side, you feel very insecure! There's not much to hold on to! That Sophomore is at the point right now!
* I see him. And I can imagine what he's thinking, right about now:

> ᵒᵒHoly Sam Houston Institute of Technology! This is worse than
> rapelling and cliff-climbing last year! At Least then we had the
> safety rope to hang on to!ᵒᴼ 12

* But that's not all, Harry. Before the end of Camp Buckner, Cadets have to do the notorious "slide for life" confidence course!
* How does that work?
* Cadets are carrying full packs. They climb up a ladder to the top of a ten-story tower. There's a cable that extends downward across a lake. They have to hang by their arms from the cable and slide — at 30 mph — down the cable to the other side. They drop off into the lake near the other side. They wade over to a pole and start climbing. They keep climbing — twenty-five feet up! And surprise! At the top there's no dock! There's a log hanging from cables, kind of swaying in the air! They climb onto the log and walk across it — twenty-five feet up! And again surprise! The log turns into nothing but a rope! It's stretched out over the water toward the bank of the lake. They "crawl" upside-down hanging onto that rope with both arms and legs until they reach the bank. Then they have to drop into the water and hoist themselves up onto the bank, finally onto land. It's not for the faint-hearted!
* If they do that, I'd say they do have self-confidence!
* It's not a matter of if they do it. They must do it. Just like the test during the academic year in Physical Education class. They must jump off the fourty-foot high tower, under full pack, into the pool — then swim to the other side! Both of these challenges are fearful for many. But there's plenty of help! And you know that many others have done them before. Yet, many Cadets have been "separated" from the Academy … because they couldn't take that one step off of either tower!

That's Self-confidence! Survival could someday depend on it! Do you remember the demoralizing defeat at Quebec in 1775, Harry? The Army had to pick itself up and start all over again in order to survive. It had to Have Courage Twice. Remember that? In short, it had to have Self-Confidence!

Speaking of the academic year, that's where we're headed next. It's the third week in August. Everyone comes together, including the rest of the Upperclass

Cadets you asked about. During Cadet Basic Training only the Upperclass Cadet Cadre is here. Plebes outnumber Upperclass Cadets by about six to one. Now Upperclass Cadets outnumber Plebes by almost three to one!
* That's a huge change! So if I'm a Plebe, that means … what?
* More "attention"! Now there are several times the number of Upperclass Cadets crawling all over you — anxious to "teach" you. It's your worst nightmare come true! You now have less physical stress, but, you'll be under more emotional stress than ever for a while!

Take for example the dining tables. During Cadet Basic Training there were one or two Upperclass Cadets at your table of ten. Now there are seven Upperclass to maybe three Plebes. Now you have a lot more requests and questions and table duties! A lot more often now, you have to put down your fork, take two or three quick chews and swallow, and give the correct response while sitting a certain way in your chair. It gets harder to have a "full and sufficient meal" in the twenty-five minutes allowed. You have to be sharper, more efficient, and more innovative to do so!
* So the stresses and the challenges don't end after Cadet Basic Training? They continue right into the academic year, even though all Cadets are going to class?
* Of course. West Point is more than a regular college. Academics. Duties. Stresses. Cadets get it all! More than ever, Plebes need those letters of encouragement from family and friends. And more than ever Plebes make the time to write letters to home. We'll look at a room of three Plebes … and especially hear the letter written by one of them:

"I'm always tired, guys! I need 24 hours straight rack time!"
　"Me too! But I want to finish up this letter to home that I
　started. Will you two do me a favor? Listen to it will you?
　Because even I can't believe what I'm telling them I do.
　Confirm I'm not exaggerating. Okay?"
"Sure. No guarantee we won't fall asleep though! But, fire
away."
　"Thanks! Here's my letter:

　'Dear Mom and Dad. This place isn't as hard as I expected
　it to be. However, it's no piece of cake either. No one likes it.
　No one. Not even me. But don't stress, Dad. We're not sup-
　posed to like it … just put up with it. I have a few minutes
　before afternoon class. So I'll tell you what I mean. Here's
　what I did today: We had inspection this morning. So we
　were up at 4:00 AM: scrubbed, cleaned and neatened-up
　every inch of our room; folded everything in sight in our
　drawers perfectly; lined-up everything that's on our shelves;
　hung our uniforms in the closet in perfect order; arranged our
　books in perfect order; and so on. I never saw a room so neat
　and clean in my life (not even yours, Mom). And I never saw
　guys dressed, shined, and polished like me and my roommates.

And get this. The Upperclass cadets who inspect us didn't think so. Can you believe it? They made this big thing about a stain on my glass. Then we got a lecture on duty, details, and conscientiousness. And we did listen very ... conscientiously. But we got gigged anyway (that means demerits that lead to punishment time). Next came duties: mail; menus; newspapers; laundry; knowledge; briefings; etc. Next, formation marching into the mess hall for breakfast, and then table duties at breakfast. After breakfast at 7:30 AM, I went to my first class — Plebe Physical Education. Boxing. Just what I didn't need. We kind of beat eachother up for an hour or so. Then I: showered; hustled back to the room; got hassled and harassed a couple of times on the way; changed into my dark class-uniform; made sure my brass and shoes and uniform were neat and shining; grabbed my books; and hustled to class. After four hours of getting hassled, harassed, and beat up, I was finally ready to become a college student again. It's no wonder some guys fall asleep right in the middle of class. I'll stop now, Mom and Dad. I have to run to an afternoon lab. Be back.

Hi. It's 11:25PM. I'm back! It's almost taps now. Only about half an hour to lights out. I just got done studying for four hours. And it's not enough. Before that, everyone did a couple hours of Sports. Then dinner. I'm falling asleep as I write. At least I didn't fall asleep in class. So, I'll sign-off for now. Love.'

Well what do you think of it guys? You still awake?"
"Hmm. ZZZZ. Hmm. ZZZZ."
ᵒᵒWoops. They're snoring. Fell asleep. Oh well. I'll join them!ᵒᵒ 13

Cadets aren't up at 4AM every day, Harry. It's more like 5:30. Otherwise, that Cadet's letter pretty accurately describes the way it is at West Point!

* It's tough. And it tells me that Plebes continue to practice the virtues all year round ... even when classes begin. But what about the Upperclass cadets? What do they do in the way of virtues?

* They teach them! When you teach the virtues you become more fixed in them yourself. And, Upperclass Cadets also continue to practice the virtues ... but slightly differently. Take, for example: Justice, Freedom, and Liberty ... they now give them out, as well as, receive them; Obedience ... they now receive it, as well as, give it; Fortitude, as in Stress ... they now judge if others can handle it, but also learn to handle new stresses of responsibility themselves; Fortitude, as in Courage ... they don't face danger, but they must have the courage of their convictions and stand up for what's right; and, Honor ... they work on turning that third level — philosophical level — of Honor into habit!

Upperclass Cadets also change their focus from Followership to learning and practicing Leadership — different kinds of Leadership.

* Different kinds?

* I should say different levels of Leadership. For example:

Seniors (Firsties): They're now pre-occupied with running the 4000 strong Corps of Cadets. That doesn't just happen by itself, you know Harry. With guidance from the Officers assigned to West Point, they actually run the day to day life of the Corps ... except for academics. They get a taste of executive leadership and decision-making. They continue to learn Appreciation, now appreciating the problems higher ranking Officers face.

Juniors (Cows): They're in charge of from ten to thirty Plebes and Sophomores each. Last year, as Sophomores themselves, they were Team-leaders. This year, as Juniors, they start to learn and practice "indirect" leadership. They've just finished their year of practicing face-to-face leadership as the Team Leader. Now they supervise the Team-Leader. They lead the leaders!

Sophomores (Yearlings): They're hot out of that pressure cooker called Cadet Field Training at Camp Buckner. They're at the peak of Self-confidence. They're fresh off of: deflecting stress; conquering fear; facing-down danger; and, learning that "cooperate and graduate" might someday mean cooperate and live! Now they must cooperate with other Upperclass Cadets to drill, direct, discipline, and develope the Plebes. Each Sophomore gets to be in charge of Plebes. And it's not to bash them or haze them. It's to teach them. At the same time, they're gaining the knack of direct — face-to-face — leadership!

So the Sophomores continue to "exercise their moral muscles", as Thomas Jefferson said when you practice making the virtues into habit. They practice the virtues they learned as Plebes. But now they look at those same virtues from a different point of view. Take moral virtues like Truth, Trust, and Honor. They have to show Plebes that they, themselves, are truthful and trustworthy and honest. That's the only way a leader can get a follower to willingly follow. The key word here is willingly!

They also learn to expand some character virtues, such as, Responsibility. This is the first time they're responsible, not just for their own behavior, but for teaching someone else virtuous behavior. Another is Consideration for Others. They learn to have concern and consideration for people, especially those they're responsible for. Then there's Patience. They learn to: first instruct; then correct; then coach. That takes Patience. Then only as a last resort, if all else fails, it's time for punishment — to get in the person's face and teach them a lesson. But it should be a useful lesson. And that's a big challenge! It takes thought, imagination, and creativeness. And it also takes another virtue. Self-Control.

We're now going to see an example of Self-Control, Harry. This Junior Cadet is about to show a Sophomore how to "get in the face" of a Plebe who thinks he's above the rules. But you'll notice there's no screaming. Here comes the Junior's platoon, lining up for morning formation.

* Why are they the only ones out there on the apron in formation this morning?
* The Junior Platoon Leader called for an early morning formation for good reason this morning. And here comes his good reason. It's a Plebe named Star who thinks the rules don't apply to him. He's ignored everyone. And as usual, he's now casually strolling out to formation — late. The young Sophomore Team Leader is about to get a lesson in the West Point way of punishment and self-control from his "boss", the Junior Platoon Leader. And so is our problem Plebe. Let's see how the Platoon Leader handles it:

"Hi, Star! Sleep well this morning? Sorry we had to wake you so early. But thanks for joining us — at this God-forsaken hour. We had to start our little question and answer game without you. But, don't worry. We believe in opportunity around here. And I know you wish to have your turn. So, as that is your wish, that is what you shall have — right now! So enlighten us Mister Star. Tell us what Sylvanus Thayer's three D's are."

"Three D's? I don't know!"

(laughing) "What? I could have sworn you said, 'I don't know'. And we know that's not one of the four responses, as in 'No Sir', don't we! So I must be hearing things! ... Mister Jones! Help Mister Star! What are the three D's?"

"Thayer's three D's are: discipline, decision, and duty, Sir!"

"Got that Mister Star? Thayer is talking about discipline! Wait! Could it be? Could that be your problem? Could it be discipline? And we all know what discipline means, don't we! Tell us all Mister Star. What does discipline mean? What are the benefits of discipline?"

"The benefits of discipline are ...... oh, I don't know!"

"You're darn right you don't know, Star ...... because you ain't got it! ..... However! It's not your fault. Who's is it? All you Cadets, listen up! It's not the fault of Star. It's my fault! I failed him! And do you know why I failed him? Because you, all of you, failed me! Some guys let Mister Star 'get over' without doing his share of duties, especially Misters Jones and Smith here — his roommates. Therefore, Mister Star doesn't have to 'cooperate to graduate', like the rest of you do. That's why he thinks he's special. So! Misters Jones and Smith! You must redeem yourselves. You do that by teaching discipline to Mister Star. How? Let's see. Start with ten pushups. Both of you. <u>Hit the apron</u>! The rest of you, listen up! Why do you think you let Mister Star 'get over'? No one? Okay! <u>I'll</u> tell <u>you</u>! Because <u>all of you</u> have no discipline, either! So who wants to redeem himself? Which of you undisciplined Plebes seek redemption for letting Mister Star here 'get over'? No one? Then Mister Star! Pick another 'volunteer'to demonstrate discipline! Come on, Star! Pick a 'volunteer' to join Smith and Jones here in pushups! Who will it be? Come on, Star. Speak up! Tell me who you think is the most <u>lacking</u> in discipline! You don't want to name him out loud, you say? Just whisper the name in my ear then."

(whispering)"I don't want to do that ...... Sir".

"Who's that? Mister <u>Bull</u>? You pick Cadet <u>Bull</u>? He's the <u>biggest</u> man in the whole Company! That took guts, Mister Star! Did you hear that, Mister Bull? Your '<u>buddy</u>' here, Mister Star, picked <u>you</u>! Hit the apron for pushups, Bull ... and stay down! Now Mister Star. Who can we pick to join these men for pushups in a show of cooperation? You know how it is, 'cooperate and graduate'? Whisper it in my ear again."

(whispering)"Come onnn ...... Sir."

"What's that you say? The <u>whole</u> platoon ... except you and me? <u>Good</u> idea! Excellent choice! The boys aren't gonna like it! You won't have many friends left around here! But you'll gain a new one. Me! Did everyone hear that!? Right now, the whole platoon — except me and Star — hit the ground! Begin with ten pushups! And on Mister Star's count! He'll lead the pushups by calling out the count!"

"Sir, permission to speak?"

"Of course, Star! It's your show!"

"Why do I have to lead the pushups, Sir?"

(laughing) "Why? Why? It was <u>your idea</u> wasn't it? You're the guy who's special! Right? You're better than everyone else! Right? <u>You're</u> above the Rules! Right? You're the reason these people are on the ground doing pushups! You're lucky! Someday you could be the reason people are on the ground ... <u>dead</u>! This is the way <u>you</u> wanted it. You think you're above everyone else. Right? Well. <u>Now</u> you are! You finally made it! So enjoy your new position now Star. <u>You</u> didn't earn it! Your buddies here are earning it for you! START THE COUNT!"

∞Just because my name's Bull doesn't make me the biggest man in the Company. But, if I have to do any more pushups because of that guy Star, he's gonna be in deep crap with <u>me</u>!∞

401

ºº Star's roommates better get him squared away or I'm gettin' on their case from now on!ºº

ºº I'll share our room's duties with Smith, but no more with Star, until he pulls his own weight!ºº

"Okay Star, stop them. EVERYONE STOP! On your feet! Mister Star here suggests we have a 'volunteer' to do extra duties … all week! Who will most benefit from extra duties, Star? Come on. Give me the name. Whisper it in my ear. Who? Bull? Cadet Bull? Again? That's favoritism, Star! You pick him for everything! What's that you say? It's because you think the 'fat-boys' need the exercise most? You hear that, Mister Bull? You're 'buddy' here is interested in your well-being! It's nice to have friends!"

ºº That's it, Star! Now you're in deep dung with me — 'fatboy Bull'!ºº

"And the rest of the platoon! As a show of cooperation with Bull! Tomorrow! We all go on a little 'spirit mission'! Everybody up to that? Unless, of course, Star here learns his 'knowledge' and comes out here 'squared away' tomorrow!"[14]

402

See, Harry? That's Patience … and Self-control!

* The Platoon Leader didn't even raise his voice! That works for me!

* It works for them, too. By "popular demand", Star begins to cooperate. He gets squared-away. And none too soon. He already had one foot out the door. The next misstep would have meant complete "separation" from the Academy! But, instead, Star will begin to get in step with the rest of his classmates.

Each new year will bring new challenges for him and his classmates. Each Cadet will gradually progress from learning followership, to learning leadership, to becoming a leader of Virtue and Knowledge. It will take four busy and long years to do so!

Most of the Jeffs and Moores, the Kahls and Williamses, the Scotts and Browns, the Stars and Joneses, the Smiths and Bulls make it all the way through West Point. They make it to the big day. GRADUATION!

On Graduation Day all of them are teary-eyed. Many openly cry … even some who can never remember crying in their life. Part of it is tears of joy, as it is with any other college on Graduation Day. But most of it is the sudden release of overwhelming stress and pressure built up and held inside for four long years. They've done it. They've gotten through all the ordeals. They have met the challenge of the most challenging college in the world!

Now, on Graduation Day, they tearfully display what has become the old familiar virtue called Cooperation! They let their feelings all hang out as they cooperate in singing these words for the last time together as cadets:

THE ALMA MATER

by: P.S. Reinicke

Hail, Alma Mater dear
To us be ever near
Help us they motto bear
Through all the years:
    Duty, be well performed
    Honor, be e'er untorn
    Country, be ever armed
West Point, by thee.

And when our work is done
Our course on earth is run
May it be said — "Well done!
    Be thou at peace!"
Ever thy line of gray
Increase from day to day
Live, serve, and die, we pray
West Point — for thee.

403

The virtue is: Dedication...to duty, honor, and country.

Now they know what they didn't know that R-Day four years ago --- who they are, and what they're made of. And, now, it's starting to sink in, that this time it's really all over, for good. Now, they'll join centuries of "zeitgeist" (time-spirit) and West Point tradition. That's why, through its graduates, West Point has never failed America. Were it to do so, thousands of those young souls left on the Plain would rise up in a ghostly long gray line to forever haunt those who would forsake their sacred obligation. Sometime during Graduation Day, the new graduates will tell loved ones and friends, in their own way, "I gave to The Corps all I had to give; what I have done, I could never do again".

THE CORPS
from: H.S. Shipman, 1902

The Corps, The Corps, And The Corps
  With Eyes Raised We Thank Our God
That We Of The Corps Are Treading
  Where They Of The Corps Have Trod.
They Are Here In Ghostly Assemblage
  The Ones Of The Corps Long Dead
Our Hearts Stand At Attention
  While We Wait For Their Passing Tread
We Sons Of Today We Salute You
  You Sons Of An Earlier Day

We follow Close Order Behind You
  Where You Have Pointed The Way
The Long Gray Line Of Us Stretches
  Through Years of The Centuries Told
And The Last Man Feels To His Marrow
  The Grip Of Your Far-off Hold.
Grip Hands, Though From The Shadows
  While We Swear As You Did Of Yore
In Living Or Dying To Honor,
  The Corps, And The Corps, And The Corps.

The virtue is: Respect. Respect those who have done what you have not.

So, Harry, that's it. There are thousands of stories inside West Point. You have seen a few of them. Now you know the way it is. You know the real story behind West Point, what it's really all about, and what I mean by "putting old souls into young bodies". We're finished. You can now give an enlightened assessment of West Point to Congress tomorrow. And now, my friend, I'm also finished. My time here with you is up.
* Oh! That's right! Tomorrow! Congress! You won't be there with me?
* If it works the way it's supposed to, you won't even remember me. When you rejoin your body ... see, it's still over there sleeping ... you'll only remember facts and events. You won't remember you were there to witness those facts and events, firsthand.
* And I won't remember, you? I don't understand!
* What it boils down to, Harry, you're not supposed to understand.

CHAPTER 2: BACK OUTSIDE OF SPACE AND TIME (HEAVEN)

* ᵒᵒ Why did I have to return so soon? I wish I could have seen what Harry says in Congress. ᵒᴼ
* ᵒᵒ You have consummated your mission, Thomas. Well done! No matter what Harry now says, we have done all we are allowed to do. You must now continue as before. ᵒᴼ
* ᵒᵒ Would you sentence me to wonder — forever — what he said? …… I hereby appeal your decision. I appeal to your Good offices. Could I not see this case to closure by seeing what he says in Congress? ᵒᴼ
* ᵒᵒ It is highly unusual for such an appeal to be granted. ……. Hmm. …… I suppose it is only fair. …… Very well. Just this one time. Your appeal is granted.ᵒᴼ
* ᵒᵒ Thankyou. I shall be grateful to you …….. forever! ᵒᴼ
* ᵒᵒ There! That is Harry speaking now, Thomas. ᵒᴼ
* ᵒᵒ Ah, yes. I see him. He has just finished enlightening Congress on how history and ideas of the great philosophers are the real story behind West Point! He is now outlining everything. ᵒᴼ

SYLLABUS OF PHILOSOPHY BEHIND WEST POINT

from: writings of the philosophers

The Spartans	– It takes hardship and sacrifice to develope character.
Socrates	– Teach by building on what's good in a person, and rebuilding the rest from scratch.
Plato	– To achieve the "Good" in good-leaders took many years at his Academy.
Aristotle	– Leaders need Virtue, and it takes years of living and practicing the virtues to form them into habits.
Epicurus	– Select a virtuous person as your role-model and act in such a way the role-model would approve.
Epictetus	– To acquire character is like the service of a soldier — long and arduous.
The Stoics	– A person must start with the Will to be virtuous, then have the Will to work hard at it.
St. Paul	– Past hardship makes leaders who can work under stress.
Machiavelli	– Knowing how a leader should not be is

as important as knowing how a leader should be.

Ignatius of Loyola	– His academy method of teaching virtue, knowledge, and professional skill produced a core of good-leaders.
Descartes	– He made Trust be earned — through his 'Method of Doubt'.
Spinoza	– Morals, ethics, and character need to be lived, not just studied.
Montesquieu	– Virtue is mostly learned, not mostly inherited.
Butler	– Consience is the will and capacity to form virtuous habits through a disciplined lifestyle.
Rousseau	– Self-government requires leaders of morals, ethics, and character.
Kant	– Duty is on a level higher than moral, ethical, and character traits because it is first our Duty to strive for those traits.
Locke	– At birth the mind is a clean slate that gets filled up through experience and observation — and that is the way it gets filled-up with the virtues.
Jefferson	– America is best "preserved, protected, and defended" by producing good-leaders trained and educated to have Virtue and Knowledge.

The virtue is: Duty and Wisdom. It is our Duty to follow the Wisdom of the wisest people who ever lived.

ᵒᵒWay to go, Harry! That was good! ᵒᵒ

* ᵒᵒThere is no sense cheering him on, Thomas. He cannot hear you. Listen now. He is beginning his final statements. ᵒᵒ

"In closing, it pleases me to summarize all I have told my esteemed colleagues today, starting with the part about costs, as follows: Some 'critics' of West Point say the cost of a West Point Officer's Commission is 4 times the cost of a Reserve Officer Training Corps (ROTC) student's Commission from a civilian college. I call that the 'Myth of the Costs'. It's like Plato's 'Myth of the Cave'. Just like the prisoners in the Cave chose to see only shadows of people on the wall in front of them and not the real people behind them, West Point's critics choose to see only 'shadows' of the real costs — the costs up front — not the real underlying costs. There are two costs: the cost to only the <u>one</u> government department — the Department of Defense; and, the <u>real</u> cost to <u>all</u> government departments — the <u>total</u> cost to taxpayers. For West Point, the Department of Defense pays the total academic costs. For civilian college ROTC, the Department of Defense pays only the tuition part of academic costs. But the <u>Statistical Abstracts of the USA</u> tell us that the tuition paid by students meets only 1/4 the total academic costs to civilian colleges in the USA, on average. Therefore, that means the total <u>real</u> academic cost to colleges is 4 times the amount colleges collect for tuition! And where does the other 3/4 of the money come from? It comes from America's taxpayers, handed out as grants through various <u>other</u> government departments! That means the <u>real</u> cost of ROTC to <u>all</u> government departments — therefore to America's taxpayers — is about <u>4 times</u> the simple cost of tuition to the Defense Department! So what it boils down to is: **the cost of ROTC and West Point to taxpayers is about the same!** But just as Plato's prisoners refuse to turn around and look at the real source of shadows on the wall in front of them, West Point's 'critics' refuse to look at the <u>real</u> costs of ROTC. They prefer the 'Myth of the Costs'. However, my esteemed colleagues and I represent America's taxpayers and what is the best buy for them. We do not represent just the Department of Defense. We must not be fooled by the 'Myth of the Costs'. <u>We</u> must look at <u>total</u> academic costs. Furthermore, we're comparing the cost of two different 'products'. West Point's 'product' includes four years of training in Virtue. What is the cost of Virtue? Virtue will save people's lives. What is the cost of people's lives?"

* ⁰⁰ Now continue Harry! Point out that those statistics also mean that even regular, <u>non</u>-ROTC, college students get 3/4 of their education costs paid indirectly by tax-

payers via other government departments! And those students have <u>no</u> obligation to our country like West Point and ROTC students have! °°
* °° He cannot say that, Thomas. That would be political dynamite! The real cost of education is one of America's best kept secrets! He would blast it wide open! Let us continue to listen. °°

> "That's right, I said Virtue. And I know my colleagues share the view that Virtue is the one investment that never fails. Indeed, it is the reason that West Point and its Long Gray Line have never failed America, and West Point is the keeper of American Virtue. It is a microcosm of what our Founding Fathers meant America to be like. It is the last living model of the Virtue they wanted, and we want for America in the future."

°° Hmm. That was a coincidence, Thomas. I heard you thinking Harry should say that next. And he did! °°

> "That's why it took <u>Thomas Jefferson</u> to finally create the United States Military Academy at West Point. It wasn't just to carry on with military studies. He wasn't passionately pro-military. He wanted to develop good-leaders for the Army's Officer Corps. He had confidence that with time and practice and education, young men could develop their 'moral sense'. They could acquire the foundation of Virtue and Knowledge that's needed to someday become Colonels and Generals of wisdom and experience to run the Army. Only then would he trust having a full-time Standing Army. So to finally found the United States Military Academy at West Point it took, as Aristotle would have said, a 'Philosopher-President'. It took Thomas Jefferson who had the unique capacity to take practical measures in pursuit of philosophically noble causes. That's why Thomas Jefferson is actually the 'philosophical father' of both America and West Point. That's why America and West Point are each considered to be not just a place, but a philosophy!"

* °° That's true, Harry. But others besides Thomas Jefferson deserve credit too.°°

> "But, of course, the 'Syllabus of Philosophy Behind West Point' shows that Thomas Jefferson was only following the wisest thinkers of all time who said that virtues need years of practice to become internalized into habits."

°° That's better, Harry! °°

> "And what should the personality profile of West Point Officers who have truly internalized Virtue look like? It may surprise you! Leaving aside religious doctrine, their personality profile should

come closer to that of a priest, rabbi, or minister than any other profession! Does that shock you? Well consider this. Like St. Ignatius' Jesuit Academy produced missionaries who could also be military leaders, West Point produces military leaders having Virtue and Knowledge who are also somewhat like missionaries. But you couldn't see the difference between a West Pointer and other Officers under normal circumstances. It's just like you couldn't see the difference between a priest without his collar and a regular person under normal circumstances. They don't wear a sign on their forehead! What's <u>inside</u> makes the difference. What's inside a priest, rabbi, or minister is what saves people's souls. And what's inside a West Point Officer is what has saved people's lives … and our Country … during times of crises!"

°° That was good, Harry! Now talk about what they have inside of them. °°
* °° I remind you again, Thomas. Harry cannot hear you. °°

"Now my colleagues may ask, what specifically is inside of West Point Officers that may save people's lives someday? What makes them different? What are the most important things West Point teaches? The answer is summed up in one word. That's right! One word! **VIRTUE**! And out of all the virtues learned, the ones that should be a <u>must</u> for military Officers are:

1.) <u>Stress</u>. Be stress tested. Living and functioning under stress for four years prepares them to save lives!
2.) <u>Honor</u>. Live it. Turn it into habit over four years. Honor breeds Trust. And for troops to willingly follow leaders, they must first trust the leaders.
3.) <u>Intelligence and Competence</u>. They're needed to win wars. That's the name of the game. And they inspire Trust in the leaders.
4.) <u>Obedience and Appreciation</u>. They make Officers loyal to and dedicated to the Constitution and our civilian government. We can trust them to never overthrow our civilian government!

As I have already said, <u>all</u> the moral, ethical, and character virtues are important in an Officer. But these are critical to America's survival!"
"Will the gentleman yield for a question?"
"Certainly. I yield to the honorable Congressman."
"How do we know applicants have the will to seriously consider a military career and are not just after a top-tier college education for free? How do we get a fair share of America's best young folks to pass up private sector salaries and opportunity to dedicate much of their adult lives to service of Country?"
°°Hmm. How would Thomas … ummm … Thomas Jefferson

answer that?[oo] "They are excellent questions![15] And they highlight two problems. First, how do we avoid wasting time and money on young folks who, secretly, would never even consider the military for a <u>career</u>? Second, how do we lure the best and brightest youth? The solution to the first problem is tighter screening of all applicants. For instance, to academic, medical, and physical screening, add psychological tests to find out about an applicant's will and intentions to at least consider the military for a <u>career</u>. Add a bonafide psychological personal interview by Admissions. The idea is to ferret out, ahead of time, those who should not be at West Point. Then once someone is in, keep it tough to <u>stay</u> in. Make the stresses great enough so that only those willing to consider a military career would be able and willing to put up with them. Make it so that even free education is not enough of an attraction to put up with all the stress!"

"But that might drive good kids away!"

"It won't if they know why West Point <u>must</u> be tough, and if they know what West Point is <u>really</u> about. Besides, stress is critical to acquiring Virtue. The West Point experience must be caring, but be a challenge they will never forget for the rest of their lives if they are to permanently acquire Virtue. It must be a life changing experience. Furthermore, we owe it to our young soldiers whose lives <u>depend</u> on their Officers being stress-tested!"

"And the second problem ... luring America's best?"

"I think the solution to that is through incentives. We can't offer high paying future jobs. But we <u>can</u> offer high prestige future positions. That's the Academy's natural role. West Point was intended by Jefferson and others to be a seminary for future Colonels and Generals of Virtue and Knowledge who America can trust to safeguard our Constitutional democracy-in-a-republic. We should reinstate that historical purpose! We need to make it the <u>prime</u> mission of West Point! After all, shouldn't that be the purpose of <u>any</u> West Point type of place? I see West Point as the first phase in the long-range program that weeds out and developes the Army's future senior Officers — the Colonels and Generals — like Thomas Jefferson meant it to be. It's the first challenge someone must complete in order to move along the track toward someday becoming a Colonel or General in America's <u>full-time</u> professional Army — the Regular Army. So here's how it would be: if you want to be a career professional Officer — not a Reserve Officer; if you get into West Point; if you get through West Point; if you retain the morals, ethics, and character you internalized at West Point (which, by definition, you should); and, if you don't screw up out in the Army (which, by definition, you shouldn't); then, you're certain to be a 'top-gun' Officer and Gentleman in the Army someday. <u>That's</u> the incentive which would lure some of America's best and brightest youth! And, therefore, we also would need to open-up West Point to college ROTC students. We would need to create a big new category of West Point nominations. Call it 'ROTC Nominations'. Here's how they would work: if you're in ROTC; if you seriously consider going for a career in the <u>full-time</u> military; if you want to be a Colonel or General; then, you have the opportunity to pursue one of the new ROTC nominations to West Point. If you choose not to switch to West Point, there would not be a lot of room at the top for you in the <u>full-time</u> Army. But there still would be opportunity in the Reserves."

"Will the gentleman yield for another question?"

"Of course. I yield to the gentleman."

"How do we open up any substantial numbers of new nominations to ROTC without expanding West Point?"

"I would break down nominations to West Point broadly like this: 50% Congressional — one per year per Senator and Representative; 40% ROTC — people in college ROTC programs; 10% Superintendent — people from the Army's enlisted ranks and all other special categories nominated by the Superintendent of West Point."

"The gentleman used the words, 'not a lot of room at the top'. Does that mean there would still be some slots for those who have not gone through West Point?"

"Yes. Broadly speaking, every West Point graduate would be a Colonel or General someday, but not every Colonel or General would be a West Point graduate. There would purposely be some slots open at the top for exceptional cases ... like the Colin Powells of this world. There are always some people who have internalized the virtues through personal adversity or other life-experiences. On a case by case basis, they could join the train to the top ... mid-journey. They wouldn't be excluded!"

* ᵒᵒ Tell them why <u>most</u> senior Officers should be West Point graduates, Harry.ᵒᴼ

* ᵒᵒWhy do you persist in thinking he hears you, Thomas? ᵒᴼ

* ᵒᵒI don't know! But, listen to what Harry is saying! ᵒᴼ

"The whole reason for making West Point the first phase of a Senior Officer Development Program is Virtue. It's to have, as Thomas Jefferson deemed to be critical, an Officer Corps of Virtue and Knowledge. But there's not room for every Officer to go through West Point. However, an organization's Virtue starts at the top. Then it trickles down. So if all senior Officers, most intermediate Officers, and many junior Officers are good-leaders of Virtue and Knowledge, that's how the nature of the Officer Corps, writ-large, will be."

"Will the gentleman yield for a comment?"

"I yield to the gentleman."

"Most professionals have tests they must pass that show they qualify to engage in their profession. For example, doctors must pass the three phases of the U.S. Medical Licensing Exam. Lawyers take a Bar exam. Architects and engineers take their professional licensing exams. And so on. But professional military Officers who are responsible for people's lives have <u>no</u> such exam to pass! Right? So is that what you're trying to do here?"

"My colleague is astute. And correct. For military Officers, qualification means not only <u>knowledge</u> in their field, but also <u>Virtue</u>. They gain knowledge in their field through college education, practical experience, and service education such as their Branch Courses, the Army War College, and the Staff and General Officers College. And they <u>do</u> have exams on knowledge given them at those Schools. But first things first. What about the other part of Officer's qualifications? VIRTUE! There's no professional test for it. You can read <u>about</u> it. You can answer questions on it. But you can only <u>internalize</u> it by living it and practicing it over long years. And you can only do that in one place. West Point (and perhaps a few other military academies). That's why West Point should be the first phase of the Professional Qualification Test for career Senior Officers. The entire four years of internalizing Virtue — learning to be a good-leader — <u>is</u> the first phase of the test. It should be the 'rite of passage' in order to continue!"

"So is that what the gentleman sees as West Point's role for the Army?"

"Yes. I see it as the critical first phase of a Senior Officer Development Program for future Colonels and Generals. Besides Officers for combat arms branches, I also see it as the Army's main source of <u>career</u> doctors, lawyers, scientists, and engineers. And, it should be the main source of the Army's career teachers at all levels. They're the Army's missionaries. They should be the ones who teach ROTC students about military science and Virtue. They should be the professors at West Point itself. Though West Point teaches Virtue, not religion, it is like Sparta and Athens and St. Ignatius' Jesuits wrapped up into one package. It has a military purpose like Sparta, intellectual purpose like Athens, and missionary purpose like the Jesuits. The Jesuits prevented the Reformation from ruining the Church. Likewise, a purpose of West Point should be to prevent decline in moral, ethical, and character values from ruining the Army!"

"So in a nutshell, how would the gentleman sum-up the reason for West Point? In other words, **WHY WEST POINT**?

"Funny you should ask! For this morning in my office, where I slept last night, I found a mysterious letter with my mail — this one that

412

I'm holding up. The handwriting actually looks like <u>mine</u>! But, I don't write letters to myself ….. especially when I'm sleeping. Do you? And the letter calls me Harry. As you all know, my name isn't Harry. Anyway, it's as if this letter knew what your question would be. And guess what? It gives exactly the same answer I would give. Weird, isn't it? I can't explain it! Oh well (chuckling), perhaps I have a guardian angel or something! … °°Hmm!°° … Anyway. The reason for West Point is still the same today as Thomas Jefferson's timeless reason for it back in 1802. As the letter says better than I can, and I'll read it:

'the reason for West Point boils down to what its mission is … which is:

to allow those persons who are able to guard the sacred deposit of the rights and liberties of fellow citizens to be called to that service without regard to birth, wealth, or other accidental condition or circumstance in order to become leaders of Virtue and Knowledge, and the future Colonels and Generals, who will preserve, protect, and defend the Constitution that contains that sacred deposit of rights and liberties'. [16]

°°Hmm! Boils down to? Why does that sound familiar?°° To do that, gentlemen, West Point not only has to put old heads onto young shoulders like other colleges do, but as someone once said, it also has to put old souls into young bodies … and put iron into those souls!"
"I see. I thank the gentleman for his concise summary."

413

"I thank my esteemed colleagues for your patience. And so, gentlemen, there you have my report. I trust that I have now set aside some old myths about West Point by clearing up, once and for all, what it is really all about and why Thomas Jefferson saw fit to found it. The fate of West Point is in your hands. The decision on whether to have a military academy, and what kind, is up to you. But remember, there are some things in life that are more important than money and the economy. This happens to be one of them! (looking up and in a low voice) How's that Thomas? How'd I do?"

"Did the gentleman have something further to say?"

"No, No. Just, I thank you all for your kind attention." (looking up) ᴼᵒSorry about adding the part about iron in the souls! But that's what it boils down to — as you would say, Thomas!ᵒᴼ

ᴼᵒDid you hear that?! Harry just spoke to me! He remembered after all! I thought he was not supposed to remember! Three huzzahs to you, Harry! You did well! And I actually like the bit you added about iron in the souls! .... Did you see Harry's face after what I just said? He looked up and smiled! It looked like he "heard" me. Did he hear me?ᵒᴼ

* ᴼᵒ I - I - I think he did hear you ...... Thomas! ᵒᴼ

* ᴼᵒThen that does it! I must speak with him! Just for one minute! I want to personally congratulate him on a job well done! He has told the American Congress everything that we ..... and you know **WHO** ..... could have hoped he would tell them. I am going to congratulate him, personally. After all, I <u>do</u> have a stake in whether we succeed in our mission with him, don't I! ᵒᴼ

* ᴼᵒ Ah, Ah, Ahhh! Not so fast! You know better than that, Thomas! <u>That</u> is against the RULES! We are not allowed to work that way! We must not do that! Why, <u>that</u> would be .... crossing the threshold! ᵒᴼ

414

NOTES

(The notes refer to sources by their number in the bibliography, eg. B21)

1.– PROLOGUE
1. From: Douglas MacArthur

2.– WEST POINT: THE PLACE
   none

3.– VIRTUE, LEADERS, AND LEADERSHIP

1. Not a fact. Strictly to demonstrate "worship" of athletes
2. Something that is generally accepted to occur
3. Bender, J. The Technique of Executive Leadership. N.Y.: McGraw-Hill, 1970 This is #21 in the bibliography and hereafter would be just "B21", for example.
4. The content is fact. The situation is invented.
5. B40
6. This chapter is from B145, B66, and other books on virtues.
7. B40, B152, B22, B42, B25 B21, B158, B147, B156
8. B42
9. For descriptive purposes, only
10. For descriptive purposes, only
11. B147
12. B156
13. Speech by H. Norman Schwarzkopf
14. B158
15. B158
16. B22; West Point students do over 20,000 hours of work in 4 years
17. God. To each his own definition

4.– THE STORY BEHIND WEST POINT: THE IDEA

1. Again, to each his own definition
2. B69
3. B11
4. For descriptive purposes only. Not historical fact
5. B139, B106
6. B139, B106
7. For descriptive purposes only
8. B134
9. For descriptive purposes only
10. B134, B18, B139

11. For descriptive purposes only
12. B134
13. B134
14. The content is based on fact. The situation is merely "imputed" — drawn from the facts.
15. B139, B11
16. B134
17. Content based on fact. Situation imputed.
18. B134, B11
19. B134
20. B71
21. Content based on fact. Situation imputed.
22. same as above
23. B134, B139, B11
24. Based on Exodus 20: 1-17
25. The content is based on The Old Testament. The comments are not.
26. B11
27. B18
28. For descriptive purposes only
29. B139, B18, B106
30. For descriptive purposes only
31. B139, B61, B106
32. B71 page 829
33. B71, B125
34. B139, B106
35. Content based on fact. Situation imputed for descriptive purposes.
36. B71
37. B71
38. B114
39. B139, B106
40. B61
41. What they say is factual. The situation is imputed.
42. B61, B114, B96
43. The situation is based on fact. The comments are imputed (not quotations)
44. B139, B106
45. The content is fact. The situation is imputed.
46. B96
47. B61, B96, B117
48. same
49. same
50. B96
51. Content based on fact. Situation is imputed. "Bonkerius" is fictitious.
52. B96
53. The point of this is historical fact. Note, drachmas were not in use at the time.
54. B96
55. B71

56. Content based on fact. Situation imputed.
57. B61, B117, B157
58. The <u>situation</u> is based on fact. The comments are imputed.
59. For descriptive purposes only. Not historical fact.
60. Not an exact translation. See B B0, or B71 page 601-608 for exact wording.
61. B61, B117, B130, B148, B144, B72. A simplified "translation".
62. Content is historical fact. Situation is imputed.
63. Based on historical fact. Situation is imputed.
64. B140, section on "Royal Pages".
65. Based on historical fact. Situation is imputed
66. B61, B117, B7, B144, B8, B10. A simplified "translation".
67. B139, B106 (sections on Alexander)
68. Based on fact. Situation imputed.
69. B139, B106, B140, B62 (sections on Alexander)
70. Referring to Socrates drinking the poison hemlock
71. B61, B144 (sections on post-Aristotle Greek philosophy)
72. Content based on fact. Situation imputed.
73. B61, B117, B144 (sections on Epicurus)
74. B60, B44 (sections on Stoicism)
75. Content based on fact. Situation imputed.
76. B60
77. Based on historical fact and Shakespeare. Caesar's thoughts are imputed.
78. Content is Stoic philosophy. The situation is imputed.
79. B71, B60, B139, B117 (sections on Roman Stoicism, Seneca, and Epictetus)
80. B134, B11, B69, Romans 5: 1-5 of Holy Bible (standard Catholic homily)
81. Based on general historical fact. Situation is for descriptive purposes.
82. B117, B29
83. Barbarians as proxy for Rome is fact. The situation is imputed.
84. Sacking of Rome is history. The situation is imputed.
85. Discussion on Augustine – B31, B117, B13; on Rome – B54, B59.
86. The dialogue is based on historical accounts of Hypatia. Situation is imputed.
87. The fact is, Charlemagne wasn't a fast learner. This scene depicts that.
88. Wild parties are historical fact. The situation is for descriptive purposes.
89. Content based on fact. The scenario shows the factual irony of the situation.
90. Content based on fact. Situation is imputed.
91. B31, B60
92. The "gossip" is factual information. Only the place is imputed.
93. Based on fact. Situation is imputed for descriptive purposes only.
94. B62, B139
95. B33
96. B159
97. Discussion based on fact. Situation is imputed.
98. B26
99. Based on fact. Situation imputed for description
100. B106, B139, B18, B117, B48. This whole section, including Bacon.

101. B19
102. Meant to give a general idea of what, in fact, was the attitude of a faction of the Church and some politicians.
103. B106, B139, B18, B117, B128, B19 for this whole section.
104. Information is historically correct. The setting is also fairly accurate.
105. This scenario contemplates what it might have been like.
106. B94, B12
107. B53, B128
108. Cromwell's comments based on fact. Hobbe's comments and thoughts represent the Opposition.
109. B127, B104
110. Content is factually correct. The situation is imputed.
111. New College Dictionary.
112. Content based on fact. The situation and reactions are imputed.
113. B118
114. B116
115. B128, B118
116. B51
117. Comments are factual information. Scenario is for descriptive purposes.
118. B57, B38
119. B143
120. Events and comments are based on fact. The situation is also probable.
121. B92
122. An imagined scenario to illustrate Kant's Categorical Imperative.
123. B93, B122, B100, B135
124. B139, B128, B106

5. – THE STORY BEHIND WEST POINT: THE HISTORY

1. Comments are based on fact. The situation is for descriptive purposes.
2. B128, B110
3. Comments based on fact. Situation is imputed for descriptive purposes.
4. Accounts of the battle are historical fact. The situation is imputed.
5. To give a flavor of feelings toward British army occupation.
6. B35, B65, B106. Situation is imputed.
7. B139
8. Content is based on historical facts. Situation is imputed.
9. same
10. Event is based on historical fact. Comments show how emotions ran.
11. Situation based on fact. Comments are fabricated.
12. Content based on historical fact. Situation is imputed.
13. An imagined scenario to impart some of the factual information.
14. Content based on fact. Situation imputed.
15. B138. Content and scenario are fact. Comments from the benches probable.

16. This chapter drawn mostly from: B14, B15, B111, B39, B47, B106
17. Circumstance based on historical fact. The rest is what they might have perhaps been ºº thinking ºº.
18. "Isaac Davis quoted from historical sources. The rest is based on fact, but the exact comments are speculative.
19. The content and quote (whites of eyes) are fact. The comments and thoughts are not quotes, but are probable.
20. The situation is factual. Comments are to show what Washington was up against when he took over.
21. The wavering support is factual. The scenario is for descriptive purposes.
22. The sayings are from Benjamin Franklin's Poor Richard's Almanac.
23. The scenarios are to show the economic mood of the colonists.
24. Problems with slaves and Indians are historical fact. Situations imputed.
25. The conditions at West Point are factual. Scenario is for descriptive purposes.
26. Situation of how Jefferson acted is based on fact.
27. Situation of British army in the South is fact. Scenario is imputed.
28. King George's reaction to surrender is history. The scenario is imputed.
29. This chapter drawn from B106, B139, B45, B39, B47, B45, B126, B137.
30. B67, B91
31. Comments based on historical fact. The scene is imputed.
32. This segment on Washington drawn from B43 and B170
33. The content is historical fact. The scenario is imputed from Shays' Rebellion.
34. Attributed to letters written by Thomas Jefferson. B80
35. Comments are to show historical concern with the Constitution in America.
36. This chapter drawn from B106, B151, B27, B65
37. A probable scenario, based on historical comments on Harmer's defeat.
38. Based on historical accounts of St. Clair's massacre, particularly in B146 on Nov. 10, 1791, Lt. Michal McDonough to his brother.
39. Comments based on facts about the Whiskey Rebellion.
40. This chapter drawn from B106, B99, B32, B84, B146.

6. THE STORY BEHIND WEST POINT: THE FOUNDING - HOW?

1. Dialogue is based on fact. Scenario imputed as probable.
2. Same
3. Based on historical writings, like the "Centinel of Kentucky". Kentucky Gazette. June 17, 1800.
4. This chapter drawn mostly from B106, B99, B161, B162, B163, B164.
5. Comments about Molly Corbin based on fact. Situation imputed.
6. B155, B162, B163, B164, B16, B113, B119, B99
7. From a letter by Steuben about a Military Establishment. N.Y. 1784
8. same as note 6.
9. B55
10. B16, B113
11. B3, B1, B58 – 6th Congress, 1st Session

12. B64, B3
13. Based on historical facts and writings. The meeting is imputed.
14. B3, B1, B58, various: especially Adams and Dexter – 5/24/00, 7/16/00, 7/25/00, Adams to Congress (speech of 11/22/00).
15. references used: B46, B68, B73, B56, B4

7. – THE STORY BEHIND WEST POINT: THE FOUNDING - WHY?

1. From B109, B105, B85
2. Based on fact, especially B2. The scenario is for descriptive purposes.
3. B79, B89
4. Based on fact, especially as told by B20.
5. Based on Kramnick, Isaac. Bolingbroke and His Circle. Cambridge: Harvard, 1968
6. B83
7. B82
8. This segment on Jefferson drawn mainly from B105, B115, B121, and B136.
9. From B131, B139, B106
10. This segment drawn from B52, B14, B97, B142, B171, B108, B132, and: Kramnick. Bolingbroke and His Circle; Wills, Gary. Inventing America. N.Y.: Doubleday, 1978
11. This segment mostly from B105, B115, B121
12. This segment on Martha Wayles Jefferson and Thomas Jefferson is taken from B136 and B50.
13. Based on fact, taken from B82. Scenario is for descriptive purpose.
14. B24
15. This segment on Jefferson in France taken from B121, B50, B83, B136.
16. Based on writings of Jefferson. The scenario is likely true, though imputed.
17. Jefferson vs Hamilton taken from B84, B98, B36, B82, B83
18. Segment leading up to 1800 uses mainly B83, B98, B136, B105, and B22.
19. Based on history. Scenario for descriptive purposes.
20. B75 vol2, pg2
21. B148, B9
22. B101, B102
23. B78
24. Kramnick, Bolingbroke and His Circle pg89.
25. B83 6:517
26. This segment on Jefferson's political philosophy comes mainly from B71, especially his Bills to reform Virginia. B77
27. B8 book, ch4, pg3; B38 pg204; B116, 1:41-42; B78 pg259; and, Harrington's Oceana pg171.
28. B36, B76 – The Anas p1210-11, 1226, and 1258
29. B24
30. B74, especially: Elbridge Gerry to T.J., May 14, 1801; T.J. to Nathanial Macon, May 14, 1801; and most important: Adams Henry. Writings of Gallatin. Phila: Lippencott, 1879, 1:24-25 - This is a letter to Jefferson from

Treas. Sec. Gallatin that shows Jefferson's personal involvment, and how everyone in his administration knew about it; see also Congressional Reference 7HID86.1, Special Collections, Library of Congress, "An Act Fixing the Military Peace Establishment of the United States", 16 March 1802.

31. From: Jefferson, Thomas (edited). The Political Writings of Jefferson, pg162.
32. B74. T.J. to James Monroe, May 21, 1784. As far back as 1784 T.J. had a comprehensive plan of defense that used a standing army on borders.
33. Special Collections, USMA Library, West Point, N.Y.; also, West Point Archives; Williams, J. "Report on the Military Academy", March 4,1808, American State Papers. 1:229-230; and B165. The Jefferson Administration did not even supply West Point with drawing and surveying instruments until long after the school opened, much less supply texts for a bonafide engineering curriculum. See also: B95, B28, B149, B56, B46, B68, and McRee, Col. "Military Academy at West Point", USMA Library, West Point, N.Y., and American Quarterly Review, Sept. 1837, pg91-92.
34. Register of Graduates; "Cadet Appointment and Application Letters", USMA Archives, W.P., NY and National Archives, Wash. DC.
35. Knight, E. (ed). Documentary History of Education in the South Before 1860 Chapel Hill: U.N.Car., 1949
36. Based on historical fact, especially as in: Dunbauld, E. Thomas Jefferson and the Law. Norman: U. Oklahoma, 1978, ch7; Novak,S. The Rights of Youth. Cambridge: Harvard, 1977, pg96; and, McRee, Col. "Military Academy "(same-N33).
37. Palmer, D. The River and the Rock. N.Y.: Hippocrene, 1991, Epilogue.
38. B74 LC20545 – 46; also Ellis, R. The Jeffersonian Crises. N.Y.: Norton, 1974.
39. Jefferson often said this, especially attributed to his First Inaugural Address.
40. B83 vol 3:194 in the Anas
41. B82. T.J. to Nathaniel Macon, May 14, 1801 - Vol 10:261
42. B83 the Anas pg190
43. B81 vol 8
44. B81 T.J. to Wm. Branch Giles, March 23, 1801, 8:25-26
45. B81 T.J. to J.W. Eppes, March 27, 1801
46. B81 T.J. to James Monroe, March 7, 1801, vol 8 pg10
47. B81 T.J. to Elias Shipman, July 12, 1801, vol8 pg67-70
48. B81 T.J. to Elias Shipman, same
49. B74 T.J. to Gideon Grange, Oct.31, 1801, LC 20210
50. B74
51. B81 vol7, p238n
52. All of this can be found in the public records, especially: "Roll of civil, military, and naval Officers, American State Papers, Class X, Misc. 1 (1834) pg260-319; "List of removals" Jefferson Papers, Lib. of Cong. 20545 - 20546 (B74); "Letters of Application and Recommendation During the Admin. of Thomas Jefferson, 1801-1809," Nat'l Archives pamphlet (1936), microcopy 418 NA; and B74

53. Library of Congress 20546
54. B76 pg254
55. Based on fact. What they are °°thinking°° is probable, but imputed.
56. "Officer Roster – 7/14/1801" in The Jefferson Papers, B74, 19697 - 19705. Results are worked out from the annotations that are on this "Officer Roster"; See also: B44 pg66-69.
57. "Register of Admissions", USMA Archives, West Point; "Miscellaneous Papers, Letters, etc", USMA Archives and Library of Congress; "Early Cadet Application Files", USMA Archives (microfilm) and Nat'l Archives (original documents and microfilm).
58. "Early Cadet Applications" (see above): Moses Elliot File; Erasmus Thompson File; John Reed File; D.B. Heil File; Bray Branch to Dearborn, War Dept. Sec's Office, Letter's Received, May 19,1908, Nat'l Archives; same for Julius Heilman; "Cadet Register of Entrants", USMA Archives; D. Tomkins for John Donnelly, Nat'l Archives; Frederick Lewis, War Dept. Sec's. Office, Letters Sent, Military Affairs, Nat'l Archives; "Cadet Reg. of Entrants", USMA Archives, Noah and Wyndham notation; "Early Cadet Applications", "Early Cadet Applications", Sylvester Roberts File.
59. USMA Archives; National Archives; "Letters Sent", "Letters Received" (various); and B46, B68, B56, B28
60. "Letters of Application — 1801-1809", Nat'l Archives pamphlet (1936), microcopy 418; and Sidney, A. "Vindication" in National Intelligencer, April 15,1803; see notes 44 to 51 above.
61. see footnote 64 forward
62. B77 pg147, B79 pg 84-94, B7, B6, B82 to Peter Carr, 1808, 2:409.
63. B74 "Thomas Jefferson's Opinion on the Constitutionality of the Residency Bill of 1790", 17:19
64. B74: to James Madison, 20 Dec. 1787, 12:438-44; to E. Carrington, 21 Dec. 1787, 12:445-47; to V. Forrest, 31 Dec. 1787, 12:475-79; to U.S. Smith, 2 Feb. 1788, 12:570-77; to A. Donald, 7 Feb. 1788, 12: 570-77; to J. Madison, 31 July 1788, 13:440-43; to J. Madison, 15 March 1789, 14:659-63; B81 to Dr. J. Priestly, 19 June 1802, 9:381
65. Based on B81 to R. Livingston, Dec.14,1800, 7:484. Scenario imputed.
66. B74 to Wm. Bache, Feb 12, 1800. In 1800 Jefferson said, "beware of a military force, even of citizens"; same – Franklin's quotation upon completing the Constitution in 1787.
67. B81 9:504; B74 TJ to James Madison, May 21, 1784; Washington's War letters to Congress, National Archives; B82 8:30 "raising..." (clarification added)
68. "Ideas on Government" in B78; Bill 79 and Bill 80 in B74 2:521-22
69. B77 pg147
70. B78 pg259 (from Montesquieu's Spirit of the Laws)
71. B74 "Bill 79", 2:257; B77 pg 667
72. B74 to Peter Carr, 19 Aug. 1785, 8:408; B124 pg 257
73. B74 to Peter Carr, 1787, 12:18
74. B74 to Peter Carr, 1787, 12:14

75. B74 to Peter Carr, 19 Aug. 1785, 8:406; B150 pg106
76. B74 to Robert Skipwith, 3 Aug. 1771, 1:76-77; B7
77. B74 "Bills 79 and 80", 2:536
78. B74 "Bill 80", 2:538-9
79. B74 to Peter Carr, 10 Aug. 1787, 12:18-19
80. B74 "Bill 80", 2:536-39; T.J. to L.W. Tazewell, 5 Jan. 1805 in B85
81. B74 to Peter Carr, 19 Aug. 1785, 8:405; B88 pg 9-18
82. B74 "Bill 80", 2:538-39; Hofstadter, R. (ed.), "John Witherspoon's Account of the College of New Jersey, 1772" in <u>American Higher Education</u>, 1: pg142
83. B74 "Bill 80", 2: 540-42
84. B83, 10: 138:141
85. B87, B70, to Peter Carr, 1 Sept. 1814, pg 223-226
86. B83 to Jos. Priestly, 10:140; B88 to Dupont deNemours, pg 126.
87. B87, B70, to Peter Carr, 7 Sept. 1814, pg224-26; B86 pg52; B74 to Pictet, 5 Feb. 1803, LC 22306; B83 to Priestly 18 Jan. 1800, 10: 140-1; B85 to Tazewell, 5 Jan. 1805
88. B86 Cabell to T.J. 14 Feb. 1816; B85 to Ticknor, 16 July 1823, 15:454-57; to Emmett, 27 April 1826, 16:169-70
89. B88 pg 9-18.
90. Comments are historical fact taken from: Sec. of War to J. Williams, 12 Dec. 1801, "Cadet's Warrant for Son of the Late Major Lillie", War Dept. Military Book No.1. Nat'l Archives, Wash. DC.; B160 Sec. War to J. Williams, 3 Dec. 1802, "Uniforms", No.1; B160 Court of Inquiry "Punishments 1802-1812", March 1816; Orderly Books, "Military duty, Steuben's Reg.'s", Corps of Artillery and Engineers, USMA Special Collections; same "Gentlemen Cadets"; Register of Cadets' and Register of Graduates, "Ratio of Graduates to Entrants 1802-1810", West Point Archives; B160 to J. Williams 16 Sept. 1802 "Cadets to have Waiters", No.1; West Point Ordnance Waste Book, "Cadets Command Companies", USMA Special Collections, No.4; B160 3 Dec. 1802; "Resistance to Training" in Orderly Book Corps of Artill. and Eng's, 18 April 1796, Special Collections West Point Library; B120; B149 <u>Memoirs 1801-07</u>, "Both factions' newspapers", Spec. Collections West Point Library; The scenario is imputed from the circumstances for descriptive purposes.
91. B165, 14 Dec. 1802 statement – (clarification in brackets)
92. Report of the Superintendent USMA 1896, Spec. Coll. West Point, P123; B 120, B153, B68; see also note 30.
93. B74 to Peter Carr, 10 Aug. 1787, 12: 15-17; B70, B87 pg 217-21
94. J. Williams to J.G. Swift in <u>Memoirs</u> B149; B107 Abraham Baldwin to Jared Mansfield, 14 April 1802; Sowerby E. ed. <u>Catalogue of the Library of Thomas Jefferson</u>. Wash. DC: Library of Congress, 1952, 4:33.
95. B107 same; Sec. of War Dearborn to Maj. Jonathan Williams, 20 Jan. 1802 in B160.
96. Dearborn to Williams, 31 May 1802, <u>Letters</u>, Nat'l. Archives M6; same on 9 July 1802; B160
97. B74 Rev. J. Madison to T.J.; 10 April 1785, 8:75-61, same to P. Carr, 10 Aug.

1787, 12:14; same 8: pg408.
98. B74 to P. Carr, 19 Aug. 1785, 8:408; same 10 Aug. 1787, 12:14; same 19 Aug 1785, 8:409
99. B74 to C.B. Brown, 15 Jan. 1800; B85; B74 to Skipwith, 3 Aug. 1771, 1:78; same to P. Carr, 10 Aug. 1787, 12:18; same to Walker Maury, 19 Aug. 1785, 8:411; B24 Ellen Wayles Randolph to T.J., 22 Feb. 1805, p267-68.
100. Orderly Books, Corp of Artillery and Engineers, Spec. Collections, West Point.
101. B149 pg27; J. Williams to Sec. Dearborn, Sept 1802 in B165; same W.A. Barron and J. Mansfield to J. Williams.
102. West Point Ordnance Waste Book, USMA Spec. Collections West Point.
103. B165, 4 Dec. 1802 "Statement".
104. B149 <u>Memoirs</u> pg27
105. B160 Dearborn to Lt. Col. Jonathan Williams, 9 July 1802; McRee, Wm. "Military Academy at West Point", <u>American Quarterly Review</u>, 6 Sept 1837, pg 91-97; Zwersher, Dorothy. "Benjamin Franklin, Jonathan Williams, and the U.S. Military Academy", (PhD dissertation, U.N.Car., 1974)
106. B149 pg37
107. B149 pg27; B165 W.A. Barron and J. Mansfield to Williams, Dec. 1802.
108. A Term was March/April through Nov. during 1802-1812 — from Report of Superintendent of USMA, 1896, pg123; vacation leave was 1 Dec. to 15 March, B160.
109. B74 T.J. "Bill 80", 2:536-39; B74 P.Carr to T.J., 18 April 1787, 11:299
110. "An Act Fixing the Military Peace Establishment of the U.S.," 16 March 1802, Congressional Reference 7HID 86-1, Special Collections, Library of Congress.
111. "Early Cadet Applications", USMA Archives, West Point; and Nat'l Archives, Wash. DC; B160, B149, B165.
112. B74 to P. Carr, 10 Aug. 1787, 12:15; B74 to Skipwith, 3 Aug. 1771, 1:76-7
113. B103 pg 221-25
114. For background on "schools" refer to: Middlekauf, RM, <u>Ancients and Axions - Secondary Education</u>, in <u>Secondary Education in 18th Century New England</u>. New Haven: Yale Press, 1963, pg 76-77 especially; Rudolph, F. <u>Essays on Education in the Early Republic</u>. Cambridge: Harvard, 1965
115. "Early Cadet Applications, Satterlee Clark", USMA Archives, West Point.
116. B85 T.J. to L.W. Tazwell, 5 Jan. 1805
117. B165 J. Williams to A. Gallatin, 19 Sept. 1807; J. Williams to President Jefferson, 5 March 1808; B74 to J. Williams, Oct. 1808; B82 to Picket, 5 Feb. 1803, 10:74
118. B83 President Jefferson, 18 March 1808 (Military Affairs,: 228) pg471 (clarification in brackets)
119. Register of Cadets, USMA Archives West Point; Register of Graduates and Former Cadets, USMA Archives West Point; Burlamaqui, Jean Jacques, <u>Principles du droit Natural</u>. Geneva: Barrillot, 1747, pg528, 87; B68 (mentions Burlemaque book)

120. B149 "Sketch of a Plan for Conducting the USMA-1808".
121. Board of Visitor Report, 1820, Spec. Collections USMA West Point; Register of Grads and Former Grads, USMA Archives West Point.
122. B95
123. B95, B28
124. Berard, A.B." Reminiscences of West Point". Michigan: Evening News Printing and Binding, 1886.
125. This segment based on: B103 pg135; Hutchison, F.A System of Moral Philosophy. N.Y.: Garland, 1967 pg 143; B74 to Skipwith, 3 Aug. 1771, 1:78; same, to Walker Maury, 19 Aug. 1785, 8:411.
126. See endnotes on "Definition of Advanced Schools". (notes 84-95.)
127. Stanhope, Philip D. (ed.) Lord Chesterfield's Letters to His Son and Others. NY: Dutton, 1959, pg52; Dumbauld, E. Jefferson and the Law; Rush, Benjamin. Essays Literary, Moral, and Philosophical. Phila.: 1798 (clarification in brackets)
128. B83, Jared Mansfield to Thomas Jefferson, 26 Jan. 1821; same, T.J. to Jared Mansfield, 13 Feb. 1821, pg 313.

8. EPILOGUE

1. The Epilogue is based on: stories and information from Cadets and former Cadets; the Bugle Notes; references from Part 3 of this book, notes B8 and B9; the events are real, the names are intentionally fictitious.
2. The R-day encounter is typical; "When Tommorrow..." - adapted from M. Freer.
3. Content based on actual experience of a former cadet. The scenario would also be accurate.
4. B78 pg259; B116 1:33
5. B138 "Benjamin Franklin's Poor Richard's Almanac, 1733-1758.
6. Based on the experience of a former Cadet
7. Taken from B76 T.J. to Benjamin Rush, 21 April 1803 pg948.
8. These 3 scenarios are based on the West Point Honor Code and are likely to have occurred many times.
9. Content taken from the Bugel Notes. The scenario is accurate.
10. This is a typical scene that probably occured hundreds of times.
11. same
12. Typical comments by cadets about "the tower".
13. The content factually describes a typical day — except room inspection isn't every day.
14. This scenario is based on actual stories by Cadets. It's meant to show that shouting and screaming are not necessary to discipline a wayward Cadet, and that imagination and creativity are more useful.
15. From here I offer my own opinions on "the way it ought to be". It's the only place in the book that has my opinions!
16. B74; B77;

ALPHABETICAL BIBLIOGRAPHY
(numbered for easy reference from Notes)

1. Adams, Charles F.,ed. The Works of John Adams. Boston, 1856
2. Adams, Pauline. Tercentenary History of the Boston Latin School. Westport, Conn: Greenwood Press, 1970
3. American State Papers – Military Affairs. Washington: Archives, 1832
4. Ambrose, Stephan. Duty, Honor, Country. Baltimore: 1966
5. Aristotle. Politics. ed. by H.Rockman. Cambridge: Harvard U-Press, 1958
6. Aristotle. Nichomachean Ethics. trans. M.O. Oswald. Book 1. Indianapolis: Bobbs – Merrill, 1962. chp 3.
7. Aristotle. Nichomachean Ethics. ed. D. Ross. London: Oxford U., 1961
8. Aristotle. Politics. trans. B. Jowett. New York: Modern Library, 1942
9. Aristotle. Politics. trans. T.A. Sinclair. Baltimore: Penguin, 1972
10. Aristotle. Ethics. trans. B. Jowett. New York: Modern Library, 1942
11. Armstrong, Karen. The History of God. New York: Ballantine, 1993
12. Aubrey, John. Aubrey's Brief Lives. Harmondsworth: Penguin, 1978
13. Augustine. City of God. Harmondsworth: Penguin, 1972
14. Bailyn, B. The Ideological Origins of the American Revolution. Cambridge: Harvard, 1967
15. Bailyn, B. Pamphlets of the American Revolution. Cambridge: Harvard, 1965
16. Bailyn, B. Origins of American Politics. New York: Vintage 1970
17. Banning, Lance. The Jeffersonian Persuasion. Ithaca: Cornell, 1964
18. Barraclough G. Concise Atlas of World History. Maplewood, N.J.: Hammond, 1988
19. Barry, M. Ignatius the Theologian. London: 1968
20. Bedini, Silvio. Thomas Jefferson: Statesman of Science. New York: MacMillan, 1990
21. Bender, J. The Technigue of Executive Leadership. New York: McGraw-Hill, 1970
22. Bennett, W. The Book of Virtues. New York: Simon and Schuster, 1993.
23. Bernardo and Bacon. American Military Policy. Harrisbury: 1961
24. Betts, E. and Bear A. The Family Letters of Thomas Jefferson. Columbia, MO.: U. Missouri, 1966
25. Bogardus, E. Leaders and Leadership. New York: Appleton, 1934
26. Bondanella, P. The Portable Machiavelli. Harmondsworth: Penguin, 1979
27. Bowen, Catherine. Miracle at Philadelphia. New York: Little, 1966
28. Boynton, E. History of West Point. New York: Van Nostrand, 1864
29. Brehier, E. The Philosophy of Plotinus. Chicago: U. Chicago, 1958 Arnold, 1963
31. Brown, P. Augustine of Hippo. London: Faber, 1967
32. Buel, R. Securing The Revolution. Ithaca: Cornell, 1972. Part 1
33. Bull, G. The Prince. Harmondsworth: Penguin, 1961
34. Cabell, N.F. Letters of T. Jefferson and J. Cabell. Richmond: Randolph, 1856
35. Chidsey, D. The French and Indian War. N.Y.: Crown, 1969

36. Christman, Margaret. The Spirit of Party. Washington D.C.: Smithsonian, 1992
37. Clausewitz. On War; and, Jomini. The Art of War. Philadelphia: 1862
38. Cole, G.D.H. The Social Contract and Discourses. London: Everyman, 1973
39. Commager, H. and Morris, R. The Spirit of Seventy-six. N.Y.: Harper, 1975
40. Conant, J.B. Education in a Divided World. Oxford: Oxford U., 1949
41. Copleston, T.C. Aquinas. Harmondsworth: Penguin, 1955
42. Cribben, J.J. Effective Managerial Leadership. N.Y.: American Management Assoc., 1972
43. Cunliffe, M. George Washington. Boston: Little, Brown, 1959
44. Cunningham, N.E. The Jeffersonian Republicans in Power. Chapel Hill: U.N. Car., 1963
45. Dann, John. The Revolution Remembered. Chicago: U. Chicago, 1980
46. Denton, E. The Formative Years of the U.S. Military Academy. Unpub. PhD Syracuse U., 1964
47. Depler, Carl. Out of Our Past. N.Y.: Harper, 1970
48. Dick, Hugh. Selected Writings of Francis Bacon. N.Y.: Modern Library, 1955
49. Diggens, John. The Lost Soul of American Politics. N.Y.: Basic Books, 1984
50. DosPassos, John. The Head and Heart of Thomas Jefferson. N.Y.: Doubleday, 1954
51. Duncan-Jones, A.E. Butler's Moral Philosophy. Harmondsworth: Penguin, 1952
52. Dworetz, S. The Unvarnished Doctrine. Durham, N.C.: Duke U., 1990
53. Elwes, R. H.M. trans. The Chief Works of Benedict de Spinoza. N.Y.: Dover, 1956
54. Ferrill, A. The Fall of the Roman Empire. London: Thomas, 1988
55. Fitzpatrick, John. The Writings of George Washington. Washington DC: 1931-1944
56. Forman, S. West Point. New York, 1950
57. Foxley, B. Emile. London: Dent, 1974
58. Gales J. and Seaton, W. Annals of Congress. Washington, 1834
59. Gibbon, Edward. The Decline and Fall of the Roman Empire. London, 1960
60. Guinagh and Dorjahn. Latin Literature in Translation. N.Y.: Longmans, 1958
61. Guthrie, W.K.C. A History of Greek Philosophy. Cambridge: Cambridge U., 1962
62. Hackett, Gen. Sir John. Warfare in the Ancient World. London: Sedgwick, 1989; also: F.F. Adcock. The Greek and Macedonian Art of War. Los Angeles: U. Cal., 1957
63. Hamilton, Madison, and Jay. The Federalist Papers. N.Y.: Penguin, 1961
64. Hamilton, Alexander. Papers of Alexander Hamilton. Washington: Library of Congress
65. Hamilton E.P. The French and Indian War. N.Y.: Doubleday, 1962
66. Harman, G. The Nature of Morality. N.Y.: Oxford U. Press, 1977
67. Hatch, Louis, The Administration of The American Revolutionary Army. N.Y., 1904
68. Holden, E. The Centennial of the U.S.M.A. West Point 1802-1902.

Washington D.C.: U.S. Gov't Printing Office, 1904

69. Holy Bible
70. Hellenbrand, H. The Unfinished Revolution. Newark: U. Delaware, 1985
71. Howe and Harrer. Greek Literature in Translation. N.Y.: Harper, 1948
72. Irwin, T. Plato's Moral Theory. Oxford: Clarenden, 1977
73. Jacobs, J.R. The Beginning of the U.S. Army. Princeton: Princeton U., 1947
74. Jefferson, Thomas. The Papers of Thomas Jefferson in the Library of Congress. Washington D.C.: On microfilm in Library of Congress
75. Jefferson, T. ed. Paul C. Ford. The Writings of Thomas Jefferson. N.Y.: 1897
76. Jefferson T. ed. Saul Padover. The Complete Jefferson. N.Y.: Tudor, 1943
77. Jefferson T. Notes on the State of Virginia. N.Y.: Norton, 1972
78. Jefferson T. ed. Gilbert Chinard. The Commonplace Book of Thomas Jefferson. Baltimore: Johns Hopkins, 1926, 1928
79. Jefferson, T. ed. Gilbert Chinard. The Literary Bible of Thomas Jefferson. Baltimore: John Hopkins, 1928
80. Jefferson, T. ed. Julian Boyd. The Papers of Thomas Jefferson. Princeton: Princeton U., 1950
81. Jefferson, T. ed. P.L. Ford. The Works of Thomas Jefferson. N.Y.: Putnam, 1905
82. Jefferson, T. ed. Bergh and Lipscomb. The Writings of Thomas Jefferson. Washington D.C., 1905
83. Jefferson, T. ed. H.A. Washington. The Writings of Thomas Jefferson. N.Y.: Derby, 1859. Published by a Joint Committee of Congress in 9 Volumes.
84. Jefferson, T. ed. Franklin Sawvel. The Complete Anas of Thomas Jefferson. N.Y., 1903
85. Jefferson, T. ed. C.E. Thurlow. The Jefferson Papers of the U. of Virginia. Charlottsville: U. Virginia, 1973
86. Jefferson, T. ed. N.F. Cabell. Letters of Thomas Jefferson and Joseph Cabell. Richmond: Randolph, 1856
87. Jefferson, T. ed. Roy J. Honeywell. The Educational Work of Thomas Jefferson. New York: Russell, 1964
88. Jefferson, T. ed. Dumas Malone. Correspondence Between Thomas Jefferson and Pierre Samuel DuPont deNemours, 1798- 1817. Boston: Houghton, 1930
89. Jefferson, T. ed. Douglas Wilson. Jefferson's Literary Commonplace Book. Princeton: Princeton U., 1989
90. Jefferson, T. ed. Betts and Bear. The Family Letters of Thomas Jefferson. Missouri: U. Missouri, 1966
91. Jensen, Merrill. The New Nation: 1781-1789. N.Y.: 1950
92. Kant, Emmanuel. Prolegomena to Any Future Metaphysics (1783) – in trans. N.Y.: Bobbs-Merrill, 1950
93. Kant, Emmanuel. trans. H.J. Paton. Groundwork of the Metaphysic of Morals 1785. N.Y.: Harper, 1964
94. Kenny A. Descartes: A Study of His Philosophy. N.Y.: Random, 1968
95. Kirshner, J.W. Sylvanus Thayer: A Biography. W. Virginia: Univ. of W. Va., 1976
96. Kirk, G.S. The Pre-Socratic Philosophers: Cambridge: Cambridge U., 1983

97. Koch, Adrienne. The Philosophy of Thomas Jefferson. N.Y.: Columbia U., 1943
98. Koch, Adrienne. The Life and Selected Writings of Jefferson: N.Y.: Random, 1944
99. Kohn, R.H. Eagle and Sword. N.Y.: Free Press, 1975
100. Korner, S. Kant. Harmondsworth: Penguin, 1955
101. Locke, John. ed. Peter Laslett. Two Treatises of Government (1690). Cambridge U., 1960
102. Locke, John. ed. Peter Laslett. Second Treatise of Government. N.Y.: New America, 1965
103. Locke, John. ed. H.R. Penniman. Some Thoughts Concerning Education: On Politics and Education. N.Y.: Black, 1947
104. Macpherson, C.B. ed. Hobbes: Leviathan. Harmondsworth: Penguin, 1951
105. Malone, Dumas. Jefferson and His Time. Boston: Little Brown, 1948-81
106. McKay Hill, Buckler. A History of World Societies. Vols. A and B. Boston: Mifflin, 1988
107. Mansfield, Jared. Mansfield Papers. West Point, N.Y.: U.S.M.A., C 1804
108. Matthews, Richard. The Radical Politics of Thomas Jefferson. Kansas: Univ., 1984
109. May, Henry. The Enlightenment in America. N.Y.: Oxford, 1976
110. Meltzer, Milton. Slavery. N.Y.: Cowles, 1971
111. Miller, John C. Origins of the American Revolution. Stanford: 1959
112. Millis, Walter. Arms and Men. N.Y.: 1956
113. Morgan, Edmund. The Genius of George Washington. N.Y., 19
114. Netzsche, Fredrick. Early Greek Philosophy. N.Y.: Russell, 1964
115. Nock, Albert. Jefferson. N.Y.: Harcourt, 1926
116. Nugent, Thomas. trans. Spirit of the Laws. N.Y.: Hafner, 1975
117. O'Conner, D.J. ed. A Critical History of Western Philosophy. N.Y.:   Free Press, 1964
118. O'Conner, D.J. ed. John Locke. N.Y.: Penguin, 1968
119. Palmer, John McAnley. Three War Statesmen. Garden City, N.Y., 1930
120. Park, Rosewell. History of West Point. Phila: Perkins, 1840
121. Parton, James. The Life of Thomas Jefferson. Boston: Osgood., 1874
122. Paton, H.J. The Categorical Imperative. London: Hutchinson, 1947
123. Pegis, A. ed. Basic Writings of St. Thomas Aquinas. N.Y.: Random, 1945
124. Pennington, H.R. ed. John Locke on Politics and Education. N.Y.: Black, 1947
125. Perrin, Bernadotte Plutarch's Lives. Cambridge, Mass.: Harvard, 1928
126. Person, Michael. Those Dammed Rebels. N.Y.: Putnam, 1972
127. Peters, R.S. Hobbes. Harmondsworth: Penguin, 1956
128. Phillips, Robert S. ed. New Encyclopedia. N.Y.: Funk and Wagnals, 1971
129. Plato. Republic trans. W.H.D. Rouse. N.Y.: Mentor, 1956
130. Plato, The Republic. trans. Benjamin Jowett. N.Y.: Random, 1937
131. Pocock, J.G.A. The Ancient Constitution and Federal Law. Cambridge: U. Press, 1951
132. Pocock, J.G.A. The Machiavellian Moment. Princeton: U. Press, 1969

133. Pocock, J.G.A. Three British Revolutions. Princeton: U. Press, 1980
134. Potter, C.F. The Story of Religion. Garden City: Garden City, 1929
135. Quinton, A.M. in Van Doren, J. ed. The Great Ideas Today. Chicago: Encyc. Brit., 1977
136. Randall, H.S. The Life of Thomas Jefferson. N.Y.: Derby, 1858
137. Randall, W. The American Revolution. N.Y.: Hammond, 1973
138. Ravitch, Diane, The American Reader. N.Y.: Harper, 1991
139. Roberts, J.M. History of the World. Harmondsworth: Penguin, 1980
140. Sekunda, N. The Army of Alexander the Great. London: Osprey, 1994
141. Sheldon, G.W. The Political Philosophy of Thomas Jefferson. Baltimore: John Hopkins, 1991
142. Sheldon, G.W. The History of Political Theory. N.Y.: Lang, 1988
143. Smith, N.K. The Philosophy of David Hume. London: Macmillan, 1941
144. Smith, F.S. The Classics in Translation. N.Y.: Schribner, 1930
145. Sober, Elliott. Core Questions in Philosophy. N.Y.: Macmillan, 1991
146. St. Claire. Papers. Washington D.C.: Library of Congress
147. Stogdill, R.M. Handbook of Leadership. N.Y.: Free Press, 1974
148. Strauss,L. Studies In Platonic Political Philosophy. Chicago: U. Press, 1983
149. Swift, J.G. Swift Papers. West Point: USMA Spec. Coll.
150. Tacitus, Cornelius. The Histories. N.Y.: Penguin, 1982
151. Taylor, R.J. Western Massachusetts in the Revolution. Providence, 1954
152. Terman, L.M. Genetic Studies of Genius. Palo Alto: Stanford U., 1926
153. Tillman, S.E. Academic History of USMA. DC.: U.S. Gov't, 1904
154. Tocqueville, Alexis. Democracy In America. N.Y.: Harper, 1969
155. Ueberhorst, Horst. Friedrick Wilhelm von Steuben. Munich: Kerlag, 1981
156. U.S.M.A. Dept. of B.S.and L. Leadership in Organizations. Garden City: Avery, 1988
157. Vlatos, G. ed. The Philosophy of Socrates. N.Y.: Anchor, 1971
158. Wakin, W. ed.   War, Morality and the Military Profession. Boulder: Westview, 1986
159. Walker, L.J. Discourses. Harmondsworth: Penguin, 1970
160. War Dept Secretary's Office. Letters, Military Affairs. Wash. D.C.: Nat'l Archives
161. Washington, G. ed. L. Osborne. Washington Speaks for Himself. N.Y., 1987
162. Weighley, R. Towards An American Army. N.Y.: 1962
163. Weighley, R. History of the U.S. Army. N.Y.: 1967
164. Weighley, R. Military Thought From Washington to Marshall. N.Y.: 1962
165. Williams, J. Papers. West Point: USMA Spec. Coll.
166. Williams, O. Modern Verse. N.Y.: Scribner, 1950 etc.
167. Williams, O. Immortal Poems. N.Y.: Pocket, 1950 etc.
168. Williams, O. Selected Poems. N.Y.: Pocket, 1950 etc.
169. Williams, O. Little Treasury of Great Poetry. N.Y.: Scribner, 1950 etc.
170. Wills, Gary.   George Washington and the Enlightenment. Garden City: Doubleday, 1984
171. Wood, Gordon. Creation of the American Republic. U.N. Car., 1969
172. Wright, L.B. First Gentlemen of Virginia. Huntington, 1940

430

EXAMPLES OF VIRTUES
(in order of appearance in the book)